THE ENGLISH UTILITARIANS

In Three Volumes

Volume 3

Leslie Stephen

THE ENGLISH UTILITARIANS

In Three Volumes

Volume 3

Leslie Stephen

continuum

This edition published by Continuum International Publishing Group, 2005

Continuum International Publishing Group
The Tower Building   15 East 26th Street
11 York Road   New York, NY 10010
London
SE1 7NX

British Library Cataloguing-in-Publication Data
A catalogue record for this book is available from the British Library.

ISBN 0 8264 8816 1 (paperback)

A reprint, in three volumes, of the 1900 edition

Library of Congress Cataloging-in-Publication Data
A catalog record for this book is available from the Library of Congress.

Printed and bound in Great Britain by MPG Books Limited, Cornwall

THE ENGLISH UTILITARIANS

THE ENGLISH UTILITARIANS

By LESLIE STEPHEN

IN THREE VOLUMES

VOL. III

JOHN STUART MILL

LONDON

DUCKWORTH and CO.

3 HENRIETTA STREET, W.C.

1900

CONTENTS

CHAPTER I

JOHN STUART MILL'S LIFE

CHAPTER II

MILL'S LOGIC

CHAPTER III

POLITICAL ECONOMY

CHAPTER I

JOHN STUART MILL'S LIFE [1]

I. CHILDHOOD

WHEN James Mill died, the spirit of his followers was entering upon a new phase. A certain chill was creeping over the confidence of previous years. The Reform Bill had been hailed as inaugurating a new era ; the Utilitarians thought that they had made a solid lodgment in the fortress, and looked forwards to complete occupation. The world was going their way ; their doctrines were triumphing ; and if those who accepted their conclusions claimed the credit of originating the movement, the true faith was advancing. Triumph by other hands should be a sufficient reward for preachers who preferred solid success to personal glory. Opinions long regarded with horror might. now be openly avowed, and might be expected to spread when the incubus of the old repressive system was removed. The position, to compare small

---

[1] Mill's *Autobiography* (1873) is the main authority. Professor Bain's *John Stuart Mill: a Criticism, with Personal Recollections* (1882), is a necessary supplement, and gives an excellent summary. The most interesting later publications are the correspondence with Gustave d'Eichthal (1898) and the correspondence with Comte. Comte's letters were published by the Positivist Society in 1877, and the whole edited by M. Lévy-Bruhl in 1899. The *Memories of Old Friends*, by Caroline Fox (1882), gives some interesting accounts of Mill's conversation in 1840, etc.

things with great, resembled that in which Protestantism
seemed to be definitely triumphing over the Papacy;
and, as in that case, the latent strength of the old order
was as yet underestimated. The party which had been
so hopeful when bound together by external pressure
seemed to lose its energy at the moment of its greatest
triumph; its disciples became languid; its cherished
plans were rejected or emasculated; and many of the
little band of enthusiasts abandoned or materially modified their doctrine. The change, indeed, meant that
many of the principles for which they contended had
won general acceptance; but, for that reason, they had
no longer a common war-cry. The consequences are
illustrated in the career of John Stuart Mill, who
succeeded to the leadership of the sect. In certain
respects, as we shall see, Mill's great aim was to soften
and qualify the teaching of his predecessors. At the
same time he adhered, even more strictly than he was
himself conscious of adhering, to their fundamental
tenets; and as a philosopher he gained in the later years
of his life a far wider authority than had ever been
exercised by his predecessors. The early disciples of
Bentham and of James Mill were few, and felt even
painfully their isolation. But in his later years John
Stuart Mill had emerged. He had become the most
prominent of English thinkers; the political liberals
referred to him as the soundest expounder of their
principles; and even in the English universities, the
strongholds in his youth of all ancient prejudices, he
had probably more followers than any other teacher. In
the following chapters I must trace the history of the intellectual change. I begin by considering Mill's personal

history.   No complete biography has appeared, nor were
the external events of his career of special interest.   Mill,
however, left an autobiography which was intended to
supply what is of most importance for us, the history of
his intellectual and moral development.   In that respect
the book is eminently deserving of study.   I must
indicate what appear to me to be the most important
of the influences there described.

John Stuart Mill, born 20th May 1806, was twenty-six
at the death of Bentham and thirty at the death of his
father.   He was therefore old enough to be deeply
affected by their personal influence ; and his precocity
had made the relation to his elders far more intimate
than is often possible.   James Mill and Bentham looked
upon him from early years as their spiritual heir.
In 1812 his father writes to Bentham[1] : 'Should I die,'
says James Mill, 'one thought that would pinch me most
sorely' would be leaving the poor boy's 'mind unmade.'
Therefore, 'I take your offer quite seriously'—an offer
apparently to be John's guardian—'and then we may
perhaps leave him a successor worthy of both of us.'
John lived till his manhood almost exclusively . their
little circle ; and no child was ever more elaborate and
strenuously indoctrinated with the views of a sect.   Had
James Mill adhered to his early creed his son would probably have become a fit subject for one of those edifying
tracts which deal with infantile conversions.   From the
earliest dawn of intellect until the age of fourteen he was
the subject of one of the most singular educational
experiments on record.

He gives in his *Autobiography* an account of his

---

[1] Bentham's *Works*, x. 472.

course of study.[1] His memory did not go back to the
time at which he began Greek ; but he was told that he
was then three years old. By his eighth year (1814)
he had read all Herodotus, Xenophon's *Cyropædia* and
Memorabilia, part of Lucian, and six Dialogues of
Plato, including the *Theætetus*, which, he 'ventures to
think,' might have been better omitted, as it 'was totally
impossible that he could understand it.' In the next
three years he had read Homer, Thucydides, parts of the
plays of Sophocles, Euripides, and Aristophanes, Demosthenes, Æschines, and Lysias, Theocritus, Anacreon,
and the *Anthology*, and (in 1817) Aristotle's *Rhetoric*, the
first 'scientific treatise on any moral or psychological
subject' which he carefully analysed and tabulated. He
did not begin Latin till his eighth year, when he read
Cornelius Nepos and Cæsar's *Commentaries*. By his
twelfth year he had read much of Virgil, Horace, Livy,
Sallust, Ovid's *Metamorphoses*, Terence, Lucretius, and a
great deal of Cicero. He had learned a little arithmetic
by his eighth year, and had afterwards gone on to conic
sections and trigonometry, and had begun the differential
calculus. His father's ignorance of the higher mathematics left him to struggle by himself with the difficulties
of his later studies ; but he was far in advance of most
boys of his age. He read, too, some books upon the
experimental sciences, especially chemistry, but had no
opportunity of seeing actual experiments. In English
he had read histories, making notes, and discussing the
results with his father in morning walks through the
green lanes near Hornsey. He had read Hume,
Robertson, and Gibbon ; Watson's *Philip II. and III.*,

---

[1] Cf. letter of 30th July 1819 in Bain's *J. S. Mill*, pp. 6 to 9.

which particularly charmed him by the accounts of the revolts in the Netherlands; Rollin's *Ancient History*, Hooke's *History of Rome*, Langhorne's *Plutarch*, Burnet's *Own Time*, the *Annual Register*, and Millar's *English Government*, besides Mosheim, M'Crie's *Knox*, and Sewell's *Quakers*. His father liked, he says, to put into his hands books illustrative of the struggles of energetic men. He read Anson and other voyages for this purpose. In a purely imaginative direction he was allowed more scanty fare. He was, however, devoted to *Robinson Crusoe*, read the *Arabian Nights* and *Don Quixote*, Miss Edgeworth, and Brooke's *Fool of Quality*; admired Joanna Baillie's plays, and was fascinated by Pope's *Homer*. He was attracted by Scott's lays, and some of Campbell's lyrics, but cared little for Shakespeare, and could make nothing of Spenser's *Faery Queen*. He attempted little Latin and no Greek composition; but he wrote a few childish 'histories,' and a little English verse. In purely literary training he was hardly above the average of clever boys. This gives his intellectual state at the age of twelve. During his thirteenth and fourteenth years he was initiated in philosophical studies. He continued to read classical literature, but was now expected to understand the thought as well as the words. He began logic by reading Aristotle, some of the scholastic treatises, and especially Hobbes's *Computatio sive Logica*. His father lectured him upon the utility of the syllogism. He made a careful study of Demosthenes, Tacitus, Juvenal, and Quintilian, and then advanced to Plato. To Plato, as he considered, he owed an especial debt, being greatly impressed by the logical method, though caring little for the more mystical or poetical doctrines congenial to those who are generally called Platonists. His faculties were also stimulated by helping his father in the proofs of the *History of India*, with whom also in the year 1819 he 'went through a complete course of political economy,' first reducing to writing his father's oral expositions, and then carefully reading Ricardo and Adam Smith.

This, he says, ended what could properly be called his lessons. The whole narrative is curiously characteristic of father and son. No one could have devoted himself more unreservedly to the education of a son. While working hard for the support of himself and his family, James Mill spared no trouble to do also the whole work of a schoolmaster. The boy prepared his lessons in the room in which the father was writing, and was constantly interrupting him for help. The father submitted, but unfortunately could not submit good-humouredly. He was 'the most impatient of men,' and the most rigorous of martinets. He did not, it seems, employ the birch, but found an equivalent in sarcastic reproaches. He was angry when his pupil failed to understand him for want—not of industry but—of knowledge, and guarded against cherishing conceit by humiliating language. When John was to leave the family, the father thought it necessary to explain that he would find himself to have learned more than other lads. But, he said, you are not to be proud of it; for it would be the deepest disgrace if you had not profited by the unusual advantage of a father willing and able to teach you. Education, like other things, was evidently a matter of sanctions; and the one sanction upon which the teacher relied was the dread of his disapproval. The child was driven, rather than attracted by sympathetic encouragement. John Mill had also to teach his younger brothers and sisters, both at this and till a much later period. Mill records his conviction that their plan (suggested probably by the Lancasterian system, in which the father was so much interested) was both inefficient and a bad moral discipline for teacher and taught. When Place went to visit Bentham and the Mills at Ford Abbey in 1814, he found the system at work. The children were regularly kept at their lessons from six to nine, and from ten to one. Their dinner had been delayed one day till six, because the girls had mistaken a word, and John, their teacher, had not detected the mistake. Place thinks that John is a ' prodigy,' but fears that he will grow up ' morose and selfish.'[1] That anticipation was happily not verified. The health of the other children, however, appears to have suffered ; and, although John speaks with the warmest appreciation of his father's character, it is evident that he felt more respect than filial affection, and that, in spite of close intellectual intercourse, there was a want of such personal confidence as gives a charm to the relation in happier cases. If I cannot say that I, like his younger children, ' loved him tenderly,' says John, ' I was always loyally devoted to him.'[2] That loyalty is shown unmistakably by every reference, and the references are very frequent, that Mill made to his father in his writings. Mill's own estimate of the result of his education is noteworthy. The experiment proves, he says, the possibility of instilling into a child an amount of knowledge such as is rarely acquired before manhood. He

[1] Given in *Dictionary of National Biography*.
[2] *Autobiography*, p. 52.

was, he considers, rather below than above par in quick-
ness of apprehension, retentiveness of memory, and energy
of character. What he did, therefore, could be done by
any child of average health and capacity.   His later
achievements, he thinks, were due to the fact that, among
other favourable circumstances, his father's training had
given him the start of his contemporaries by 'a quarter
of a century.' [1]   His opinion is probably coloured by
his tendency to set down all differences between men
as due to external circumstances. He and his father, as
Professor Bain notes, inclined to the doctrine of Helvétius that children all start alike.[2]   Mill, by those who
dissent from this view, will probably be held to have
been endowed by nature with an extraordinary power of
acquiring and assimilating knowledge, and presumably
had from infancy whatever intellectual qualities are implied in that gift. His experience in teaching his own
family might have taught him that the gift is not shared
by the average child. So far, however, as Mill's judgment refers to his own case, it asserts what I take to be a
truth not always admitted. He is sometimes noticed as
an example of the evils done by excessive instruction.
Yet, after all, he certainly became one of the leading
men of his generation, and, if this strenuous education
was not the sole cause, it must be reckoned as having
been one main condition of his success. His father's
teaching had clearly one, and that the highest, merit.
The son had been taught really to use his mind ; he had
been trained to argue closely ; to test conclusions instead
of receiving them passively, and to systematise his knowledge as he acquired it. The course of strenuous mental

[1] *Autobiography*, p. 30.   [2] Bain's *J. S. Mill*, p. 84.

gymnastics qualified him to appear in early youth as a vigorous controversialist, and to achieve an immense quantity of valuable work before he passed middle age. It seems improbable that more could have been made of his faculties by any other system ; and he gave a rarely approached instance of a life in which the waste of energy is reduced to a minimum.

Mill's verdict must, however, be qualified upon another ground, which he might have been expected to recognise. No one was more anxious to assert in general that an education is good in proportion as it stimulates the faculties instead of simply storing the mind with facts. Undoubtedly Mill's knowledge was of use to him. He became widely read and interested in a large circle of subjects. But we cannot hold that the mere knowledge gave him a 'quarter of a century' start. The 'knowledge' which can be acquired by a child of fourteen is necessarily crude ; the *Theaetetus* or the history of Thucydides could not represent real thought for him ; and one would rather say that a year's activity at twenty would have enabled him, if he had read only a quarter as much by fourteen, to make up the deficiency. The knowledge was no doubt a useful foundation ; but, so far as it was acquired at the cost of excessive strain, the loss would greatly overbalance the gain. It seems clear that Mill's health did in fact suffer ; and a loss of energy was far more serious than any childish knowledge could compensate. I cannot help thinking, with the so-called 'Philistine,' that a little cricket would have been an excellent substitute for half the ancient literature instilled into a lad who was not prepared really to appreciate either the thought or the literary charm.

The system had further and permanent results. Mill saw little of other boys. His father was afraid of his being corrupted or at least vulgarised by association with the average schoolboy. He had leisure enough, he declares, though he was never allowed a holiday; but his leisure was dedicated to quiet and 'even bookish' amusements. He was unready and awkward; untrained in the ordinary accomplishments which come from the society of contemporaries. The result was—besides the trifling loss of mere physical accomplishments—that Mill was a recluse even in childhood. There was another special reason for this isolation. Mill himself says that he was brought up without any religious instruction; and though Professor Bain tells us that the boy went to church in his infancy, it must have been at so early a period as to leave no mark upon his memory.[1] Up to the age of fourteen, therefore, Mill, while kept apart from the ordinary influences, was imbibing with astonishing rapidity a vast amount of knowledge, and inevitably taking for granted the general opinions of his father's party.

At the end of his fourteenth year Mill went to the south of France, and stayed for a year with Sir Samuel, the brother of Jeremy, Bentham. There he learned French, attended various courses of lectures, and carried on his study of mathematics and of political economy. His intellectual appetite was still voracious and his hours of study were probably excessive. The period, however, was chiefly remarkable for the awakening of other tastes. The lessons of fencing and riding masters seem to have been thrown away; but he learned something of botany

---

[1] Mill's *Autobiography*, p. 43; Bain's *James Mill*, p. 90.

from George, the son of Sir Samuel, afterwards eminently distinguished in the science. Mill's taste, though it did not develop into a scientific study, made him a good field botanist, and provided him with almost his only recreation. It encouraged the love of walking, which he shared with his father; and in a tour in the Pyrenees he learned to enjoy grand natural scenery. He appears, too, to have lost some of his boyish awkwardness in the new society. The greatest advantage, however, according to himself, was his 'having breathed for a whole year the free and genial atmosphere of continental life.'[1] His comments upon this are remarkable. He could not then, as he remarks, know much of English society. He did not know its 'low moral tone,' the 'absence of high feelings' and 'sneering depreciation of all demonstrations of them,' nor, therefore, perceive the contrast with the French, who cultivate sentiments elevated by comparison at least, and who, by the habitual exercise of the feelings, encourage also a culture of the understanding, descending to the less educated classes.[2] Still, he was impressed by French amiability and sociability, and the English habit of 'acting as if everybody else was either an enemy or a bore.'

I do not venture to pronounce any opinion upon this estimate of the contrast between English and French society. Whatever truth it contains would be intensified for Mill by the fact that a large class of Englishmen clearly regarded the Utilitarians as 'enemies,' and all

[1] *Autobiography*, p. 58.

[2] Mill does not here make especial reference to his father, of whom, however, he had said before that he shared the ordinary English weakness of starving the feelings from dislike of expressing them. One would be inclined to guess that James Mill exaggerated rather than shared that feeling.

men felt them to be bores.   The 'practical' Briton no doubt treated the views of the philosophical Radical with an application of what he meant for humour and Mill received as brutality.   But the estimate is characteristic. Mill's Spartan discipline was already rousing him to a dumb sense of the value of the emotions.   Though he, with his school, was bound to denounce 'sentimentaliom,' he was beginning to see that there was another side to the question.   And, in the next place, Mill's appreciation of French courtesy fell in with a marked tendency of his thought.   He had, of course, at this time only laid the foundation of an acquaintance with France and Frenchmen, which, however, became much closer in the following years.   He acquired a cordial sympathy with the French liberals; he grew to be thoroughly familiar with French politics, and followed the later history of his friends with sympathy and admiration.   In his early essays, he is constantly insisting upon the merits of French writers and lamenting the scandalous ignorance of their achievements prevalent in England; the French *philosophes* of the eighteenth century became his model;[1] and he pushed his zeal, as he thinks, even to excess; while, as we shall afterwards see, some contemporary French writers exercised an influence upon his own views of the highest importance.   He did not learn German till some time later; and never became a profound student of German literature and philosophy.   But France was a kind of second country to him; and excited what may almost be called a patriotic sentiment.   Patriotism, indeed, was scarcely held to be a virtue by the Utilitarians.   It meant for them the state of mind of the country squire or his

[1] *Autobiography*, p. 108.

hanger-on the parson; and is generally mentioned as giving a sufficient explanation of unreasoning prejudice. Mill's development, I doubt not, was furthered by this enthusiasm; it gave him a wider outlook, and stimulated many impulses which had been hampered by the narrowness of his party. For many years, however, it contributed to make him something of an alien; and I do not think that incapacity to sympathise even with the stupid prejudices of one's countrymen is an unmixed advantage.

Mill returned to England in July 1821. He took up his old studies, taught his brothers and sisters, read Condillac and a history of the French revolution, of which, in spite of his previous stay in France, he had known very little, and decided that it would be 'transcendent glory' to be 'a Girondist in an English convention.' Meanwhile, a profession had to be chosen. He was intended for the bar, and began to study Roman law under John Austin. He set to work upon Bentham, and the reading of Dumont's *Traités de Législation* formed an epoch in his life. His botanical studies had fostered his early taste for classification, already awaked by his early logical studies. He was now delighted to find that human actions might be classified as well as plants, and, moreover, classified by the principle of utility, that is to say, by reference to a guiding rule for all known conduct. 'Utility' took its place as 'the keystone which held together the detached and fragmentary parts of his knowledge and beliefs.'[1] He had now a philosophy and even, 'in one of the best senses of the word, a religion, the inculcation and diffusion of which could be made the principal outward purpose of a life.' The very modera-

[1] *Autobiography*, p. 66.

tion of the creed was among its claims. Mill was not roused, like Shelley, to an enthusiastic vision of an abrupt regeneration of man.   His religion was strictly scientific; it recognised the necessity of slow elaboration, but offered a sufficiently wide vista of continuous improvement to be promoted by unremitting labour. He now enlarged his philosophical reading; he studied Locke, Helvétius, and Hartley, Berkeley, and Hume's *Essays*, besides Reid, Dugald Stewart, and Brown's essay upon Cause and Effect.   These studies were carried on while he was reading his father's *Analysis* in manuscript, and no doubt discussing with his father the points raised by the argument.   The last book which he mentions as affecting his early development is ' Philip Beauchamp's ' treatise upon the utility of religion.   The ' searching character of its analysis,' he says, produced a great effect upon him, of which some results will appear hereafter.

II. EARLY PROPAGANDISM

In 1822—at the age, that is, of sixteen—Mill began to compose ' argumentative ' essays, which were apparently crude enough, but which were profitable exercises. Already, too, he was beginning to take a position in the Utilitarian circle. John Austin (1790-1859), his tutor, a man of lofty, if over-fastidious character, encouraged the boy by his kind interest.   Another important friend was George Grote, who, as I have said, had already become a writer in the cause.   To both these men, his seniors by sixteen and twelve years respectively, a boy of sixteen or seventeen would naturally look up with respectful admiration.   With Grote, as with John Austin, he held much 'sympathetic communion,' but his first ally among men whom he could feel to be contemporaries was Austin's younger brother Charles. He was a man who gave the impression, according to Mill, of 'boundless strength,' with talents and will which seemed capable of 'dominating the world.' Instead of being, like his brother John, incapacitated for life by over-refinement, he made a fortune at the bar; and his energy was, after a time, entirely diverted from the Utilitarian propaganda. For the present, however, he was defending the true faith in an uncongenial atmosphere. He was, says Mill, the 'really influential mind among these intellectual gladiators'—the young Cambridge orators. James Mill, as I have said, had been encouraged by hearing that the cause of Utilitarianism was being upheld even in one of the universities, which he took to be the natural centres of obscurantism. John Mill visited Austin at Cambridge in 1822, and the boy of sixteen greatly impressed the undergraduates by his conversational power. The elder Mill was urged to send his son to Trinity College. He would no doubt have feared to expose the youth to such contagion.[1] John Mill himself long held the universities to be mere institutions for supporting the established creed. 'We regard the system of these institutions,' he said in 1836, 'as administered for two centuries past, with sentiments little short of utter abhorrence.'[2] It is

---

[1] It was not necessary at this time for an undergraduate to sign the Thirty-nine Articles as Bain supposes. From 1773 a graduate had to make the declaration that he was a '*bona fide* member of the church of England,' whatever that may mean; but any one might be a member of the University and pass the examinations. Sylvester, for example, though a Jew, was second wrangler in 1837.

[2] *Dissertations*, i. 193.

idle to ask whether closer contact with the average
English youth would or would not have been beneficial,
but the sentiment marks the degree in which Mill was
an alien among men of his own class in English society.
Meanwhile, he formed, in the winter of 1822-23, a little
society of his own. He called it the Utilitarian Society,
adopting the title which had been cursorily used by
Bentham[1] from Galt's *Annals of the Parish*. He mentions
among its members, which never amounted to ten, William
Eyton Tooke, son of Thomas Tooke, the economist,
who died young ; William Ellis (1800-1881), known,
says Mill, for his 'apostolic exertions for the improvement of education,' chiefly in the direction of promoting
the study of political economy in schools ; George John
Graham, afterwards an official in the Bankruptcy Court ;
and Graham's special friend, John Arthur Roebuck
(1801-1879), who was to become one of the most
thoroughgoing Radicals of the following period, though
in later years the faithful Abdiel became an Ishmael, and
finally a Tory. With these youths, all apparently Mill's
seniors by a few years, he discussed the principles of the
sect, and became, as he says, 'a sort of leader.' He tried
hard to enlist recruits, and soon became an effective com-
batant in the actual warfare of the time. The society was
broken up in 1826.

Mill had already received the appointment which decided the future course of his life. He was appointed
to a clerkship in the India House, 21st May 1823,

---

[1] The name soon became popular. Southey, writing to Henry Taylor (12th
April 1827), calls them 'Futilitarians' (*Life and Correspondence*). Taylor
was on friendly terms with the set, and gives some account of them and the
later debating society. See *Autobiography*, i. 77-95 ; and *Correspondence*,
pp. 30, 72.

having just finished his seventeenth year. He received successive promotions, till in 1856 he became chief of the office with a salary of £2000 a year. Mill gives his own view of the advantages of the position, which to a man of his extraordinary power of work were unmistakable. He was placed beyond all anxiety as to breadwinning. He was not bound to make a living by his pen, and could devote himself to writing of permanent value. He was at the same time brought into close relation with the conduct of actual affairs ; forced to recognise the necessity of compromise, and to study the art of instilling his thoughts into minds not specially prepared for their reception. Mill's books show how well he acquired this art. Whatever their other merits or defects, they reconcile conditions too often conflicting ; they are the product of mature reflection, and yet presented so as to be intelligible without special initiation. He is unsurpassable as an interpreter between the abstract philosopher and the man of common-sense. The duties were not such as to absorb his powers. Though his holidays were limited to a month, he could enjoy Sunday rambles in the country and pedestrian tours at home and abroad; and though conscientiously discharging his official duties, he managed to turn out as much other work as might have occupied the whole time of average men. The Utilitarians were beginning to make themselves felt in the press. Mill's first printed writings were some letters in the *Traveller* in 1822, defending Ricardo and James Mill against some criticism by Torrens. He then contributed three letters to the *Morning Chronicle*, denouncing the prosecution of Carlile, which then excited the rightful wrath of the Utilitarians. Two letters in

continuation were too outspoken to be published.[1]   Mill
contributed to the *Westminster Review* from its start in
the spring of 1824, helping his father's assault upon the
Edinburgh.   He was, he says, the most frequent writer
of all, and between the second and eighteenth number
contributed thirteen reviews.   They show that he was
reading widely.   An article upon Scott's *Napoleon* in
1828 shows that he had fully made up his deficiencies as
to the history of the French revolution.   He had not,
however, as yet attained his full powers of expression;
and neither the style nor the arrangement of the matter
has the merits of his later work.[2]   The most remarkable
by far is the review of Whately's *Logic* in January 1828.
It shows some touches of youthful arrogance, though
exceedingly complimentary to the author reviewed.   But
the knowledge displayed and the vigour of the expression
are surprising in a youth of twenty-one; and it proves
that Mill was already reflecting to some purpose upon
the questions treated in his *Logic*.

While thus serving an apprenticeship to journalism,

[1] About this period, Mill, then aged seventeen or eighteen, took part with
some friends in distributing a pamphlet called 'What is Love?' advocating
what are now called Neo-Malthusian principles.   The police interfered, and
some scandal was caused.   An allusion to this performance—which shows
Mill's enthusiasm and honesty, if not his discretion—appeared in an article
by Abraham Hayward upon Mill's death.   Hayward was attacked by
W. D. Christie in an indignant pamphlet, which gives a sufficient statement
of the facts.   See Cobbett's *Political Works*, vi. 421 (August 1824), for a reference to this affair.

[2] Bain thinks that J. S. Mill wrote the article in the Review upon the
Carlile prosecutions in July 1824.   I cannot admit this opinion.   If so, Mill
was a more capable journalist than the other articles would imply.   But—
apart from questions of style—I cannot think that Mill would have gone
out of his way to avow a belief in Christianity, as is done by the writer of
the article.

Mill was going through a remarkable mental training. About the beginning of 1825 he undertook to edit Bentham's *Rationale of Evidence*. He says that this work ' occupied nearly all his leisure for about a year.' That such a task should have been accomplished by a youth of twenty in a year would seem marvellous even if he had been exclusively devoted to it. He had to condense large masses of Bentham's crabbed manuscript into a continuous treatise ; to ' unroll' his author's involved and parenthetic sentences ; to read the standard English textbooks upon evidence ; to reply to reviewers of previous works of Bentham, and to add comments especially upon some logical points. Finally, he had to see ' five large volumes through the press.'[1] That this was admirable practice, and that Mill's style became afterwards ' markedly superior' to what it had been before, may be well believed. It is impossible, however, not to connect the fact that Mill had gone through this labour in 1825 with the singular mental convulsion which followed in 1826.

He was, he says, in a ' dull state of nerves' in the autumn of that year. It occurred to him to ask whether he would be happy supposing that all his objects in life could be realised. ' An irrepressible consciousness distinctly answered "No."' The cloud would not pass away. He could think of no physician of the mind who could ' raze out the rooted trouble of the brain.' His father had no experience of such feeling, nor could he

---

[1] In the collective edition of Bentham's *Works* the treatise occupies about 900 double-column pages of some 500 words to a column. If 300 days were given to the task, this would mean an average output of 1500 words a day.

give the elder man the pain of thinking that all the educational plans had failed. The father's philosophy, indeed,
both explained, and showed the hopelessness of, the evil.
Feelings depend upon association. Analysis tends to
destroy the associations, and therefore to ' wear away the
feelings.' Happiness has for its main source the pleasure
of sympathy with others. But the knowledge that the
feeling would give happiness could not suffice to restore
the feeling itself. It seemed to be impossible to set to
work again and create new associations. Mill dragged
on mechanically through the winter of 1826-27, and the
gloom only gathered. He made up his mind that he
could not bear life for more than a year. The first ray
of hope came from a passage in which Marmontel de-
scribes his father's death and his resolution to make up
the loss to his family. Gradually he recovered, though
he suffered several relapses. He learned, he says, two
lessons : first, that though happiness must be the end, it
must not be the immediate or conscious end, of life. Ask
whether you are happy and you will cease to be happy.
Fix upon some end external to happiness, and happiness
will be ' inhaled with the air you breathe.' And in the
second place, he learned to make the ' cultivation of the
feelings one of the cardinal points in his ethical and
philosophical creed.' He could not, however, for some
time apply his new doctrine to practice. He mentions
as a quaint illustration of this period one ingenious mode
of self-torment. He had from childhood taken pleasure
in music. During the period of depression even music
had lost its charm. As he revived, the charm gradually
returned. Yet he teased himself by the reflection that,
as the number of musical notes is limited, there must

come a time when new Mozarts and Webers would no longer be possible. This, he says, was like the fear of the Laputans that the sun would in time be burnt out, a fear, it may be remarked, which modern science has not diminished. He might have noticed that, as the number of combinations of twenty-six letters is finite, new Shakespeares and Dantes will become impossible. He observes, however, that this was connected with the ' only good point in his very unromantic and in no way honourable distress.' It showed an interest in the fortunes of the race as well as in his own, and therefore gave hopes that if he could see his way to better prospects of human happiness his depression might be finally removed. This state of mind made his reading of Wordsworth's *Excursion* in the autumn of 1828 an important event in his life. He could make nothing of Byron, whom he also studied for the first time. But Wordsworth appealed to the love of scenery, which was already one of his passions, and thus revealed to him the pleasure of tranquil contemplation and of an interest in the common feelings and destiny of human beings. From the famous *Ode*, too, he inferred that Wordsworth had gone through an experience like his own, had regretted the freshness of early life, and had found compensation by the path along which he could guide his reader.

The effect upon Mill of Wordsworth's poetry is remarkable, though I cannot here discuss the relation. Readers of the fourth book of the *Excursion* (called ' Despondency corrected') may note how directly the poet applies his teaching to the philosopher. He asks, for example, whether men of science and those who have ' analysed the thinking principle' are to become a 'degraded race,' and declares that it could never be intended by nature

> 'That we should pore, and dwindle as we pore,
> Viewing all objects unremittingly
> In disconnexion dead and spiritless;
> And still dividing, and dividing still,
> Break down all grandeur, still unsatisfied
> With the perverse attempt, while littleness
> May yet become more little; waging thus
> An impious warfare with the very life
> Of our own souls!'

This is the precise equivalent of Mill's doctrine about the danger of the habit of analysis, and James Mill, if Wordsworth had ever read him, would have made an admirable example for the excellent pedlar.

It is characteristic of Mill that he does not explicitly attribute this mental crisis to the obvious physical cause. As Professor Bain tells us, he would never admit that hard work could injure anybody. Disbelief in that danger is only too common with hard workers. Mill intimates that his dejection was occasioned by a 'low state of nerves,' but adds that this was one of the accidents to which every one is occasionally liable.[1] A man would at least be more liable to it who, like Mill, had been kept in a state of severe intellectual tension from his earliest infancy, and who had gone through such labours as the editing Bentham's *Rationale of Evidence*. That his health was permanently affected seems to be clear. Ten years later (1836) he was 'seized with an obstinate derangement of the brain.' One symptom was a 'ceaseless spasmodic twitching over one eye,' which never left him. In 1839 another illness forced him to take a month's holiday, which he spent in Italy. It left permanent weakness in the lungs and the stomach. An accident in

[1] *Autobiography*, p. 133.

1848 led to a long illness and prostration of the nervous system ; and in 1854 another serious illness, which he met by an eight months' tour in Italy, Sicily, and Greece, led to the 'partial destruction of one lung' and great 'general debility.'[1] In spite of these illnesses, Mill continued to labour as strenuously as before, and until the illness of 1848 at least showed no signs of any decline of intellectual energy. They must be remembered if we would do full justice to his later career.

It is, meanwhile, remarkable that his energetic course of self-education seems hardly to have been interrupted by the period of dejection. In the year 1825, while, one might have supposed, fairly drowned in Bentham's manuscript, he contributed an article upon Catholic Emancipation to a *Parliamentary History*, started by Mr. Marshall of Leeds. He wrote others upon the commercial crisis and upon the currency and upon reciprocity in commerce for the two subsequent annual issues. He thinks that his work had now ceased to be 'juvenile,' and might be called original, so far as it applied old ideas in a new connection. At the same time he learned German, forming a class for the purpose. He also set up a society which met two days a week at Grote's house in Threadneedle Street and discussed various topics from half-past 8 till 10 A.M. These meetings lasted till 1830. The young men discussed in succession political economy, logic, and pyschology. Their plan was to take some text-book, and to discuss every point raised thoroughly— sometimes keeping to a single question for weeks—until every one was satisfied with at least his own solution of the question. Ricardo, James Mill, and their like supplied the chief literature ; but in logic they went further, and,

[1] Bain's *J. S. Mill*, pp. 43, 45, 90, 95.

being disgusted with Aldrich, reprinted the *Manuductio ad Logicam* of the Jesuit Du Trieu. The result of these arguments appears in the review of Whately. Mill, helped by Graham and Ellis (his old allies in the Utilitarian Society), started 'most of the novelties'; while Grote and the others formed a critical tribunal. The results formed the materials of several of Mill's writings. These occupations might have been enough for a youth of twenty, but another field for discussion offered itself. The followers of Owen were starting weekly public discussions in 1825. The Utilitarians, headed by Charles Austin, went in a body, and a series of friendly but very energetic debates went on for three months. This led to the foundation of a debating society, upon the model of the 'Speculative Society' of Edinburgh. After a failure at starting, the society became active, and until 1829 Mill took part in nearly every debate. Besides the Utilitarians, it included Macaulay, Thirlwall, Praed, the Bulwers, Fonblanque, and others. Charles Buller and Cockburn came in as Radicals, and the Tories, of whom there had been a lack in those days of reforming zeal, were reinforced by Shee (afterwards judge) and A. Hayward. Maurice and Sterling were representatives of a liberalism widely differing from Utilitarianism, and accepting Coleridge in place of Bentham as intellectual guide. Mill learned to speak fluently, if not gracefully, and improved his style by preparing written speeches. It is not strange that, with all these occupations, he felt it a relief when, in 1828, he was released from contributing to the *Westminster*. Bowring, the editor, had made arrangements with Perronet Thompson, and it was no longer an organ of the orthodox

Utilitarians. In 1829 Mill gave up the Speculative Society and resolved to devote himself to private studies and prepare for more elaborate work. New thoughts were being suggested from various quarters. Macaulay's attack upon his father's political theory led him to recognise the inadequacy of the Utilitarian system, and forced him to consider the logical problems involved. He came under the influence of the St. Simonians at the same period. An enthusiastic disciple of the school, Gustave d'Eichthal, two years senior to Mill, was taken by young Tooke to the debating society in May 1828, and was surprised by Mill's skilful and comprehensive summing up of a discussion. He endeavoured to make proselytes of the pair, then full of the enthusiasm and expecting the triumph of their party. Tooke, apparently Mill's warmest friend at the time, committed suicide early in 1830, in an access of excitement produced by fever ascribed to overwork and tension of mind. Mill became a half-convert. He was greatly impressed by the St. Simonian doctrine of the alternation of 'critical' and 'constructive' periods. He admitted the necessity of something better than the negative or 'critical philosophy' of the eighteenth century.[1] He desired the formation of a spiritual power. He protested, however, against the excessive spirit of system and against premature attempts to organise such a power. Yet by degrees he modified his objections, and on 30th November 1831 declares his belief that the St. Simonian ideal will be the final state of the human race. Were England ripe for an 'organic view,' which it certainly is not, he might renounce everything in the world

[1] D'Eichthal, *Correspondence*, p. 30.

to become—not one of them, but—like them. Mill
kept, as he says, a bureau of St. Simonianism for a
time, and suggested to d'Eichthal the names of many
persons to whom the publications of the party might be
sent.   Bulwer, Sterling, Whately, Blanco White, W. J.
Fox, and Dr. Arnold were among them.[1]   Meanwhile,
his speculations caused him to be much troubled
by the doctrine of Philosophical Necessity ; and he
worked out a solution which was ultimately published in
the *Logic*.   While his mind was thus fermenting with
many new thoughts, often, as he says,[2] new only to him,
he was profoundly moved by the French revolution of
July 1830.   He went at once to Paris with Roebuck
and Graham ; was introduced to Lafayette, made friends
with other popular leaders, and came back prepared to
take an active part as a writer on behalf of the Reform
agitation.   For some years he was an active journalist,
contributing to the *Examiner* under Fonblanque.   A
series of articles called ' The Spirit of the Age ' in this
paper led to his acquaintance with Carlyle, who took
him to be a ' new Mystic.'[3]   In 1830 and 1831 he wrote
his essays on *Some Unsettled Questions of Political Economy*,
the fruit of the discussions with Graham (not published
till 1844), and in 1832 wrote articles upon foundations

[1] D'Eichthal, *Correspondence*, p. 147.   The St. Simonians excited some
interest in England at the time.   See, *e.g.*, Carlyle's *Sartor Resartus*, book iii.
ch. 12 ; Carlyle's *Correspondence with Goethe*, 214, 226, 258; *Tennyson's Life*,
i. 99 ; Todhunter's *Whewell*, i. 240 ; Hodder's *Shaftesbury*, i. 126.   Shaftesbury's notice was called to St. Simonianism by Southey, who wrote an article
upon it in the *Quarterly* for July 1831—a mere shriek of alarm.

[2] *Autobiography*, p. 168.

[3] Seven articles appeared from January to May 1831.   As Mill says in his
Autobiography (p. 175) they are ' lumbering in style,' and of no great interest
in substance, except as showing the St. Simonian influence.

and upon the ' currency juggle,' which are the first of his collected dissertations.

I have now followed Mill's mental history until the period at which the follower was fully competent to become the guide. It would be difficult to mention any thinker who has gone through a more strenuous and continuous discipline. From his earliest infancy till the full development of his powers he had been going through a kind of logical mill. No student in the old schools employing every waking hour in ' syllogising ' could have been more assiduously trained to the use of his weapons. If his boyish years had been passed in a kind of intellectual gymnasium, he had as a youth proved and perfected his skill in the open arena. His official position was making him familiar with business and with the ordinary state of mind of the commonplace politician. He had been interested in fresh lines of thought through the writings of French Liberals, and especially the St. Simonians, and through his arguments with the Socialists who followed Owen, and with the young men who looked up to Coleridge as their great teacher. His own experience had brought home to him the sense of a certain narrowness and rigidity in the Utilitarians; his friendly controversies had led him to regard opponents with more toleration than his party generally displayed, and he was sincerely anxious to widen the foundations of his creed, and to assimilate whatever was valuable in conflicting doctrines. Meanwhile his practice as a writer had by this time enabled him to express himself with great clearness and vigour ; and young as he still was, he was better qualified than any of his contemporaries to expound the views of his party.

One point, however, must be marked. Mill's training
left nothing to be desired as a system of intellectual
gymnastics. It was by no means so well calculated
to widen the mental horizon. His philosophical reading was not to be compared to that, for example,
of Sir William Hamilton, who was at this time
accumulating his great stores of knowledge. He
learned German, as people were beginning to learn
it, but he did not make himself familiar with German
thought. On 13th March 1843, having just sent
a copy of his *Logic* to Comte, he observes that he
owes much to German philosophy as a corrective to
his exclusive Benthamism. He has not, he adds, read
Kant, Hegel, or any chief of the school, but knows of
them from their French and English interpreters—
presumably Cousin, Coleridge, and Sir W. Hamilton.
He tried some of the originals afterwards, but found
that he had got all that was useful in them, and the
remainder was so *fastidieux* that he could not go on
reading.[1] Considering all his occupations, his official
duties, his editing of Bentham, his many contributions
to journalism, and the time taken up by the little societies
of congenial minds, the wonderful thing is that he read
so much else. He kept himself well informed on the
intellectual movement of France ; he had made a special
study of the French revolution ; and was fairly familiar
with many other provinces of historical inquiry. It was
impossible, however, that he should become learned in
the strict sense. His studies, that is, were more remarkable for intensity than for extent. The vigorous discussions with his friends upon political economy, logic,

[1] *Correspondence with Comte*, pp. 169-70.

and psychology, while implying an admirable training, implied also a limitation of study; they did not get beyond the school of Ricardo in political economy, nor beyond the school of James Mill in psychology, nor beyond a few textbooks in formal logic. They argued the questions raised thoroughly, and until they had fully settled their own doubts. But it would be an inevitable result that they would generally be satisfied when they had discovered not so much a thorough solution as the best solution which could be given from the Utilitarian point of view. The more fundamental questions as to the tenability of that view would hardly be raised. Therefore, though Mill deserves all the credit which he has received for candour, and was, in fact, most anxious to receive light from outside, it is not surprising that he will sometimes appear to have been blind to arguments familiar to thinkers of a different school. The fault is certainly not peculiar to Mill; indeed, it is his genuine desire to escape from it which makes it necessary to ask why the escape was not more complete. Briefly, at any rate, Mill, like most other people, continued through life to be penetrated by the convictions instilled in early youth.

III. THE PHILOSOPHICAL RADICALS

The period which followed the Reform Bill showed a great change in Mill's personal position. The Utilitarians had taken their part in the agitation, and expected to share in the fruits of victory. Several of them were members of the first reformed parliament, especially Grote and Roebuck, who now entered the House for the first time. Charles Buller (1806-1848) and Sir William

Molesworth (1810-1855) were also new members, and
both were among the youngest recruits of the Utilitarian
party.   Buller had been a pupil of Carlyle, and afterwards one of the Cambridge orators.   He was evidently
a man of very attractive nature, though he seems to have
been too fond of a joke—the only Utilitarian, probably,
liable to that imputation—and was gaining a high reputation by the time of his early death.   Molesworth, after a
desultory education, which included a brief stay at Cambridge about Buller's time, and some study on the Continent, became a friend of Grote upon entering parliament.
He was a man of many intellectual interests, and an
ardent Utilitarian.   These and a few more formed the
party known as 'the philosophical Radicals.'   Mill,
whose position was incompatible with parliamentary
ambition, was to be the exponent of their principles in
the press.   Whatever their failings, they certainly formed
an important section of the most intelligent politicians of
the time.   Mill became their chief exponent in the press,
and began operations by articles in the *Examiner* and the
Monthly Repository (edited by W. J. Fox).   He says[1]
that his writings between 1832 and 1834 would fill a
large volume.   Molesworth then proposed to start a new
quarterly, to be called the *London Review*, which should
represent the true creed more faithfully than the recreant
Westminster.   He stipulated that Mill should be the
virtual, though he could not, on account of his official
position, be the ostensible, editor.   The first number of
the *London* accordingly appeared in April 1835.   A
year later Molesworth bought the *Westminster*, and the
review was now called the *London and Westminster*.

[1] *Autobiography*, p. 198.

Molesworth, having become tired of carrying on a review which did not pay, handed it over to Mill in 1837, who continued it till 1840, when he transferred it to Mr. Hickson.[1] The vitality of unprofitable reviews is one of the mysteries of literature. Mill lost money and spent much time in this discouraging work ; but he would doubtless have grudged neither had he succeeded in doing a real service to his party.

The 'philosophical' Radicals, however, were doomed to failure. One among many obvious reasons is suggested by the name. Philosophical in English is synonymous with visionary, unpractical, or perhaps, simply foolish. The philosophers seemed to be men of crotchets, fitter for the study than the platform. They had, as Mill says, little enterprise or activity, and left the lead to the 'old hands,' Hume and O'Connell. About 1838, indeed, Mill appears to have become quite alienated from them. He thought them 'craven,' and they thought him 'mad.'[2] He admits, indeed, that the men were less to blame than the times. Mill, however, held then, and seems to have always believed, that what was wanting was mainly a worthy leader. His father, he thinks, might have forced the Whigs to accept the Radical policy had he been in parliament. For want of such a leader, the philosophical Radicals became a mere left wing of the Whigs. For a time, Mill had some hopes of Lord Durham, who represented Radical leanings in the upper sphere. Durham's death in 1840

---

[1] *Autobiography,* pp. 199, 206, 220; Bain's *J. S. Mill,* p. 58. Mill at first supervised rather than edited the *Review.* His sub-editors were Thomas Falconer and afterwards John Robertson.

[2] Bain's *J. S. Mill,* p. 160 (quotation from Fonblanque). See also pp. 56, 82.

put an end to any such hopes ; and the philosophical Radicals had pretty well ceased by that time to represent any real political force. In truth, however, it is difficult to believe that any leader could have made much out of the materials at his disposal. The Reform Bill had transferred power to the middle classes. They had resented their own exclusion from influence, and it had been impossible to prevent the great towns from acquiring a share in the representation without risk of violent revolution. But it did not at all follow that the majority of the new constituents accepted the programme of the extreme reformers. They had forced the doors for themselves, but had no desire to admit the crowd still left outside. Only a small minority desired the measures which the Radicals had contemplated, which involved organic constitutional changes, and would possibly lead to confiscation. When the Chartists proposed a sweeping reform the middle classes were frightened by the prospect of revolution. They were quite willing to leave the old aristocratic families in power, if only the policy were modified so as to be more congenial to the industrial interests. Statesmen brought up under the old system were still the office holders, and were only anxious to steer a middle course. All this is now obvious enough ; and it meant at the time that the philosophical Radicals found themselves, to their surprise, without any great force behind them, and were only able to complain of the half-hearted policy of the Whigs, and to weaken the administration until the Conservatives under Peel could take advantage of a situation which had become intolerable. The favourite measure of the philosophical Radicals was the ballot. They attributed the slackening of zeal for Radicalism to the fact that the aristocracy were trying to maintain their old power by bribery and intimidation. The ballot would be the most obvious check to this policy.

Under these conditions Mill's position is characteristic. He wrote much and forcibly. Some of his articles of this period in the *Westminster* are collected in the first volume of the *Dissertations*. He omitted others which refer to matters of more ephemeral interest. They show great power, but they also indicate the real difficulty. Mill writes as a philosopher and an expounder of general ideas. But he also writes as a partisan—insisting, for example, upon the ballot of which he afterwards came to disapprove—and it is always a very difficult matter to reconcile the requirements imposed by these different points of view. Mill was scarcely immersed enough in the current of political agitation to plant telling personal blows ; and, on the other hand, his theories seem to be cramped by the necessity of supporting a platform. He aimed, he says, at two points. He tried, and, he thinks, with partial success, to supply a philosophy of Radicalism, wider than Bentham's, and yet including what was permanently valuable in Bentham. He tried also, and this aim was ' from the first chimerical,' to rouse the Radicals to the formation of a powerful party. The articles upon Durham were partly prompted by this purpose ; and, though unsuccessful in that respect, he spoke, he thinks, the ' word in season,' which at a critical moment directed public opinion towards the concession of self-government to the Colonies.[1]

The articles in the *Westminster* show, now that we can

[1] *Autobiography*, pp. 214-17.

see later developments, how clearly he saw the real
difficulty, and yet how far he was from estimating its
full significance. They are of essential importance to an
understanding of his whole career.[1] In the article which
was his farewell to politics for the time, he elaborately
states the problem. He considers what are a man's
'natural' politics. He claims more than the usual faith
in the influence of reason and virtue over men's minds ;
but then it is in the influence ' of the reason and virtue
upon their own side of the question.' A man is made a
Liberal or a Conservative on the average by his position ;
he is made a Liberal or a Conservative of a particular
kind by his 'intellect and heart.' In other words, parties,
in the main, represent classes ; and the fundamental
opposition is between the ' privileged ' and the ' disqualified ' classes. The line, then, as with the old Radicals, is
drawn between the privileged, who are chiefly the landowners and their adherents, clerical, legal, and military,
and the ' disqualified,' who are chiefly the lower middle
classes and the working classes. Now, the Radical party
ought to combine the whole strength of the disqualified
against the privileged. Why do they not? Among the
superficial reasons is that want of a leader, which Mill
hoped to supply by Durham. Another personal reason
is that, as he complains rather bitterly,[2] the Radicals
never spoke so as to secure the sympathy of the working
classes. This points to the real difficulty. There was
a gulf between the middle and the working classes, as
well as between the ' privileged ' and the ' disqualified.'

---

[1] See articles in *Westminster Review* : Oct. 1837, ' Parties and the Ministry ' ; Jan. 1838, 'Radicalism in Canada ' ; April 1839, ' Reorganisation of
the Radical party.'   [2] ' Parties and the Ministry.'

The real aim of Mill's articles is to show how this gulf could be surmounted. All the ' disqualified ' might be brought into line if only the philosophical Radicals could be got to attract the working classes, and the working classes to follow the Radicals. Mill therefore endeavours to prove that the Radical measures were in fact intended for the benefit of the working classes, and might consequently be made attractive. The position was in fact precisely this. The Chartist agitation was becoming conspicuous, and the Chartists had broken off from the Radicals. Mill had to persuade them that they did not know their true friends. His sincerity and the warmth of his sympathy are unmistakable, but so is the difficulty of the task.

In the first place, he repudiates universal suffrage (one of the six points). He thinks it bad in point of policy, because to propose it would alienate the whole middle class at once, who would see in it a direct attack upon property. But universal suffrage was also bad in itself, because the mass of the very lowest class was ignorant, degraded, and utterly unfit for power. The intelligent working man ought to recognise the fact, and therefore not to grant the suffrage to the lowest class. What, then, was to be done ? The answer, given emphatically in his last article, is that we should govern for the working classes by means of the middle classes. That, he says, should be the motto of every Radical. The ideal is a government which should adopt such a policy as would be adopted under universal suffrage in a country where the masses were educated so as to be fit for it. In other words, the great aim of Radicals should be to redress practical grievances.

Did, then, the Radical platform aim at such redress ? Mill's proof that it did is significant. The Radicals were unanimous against the Corn-laws ; and the Corn-laws, as he argues,[1] injure the poor man because they lower the rate of profit, and are ruining the small capitalist and destroying our trade. The philosophical Radicals were supporters of the new Poor-law. It had often been said that the sinecurists were in fact rich paupers living on other men's labours. Mill inverts the argument by saying that the paupers under the old system were poor sinecurists, equally living upon other men's labours. To say nothing of some smaller grievances, such as taxes on articles consumed by the poor, flogging in the army, and enclosure of commons, which were attacked by the Radicals, the Radicals also wished to discharge 'one of the highest duties of government' by setting up a system of national education. It is now easy to see why these proposals failed to satisfy the class to whom the Radicals were to appeal. A great part of them, he says, were 'Owenites' or, in other words, inclined to Socialism. They had, as Mill regretfully admits, crude views upon political economy. Thus, the Chartists were not hearty, even in the anti-Corn-law agitation. They did not see that a rise of profits was at all for their benefit. They held, as Mill observes, that whatever profit was gained would go to their masters. On the other hand, they did not admire the new Poor-law. They thought that, as Cobbett had told them, it robbed them of their rights, and did not object to having small sinecures. National education, however desirable, did not seem worth a struggle till they

[1] ',Ministers and Parties.'

had got higher wages.   Then, as Mill again admits, they
would not see that the competition which injured them
was their own competition, and due to their disregard of
Malthus.   They objected to competition in general,
which meant, as they thought, the grinding down of their
class by the wicked capitalist.   Mill remarks that Owen
was not really opposed to rights of property ; and one
of his recommendations is that the law of partnership
should be reformed so as to facilitate the growth of co-
operative societies.   Even if this failed, it would tend to
educate the poor in sound economic principles.   Meanwhile, however, the principles of their actual leaders
were anything but 'sound.'   Mill incidentally speaks
of the 'Oastlers and Stephenses' as representing only
the worst class of the 'operative Radicals.'   Oastler
was at this time conspicuous for his support of the
factory legislation.   He was allied with Lord Ashley,
and represented the alliance of Socialism with Toryism
or 'New Englandism.'   Now the factory legislation,
which naturally seemed to the working classes the
greatest step towards a recognition of their interest, is
not mentioned by Mill, and for the good reason that
he and his school were opposed to it on principle.   He
refers incidentally to measures such as the Eight Hours
Bill as belonging to the quack schemes of reform.[1]

Briefly, the difficulty was that the working classes
were already looking in the direction of Socialism, and
that Mill remained a thorough individualist.   With his
sanguine belief in the power of education, he thought,
with a certain simplicity, that the Owenites, with whose
ultimate views he fully sympathised, might be taught to

[1] See 'Claims of Labour' in *Dissertations*, ii. 192.

give up their crude political economy.   Their education required more time and labour than he imagined.

This indicates a critical point.   The classes which had been disappointed by the Reform Bill, and had hoped for great social changes, were discontented, but looked for remedies of a very different kind from Mill's.   They could not see a philanthropy which was hidden behind Malthus and Ricardo, and which proposed to improve their position by removing privileges, indeed, but not by diminishing competition.   If this applied to Mill, it applied still more to his friends.   They represented rather intellectual scorn for old prejudices and clumsy administration than any keen sympathy with the sufferings of the poor.   The harsher side of the old Utilitarianism was, therefore, emphasised by them, and Mill's attempts to enlarge and soften its teaching were regarded by his allies with a certain suspicion.   They thought that his sympathy with the Socialist ends implied a tendency to look too favourably upon its means.   The articles upon Bentham and Coleridge,[1] in which he tried to inculcate a wider sympathy with his opponents, scandalised such friends as Grote, and he ceased to represent even his own allies.   Philosophical Radicalism died out. Its adherents became Whigs, or joined the Cobden form of Radicalism, which was the very antithesis of Socialism. Their philosophy suited neither party.   To the class which still retained the leading position in politics, they appeared as destructives ; and to the classes which were turning towards Chartism, they appeared as the most chilling critics of popular aspiration.   The Free-trade movement, which was gathering strength as the manufacturing

[1] August 1838, and March 1840.

interest grew stronger, had no doubt an affinity for one important part of their teaching. But such men as Cobden and Bright, though they accepted the political economy of the Utilitarians, could not be counted as products or adherents of the Utilitarian philosophy. The agreement was superficial in other respects, though complete in regard to one important group of measures. This marks an essential point in Mill's political and social doctrine. For the present, it is enough to note that the philosophical Radicals who had expected to lead the van had been left on one side in the political warfare, and by 1840 were almost disbanded. Grote, the ablest of Mill's friends, retired from parliament to devote himself to his *History of Greece* about the same time as Mill set to work upon the completion of his *Logic*.

One characteristic of Mill as an editor may be noted before proceeding. Under his management, a large number of distinguished contributors were enlisted. Professor Bain mentions Bulwer, Charles Buller, Roebuck, James and Harriet Martineau, W. J. Fox, Mazzini, and others. The independent authorship of many articles was indicated by appending letters, although Mill could not introduce the more modern plan of full signatures. He occasionally attaches notes to express his personal dissent from some of the opinions advocated, and aims at representing various shades of thought. He was especially anxious to help rising men of genius. In the *London Review* in 1835 he wrote one of the first appreciations of Tennyson, and answered some depreciatory criticisms of the *Quarterly Review* and *Blackwood*.[1]

---

[1] Browning believed that he had written in 1833 a review of *Pauline* for *Tait's Magazine*, where, however, it was supplanted by a less favourable notice.—Mrs. Orr's *Life of Browning*, p. 59.

On the publication of Carlyle's French Revolution he called attention to its merits in an article (July 1837), which, though rather clumsy in form, shows no want of generous appreciation of Carlyle's historical powers; and in a later number (October 1839) admitted, with a note to explain his personal reservations, an exposition of Carlyle by Sterling. To his review of Carlyle's book, as to the Durham article, he attributes considerable success.[1] It set people right, he thinks, in regard to a writer who had set commonplace critics at defiance. From a letter quoted by Professor Bain,[2] he reckoned at the time as a third success the result of his constant 'dinning into people's ears' that Guizot was 'a great thinker and writer.' His opinion of Guizot was to change; but the article republished in the Dissertations from the Edinburgh Review of 1845 shows that he retained a high admiration for Guizot's work. Other articles upon Carrel, A. de Vigny, and Michelet in the same collection show his constant desire to rouse Englishmen to an appreciation of French literature. Tocqueville's Democracy in America was twice reviewed by him, and had an important influence upon his thought.[3] The rigid Utilitarianism of Grote was a little scandalised by the width of Mill's sympathies even with his opponents. The orthodoxy of a man who could see and even insist upon the good side of Coleridge and Carlyle was precarious. In any case, we may admit that Mill showed the generous desire to meet and encourage whatever seemed good in others, which is one of his strong claims upon our personal respect.

[1] Autobiography, p. 217.　　[2] Bain's J. S. Mill, p. 59.
[3] Autobiography, p. 191,

For many years Mill's relation to Carlyle, who represented a Radicalism of a very different type, was significant. The first personal acquaintance began in 1831, when Carlyle came to London, and desired to see the author of the articles upon the 'Spirit of the Age.' For a time there was a warm liking on both sides. Mill appeared as a candid and eager disciple, and Carlyle hoped that he would become a 'mystic.' During Carlyle's subsequent retirement at Craigenputtock, they carried on an intimate correspondence.[1] Mill's letters, of which Froude gives an interesting summary, show Mill's characteristic candour and desire to profit by a new light. Though he speaks with the deference becoming to the younger man, and to one who admits his senior's superiority as a poet, if not as a mere logician, he confesses with a certain shyness to a radical dissent upon very vital points. But the most remarkable characteristic is Mill's conviction that he has emerged from the old dry Benthamism into some higher creed. What precisely that may be is not so obvious. When in 1834 Carlyle finally settled in London, the intercourse became frequent. Mill supplied Carlyle with books on the French revolution, and was responsible for the famous destruction of the manuscript of the first volume. The review in the *Westminster* was perhaps prompted partly by remorse for this catastrophe, though mainly, no doubt, by a generous desire to help his friend. At one time Carlyle hoped to be under-editor to the newly started *London Review*; and, as the old tutor of Charles

[1] Froude's *Carlyle: First Forty Years*, ii. 360. The letters are in existence, but have not been published. Mr. A. Carlyle has kindly allowed me to read them.

Buller, he was naturally acquainted with the Utilitarian circle. The divergence of the whole creed and ways of thought of the men was certain to cool the alliance. Carlyle expresses respect for the honesty of the Utilitarians, and considered them as allies in the war against cant. But his 'mysticism' implied the conviction that their negative attitude in regard to religion was altogether detestable; while, in political theories, he was at the very opposite pole. Mill sympathised with his *Chartism* (1839) and *Past and Present* (1843), published at this period, as remonstrances against the sins of the governing classes; but altogether rejects what he took to be the reactionary tendency of the Carlylese gospel. Ultimately, when Carlyle attacked the anti-slavery agitators in 1849, Mill made an indignant reply,[1] and all intercourse ceased.[2] Mill's judgment of Carlyle, as given in his *Autobiography*, shows the vital difference. Carlyle was a poet, he says, and a man of intuitions; and Mill was neither. Carlyle saw at once many things which Mill could only 'hobble after and prove' when pointed out. 'I knew that I could not see round him, and could never be certain that I saw over him, and I never presumed to judge him with any definiteness until he was interpreted to me by one greatly superior to us both, who was more a poet than he and more a thinker than I, whose own mind and nature included his and infinitely more'[3]; in short, by Mrs. Taylor, of whom I shall speak directly. Carlyle's aversion to scepticism (in some sense), to Utilitarianism, to logic, and to political economy—the

[1] 'Negro Question' in *Fraser's Magazine*, Feb. 1849.
[2] A friendly message, as the Carlyle letters show, passed between them in 1869.   [3] *Autobiography*, pp. 175-76.

'dismal science'—was indeed too inveterate to allow of any real alliance; and though Mill did his best to appreciate Carlyle, he learned from him only what one learns from an antagonist, that is, to be more confident in one's own opinions.

IV. PHILOSOPHIC LEADERSHIP

As philosophical Radicalism sank into impotence, Mill's occupation as its advocate was gone. He now again became a recluse. For many years he withdrew altogether from London society. This was obviously due in part to the connection to which he ascribed the greatest possible importance. The 'most valuable friendship of his life,' as he calls it, had been formed in 1830 with Mrs. Taylor, who was two years his junior. Her husband was a man in business,[1] a 'most upright, brave, and honourable man,' according to Mill, and regarded by her with the 'strongest affection' through life.[2] Taylor was, however, without the tastes which would have qualified him to be a worthy intellectual companion for his wife. In this respect Mill was greatly his superior; and his intimacy with Mrs. Taylor rapidly developed. He dined with her twice a week, her husband dining elsewhere. She was an invalid for many years, and had to live in country lodgings apart from her husband. He travelled with her on the Continent during his illness of 1836. Although Taylor himself behaved with singular generosity, and Mill himself states that his own relation to Mrs. Taylor was one of 'strong affection and confidential

---

[1] A 'drysalter' or 'wholesale druggist in Mark Lane,' according to Bain, 164 n.   [2] *Autobiography*, p. 185.

intimacy only,' the connection naturally provoked censure. His father bluntly condemned him for being in love with another man's wife. His mother and sisters disapproved, and were finally estranged by his marriage in later years.[1] Mrs. Grote gave him up, apparently upon this ground, although he continued his intercourse with Grote. Roebuck states that a remonstrance which he imprudently made to Mill led to the cessation of their friendship, which Mill attributes (with less probability) to differences of opinion as to Byron and Wordsworth.[2] Mill, who worshipped Mrs. Taylor as an embodiment of all that was excellent in human nature, resented such disapproval bitterly ; any reference to Mrs. Taylor produced excitement, and he avoided collisions with possible censors by retiring from the world altogether. On giving up the *Westminster Review*, he could, as he put it,[3] indulge the inclination, 'natural to thinking persons when the age of boyish vanity is once past, for limiting his own society to very few persons.' Englishmen, as he says in his customary tone of disapproval, consider serious discussion as ' ill-bred,' and have not the French art of talking agreeably on trifles. Men of mental superiority are ' almost without exception greatly deteriorated' if they condescend to join in such society. The ' tone of the feelings is lowered,' and they adopt the low modes of judgment which alone can meet with sympathy. When the character, moreover, is once formed, agreement on cardinal points is felt to be a necessary condition of ' anything worthy the name of friendship.'

[1] Bain's *J. S. Mill*, p. 172.
[2] Leader's *Roebuck*, p. 39 ; and Mill's *Autobiography*, p. 150.
[3] *Autobiography*, p. 227.

Mill accordingly shut himself up in his office, and except occasional intercourse with Grote, Professor Bain, and a few others, lived as a solitary or sat at the feet of his Egeria. His admirers, who were soon to be a rapidly increasing class, heard generally that a sight of him was a rare privilege, scarcely to be enjoyed except at meetings of the Political Economy Club. There the conversation turned upon sufficiently solid topics. Whether a life of seclusion be really wise is a topic for an essay. Mill's unequivocal condemnation of the society of which he had so little experience may appear to be censorious. A philosopher may be as austere as a religious Puritan ; and Mill might have been a wiser man had he been able to drop his dignity, indulge in a few amusements, and inter- pret a little more generously the British contempt for high-flown sentiment. His incapacity for play, as he admitted to Comte, was a weak side of his character. Sydney Smith was for a short time (1841-43) a member of the Political Economy Club, and there met Mill on two or three occasions. One would like to know what impression they made upon each other, and especially what Mill thought of the jovial, life-enjoying, and sociable parson. Probably, one fears, he would have taken the superabundant fun of the canon as one more proof of the frivolity of British society, and set his colleague down as a mere sycophant and buffoon. I will not compare the merits of such opposite types. If Mill's retirement is indicative of some weakness, it must also be admitted that it was also dictated by a devotion to great tasks requiring and displaying remarkable strength. He now set to work vigorously, and in the course of the next few years produced his most elaborate and important works.

Both of them were the outcome of his early training. The discussions at Grote's house had suggested to him the plan of a book upon logic. The end, speaking roughly, was to set forth articulately the theory of knowledge implicitly assumed in the writings of his school. Fully accepting the main principles of Bentham and James Mill, and regarding them as satisfactory, after close investigation, he had yet become aware of certain difficulties which might be solved by a more thorough inquiry. He was afterwards stimulated by the controversy between his father and Macaulay ; and this led him, as he thought, to perceiving the true logical method of political philosophy. About 1832 he took up the subject again, and tried to solve the ' great paradox of the discovery of new truths by general reasoning.' This led to his theory of the syllogism, given in the second book of his *Logic*. He now felt that he could produce a valuable work, and wrote the first book. He was stopped by fresh difficulties, and made a halt which lasted for five years. He ' could make nothing satisfactory of induction.' In 1837, while weighted by the *Review,* he received a fresh impulse. Whewell's *History of the Inductive Sciences* and Herschel's *Discourse on the Study of Natural Philosophy* provided him with materials which had before been lacking. In two months, during intervals snatched from other works, he had written a third, ' the most difficult third,' of the book. This included the remainder ' of the doctrine of reasoning ' and the greater part of the book upon induction. He had now ' untied all the really hard knots,' and completion was only a question of time. Comte's *Philosophie Positive* now became known to him and greatly stimulated him,

though he owed little of definite result to it. In July
and August 1838 he managed to finish his third book ;
and his doctrine of 'real kinds' enabled him to turn the
difficulty which had caused the five years' halt. Other
chapters on 'language and classification' and upon fallacies were added in the same autumn, and the remainder
of the work in the summer and autumn of 1840.
Finally, the whole book was rewritten between April
1841 and the end of the year, much matter being introduced in the process which had been suggested by
Whewell's *Philosophy of the Inductive Sciences* and by
Comte's treatise.[1] He offered the finished book to
Murray, who declined it ; and it was finally accepted by
Parker, who published it in the spring of 1843.

The significance of these dates will appear hereafter.
It is here enough to say that the book was the product
of strenuous, long-continued thought, and of influences
from various quarters. The success greatly exceeded
his anticipations. No one since Locke had approached
him in the power of making the problems of philosophy
interesting to the laity. One remark which he makes
is important. He held that the philosophy which he
assailed was the great support of all deep-seated and
antiquated prejudice. He was therefore attacking false
philosophy in its stronghold ; and so far as he succeeded,
not merely exposing philosophic fallacies, but essentially
contributing to the triumph of reason. Though retiring
from active politics, he was elucidating the principles
which underlie all political theory.

The *Logic*, in short, was intended not merely as a
discussion of abstruse problems, but as indirectly bearing

[1] *Autobiography*, pp. 122, 159, 181, 209, 221.

upon the purposes to which his life was devoted. He
was led by the course of his speculation to propose the
formation of a new science to be called ' ethology.' This
ethology (of which I shall have to speak in its place) is
described by Mill as the Science which corresponds to
the Art of Education.[1]   Education is to be taken in the
widest sense of the word : as the training given by the
whole system of institutions which mould the character
and the thought of mankind.   Mill had recognised the
immense difficulties in the way of all his schemes of
reform which resulted from the ignorance and stupidity
of the classes to whom power was inevitably passing.
Whether that transition would be beneficial or the
reverse depended essentially upon the degree in which
men could be prepared for their new duties. Believing
that such a preparation was possible, he desired to determine the general principles applicable ; to give, as he
says, the science corresponding to the art.

This scheme is noticed in the remarkable correspondence with Comte, which began in 1841 during the
final stage of the composition of the *Logic*, and lasted
until 1846.   Some knowledge of Comte's doctrines was
spreading in England.[2]   Mill had read an early work of
Comte's (the *Traité de Politique Positive*, 1822), and

1 *Logic*, bk. vi. ch. v. § 4.
2 Bain's *J. S. Mill*, p. 70.   There was a review of Comte by Brewster in the
Edinburgh Review for August 1838, and an article by William Smith, author
of *Thorndale*, in *Blackwood* for March 1843.   G. H. Lewes spoke favourably
of Comte (to whom he had been personally introduced by Mill) in an article
upon ' Modern French Philosophy ' in the *Foreign Quarterly* in 1843.   His later
accounts of Comte in the *Biographical History of Philosophy* (1st edition, 1845-46),
and in letters published in the *Leader* in 1852, and afterwards collected as
Comte's Philosophy of the Sciences, are also noticeable.   Miss Martineau's
abridged translation appeared in 1853.

criticised it sharply in his letters to d'Eichthal in 1828,
though preferring it to other works of the St. Simonians.
On taking up in 1837 the two first volumes of Comte's
Philosophie Positive (all then published), he had been
deeply impressed ; he read their successors, and in
November 1841 he wrote to Comte as an unknown
admirer, and indeed in the tone of an ardent disciple.
He has, as he says, definitively left the 'Benthamist
section of the revolutionary school,' though he regards
it as the best preparation for true positivist doctrine.
He accepts Comte's main positions, though on some
'secondary' questions he has doubts which may disappear.[1] He had even thought of postponing the publication of his *Logic* until he had seen the completion of
Comte's treatise ; and, had he been able to see the whole
in time, would perhaps have translated it instead of
writing a new book.[2] Two-thirds, however, of the
Logic was substantially finished before he had read
Comte, and it is adapted to the backward state of
English opinion. Mill holds, as he held when writing
to d'Eichthal, that a constructive should succeed to a
critical philosophy, and sees the realisation of his hopes
in the new doctrine. He holds with Comte that a
'spiritual power' should be constituted, which cannot
be reached through simple liberty of discussion ;[3] and
believes in a religion of humanity, destined to replace
theology.[4] It is not surprising that Comte took Mill
for a thorough convert. A discord presently showed
itself. 'You frighten me,' Mill said to Comte, 'by the
unity and completeness of your convictions,' which seem

[1] *Correspondence*, pp. 2, 3.   [2] *Ibid.* p. 77.
[3] *Ibid* p. 29, cf. 414.   [4] *Ibid.* p. 135.

to need no confirmation from any other intelligence. Comte, in fact, had a rounded and definitive scheme. He had ceased to read other speculations as a mathematician might decline to read the vagaries of circle-squarers. His whole system was demonstrated, once for all. In 1843 Mill began an argument as to the equality of the sexes, which lasted for some months, and ended characteristically. Comte said [1] that further argument would be useless, as Mill was not yet prepared to accept 'fundamental truths.' Mill agreed to drop the discussion, and added that his own opinions had only been confirmed. The supposed convert announced himself as an independent, though respectful, junior colleague, with a right to differ. Mill, according to Bain, became 'dissatisfied with the concessions which he had made.' In truth, the divergence was hopeless, and implied a difference of first principles. Meanwhile, the misunderstanding had further consequences. When Comte was expecting to be dismissed from his post, Mill generously declared (June 1843) that, so long as he lived, he would share his last *sou* with his friend.[2] Mill was at this time in anxiety caused by the repudiation of American bonds, in which he had invested some of his own money and some of his father's, for which he was responsible. Comte declined to take money from a fellow-thinker, but afterwards, when he actually lost his post in July 1844, accepted help from Mill's richer friends, Grote, Molesworth, and Raikes Currie. Comte took their gift to be a tribute from disciples, and was offended when, after the first year, they declined to continue the subsidy. Instead of being disciples, they

[1] *Correspondence*, p. 273.   [2] *Ibid.* p. 206.

were simply persons interested in a philosopher, many of whose tenets they utterly repudiated, and thought that they had done quite enough to show their respect. Mill, as the mediator in an awkward position, acted with all possible frankness and delicacy, but the divergence was growing. When, in 1845, Comte proposed to start a review to propagate his doctrine, Mill had to point out that he and his friends were partial allies, not subjects, and that positivism was not yet sufficiently established to set up as a school.[1] Gradually the discord developed, and the correspondence dropped. Comte's last letter is dated 3rd September 1846, and a letter from Mill of 17th May 1847, speaking of the Irish famine, produced no reply. Mill recognised the hopeless differences, and came to think that Comte's doctrine of the spiritual power implied a despotism of the worst kind. He expressed his disapproval in his final criticism of Comte, and in the later editions of the *Logic* considerably modified some of his early compliments.[2]

On 3rd April 1844 Mill informs Comte that he has put aside the Ethology, his ideas being not yet ripe, and has resolved to write a treatise upon Political Economy. He is aware of Comte's low opinion of this study, and explains that he only attaches a provisional value to its sociological bearing. The book, he explains, will only take a few months to write. The subject, indeed, had been never far from his thoughts since his father had in early days expounded to him the principles of Ricardo. He had discussed economic questions with the meetings at Grote's house ; he had written his *Essays upon*

[1] *Correspondence*, p. 402.
[2] See Bain's *J. S. Mill*, p. 72, for an account of the changes.

Unsettled Questions; and had been taking a part by his reviews and articles in controversies upon such topics as the Corn-laws, the currency, and the Poor-law. He thus had only to expound opinions already formed, and the book was written far more rapidly than the *Logic*. Begun in the autumn of 1845, it was finished by the end of 1847. Six months out of this were spent in writing an elaborate series of articles in the *Morning Chronicle* during the disastrous winter of 1846-47, urging the formation of peasant properties on the waste lands of Ireland.[1] The articles, of which four or five often appeared in a week, were remarkable in the journalism of the day; but his proposals failed to attract attention from English stupidity and prejudice. He tells Comte in his last letter that the English wish to help Ireland; but, from their total ignorance of Continental systems, can only think of enabling the population to live as paupers, instead of introducing the one obvious remedy. His friend and colleague in the India House, W. T. Thornton, was writing about the same time his *Plea for Peasant Proprietors*.[2] Thornton was one of the few who from this period saw much of Mill; and his influence at a later time was remarkable. The *Political Economy* represents essentially a development of the Ricardo doctrine. One point requires notice here. Mill tells us that he had turned back from his 'reaction against Benthamism.'[3] At the height of that reaction he had

[1] *Autobiography*, p. 235. Mill, as we have seen, spoke of the *Political Economy* to Comte in April 1844. Possibly, therefore, some preparation may have been made for it in the interval before the autumn of 1845.

[2] Published in 1848 before the appearance of Mill's *Political Economy*. Mill read the proofs of his friend's book. Bain's *J. S. Mill*, p. 86 *n*.

[3] *Autobiography*, p. 231. The dates of these changes are rather vaguely indicated.

become more tolerant of compromise with current opinions. By degrees, however, he had become more than ever opposed to the established principles. He was less of a democrat, indeed, because more convinced of the incapacity of the masses ; but more of a Socialist, in the sense that he looked forward to a complete, though distant, revolution in the whole structure of society. In the first edition of the *Political Economy* he had spoken decidedly against the possibility of Socialism. The events of 1848 seemed to open new possibilities for the propagation of novel doctrines. He accordingly modified this part of his book, and the second edition (1849) represented a 'more advanced opinion.'[1] How far Mill could be called a Socialist will have to be considered hereafter. This tendency, at any rate, marks one characteristic. Mill points out, as one condition of its very remarkable success, that he regarded political economy, not as a 'thing by itself, but as part of a greater whole.' Its conclusions, he held, were valid only as conditioned by principles of 'social philosophy' in general ;[2] and the book, instead of being ostensibly a compendium of abstract scientific principles, is therefore written with constant reference to wider topics and to the application of the doctrines to concrete facts. How far Mill succeeded in giving satisfactory theories is another question, but one thing at least he achieved. The *Political Economy* became popular in a sense in which no work upon the same topic had been popular since the *Wealth of Nations*; and it owed its success in a great degree to the constant endeavour to trace the bearings of merely abstract formulæ upon the general questions of

[1] *Autobiography*, p. 235.   [2] *Ibid.* p. 236.

social progress. He stimulated the rising interest in those important problems, and even if his solutions did not carry general conviction, they brought to him in later years a following of reverent disciples.

These two books, the *Logic* and the *Political Economy*, contain in fact a nearly complete statement of Mill's leading position. Although in later years he was to treat of political, ethical, and philosophical topics, his leading doctrines were now sufficiently expounded ; and the later writings were rather deductions or applications than a breaking of new ground. None of them involved so strenuous and long-continued a process of mental elaboration. The success of these two books gave him a position at the time unrivalled. He was accepted as the Liberal philosopher ; and could speak as one of unquestioned authority.

Professor Bain thinks that Mill's energy was henceforth less than it had been. The various attacks from which he had suffered had probably weakened his constitution. It must be noticed, however, as Professor Bain also remarks, that there were sufficient causes for some decline of literary activity, and he certainly did an amount of work in the remaining twenty-five years of his life which would have been enough to absorb the powers of most men even of high ability. The publication of new editions of his great books, which involved revision and replies to criticism, and the composition of occasional review articles, occupied some of the leisure from his official duties. The severe illness of 1854 made necessary a long foreign tour. In 1856 he became head of his department, and more work was thrown upon him. On the extinction of the East India Company in 1857, he drafted a petition to parliament on their behalf. It is remarkable that, like his father in 1833, he became the apologist of a system generally condemned by the Liberals of the day. His belief—whatever its value—was that the government of India could not be efficiently carried on by the English parliament ; that Indian appointments would become prizes to be won by jobbery ; and that the direct rule of English public opinion would imply a disregard of native opinions and feelings. The company, however, came to an end ; and Mill, refusing to accept a place on the new Councils, retired at the beginning of 1858 on a pension of £1500 a year.

V. MINOR WRITINGS

A great change was now to take place in his life. Mr. Taylor had died in July 1849 ; and in April 1851 his widow became Mill's wife. They co-operated in one remarkable work, which is to be connected with the development of his opinions at the time. Mill had welcomed the French revolution of 1848 with enthusiasm. He saw in it the victory of the party to which he had been most attached from his youth ; and in 1849 he wrote a vigorous vindication of its leaders against the criticisms of Brougham.[1] He spoke with much sympathy even of the Socialism of Louis Blanc, though, of course, admitting that it contained many grave errors. The 'success of an unprincipled adventurer in December 1851 ' put an end to his hopes for the immediate future. He felt painfully that even the recognition of many opinions for which he had contended in his youth had brought less benefit than

[1] Article in *Dissertations*, ii., republished from *Westminster Review* of April 1849.

he had anticipated. He became convinced that a great change in the 'fundamental conditions of (men's) modes of thought' was essential to any great improvement in their lot.[1] During 1854 he had planned an essay upon *Liberty*, which was essentially an attempt to point out certain conditions of such improvements. During the last two years of his official life, he went over this elaborately with his wife. After being twice written, he tells us, every sentence was carefully weighed and criticised by them both. He intended to make a final revision during the winter of 1858-59. That was not to be given. The book, however, is not only characteristic, but is, from a purely literary point of view, the best of Mill's writings. Mrs. Mill died at Avignon from a sudden attack of congestion of the lungs. The blow was crushing. Mill felt that 'the spring of his life was broken.' He withdrew for a time into complete isolation, though he soon found some solace in work. He bought a house at Avignon, and spent half his time there to be near his wife's grave. The rest of his time was spent at Blackheath. His stepdaughter, Miss Taylor, lived with him, and he expresses his gratitude for having drawn two such prizes in 'the lottery of life.' Other friends and disciples were to gather round him in later years.

It is necessary to say something of the woman to whom Mill was thus devoted. Yet it is very difficult to speak without conveying some false impression. It is impossible, on the one hand, to speak too respectfully of so deep and enduring a passion. Mill's love of his wife is a conclusive answer to any one who can doubt the tenderness of his nature. A man who could love so

[1] *Autobiography*, p. 238.

deeply must have been lovable himself. On the other hand, it is necessary to point out plainly certain peculiarities which it reveals. Mill speaks of his wife's excellences in language so extravagant as almost to challenge antagonism.[1] I have already quoted the passage in which he says that her qualities included Carlyle's and his own and 'infinitely more.' In other passages, he seems to be endeavouring to outdo this statement : her judgment, he declares, was ' next to infallible ' ; ' the highest poetry, philosophy, oratory, and art seemed trivial by the side of her, and equal only to expressing some part of her mind ' ; and he prophesies that ' if mankind continue to improve, their spiritual history for ages to come will be the progressive working out of her thoughts and realisation of her conceptions.' 'Only John Mill's reputation,' said Grote, ' could survive such displays.'[2] The truth seems to be that in Mill's grief one exquisite pang came from the thought that his wife had left nothing by which her excellence could be made manifest to others. The only article which he could call hers was that upon the ' enfranchisement of women,' the prefatory note to which includes the phrases cited. He feels that it would hardly justify his words ; and has to add that she would, had she pleased, have excelled it in eloquence and profundity. Even that has to be qualified by saying that she could have written nothing on a single subject which would have adequately shown ' the depth and compass of her mind.' His readers, therefore, have to take his statements on faith, and he

[1] See reference to Mrs. Mill in the suppressed dedication of the *Political Economy* given in Bain's *J. S. Mill*, p. 175 ; the dedication of the *Liberty* ; the note in *Dissertations*, ii. 412 ; and *Autobiography*, pp. 184-90 and 240-42.

[2] Bain's *J. S. Mill*, p. 167.

tries to make up for the want of proof by vehemence of asseveration. The only way of accepting such utterances fairly is to regard them as a cry of poignant anguish, not as a set of statements to be logically criticised. The accumulation of superlatives, meanwhile, has the disadvantage that it leaves us without any distinctive characteristic. The figure invested with such a blaze of light has neither distinct form nor colouring. Mill was, I think, always at his feeblest in describing character, and that was a natural weakness of one who, with all his perspicacity, was essentially a bad judge of men.

Apart from the revelation of Mill's character, the only question is whether any intellectual influence is to be attributed to Mrs. Mill. It is easy to suggest that he admired her because she was skilful in echoing his own opinions. To this Professor Bain replies that Mill generally liked intelligent opposition, and holds that in fact Mrs. Mill did set his mind to work by stimulating conversation.[1] This may be true within limits. Mill, however, himself assigns coincidence on cardinal points of opinion as a necessary condition of friendship.[2] It is plain that such an agreement existed between himself and his wife. That he could detect no error in her proves simply that she held what he thought to be true, that is, his own opinions. He has indeed said enough to explain the general relation. She had nothing to do with the *Logic*, except as to the minuter matters of composition ; he had already come to believe in woman's rights before he knew her ; she did not affect the logical framework of the *Political Economy*, but she suggested the chapter to which he attributes most influence upon

[1] Bain's *J. S. Mill*, p. 173.   [2] *Autobiography*, p. 229.

the future of the labouring classes ; and gave to the book
' the general tone by which it is distinguished from
previous treatises.' 'What was abstract and purely
scientific,' he says by way of summary, 'was generally
mine ; the properly human element came from her.' [1]
In other words, her influence was rather upon his
emotions than upon his intellect, and led him to apply
his abstract principles to the actual state of society and
to estimate their bearing upon human interests and
sympathies more clearly and widely than he would otherwise have done. Undoubtedly we may gladly admit the
importance of this element in Mill's life ; we can fully
believe that this, the one great affection of his life, had
enabled him to breathe a more genial atmosphere and
helped to save him from the rigidity and dryness of some
of his allies. It is, however, impossible to attribute to
Mrs. Mill any real share in framing his philosophical
doctrines ; and the impossibility will be the more
evident when we have noticed to what an extent they
were simply the development of the creed which he
had been imbibing from his earliest years. Mill was
essentially formed by Bentham, James Mill, and Ricardo ;
while the relation to Mrs. Mill encouraged him to a
more human version of the old Utilitarian gospel. The
attribution of all conceivable excellences to his wife shows
that he loved, if I may say so, with his brain. The love
was perfectly genuine and of most unusual strength ; but
he interpreted it into terms of reason, and speaks of an
invaluable sympathy as if it implied a kind of philosophical inspiration.

Mill, now released from his official labours, settled

[1] *Autobiography*, p. 244-47.

down as he expected 'for the remainder of his existence into a purely literary life.'[1]   For six or seven years (end of 1858 to summer of 1865) he carried out this design, and wrote much both on political and philosophical topics. He first published the *Liberty*, in which, after the death of his wife, he resolved to make no further alterations. He gave the weight of his approval to the congenial work of his friend, Professor Bain, by a review in the *Edinburgh* of October 1859.   He put together, from previously written papers, his short treatise upon *Utilitarianism*.[2]   In October 1863 he reviewed in the *Edinburgh* the recently published lectures of his old friend, John Austin, the representative Utilitarian jurist. Two articles upon Comte[3] in 1864 gave his final judgment of one of the thinkers to whom he owed most outside of the Utilitarian circle.   His most elaborate performance, however, was his examination of Sir William Hamilton's philosophy.   This was suggested by the recent publication of Hamilton's *Lectures*, which he at first intended only to review.   The work swelled upon his hands; he read all Hamilton's writings three times over, and much other literature; he completed the book in the autumn of 1864, and published it in the following spring.   It involved him in some very sharp controversies, and contained his final and most elaborate protest against the Intuitionist school.   This, too, with the three posthumous essays,[4] gives his position upon

---

[1] *Autobiography*, p. 262.

[2] First in *Fraser's Magazine* in 1861 ; republished in 1863.

[3] First in the *Westminster* for 1864 ; reprinted separately in 1865.

[4] The essays upon *Nature* and *The Utility of Religion* are stated to have been written between 1850 and 1858; that upon *Theism* between 1868 and 1870.

the general philosophical questions which were not treated in the *Logic*. In his earlier books he had been systematically reticent to a degree of which he afterwards disapproved.[1] The intelligent reader, indeed, could perceive to what conclusions his principles led ; but the intelligent reader is a rarity. When, in 1865, his political opponents tried to turn his unpopular opinions to account, the only phrase upon which they could fix was the really very orthodox sentiment (in the examination of Hamilton) that he would go to hell rather than worship an unjust God. He had intended, it may be noticed, to publish the essay upon *Nature* himself ; but the others were to be still held back. These last utterances, however, taken together, give a sufficient account of Mill's final position in philosophy.

VI. POLITICAL ACTIVITY

Meanwhile, he had been again drawn to politics. After the long period of indifference which followed the final decay of the philosophical Radicals, the English democracy was showing many symptoms of revived animation. The new Reform Bill was becoming the object of practical political agitation ; and it seemed that the hopes entertained of the Reform Bill of 1832 had now at last a prospect of realisation. Mill thought in 1861 that there was 'a more encouraging prospect of the mental emancipation of England,' and that things were looking better for the general advance of Europe.[2] The surviving Utilitarians had declined from the true faith. John

[1] *Autobiography*, p. 230. He defends this reticence in a letter to Comte of 18th December 1841.—*Correspondence*, p. 12.

[2] *Autobiography*, p. 240.

Austin before his death had become distinctly Conservative ; and the sacred fire of Benthamism was nearly
extinct. Mill himself had changed in some respects.
While more awake to certain dangers of democracy,
he was the more strongly convinced of the possibility of
meeting them by appropriate remedies. Meanwhile Radicalism in various forms was raising its head, and willing
to accept Mill, now a writer of the first celebrity, as its
authorised interpreter. He wrote much at this period,
which defines his position and shows his relation to the
new parties. His first publication was a pamphlet on
Parliamentary Reform, suggested by the futile Reform
Bill of Lord Derby and Disraeli in 1859. He now
objected to the ballot, the favourite nostrum of the
philosophical Radicals to which Grote still adhered, but
his main suggestions were in harmony with the scheme
proposed by Mr. Hare. After the publication of his
own pamphlet, he became acquainted with this scheme,
of which he immediately became an ardent proselyte. In
1860 and 1861 he wrote two treatises. He expounded
his whole political doctrine in his *Considerations on
Parliamentary Government* (1861), and he wrote for
future publication—' at the time when it should seem
most likely to be useful '—his *Subjection of Women*.[1] In
this, as he intimates, ' all that is most striking and profound belongs to his wife ' ; while it appears that his
stepdaughter had also some share in the composition.
The outbreak of the civil war in America led him to
pronounce himself strongly in support of Bright and
other sympathisers with the cause of union.[2] Although
his opinions were opposed to those commonest among the

[1] Published in 1869.　　[2] Article in *Fraser's Magazine*, January 1862.

English upper classes, they fell in with those of the Radicals, and made him at once a representative of a great current of opinion. His occupation with Hamilton now withdrew him for a time to another department of thought.

In the beginning of 1865 Mill published popular editions of his *Political Economy*, his *Liberty*, and his *Representative Government*. At the general election of that year he was invited to stand for Westminster. Mill accepted the invitation, though upon terms which showed emphatically that he would make no sacrifice of his principles. He declined to incur any expense. He would not canvass, although he attended a few public meetings in the week preceding the nomination. He declared that he would answer no questions about his religious beliefs, but upon all other topics would answer frankly and briefly. 'Did you,' he was asked at one meeting, ' declare that the English working classes, though differing from some other countries in being ashamed of lying, were yet " generally liars " ? ' His answer, ' I did,' produced, he says, ' vehement applause.' It certainly deserved the applause. Upon some points, too, of the Radical creed, Mill's views were not acceptable. His condemnation of the ballot, and his adherence to women's suffrage and to minority representation marked his opposition to some democratic tendencies. These opinions, however, referred to questions not prominent enough at the time to be important as disqualifications in a candidate. His election by a considerable majority roused great interest. He came in upon a wave of enthusiasm, which accompanied the beginning of a new political era. The Radicalism which was to succeed was, indeed, very unlike the old Radi-

calism of 1832 ; but, for the time at least, it believed
itself to be simply continuing the old movement, and
was willing to accept the most distinguished representative of the creed for one of its leaders.

In his *Autobiography* Mill shows a certain self-com-
placency in describing his proceedings in the new
parliament, which is not unnatural in a man called
from his study by the strong demand from practical
politicians. The voice which had been crying in the
wilderness was now to be heard in the senate, and
philosophy to be married to practice. Mill took up his
duties with his usual assiduity ; he watched business as
closely as the most diligent of partisans, and was as
regular in the House as he had been in his office. The
scenes in which he appeared as an orator were remarkable. His figure was spare and slight, his voice weak ;
a constant twitching of the eyebrow betrayed his nervous
irritability; he spoke with excessive rapidity, and at times
lost the thread of his remarks, and paused deliberately to
regain self-possession.[1] But he poured out continuous
and thoroughly well-arranged essays—lucid, full of
thought, and frequently touching the point epigram-
matically. His old practice at debating societies and
the Political Economy Club had qualified him to give
full expression to his thoughts. A general curiosity to
see so strange a phenomenon as a philosopher in parliament was manifest, and Mill undoubtedly introduced an
order of considerations far higher than those of the
average politician. The tone of the debates, as was said
by competent witnesses, was perceptibly raised by his

[1] I heard some of his first speeches from the press gallery of the House of
Commons.

speeches. The accepted leaders, such as Bright and Gladstone, welcomed him cordially, and were doubtless pleased to find that they had been talking so much philosophy without knowing it. The young men who were then entering public life looked up to him with reverence; and, for a time, even the squires, the embodiments of Tory prejudice, were favourably impressed. That could not be for long. One of the hits to which Mill refers with some glee in the *Autobiography*[1] gave the nickname of the 'stupid party' to the Conservatives. It expressed his real view a little too clearly. Between him and the typical 'John Bull' a great gulf was fixed. He could never contrive, though he honestly tried, to see anything in the class which most fully represents that ideal, except the embodiment of selfish stupidity generated by class prejudice. And the country-gentlemen naturally looked upon him as their ancestors would have looked upon Sieyès, could the Frenchman have been substituted for Charles Fox. They could dimly understand Whiggism, embodied in a genial, hearty member of their own class; but the flavour of the French philosophy, or its English correlative, was thin, acid, and calculated to set their teeth on edge. They showed the feeling after a time, and Mill retorted by some irritability as well as scorn. He did not, I fancy, obtain that kind of personal weight which is sometimes acquired by a man who, though he preaches equally offensive doctrines, is more obviously made of the same flesh and blood as his adversaries.[2]

[1] *Autobiography*, p. 289.
[2] Disraeli is said to have summed up the impression made upon practical politicians by calling him a 'political finishing governess.'

Mill took a part in various parliamentary proceedings. He helped to pass the Reform Bill of 1867 ; he acted as a mediator between the ministers and the Radicals who were responsible for the famous meeting in Hyde Park ; and he made a weighty protest on behalf of a generous and thoroughgoing Irish policy. He thought that a separation would be mischievous to both parties ; but he advocated a scheme for giving a permanent tenure to existing tenants, with a due regard to vested interests.[1] He obtained little support for a policy which, at least, went to the root of the great difficulty ; but the wisdom of his view, whatever its shortcomings, is more likely to be recognised now. The main peculiarity of Mill's position, however, is all that I am able to notice. In spite of his philosophy, he appeared to be a thorough party man. He fully adopted, that is to say, the platform of the Radical wing, and voted systematically with them on all points. His philosophy led him, as he says,[2] to advocate some measures not popular with the bulk of the Liberal party. Of these the most important were the extension of the suffrage to women and the provision of representation for minorities. Many people, he observes, took these to be ' whims of his own.' Mill, in fact, was contributing to the advance of democracy. In his eyes, these measures were of vital importance as safeguards against democratic tyranny. The democrat was, of course, content to accept his alliance, and to allow him to amuse himself with fanciful schemes, which for the time could make no difference. Mill, on the other hand, thought that by helping the democrat's immediate purposes, he was also gaining ground for the popularisa-

[1] See his pamphlet, *England and Ireland*, 1869.   [2] *Autobiography*, p. 286.

tion of these subsidiary though essential changes. The relation is significant ; for, whatever may be the value of Mill's proposals, there can be no doubt that in many ways the democratic changes which he advocated have led to results which he would have thoroughly disapproved. The alliance, that is, for the time, covered very deep differences, and Mill was virtually helping Demos to get into power, in the expectation that, when in power, Demos would consent to submit to restrictions, not yet, if they ever will be, realised. There is the further question, not here debatable, whether, if realised, they would act as Mill supposed. Anyhow, for the present, the philosopher was really the follower of the partisan. Mill made himself unpopular with a class wider than that which constituted the ' stupid party.' He took a very active part in the agitation provoked by Governor Eyre's action in the Jamaica insurrection. That he was right in demanding a thorough investigation seems to be undeniable. It seems also that a more judicial frame of mind would have restrained him from apparently assuming that such an investigation could have but one result. People of a high moral tone are too apt to show their virtue by assuming that a concrete case comes under a simple moral. law, when in fact most such cases are exceedingly complex. Mill, at any rate, and his committee impressed many people besides their strongest opponents as allowing their indignation to swamp their sense of fairplay. Governor Eyre appeared .to be a victim of persecution instead of a criminal, and there was, though Mill could not see it, a generous element in the feeling that allowance should be made for a man placed in a terribly critical position.

After the dissolution of parliament, Mill incurred further odium by subscribing to the election expenses of Bradlaugh. Nothing could be more in harmony with his principles than the support of an honest and straightforward man, attacked by the bitterest theological prejudice. His seat, however, for Westminster was lost (1868), and, refusing some other offers, he was glad to retire once more to private life, and to literary and philosophical pursuits. His strength was apparently failing, and he achieved little more. His parliamentary activity had enlarged his circle of acquaintance, and during these years he became far more sociable. Admiring friends gathered round him ; his old allies, such as Hare and W. T. Thornton, the economist Cairnes, and such rising politicians as Henry Fawcett, Mr. Courtney, and Mr. Morley, looked up to him, and had frequent meetings with him. One characteristic point must be noticed, his withdrawal of the 'wage fund' theory when impugned by W. T. Thornton in 1869. The candour which he showed on this occasion, and his generous appreciation of his friend, was eminently characteristic. In the same year appeared his edition of his father's *Analysis*, which, he says,[1] 'ought now to stand at the head of the systematic works on Analytic Psychology.' He was preparing for other writings, but his task was done. He died at Avignon, 8th May 1873, of a sudden attack, having three days before walked fifteen miles on a botanical excursion.

The impression made upon T. H. Green [2] by some of Mill's letters was that he must have been an 'extra-

---

[1] *Autobiography*, p. 308.

[2] Green's *Miscellaneous Works*, iii. cxliv.

ordinarily good man.' The remark came from a philosophical opponent, and might be echoed by many admirers and generous adversaries. The reverence of his personal friends is sufficiently indicated by the articles of Mr. John Morley,[1] written at the time of their loss. Mill's moral excellence, indeed, is in some directions beyond all dispute. No human being ever devoted himself more unreservedly to a worthy end from his earliest to his latest years ; the end was the propagation of truths of the highest importance to mankind, and the devotion implied entire freedom from all meaner or subsidiary ambitions. A man of whom that can be said without fear of contradiction has certainly extraordinary goodness. When we add that he was singularly candid, fair in argument, most willing to recognise merits in others, and a staunch enemy of oppression in every form, we may say that Mill possessed in an almost unsurpassable degree the virtues peculiarly appropriate to a philosopher. A complete judgment, however, must take other characteristics into account. One remark is obvious. Mill observes [2] that the description of a Benthamite as 'a mere reasoning machine,' though untrue of many of his friends, was true of himself during 'two or three years'—before, that is, he had learned to appreciate the value of the emotions. Many readers thought it true of him to the last. Though the phrase may be understood so as to imply the very contradictory of the truth, I take it to imply one aspect of his character which cannot be neglected. The *Autobiography*, though a very interesting, is to many readers far from an attractive, work ; and its want of

---

[1] *Miscellanies* (second series).　　　　[2] *Autobiography*, p. 109.

charm is, I think, significant of the weakness which is
caricatured by the epithet 'reasoning machine.' Omit-
ting the pages about his wife, there is a singular absence
of the qualities which make so many autobiographies
interesting : there is no tender dwelling upon early days
and associations ; his father is incidentally revealed as an
object of profound respect, but without illusion as to his
harsher qualities ; hardly any reference is made to his
mother or his brothers and sisters ; his friends are briefly
noticed and their intellectual merits duly set forth, but
there is no warm expression of personal feeling towards
any one of them ; his remarks upon his countrymen in
general are contemptuous ; and, though he is desirous of
the welfare of the species, he is as fully convinced as
Carlyle, that men are 'mostly fools.' Old institutions
awake no thrill ; they are simply embodiments of prejudice ; and the nation is divided between those who
have a 'sinister interest' in abuses, and the masses who
are still too brutalised to be trusted. At the bottom of
his heart he seems to prefer a prig, a man of rigid
formulæ, to the vivid and emotional character, whose
merits he recognises in theory. He complains frequently
of the general decay of energy, and yet his ideal would
seem to be the thoroughly drilled thinker, who is the
slave of abstract theories. His 'zeal for the good of
mankind' was really to the last what he admits it to
have been at the early period, a 'zeal for speculative
opinions.' The startling phrases about his wife are in
contrast to this coolness, but they are so hysterical as to
check full sympathy. From such remarks, some people
have inferred that Mill was really a frigid thinker, a
worthy prophet of the dismal science, which leaves out

of account all that is deepest and most truly valuable in human nature.

A reply even to an unjust estimate should admit what there is of truth in it. In the first place, of course, Mill was not, and never took himself to be, a poet. He had no vivid pictures of concrete facts ; he was not, as he puts it in contrasting himself with Carlyle, a man of intuitions, and he formed his judgments of affairs by analysing and reflecting and expressing the result in abstract formulæ. That is only to say that his predominant faculty was logical, and that the imagination was comparatively feeble. He was sensitive to some poetry, to Shelley as well as to Wordsworth ; but he is more impressed by its philosophical than its direct æsthetical value. He was certainly less deficient than James Mill in this direction ; but in another quality the contrast with his father is significant. James Mill, whatever his faults, was a man, and born to be a leader of men. He was rigid, imperative, and capable of controlling and dominating. John Stuart Mill was far weaker in that sense, and weaker because he had less virility. Mill never seems fully to appreciate the force of human passions ; he fancies that the emotions which stir men to their depths can be controlled by instilling a few moral maxims or pointing out considerations of utility. He has in that respect less ' human nature ' in him than most human beings ; and has not, like Carlyle's favourite Ram Dass, fire enough in his inside to burn up the sins of the world. One effect is obvious even in his philosophy. A philosopher, I think, owes more than is generally perceived to the moral quality which goes into masculine vigour. To accept, as well as to announce, a doctrine which clashes with the opinions accepted in his class requires an amount of vigour and self-reliance which is only possessed by the few.   Mill held very unpopular opinions, but they had been instilled into him from childhood; they were those of the whole world in which he lived, and it would have required more vigour to abandon than to maintain them.   It is impossible to read the *Autobiography* without wondering whether a different education might not have made him a Coleridgean instead of a Benthamite.   If he disbelieved in innate principles and in the boundless power of 'association,' it was partly because the influence of his own idiosyncrasy was so slightly marked in his intellectual development. He was one of the most remarkable instances of the power of education to mould the intellect, because few intellects so powerful have been so amenable.

The want of the qualities which make a man self-assertive and original implies, however, no coldness of the affections.   Mill was a man of great emotional sensibility, and of very unusual tenderness.   Besides his great attachment, he was deeply devoted to a few friends, and, in certain cases, greatly overestimated their qualities.   His devotion to speculative pursuits made most of his attachments the product of intellectual sympathy; and he either did not form, or could not keep up, intimacies formed with persons incapable of such sympathy.   Unless he could talk upon serious matters with man or woman, he would have no common bond with them ; and he was too sincere to express it. His feelings, however, were, I take it, as tender as a woman's.   They were wanting, not in keenness, but in the massiveness which implies more masculine fibre.

And this, indeed, is what seems to indicate the truth. Mill could never admit any fundamental difference between the sexes. That is, I believe, a great but a natural misconception for one who was in character as much feminine as masculine. He had some of the amiable weaknesses which we at present—perhaps on account of the debased state of society—regard as especially feminine. The most eminent women, hitherto at least, are remarkable rather for docility than originality. Mill was especially remarkable, as I have said, for his powers of assimilation. No more receptive pupil could ever be desired by a teacher. Like a woman, he took things—even philosophers—with excessive seriousness ; and shows the complete want of humour often—unjustly perhaps—attributed to women. Prejudices provoke him, but he does not see the comic side of prejudice or of life in general. When Carlyle, in his hasty wrath, denounces 'shams' with a huge guffaw, Mill patiently unravels the sophistry, and tries to discover the secret of their plausibility. Mill's method no doubt leads as a rule to safer and more sober results. The real candour, too, and desire of light from all sides is most genuine and admirable. It may lead him rather to develop and widen the philosophy in which he was immersed than to strike out new paths. One misses at times the flashes of intuition of keener philosophers, and still more the downright protests of rough common-sense, which can sweep away cobwebs without trying elaborately to pick them to pieces.

On the other hand, he has in the highest degree the power of single-minded devotion, which is pre-eminently, though not exclusively, a feminine quality. His intellect fitted him for abstract speculation, rather than for immediate practical applications. But he was from his youth upwards devoted to the spread of principles which he held to be essential to human happiness. No philanthropist or religious teacher could labour more energetically and unremittingly for the good of mankind. He never forgets the bearing of his speculations upon this ultimate end. Whatever his limitations, he brought the whole energy of a singularly clear, comprehensive, and candid intellect to bear upon the greatest problems of his time; and worked at them with unflagging industry for many years. He was eminently qualified to bring out the really strong points of his creed; while his perfect intellectual honesty forced him frankly to display its weaker side. Through Mill English Utilitarianism gave the fullest account of its method and its presuppositions. In summarising his work, I must dwell less than I have hitherto done upon surrounding conditions; and take his books, nearly in the order of publication, as representing the final outcome of Utilitarianism. He virtually answers in the *Logic* the question, what are the ultimate principles by which the Utilitarians had more or less unconsciously been guided. I shall first deal with this. I shall then take his *Political Economy*, as showing how these principles applied to sociology, which ought, upon his showing, to be the crowning science. Then I shall take the political speculations, which are a further application of the same principles; and, finally, deal with his views in ethics and in philosophy generally.

CHAPTER II

MILL'S LOGIC

I. INTUITIONISM AND EMPIRICISM

MILL'S *System of Logic* may be regarded as the most important manifesto of Utilitarian philosophy. It lays down explicitly and in their ripest form the principles implicitly assumed by Bentham and the elder Mill. It modifies as well as expounds. It represents the process by which J. S. Mill, on becoming aware of certain defects in the Utilitarians' philosophy, endeavoured to restate the first principles so as to avoid the erroneous conclusions. The coincidence with his predecessors remains far closer than the divergence. The fundamental tenets are developed rather than withdrawn. The *Logic* thus most distinctly raises the ultimate issues. It has the impressiveness which belongs in some degree to every genuine exertion of a powerful mind. Mill is struggling with real difficulties ; not trying to bolster up a theory commended to him by extraneous considerations. He is doing his best to give an answer to his problem ; not to hide an evasion. His honourable candour incidentally reveals the weakness as frankly as the strength of his position. He neither shirks nor hides difficulties, and if we are forced to admit that some of his reasoning is fallacious, the admission scarcely adds to the statement that he is writing a treatise upon philosophical problems. His frankness has made the task of critics comparatively easy. It takes so many volumes to settle what some philosophers have meant that we scarcely reach the question whether their meaning, or rather any of their many possible meanings, was right. In the case of Mill, that preparatory labour is not required. His book, too, has been sufficiently tested by time to enable us to mark the points at which his structure has failed to stand the wear and tear of general discussion. I must try to bring out the vital points of the doctrine.

Mill, I have said, had a very definite purpose beyond the purely philosophical. 'Bad institutions,' he says,[1] are supported by false philosophy. The false philosophy to which he refers is that of the so-called 'intuitionist school.' Its 'stronghold,' he thought, lay in appeals to the mathematical and physical sciences. To drive it from this position was to deprive it of 'speculative support'; and, though it could still appeal to prejudice, the destruction of this support was an indispensable step to complete victory. Mill wished to provide a logical armoury for all assailants of established dogmatism, and his success as a propagandist surprised him. The book was read, to his astonishment, even in the universities. Indeed, I can testify from personal observation that it became a kind of sacred book for students who claimed to be genuine Liberals. It gave the philosophical creed of an important section of the rising generation, partly biassed, it may be, by the application to 'bad institutions.' Mill's logic, that is,

---

[1] *Autobiography*, p. 226.

fell in with the one main current of political opinion. His readings in logic with Grote and other friends enabled him to fashion the weapons needed for the assault.   Thus in its origin and by its execution the task was in fact an attempt to give an organised statement of sound philosophy in a form applicable to social and political speculations.

Mill considered that the school of metaphysicians which he attacked had long predominated in this country.[1] When Taine called his view specially English, Mill protested.   The Scottish reaction against Hume, he said, which 'assumed long ago the German form,' had ended by 'prevailing universally' in this country.   When he first wrote he was almost alone in his opinions, and there were still 'twenty *a priori* and spiritualist philosophers for every partisan of the doctrine of Experience.'[2]   The philosophical world, he says elsewhere,[3] is 'bisected' by the line between the 'Intuitional' and the 'Experiential' schools.   Mill's conviction that a majority of Englishmen were really 'intuitionists' in any shape is significant, I think, of his isolated position.   Undoubtedly most Englishmen disliked Utilitarians, and respectable professors of philosophy were anxious to disavow sympathy with covert atheism.   Yet the general tendency of thought was, I suspect, far more congenial to Mill's doctrine than he admitted.   Englishmen were practically, if not avowedly, predisposed to empiricism.   In any case, he was carrying on the tradition which Taine rightly,

[1] *Logic*, p. 369 (bk. iii. ch. xxi. § 1).   I quote from the popular edition of 1898.   Book, chapter, and section are generally applicable to former editions.

[2] See letter in note to chapter upon Mill in Taine's *History of English Literature*.

[3] James Mill's *Analysis*, i. 352 *n*.

as I should say, regarded as specifically English. Its
adherents traced its origin back through James Mill to
Hartley, Hume, Locke, Hobbes, and Francis Bacon,
and perhaps it might even count among its remoter
ancestors such men as William of Ockham and Roger
Bacon. The series of names suggests some permanent
congeniality to the national character.[1] Although, moreover, this tradition had in later times been broken by
Reid and his followers, their condemnation did not really
imply so fundamental an antithesis of thought as Mill
supposed. They and the empiricists had, in their own
opinion at least, a common ancestor in Bacon, if not in
Locke. But, however this may be, the Scottish school
had maintained the positions which Mill thought himself
concerned to attack ; and for him represented the rejection of ' experience.'

Experience is a word which requires exposition ; but
in a general way the aim of the Utilitarians is abundantly
clear. They attacked ' intuitions ' as Locke had attacked
' innate ideas.' The great error of philosophy, according
to them, as according to Locke, has been the attempt to
transcend the limits of human intelligence, and so to
wander into the regions of mysticism ; to seek knowledge by spinning logical structures which, having no
base in fact, ended in mere scholastic logomachy ; or to
override experience by claiming absolute authority for
theories which dispense with further proof for the simple
reason that no proof of them can be given. To limit
speculation and to make it fruitful by forcing it from
the first to deal with facts ; to trace all its evidence to

[1] See an interesting article in G. Croom Robertson's *Philosophical Remains*
(1894), pp. 28-45.

experience or the observation of facts ; and to insist upon its verification by comparison with facts, is the main and surely the legitimate purpose of the Utilitarians as of all their philosophical congeners.   The gulf between the world of speculation and the world of fact is the great opprobrium of philosophy.   The necessity for finding a basis of fact was emphasised at this time by the rapid development of the sciences which may be called purely empirical, and which had sprung, in any case, from methods of direct observation.   This development suggested the elaborate treatise written from a different point of view by Whewell.   The great ambition of the Benthamites had been to apply scientific methods to all the problems of legislation, jurisprudence, economics, ethics, and philosophy.   Mill could now show, with the involuntary help of Whewell, what those methods really implied.   The questions remain : What are facts ? and, What is experience ? and, What are the consequent conditions of reasoning about facts ?   Admitting that, somehow or other, a vast and rapidly growing body of knowledge has been attained in the physical sciences, we may ask how it has been gained, and proceed to apply the methods in what have been called the moral sciences. Kant's famous problem was, How is *a priori* synthetic knowledge possible ?   Mill denies that any such knowledge exists.   His problem is therefore, How can knowledge be explained without *a priori* elements ?   When this can be satisfactorily done, we shall be able to show how both moral and physical science can be fairly based upon experience.

Mill's view of the proper limits of his inquiry is characteristic.   He accepts Bacon's account of logic.

It 'is the *ars artium*, the science of science itself.'[1]
It implies an investigation into the processes of inference generally. It is not limited to the old formal
logic, but includes every operation by which knowledge
is extended. It is thus, as he afterwards puts it,
the 'theory of proof.'[2] The book, indeed, owes its
interest to the width of the field covered. It has
not the repulsive dryness of formal logic, but would
lead to a natural history of the whole growth of
knowledge, and makes constant reference to the actual
development of thought. On the other hand, Mill
gives notice that he has no more to do with metaphysics than with any of the special sciences. Logic, he
declares, is common ground for all schools of philosophy.
It is, he says, the office of metaphysics to decide what are
ultimate facts, but for the logician it is needless to go
into this analysis.[3] Accordingly, he often in the course
of the book considers himself entitled to hand over
various problems to the metaphysicians.[4] The possibility
of really keeping to this distinction is doubtful. Since
Mill's very aim is to show that all knowledge comes from
observation of 'facts,' it is apparently relevant to inquire

[1] *Logic*, Introduction, § 5.
[2] *Ibid.* p. 29 (bk. i. ch. iii. § 1).
[3] *Ibid.* p. 8 § 7.
[4] See John Grote's *Exploratio Philosophica* (1865), p. 209 *n*. This book is,
I think, by far the most interesting contemporary discussion of Mill, Hamilton,
and Whewell. It was, unfortunately, desultory and unfinished, but it is full
of acute criticism, and charmingly candid and modest. Mill's *Logic* is especially
discussed in chapters viii. and ix. Grote holds, and I think truly, that Mill's
attempt to divide metaphysics from logic leads to real confusion, and especially
to an untenable mode of conceiving the relation between 'things' and thoughts.
I cannot discuss Grote's views; but the book is full of interesting suggestions,
though the results are rather vague. See the excellent account of Grote by
the late Croom Robertson in the *Dictionary of National Biography*.

what are these 'ultimate facts.' Indeed, his statement, though made in all sincerity, almost suggests a controversial artifice. Logic, as Mill of course admits, affects metaphysics as it affects all sciences ; but in one way it affects them very differently. It justifies astronomy, but it apparently makes metaphysics superfluous. Inquiry into the 'ultimate facts' turns out to be either hopeless or meaningless. Mill does not directly assert that all 'ontological' speculations are merely cobwebs of the brain. But he tries to show that, whatever they may be, they are strictly irrelevant in reasoning. All metaphysicians are expected to grant him certain postulates. These once granted, he will be able to account for the whole structure of knowledge. 'Intuitions,' transcendental speculations, and ontology will then be deprived of the whole conditions under which they thrive. I do not now assert, he virtually says, that your doctrine is wrong, but I shall show that it is thrown away. It is a pretence of explaining something which lies altogether beyond the limits of real knowledge, and therefore admits of no explanation.

Mill starts from the classification given in old logical textbooks, to which, different as are his conclusions, he attached a very high value.[1] The schoolmen had by their elaborate acuteness established a whole system of logical distinctions and definitions which are both

---

[1] Mill, in his review of Whately, refers to Du Trieu (whose treatise had been privately printed by him and his friends), Crakenthorpe, and Burgersdyk ; and in the *Examination of Hamilton's Philosophy* (ch. xxii.) quotes also Sanderson, Wallis, Aldrich, Keckermann, Bartholinus, and Du Hamel as the 'authorities nearest at hand.' There is nothing, as I am told by the learned, exceptionally interesting in Du Trieu ; and the selection was probably accidental.

important and accurate, however sterile the inquiries in
which they were used. The machinery was excellent,
though its contrivers forgot that a mill cannot grind out
flour if you put in no grain. Mill begins accordingly
by classifying the various kinds of words in the light
afforded by previous logical systems.

He is to give a theory of proof. That which is to be
proved is a proposition ; and a proposition deals with
names, and moreover with the names of 'things,' not
merely with the names ' of our ideas of things.'[1]   That,
in some sense, reasoning has to do with things is of
course his essential principle ; and the problem consequently arises, What are empirical ' things'?[2]   Though
we cannot ask what are 'ultimate things,' the logician
must enumerate the various kinds of things to which
reference may be made in predication. Mill makes out
a classification which he proposes to substitute, provisionally at any rate, for the Aristotelian categories.[3]   The
first and simplest class of nameable things corresponds
to things 'in the mind,' that is, 'feelings,' or 'states of
consciousness,' sensations, emotions, thoughts, and volitions.   The second class corresponds to things 'external
to the mind':[4] and these are either 'substances' or
'attributes.' Here our task is lightened by a welcome
discovery.   All philosophers, it appears, are now
agreed upon one point. Sir W. Hamilton, Cousin,
Kant, nay, according to Hamilton—though that is
too good to be true—nearly all previous philosophers
admit one truth.[5]   We know, as they agree, nothing
about 'objects' except the sensations which they give

[1] *Logic*, p. 15 (bk. i. ch. ii. § 1).   [2] *Ibid.* p. 29 (bk. i. ch. iii. § 1).
[3] *Ibid.* p. 49 (bk. i. ch. iii. § 15).   [4] *Ibid.* p. 35 (bk. i ch. iv. § 6).
[5] *Ibid.* p. 38 (bk. i. ch. iv. § 7).

us and the order of those sensations.   Hence the two
'substances,' body and mind, remain unknowable 'in
themselves.'   Body is the 'hidden external cause' to
which we refer our sensations;[1] and as body is the
'mysterious something which excites the mind to feel,
so mind is the mysterious something which feels and
thinks.'   The mind is, as he says in language quoted
from his father, 'a thread of consciousness,' a series of
'feelings': it is the 'myself' which is conceived as
distinct from the feelings but of which I can yet know
nothing except that it has the feelings.

Thus, although we know nothing of minds and of
bodies 'in themselves,' we do know their existence.
That is essential to his position.   The 'thread of consciousness' is a 'final inexplicability' with him, but
it corresponds to some real entity.   And, on the other
side, we must believe, in some sense, in things.   The
thing, though known only through the sensations which
it excites, must be something more than a mere sensation, for the whole of his logic defends the thesis that
in some way or other thought has to conform to facts or
to the relations between 'things.'   Knowledge, however,
is confined entirely to the sensations and the attributes;
and the two are at bottom one.   The 'verbal' distinction
between a property of things and the sensation which
we receive from it, is made, he says, for convenience of
discourse rather than from any difference in the nature of
the thing denoted.[2]   This brings us to a critical point.
Attributes, he says, following the old distribution, are
of Quality, Quantity, and Relation.   Now Quality and

[1] *Logic*, p. 40 (bk. i. ch. iv. § 8).
[2] *Ibid.* p. 41 (bk. i. ch. iii. § 9).

Quantity mean simply the sensations excited by bodies.
To say that snow is white, or that there is a gallon of
water, means simply that certain sensations of colour or
size are excited in us by snow or a volume of water.
The attribute called 'Relation' introduces a different
order of feelings. A 'relation' supposes that two
things are involved in some one fact or series of facts.[1]
But it is still an 'attribute' or a 'state of consciousness.' It is a feeling different from other feelings by
the circumstance that two 'things' instead of one are
involved. This is the explanation which, as we have
seen, he praises so warmly in his father's *Analysis*, and
now adopts for his own purposes. It enables him to
classify predications. All predication is either an assertion of simple existence or an assertion of 'relations.'
By classifying the possible relations, therefore, we obtain
the possible forms of predication. It turns out accordingly that we can make five possible predications : we can
predicate, *first*, simple existence ; or *secondly*, 'coexistence' ; or *thirdly*, 'sequence' (these two being equivalent,
as he adds, to 'order in place' and 'order in time') ; or
fourthly, we may predicate 'resemblance' ; or *fifthly*, and
this is only to be stated provisionally, we may predicate
'causation.'[2]

So far, Mill's view corresponds to the psychology of
the *Analysis*, which gives a similar account of the various
terms employed. J. S. Mill has now the standing
ground from which he can explain the whole development of knowledge. At this point, however, he has to
diverge from his father's extreme nominalism. Predica-

---

[1] *Logic*, p. 43 (bk. i. ch. iv. § 10).
[2] *Ibid.* p. 68 (bk. i. ch. v. § 6).

tion, according to the elder, is a process of naming.   A predicate is a name of the same thing of which the subject is a name ; and to predicate is simply to assert this identity of names.   This doctrine, as Mill thinks, is equally implied in the *dictum de omni et nullo* which is taken as the explanation of the syllogism.   We have arbitrarily put a number of things in a class, and to 'reason' is simply to repeat of each what we have said of all.   This is to put the cart before the horse, or to assume that the classification precedes the reason for classification, though probably the theory ' thus nakedly stated' would not be granted by any one.[1]   What, then, is the true theory ?   That is explained by the distinction between 'connotation' and 'denotation,' which Mill accepted (though inverting the use of the words) from his father.   A general name such as 'man' *de*notes John, Thomas, and other individuals.   It *con*notes certain 'attributes,' such as rationality and a certain shape.   When, therefore, I say that John is a man, I say that he has the attributes 'connoted'; and when I say that all men are mortal, I assert that along with the other attributes of man goes the attribute of mortality.[2] Predication, then, in general, involves the attribute of 'relation.'   We may assert the simple existence of a 'quality,' or, which is the same thing, of a 'sensation' ; but to say that John is a man, or that men are mortal, or to make any of the general propositions which constitute knowledge, is to assert some of those 'relations' which are perceived when we consider two or more things together.

---

[1] *Logic*, p. 61 (bk. i. ch. v. § 3).
[2] *Ibid.* p. 63 (bk. i. ch. v. § 4).

'Things,' then, so far as knowable are clusters (in Hartley's language) of 'attributes'; and the attributes may be equally regarded as 'feelings.' To predicate is to refer a thing to one of the clusters, and therefore to assert its possession of the attributes connoted. I will only note in passing that by declining to go into the metaphysical question as to the difference between 'attributes' and 'sensations,' or thoughts and things, Mill leaves an obscurity at the foundation of his philo. sophy. But leaving this for the present, it is enough to say that we have our five possible types of predication.[1] All propositions may be reduced to one of the forms. Things exist or coexist or follow or resemble or are cause or effect.[2] The next problem, therefore, is, How are these propositions to be proved? or, by what tests is our belief to be justified?

What may be the nature of belief itself is a question which Mill leaves to the analytical psychologist,[3] who, as he admits, will probably find it puzzling, if not hopeless. But as we all agree that somehow or other we

---

[1] It would be interesting to compare this part of Mill with the correspond-ing part of Hume's *Treatise*. Hume, like Mill, begins by accepting causation as one of the relations involved, and then explains it as merely derivative. His treatment of relations generally, especially the division of relations into the two classes, which do or do not depend upon the 'ideas' themselves,* has a bearing upon Mill's doctrine too intricate to be considered here. I do not think that Mill was very familiar with Hume's writings. A note to the con-cluding chapter of the *Examination of Hamilton* seems to imply that he was not acquainted with the *Treatise*; nor does he appear from his posthumous *Essays* to have studied Hume's writings upon theology. Whether T. H. Green was right in holding that Hume had a more distinct view than his successor of some metaphysical difficulties, I need not inquire.

* *Treatise of Human Nature*, pt. vi. sec. 1.

[2] *Logic*, p. 70 (bk. i. ch. v. § 7).
[3] *Ibid.* p. 434 (bk. iv. ch. iii. § 2 *n.*).

attain knowledge, we may inquire what is implied in the process.   Now, some part of our knowledge obviously depends upon 'experience.'   We know of any particular fact from the testimony of our senses.   We know that London Bridge exists because we have seen and touched it ; and it would be obviously hopeless to try to deduce its existence from the principle of the excluded middle. London Bridge would then be something independent of time and place.   But do we not want something more than bare experience when we lay down a general rule as a law of nature ?   Then we not only say 'is,' but 'must be' ; and this, according to the Intuitionist, marks the introduction of something more than an appeal to ' experience.'   There are truths, he says, which represent ' laws of thought ' ; which are self-evident, or perceived by 'intuition' ; or the contrary of which is 'inconceivable.'   Without some such laws, we could not bind together the shifting data of experience, or advance from ' is ' to 'must be,' or even to 'will be.'   We lose all certainty, and fall into the scepticism of Hume, which makes belief a mere 'custom,' regards all things as distinct atoms conjoined but not connected, and holds that 'anything may be the cause of anything.'   Mill's aim is to explode the intuitions without falling into the scepticism.   Necessary truths, he holds, are mere figments.   All knowledge whatever is of the empirical type.   ' This has been ' justifies ' this will be.'   Empirical truths clearly exist, and are held undoubtingly, although they have no foundation except experience.   Nobody ever doubted that all men die ; yet no 'proof' of the fact could be ever suggested, before physiology was created, except the bare fact that all men have died.   If physiology has made the necessity more evident, it has not appreciably strengthened the conviction. We all believe even now that thunder will follow lightning, though nobody has been able to show why it should follow. The ultimate proof in countless cases, if not in all, is simply that some connection has been observed, and, in many such cases, the belief reaches a pitch which excludes all perceptible doubt. As a fact, then, belief of the strongest kind can be generated from simple experience. The burthen of proof is upon those who assume different origins for different classes of truth.[1]

II. SYLLOGISM AND DEFINITION

This main thesis leads to two lines of argument. First of all, Mill seeks to show that the methods of proof expounded by his adversaries do not really take us beyond experience ; and, secondly, he seeks to show that experience gives us a sufficient basis of knowledge. Let us first notice, then, how the ground is cleared by examining previous accounts of the process of inference. The old theory of reasoning depends upon the syllogism. That gives the type of the whole process by which knowledge is extended. All men are mortal ; Socrates is a man, therefore Socrates is mortal. Stewart and Brown had both attacked the syllogism on the familiar ground that it is tautologous. The major has already asserted the minor. To say that one man is mortal when you have already said that all men are mortal, is merely to repeat yourself. There can be no

[1] *Logic*, p. 152 (bk. ii. ch. v. § 4).

real inference, and no advance to new knowledge. So long as the syllogism is to be explained on the old terms, Mill thinks this criticism fatal; but he holds, too, that by a different interpretation we may assign a real and vitally important meaning to this venerable form of argument. In several places[1] he gives a view which seems to be much to the purpose. The syllogism, it would seem, corresponds really, not to a mode of reasoning, but to a system of arguing. When a disputant bases some statement upon an inference, we may challenge either the truth of the rule or the statement of fact. The cogency of the argument depends upon the applicability of the rule to the fact. If men be not mortal, or, again, if Socrates be not a man, the inference is not valid; and these two distinct issues, the issue of law and the issue of fact, may be raised in any case.[2] The value of the syllogism is that it raises these issues distinctly. The argument is thus put in such a form as to be absolutely conclusive if the premises be themselves granted. It therefore provides a test of the validity of the logic. Granting the premises, a denial of the inference must involve a contradiction. That is the only test in pure logic. The syllogism must, therefore, be in a sense tautologous, for otherwise it could not be conclusive. Acceptance of the premises must be shown from the form of statement to necessitate the admission of the inference. This follows, and the logical link is complete and irrefragable, if the

[1] Especially the early review of Whately.

[2] This suggests a parallel to the old English system of pleading—as a preparatory process for bringing out the issues really involved in a dispute—which is said to have been thoroughly logical, though it became excessively cumbrous and technical.

middle term be identical in both premises, and not otherwise. This is what Mill indicates by saying that 'the rules of the syllogism are rules for compelling a person to be aware of the whole of what he must undertake to defend if he persists in maintaining his conclusion.'[1] Ratiocination, as he sums up his view elsewhere, 'does not consist of syllogisms', but the syllogism is a useful formula into which it can 'translate its reasonings,' and so guarantee their correctness.[2]

If this be granted, we must consider the essential step of inference to be embodied in, but not created by, the syllogism. Correct reasoning can always be thrown into this form. The syllogism emerges when the reasoning is complete. 'The use of the syllogism is no other,' says Mill, 'than the use of general propositions in reasoning.' It is a security for correct generalisation.[3] We have, then, still to ask what is the reasoning process for which the syllogism provides a test. Generalisation implies classification. Our general rule or major premise states some property of a class to which the individual belongs. The question is how this reference to a class enables us to draw inferences which we could not draw from the individual case. To this Mill gives a simple answer, which is already implied in his theory of predication. When I say that Socrates is a man, I say that he has the attributes connoted by the name. He is a rational, featherless biped, for example. But I already know by observation that

---

[1] *Logic*, p. 527 (bk. v. ch. vi. § 3). So in *Examination of Hamilton*, ch. xxii., 'The syllogism is not the form in which we necessarily reason, but a test of reasoning.'

[2] James Mill's *Analysis*, ii. 427.

[3] *Logic*, p. 131 (bk. ii. ch. iii. § 5).

with these attributes goes the attribute of mortality. The essence of the reasoning process is therefore that, from the possession of certain attributes, I infer the possession of another attribute which has coexisted with them previously. That I do, in fact, reason in this way in countless cases is undeniable. I know that a certain quality, say malleability, goes along with other qualities of colour, shape, and so forth, by which I recognise a substance as gold. I can, it may be, give no other reason for believing the future conjunction of those qualities than the fact of their previous conjunction. The belief, that is, is as a matter of fact generated simply by the previous coincidence or corresponds to constant association. Whether this exhausts the whole logical significance may still be disputed ; but, at any rate, upon these terms we can escape from the charge of tautology. The rule in the major premise registers a number of previous experiences of coexistence. When we notice some of the attributes in a given case, we make an addition to our knowledge by applying the rule, that is, by inferring that another attribute may be added to the observed attributes. This, then, gives a rational account of the advance in knowledge made through the syllogism in the case where the class can be defined as a simple sum of attributes.

But is this an adequate account of the reasoning process in general? There is another view which suggested difficulties to Mill. His solution of these difficulties, marked, as we learn from the *Autobiography*, an essential stage in the development of his doctrine. Reference to a class is, upon his interpretation, implied in the syllogism ; and classification implies definition.

A class means all things which have a certain list of attributes stated in the definition. May we not then infer other properties from the definition? May not mortality, for example, be deducible from the other attributes of man? The assumption that we can do so is connected with the fallacy most characteristic of the misuse of the syllogism. It is plain that we may create as many classes as we please, and make names for combinations of attributes which have no actual, or even no possible, existence. Any inferences which we make on the strength of such classification must be nugatory or simply tautologous. I show that a certain proposition follows from my definition ; but that gives no guarantee for its conformity to the realities behind the definition. Your 'proof' that a man is mortal means simply that if he is not mortal you don't call him a man. The syllogism treated on that system becomes simply an elaborate series of devices for begging the question. From such methods arise all the futilities of scholasticism, and the doctrine of essences which, though Locke confuted it,[1] has 'never ceased to poison philosophy.'[2] It may, I suppose, be taken for granted that the syllogism was constantly applied to cover such fallacies, and so far Mill is on safe ground. The theory, however, leads him to a characteristic point. Already in the early review (January 1828), he had criticised Whately's account of definition. A 'real definition,' as Whately had said, 'explains and unfolds "the nature" of the thing defined, whereas a "nominal definition" only explains the name.' Whately goes on

---

[1] *Logic*, p. 72 (bk. i. ch. vi. § 2).
[2] *Ibid.* p. 115 (bk. ii. ch. ii. § 2).

to point out that the only real definitions in this sense
are the mathematical definitions.   It is impossible to
discover the properties of a thing, a man, or a plant
from the definition.   If it were possible, we might
proceed to ' evolve a camel from the depths of our consciousness,' and nobody now professes to be equal to
that feat.   When, however, we ' define' a circle or a line
and so forth, we make assertions from which we can
deduce the whole theory of geometry.   A geometrical
figure represents a vast complex of truths, mutually
implying each other, and all deducible from a few
simple definitions.   The middle term is not the name
of a simple thing, or of a thing which has a certain
set of coexisting attributes, but a word expressive of a
whole system of reciprocal relations.   If one property
entitles me to say that a certain figure is a circle, I am
virtually declaring that it has innumerable other properties, and I am thus able to make inferences which,
although implicitly given, are not perceived till explicitly
stated.   By assigning a thing to a class, I say in this case
that I may make any one of an indefinite number of
propositions about it, all mutually implying each other,
and requiring the highest faculties for combining and
evolving.   Pure mathematics give the one great example
of a vast body of truths reached by purely deductive
processes.   They appear to be evolved from certain
simple and self-evident truths.   Can they, then, be
explained as simply empirical ?   Do we know the properties of a circle as we know the properties of gold,
simply by combining records of previous experience ?
Or can we admit that this great system of truth is all
evolved out of ' definitions ' ?

Mill scents in Whately's doctrine a taint of *a priori* assumption, and accordingly meets it by a direct contradiction. A geometrical definition, he says, is no more a 'real' definition than the definition of a camel. No definition whatever can 'unfold the nature' of a thing. He states this in his review, though it was at a later period,[1] when meditating upon a passage of Dugald Stewart, that he perceived the full consequences of his own position. In answering Whately, he had said that all definitions were 'nominal.' A 'real definition' means that to the definition proper we add the statement that there is a thing corresponding to the name.[2] The definition itself is a 'mere identical proposition,' from which we can learn nothing as to facts. But it may be accompanied by a postulate which 'covertly asserts a fact,' and from the fact may follow consequences of any degree of importance. This distinction between the definition and the postulate may be exhibited, as he remarks, by substituting 'means' for 'is.' If we say : a centaur 'means' a being half man and half horse, we give a pure definition. If we say : a man 'is' a featherless biped, our statement includes the definition—man 'means' featherless biped ; but if we said no more, no inference could be made as to facts. If we are really to increase our knowledge by using this definition, we must add the

---

[1] *Autobiography*, p. 181. The passage to which Mill refers is apparently that in Stewart's *Works*, iii. 24-36 and 113-52. Stewart quotes a passage from Dr. Beddoes' *Observations on the Nature of Demonstrative Evidence* (1793), which anticipates Mill's view that the 'mathematical sciences are sciences of experiment and observation, founded solely on the induction of particular facts.' Stewart professes to follow Locke (see Locke's *Essay*, bk. iv. ch. xii. § 15), and gives some references to other discussions on the questions.

[2] *Logic*, p. 94 (bk. i. ch. viii. § 5).

'covert' assertion that such featherless bipeds exist.
The mathematical case is identical.   Stewart had argued
that geometrical propositions followed, not from the
axioms but, from the definitions.   From the bare axiom
that if equals be added to equals the wholes are equal,
you can infer nothing.   You must also perceive the
particular figures which are compared.   Of course the
truth of the axioms must be admitted ; but they do not
specify the first principles from which geometry is evolved.
In other words, geometry implies 'intuition,' not the *a
priori* 'intuitions' to which Mill objected, but the direct
perception of the spatial relations.   We must see the
figure as well as admit the self-evident axiom.   Mill, on
considering this argument, thought that Stewart had
stopped at a half truth.[1]   He ought to have got rid of
the definitions as well as the axioms.   Every demonstration in Euclid, says Mill, might be carried on without
them.   When we argue from a diagram in which there
is a circle, we do not really refer to circles in general, but
only to the particular circle before us.   If its radii be
equal or approximately equal, the conclusions are true.
We afterwards extend our reasoning to similar cases ; but
only one instance is demonstrated.   The definition is
merely a 'notice to ourselves and others,' stating what
assumptions we think ourselves entitled to make ; and in
this way it resembles the major in the syllogism.   The
demonstration does not 'depend upon' it, though if we
deny it, the demonstration fails.   By this argument,
Mill conceives that the case of mathematics is put on
a level with other cases.   We always argue from facts,
and moreover from 'particular facts,' not from defini-

[1] *Logic*, p. 125 (bk. ii. ch. iii. § 3).

tions. We start from an observation of this particular circle—a sensible 'thing' or object, as in arguing about natural history we start from observation of the camel. Hence we may lay down the general proposition, applicable to geometry as well as to all ordinary observation, that 'all inference is from particulars to particulars.'[1] This is the 'foundation' both of Induction, which is 'popularly said' to reason from particulars to generals, and of Deduction, which is supposed to reason from generals to particulars.[2] This sums up Mill's characteristic position.

III. MATHEMATICAL TRUTHS

This attempt to bring all reasoning to the same type forces Mill to ignore what to others seems to be of the essence of the case. There are, he says, two statements: 'There may exist a figure bounded by three straight lines'; that is the fruitful statement of facts. 'This figure is called a triangle'; that is the merely nominal definition or explanation of words. Moreover, as he says, we may drop the definition by substituting the equivalent words or simply looking at the thing. It does not follow that we can dispense with the mode of apprehension implied by the definition. Whether we use the word triangle, or the words, 'three lines enclosing a space,' or no words at all, we must equally have the conceptions or intuitions of lines and space. All demonstration in geometry consists in mentally rearranging a combination of lines and angles so as to show that one figure may be made to coincide absolutely with

[1] *Logic*, p. 126 (bk. ii. ch. iii. § 4).   [2] *Ibid.* p. 107 (bk. ii. ch. i. § 3).

another figure. The original fact remains unaltered, but the ways of apprehending the fact are innumerable. Newton and his dog Diamond might both see the same circular thing ; but to Diamond the circle was a simple round object ; to Newton it was also a complex system of related lines, capable of being so regarded as to embody a vast variety of elaborate formulæ.[1] Geometry, as Mill undeniably says, deals with facts. Newton and Diamond have precisely the same fact before them. It remains the same, whether we stop at the simplest stage or proceed to the most complex evolution of geometry. The difference between the observers is not that Newton has seen new facts, but that he sees more in the same fact. The change is not in the things but in the mind, which, by grouping the things in the way pointed out by the definitions, is able to discover countless new relations involved in the same perception. This again may suggest that even the fact revealed to simple perception is not a bare 'fact,' something, as Mill puts it, 'external to the mind,' but is in some sense itself constituted by the faculty of perception. It contains already the germ of the whole intellectual evolution. The change is not in the thing perceived, but in the mode of perceiving. And, therefore, again, we do not acquire new knowledge, as we acquire it in the physical sciences, by observing new facts, discovering resemblances and differences, and generalising from the properties common to all ; but by contemplating the same fact. All geometry is in any

[1] Whiston (*Memoirs*, i. 35) reports that Newton saw by intuition, or previously to formal demonstration, the equality of all parallelograms described about the conjugate diameters of an ellipse. Most of us can only learn the fact by painful construction.

particular space—if only we can find it. We do not proceed by comparing a number of different regions of spaces, and inquire whether French triangles have the same properties as English triangles. To Mill, however, the statement that geometry deals with fact leads to another conclusion. We must deal with these facts as with other facts, and follow the method of other natural sciences. We really proceed in the same way whether we are investigating the properties of an ellipse or a camel. In either case we must discover truth by experience.

What, then, is really implied in the doctrine that all knowledge rests upon experience? One of Mill's intellectual ancestors lays down the fundamental principle. It is absurd, says Hume,[1] to try to demonstrate *matter of fact* by *a priori* arguments. 'Nothing is demonstrable unless the contrary implies a contradiction. Nothing that is distinctly conceivable implies a contradiction. Whatever we conceive as existent we can also conceive as non-existent. There is no being, therefore, whose non-existence implies a contradiction.' 'Matter of fact,' then, must be proved by experience; but, given a 'fact' we may deduce necessary consequences. All necessity may be hypothetical; there is an 'if' to every 'must,' but remembering the 'if' the 'must' will be harmless. It can never take us beyond experience. The existence of space itself cannot be called necessary; but space once given, all geometry may 'necessarily' follow, and imply relations running through the whole fabric of scientific knowledge. Mill agrees that a 'hypothetical' necessity

[1] Hume's *Works* (Grose and Green), ii. 432 and iv. 134. Hume's statement is criticised by G. H. Lewes in his *Problems*, etc., i. 391, but, I think, on an erroneous interpretation.

of this kind belongs to geometry ; and adds, that in any science whatever, we might, by making hypotheses, arrive at an equal necessity.[1] But then, he goes on to urge, the hypotheses of geometry are not 'absolute truths,' but 'generalisations from observation,' or 'inductions from the evidence of our senses,'[2] which, therefore, are not necessarily true. This led to his keenest controversies, and, in my opinion, to his least successful answers. He especially claims credit in his *Autobiography* for having attacked the 'stronghold' of the intuitionists by upsetting belief in the *a priori* certainty of mathematical aphorisms. In fact, his opponents constantly appealed to the case of mathematics, and Mill assumes that they can be met only by reducing such truths to the case of purely empirical truths. He argues boldly that the 'character of necessity ascribed to the truths of mathematics' is 'an illusion.'[3] Geometry and arithmetic are both founded upon experience or observation. He goes indeed still further at times. At one place he even holds that the principle of contradiction itself is simply 'one of our first and most familiar generalisations from experience.' We know, 'by the simplest observation of our own minds,' that belief and disbelief exclude each other, and that when light is present darkness is absent.[4] Mill thought himself

---

[1] *Logic*, p. 149 (bk. ii. ch. v. § 1).   [2] *Ibid.* p. 151 (bk. ii. ch. v. § 4).

[3] *Ibid.* p. 147 (bk. ii. ch. v. § 1).

[4] *Ibid.* p 183 (bk. ii. ch. vii. § 5). In the *Examination of Hamilton* he is less confident. It is 'not only inconceivable to us, but inconceivable that it should be made conceivable' that the same statement should be both true and false (ch. vi. p. 67). Afterwards (ch. xxi. p. 418) he will only decide that such laws are now 'invincibly' laws of thought, though they may or may not be 'capable of alteration by experience.'

bound, we see, to refer to experience not only our knowledge of facts, but even the capacities, which are said by another school to be the conditions of perceiving and thus acquiring experience. If he had studied Kant, he might have reached a better version of his own view. As it was, he was led to accepting paradoxes which he was not really concerned to maintain. He had to choose between a theory of 'intuitions'—so understood as to entitle us to assert matter of fact independently of experience—and a theory which seems to make even the primary intellectual operations mere statements of empirical fact. Since necessary statements about matters of fact must be impossible, he argues that we cannot even draw necessary inferences from observed fact. Not content with saying that all necessity is hypothetical, he argues that all necessity, even the logical necessity of contradiction, is a figment. If he does not carry out a theory which would seem to make all reasoning unsatisfactory, he maintains, at least, that the hypotheses or assumptions involved in geometry, and even in arithmetic, are generalised from experience, and 'seldom, if ever, exactly true.' If the assumptions are inaccurate or uncertain, the whole superstructure of science must also be uncertain.

The nature of his argument follows from his previous positions. He treats space and number as somehow qualities of the 'things,' or as attributes which we observe without in any sense supplying them. His argument upon geometry begins by asserting that there are no such 'real things' as points or lines or circles. Nay, they are not even possible, so far as we can see, consistently with the actual constitution of the universe. It is 'customary' to answer that such lines only exist in our minds, and have therefore nothing to do with outward experience.[1] This, however, is incorrect psychologically, because our ideas are copies of the realities. A line without breadth is 'inconceivable,' and therefore does not exist even in the mind. Hence we must suppose that geometry deals either with 'non-entities' or with 'natural objects.'[1] Arithmetic fares little better. When we say that two and one make three, we assert that the same pebbles may, 'by an alteration of place and arrangement' — that is, by being formed into one parcel or two—be made to produce either set of sensations.[2] Each of the numbers, 2, 3, 4, etc., he says elsewhere, 'denotes physical phenomena and connotes a physical property of those phenomena.'[3] Arithmetic owes its position to the 'fortunate applicability' to it of the 'inductive truth' that the sums of equals 'are equal.'[4] It is obvious to remark that this is only true of certain applications of arithmetic. When we speak of the numbers of a population, we imply, as Mill admits, no equality except that each person is a unit.[5] We may speak with equal propriety of a number of syllogisms or of metaphors, in which we have nothing to do with 'equality' or 'physical properties' at all. Further, as he observes,[6] it is the peculiarity of the case that counting one thing is to count all things. When I see that four pebbles are two pairs of pebbles, I see the same truth for all cases, including, for example, syllogisms. Mill admits, accordingly, that 'in questions

---

[1] *Logic*, p. 148 (bk. ii. ch. v. § 1).   [2] *Ibid.* p. 168 (bk. ii. ch. vi. § 2).
[3] *Ibid.* p. 400 (bk. iii. ch. xxiv. § 5).   [4] *Ibid.* p. 401 (bk. iii. ch. xxiv. § 5).
[5] *Ibid.* p. 170 (bk. ii. ch. vi. § 3).   [6] *Ibid.* p. 167 (bk. ii. ch. vi. § 2).

of pure number'—though only in such questions—
the assumptions are 'exactly true,' and apparently
holds that we may deduce exactly true conclusions.
That ought to have been enough for him.   He had
really no sufficient reason for depriving us of our
arithmetical faith.   He can himself point out its harm-
lessness.   As he truly says, 'from laws of space and
number alone nothing can be deduced but laws of space
and number.'[1]   We can never get outside of the world
of experience and observation by applying them.   If
we count, we do not say that there must be four things,
but that wherever there are four things there are also
two pairs of things.   The unlucky 'pebble' argument
illustrates one confusion.   'Two and two *are* four' is
changed into 'two and two *make* four.'   The statement
of a constant relation is made into a statement of an
event.   Two pebbles added to two might produce a
fifth, but the original two pairs would still be four.
The space-problem suggests greater difficulties.   Space,
he argues, must either be a property of things or an
idea in our minds, and therefore a 'non-entity.'   If we
consider it, however, to be a form of perception, the
disjunction ceases to be valid.   The space-perceptions
mark the border-line between 'object' and 'subject,' and
we cannot place its product in either sphere exclusively.
The space-relations are 'subjective,' because they imply
perception by the mind, but objective because they imply
the action of the mind as mind, and do not vary from
one person or 'subject' to another.   To say whether
they were objective or subjective absolutely we should
have to get outside of our minds altogether—which is an

[1] *Logic*, p. 212 (bk. iii. ch. v. § 1).

impossible feat. Therefore, again, it is not really to the purpose to allege that such a 'thing' as a straight line or a perfect circle never exists. Whether we say that a curve deviates from or conforms to perfect circularity, we equally admit the existence of a perfect circle. We may be unable to mark it with finger or micrometer, but it is there. If no two lines are exactly equal, that must be because one has more space than the other. Mill's argument seems to involve the confusion between the statement that things differ in space and the statement, which would be surely nonsense, that the space itself differs. It is to transfer the difference from the things measured to the measure itself. It is just the peculiarity of space that it can only be measured by space; and that to say one space is greater than another, is simply to say, 'there is more space.' As in the case of number, he is really making an illegitimate transfer from one sphere to another. A straight line is a symmetrical division of space, which must be taken to exist, though we cannot make a perfectly straight line. Our inability does not tend to prove that the 'space' itself is variable. In applying a measure we necessarily assume its constancy; and it is difficult even to understand what 'variability' means, unless it is variability in reference to some assumed standard. If, as Mill seems to think, space is a property of things, varying like other properties, we have to ask, In what, then, does it vary? All other properties vary in respect of their space-relations; but, if space itself be variable, we seem to be reduced to hopeless incoherence.

Thus, to ascribe necessity to geometry as well as to arithmetic is not to ascribe 'necessity' to propositions

(to use Hume's language again) about ' matters of fact.'
The ' necessity' is implied in a peculiarity which Mill
himself puts very forcibly,[1] and which seems to be all
that is wanted. An arithmetical formula of the simplest
or most complex kind is an assertion that two ways of
considering a fact are identical. When I say that two
and two make four, or lay down some algebraical
formula, such as Taylor's theorem, I am asserting the
precise equivalence of two processes. I do not even
say that two and two must make four, but that, if they
make four, they cannot also or ever make five. The
number is the same in whatever order we count, so
long as we count all the units, and count them correctly.
So much is implied in Mill's observation that counting
one set of things is counting all things. The concrete
circumstances make no difference. The same is true of
geometry. The complex figure may be also regarded as
a combination of simpler figures. It remains precisely
the same, though we perceive that besides being one
figure it is also a combination of figures. This runs
through all mathematical truths, and, I think, indicates
Mill's precise difficulty. He says quite truly that to
know the existence of a fact you must always have something given by observation or experience. The most
complex mathematical formulæ may still be regarded as
equating different statements of the same experience.
The difference is only that the experience is evolved
into more complex forms, not by any change in the data
supplied, but by an intellectual operation which consists
essentially in organising the data in various ways. The
reasoner does not for an instant desert fact ; he only

[1] *Logic*, p. 402 (bk. iii. ch. xxiv. § 6).

perceives that it may be contemplated in different ways, and that very different statements assert the very same fact or facts. Our experience may be increased, either by the entrance of new objects into our field of observation, or by the different methods of contemplation. The mathematician deals with propositions which remain equally true if we suppose no change whatever to take place in the world, or, as Mill puts it, 'if all the objects of the universe were unchangeably fixed.' [1] His theories, in short, construct a map on which he can afterwards lay down the changes which involve time. The filling up of the map depends entirely upon observation and experience ; but to make the map itself a mere bundle of accidental coexistences is to destroy the conditions of experience. The map is our own faculty of perception.

'There is something which seems to require explanation,' says Mill,[2] 'in the fact that an immense multitude of mathematical truths . . . can be elicited from so small a number of elementary laws.' It is puzzling when you identify Newton with Diamond on the ground that they both see the same 'fact.' But it is no more puzzling than anything else, as indeed Mill proceeds to show, when we observe the method by which in arithmetic, for example, an indefinite number of relations is implied by the simple process of counting. The fact is the same for all observers, in so far as they have the same data ; but to perceive the data already implies the germ of thought from which all the demonstrative sciences are

[1] *Logic*, fourth edition, i. 356 (bk. iii. ch. v. § 1). This phrase is omitted in the last edition (p. 211), but the meaning is apparently not altered.

[2] *Ibid.* p. 399 (bk. iii. ch. xxiv. § 5).

evolved. The knowledge can be transformed and complicated to an indefinite degree by simply identifying different ways of combining the data. Mill, in his anxiety to adhere to facts and experience, fails to recognise adequately the process by which simple observation is evolved into countless modifications. The difficulty appears in its extreme form in the curious suggestion that even the principle of contradiction is a product of experience. Mill is so resolved to leave nothing for the mind to do, that he supposes a primitive mind which is not even able to distinguish 'is not' from 'is.' It is hard to understand how such a ' mind,' if it were a 'mind,' could ever acquire any 'experience' at all. So when Mill says that the burthen of proof rests with the intuitionist, he is, no doubt, quite right in throwing the burthen of proof upon thinkers who suppose particular doctrines to have been somehow inserted into the fabric of knowledge without any relation to other truths; but it is surely not a gratuitous assumption that the mind which combines experience must have some kind of properties as well as the things combined. If it knows no 'truths' except from experience, it is at least possible that it may in some way react upon the given experience. This, at any rate, should be Mill's view, who takes 'mind' and 'body' to be unknowable, and all knowledge of fact to be a combination of 'sensations.' He only requires to admit that knowledge may be increased either by varying the data or by varying the mind's action upon fixed data. In neither case do we get beyond 'experience.' In many places, Mill seems to interpret his view in consistency with this doctrine. His invariable candour leads him to make admissions, some of which I have noticed. Yet his prepossessions lead him to the superfluous paradoxes which, for the rest, he maintains with remarkable vigour and ingenuity.

One other device of the enemy raised the troublesome question of inconceivability as a test of truth, which brought Mill into conflict not only with Whewell and Hamilton, but with Mr. Herbert Spencer. I will only notice the curious illustration which it affords of Mill's tendency to confound statements of fact with the purely logical assertion that two modes of stating a fact are precisely equivalent. The existence of Antipodeans, in his favourite illustration,[1] was declared to be 'inconceivable.' Disbelief in their existence involved the statement of fact: gravity acts here and at the Antipodes in the same direction. That statement could of course be disproved by evidence ; and there is no reason to suppose that the truth, once suggested, would be less 'conceivable' to Augustine or, say, to Archimedes, than to Newton. It also involved the assertion : men (if the direction of gravity were constant) would drop off the earth at the Antipodes as they here drop off the ceiling. The denial of that statement is still 'inconceivable,' though the statement ceases to be applicable. Mill, however, infers that, as an 'inconceivability' has been surmounted, 'inconceivability' in general is no test of truth. 'There is,' he says,[2] 'no proposition of which it can be asserted that every human mind must eternally and irrevocably believe it,' and he tries, as I have said, to apply this even to the principle of contradiction. In other words, because our logic requires a basis in fact, and the fact must be given by experience,

---

[1] See *Logic*, p. 177 (bk. ii. ch. vii. § 3), and p. 493 (bk. v. ch. iii. § 3).

[2] *Ibid.* p. 370 (bk. iii. ch. xxi. § 1).

the logic is itself dependent upon experience. If ' inconceivable ' be limited, as I think it should be limited in
logic, to the contradictory, an inconceivable proposition is
incredible because it is really no proposition at all. We
may, no doubt, believe statements which are implicitly
contradictory ; but when the contradiction is made
explicit, the belief becomes impossible. Similarly we
may disbelieve statements which appear to be contradictory ; and when the error is exposed, we may believe
what was once ' inconceivable.' That only shows that
our thoughts are often in a great muddle, and in great
need of logical unification. It does not prove any
incoherence in the logical process itself.

IV. CAUSATION

We can now proceed to what may be called the constructive part of the logic. We have got rid of proofs
from intuitions, from definitions, and from inconceiva-
bilities, and the question remains how we can prove
anything. All knowledge is inductive. It is all derived
from facts ; it proceeds from particulars to particulars ;
the previous coexistence of sequences which have been
observed constitute our whole raw material. What,
then, serves to bind facts together ? or how are we
to know that facts are bound together, or that any
two given facts have this relation ? The fundamental
postulate of science is the so-called ' uniformity of
nature.' But Nature, as it is seen by the unscientific
mind, is anything but uniform. There are, it is true,
certain simple uniformities which frequently recur. Fire
burns, water drowns, stones thrown up fall down ; and

such observations are the germs of what we afterwards call scientific 'laws.' But things are constantly happening of which we can give no account. Catastrophes occur without any assignable 'antecedent'; storm and sunshine seem to come at random; and the same combination of events never recurs in all its details. Variety is as manifest as uniformity. How can cosmos be made out of chaos? How do we come to trace regularity in this bewildering world of irregularities? From any fact taken by itself, as Hume had fully shown, we can deduce no necessity for any other fact. The question is, whether we are to account for the belief in uniformity by an 'intuition' or by James Mill's universal solvent of 'association of ideas.' J. S. Mill was fully convinced of the efficacy of this panacea, but he sees difficulties over which his father had passed. If association explains everything, the tie between ideas ought to be stronger, it might be supposed, in proportion to the frequency of their association. The oftener two facts have been joined, the more confidently we should expect a junction hereafter. But this does not hold true universally. A chemist, as Mill observes, analyses a substance; and assuming the accuracy of his results, we at once infer a general law of nature from 'a single instance.' But if any one from the beginning of the world has seen that crows are black, and a single credible witness says that he has seen a grey crow, we abandon at once a conjunction which seemed to rest upon invariable and superabundant evidence. Why is a 'single instance' sufficient in one case, and any number of instances insufficient in the other? 'Whoever can answer this question,' says Mill, 'knows more of the philosophy of logic than the wisest of the ancients, and has solved the problem of induction.'[1]

Here Mill again professes to set metaphysics aside. He has nothing to do with ' ontology.' He deals with ' physical,' not ' efficient,' causes. He does not ask whether there be or be not a ' mysterious' tie lying behind the phenomena and actually producing them.[2] He is content to lay down as his statement of the ' law of causation' that there is an invariable succession between ' every fact in nature' and ' some other fact which has preceded it.' This, he assumes, is a truth, whatever be the nature of things in themselves. The true account is rather that he will show that ' ontology' is a set of meaningless phrases. He can answer his problem without it. Causation is, in fact, conceived by him as it was conceived by all the psychologists, including Brown ; and he has simply to show that Brown's supposed ' intuition' is a superfluity. His treatment of the question gives the really critical part of his philosophy. It leads to some of the results which have been most highly and, as I think, most deservedly praised. It also leads to some of his greatest errors, and shows the weak point of his method.

Mathematical knowledge, as Mill remarks, has nothing to do with causation. Every geometrical or arithmetical formula is true without supposing change. One theorem does not 'cause' the others ; it 'implies' them. The most complex and the most simple are mutually involved in the single perception, though our knowledge of one may be the cause of our knowing the others. Their necessity

---

[1] *Logic*, p. 206 (bk. iii. ch. iii. § 3).
[2] *Ibid*. p. 213 (bk. iii. ch. v. § 2).

is another way of stating this implication. We can show that to deny one theorem while admitting another is to be contradictory. The whole of physical science, however, from first to last, is a process of stating the changes of phenomena in terms of time and place, and therefore brings them all within the range of mathematical methods. Science is not fully constituted till it becomes quantitative or can speak in terms of definite relations of magnitudes. How, then, are its laws necessary? It is contradictory to say that the same thing has different space-relations at the same time; but there is no contradiction in saying that it is here now and somewhere else to-morrow. The formula of the 'uniformity of nature,' whatever may be its warrant, transfers the necessity of the geometrical theorem to the laws of phenomena. We assume that things are continuous or retain identity in change. We are no more permitted to say that the combination of the same elements may produce a compound of different properties, than to say that the product of two numbers may sometimes give one result and sometimes another. Every change is regarded as regular, or as having a 'sufficient reason.' The same series of changes therefore must take place under the same conditions, or every difference implies a difference in the conditions. So far as we carry out this assumption, we resolve the shifting and apparently irregular panorama into a system of uniform laws. Each law may be, and if it be really a law must be, absolutely true, not in the sense that it states a fact unconditionally, but that it is stated so that the conditions under which it is absolutely true are fully specified. If we could reach a complete science of all physical phenomena, we should have a system of con-

nected laws as infallible and mutually consistent as those
of geometry or arithmetic. But in order thus to organise
our knowledge, we have to alter—not the facts—but the
order of grouping and conceiving them. We have to
see identities where there were apparent differences, and
differences in apparent identities, and to regard the
whole order of nature from a fresh point of view. The
fact remains just as it was; but the laws—that is, the
formulæ which express them—are grouped upon a new
system. The questions remain, What is the precise
nature of the scientific view? and What is our guarantee
for a postulate which it everywhere implies?

The chapter upon causation[1] is a vigorous assertion
of Mill's position. He accepts the traditional view
of his school, that cause means invariable sequence;
but he makes two very important amendments to the
previous statements. A simple sequence of two events
is not a sufficient indication, however often repeated,
that they are cause and effect. We speak, he says, of a
particular dish 'causing' death; but to be accurate we
must also include, as part of the cause, all the other
phenomena present, the man as well as the food, the
man's state of health at the time, and possibly even the
state of the atmosphere or the planet. The real cause
must include all the relevant phenomena. The cause, therefore, is, 'philosophically speaking,' the 'sum total of the
conditions,' positive and negative, 'taken together, the
whole of the contingencies of every description, which,
being realised, the consequent invariably follows.'[2]
Mill's second amendment is made by saying that the
cause does not signify simply 'invariable antecedence,'

---

[1] *Logic*, bk. iii. ch. v.   [2] *Ibid.* p. 217 (bk. iii. ch. v. § 3).

but also 'unconditional' sequence. There may be 'invariable' sequences, such as day and night—a case often alleged by Reid and others, which are not 'unconditional.' The sun, for anything we can say, might not rise, and then day would not follow night. The real condition, therefore, is the presence of a luminous body without the interposition of an opaque screen.[1] These are undoubtedly material improvements upon previous statements; and this view being admitted, it follows, as Mill says, that the state of the whole universe is the consequence of its state at the previous instant. Knowing all the facts and all the laws at any time we could predict all the future history of the universe.[2] Some curious confusions, it must be noticed, result apparently from Mill's use of popular language. The most singular is implied in his discussion of the question whether cause and effect can ever be simultaneous. Some 'causes,' he says, leave permanent effects; a sword runs a man through, but it need not remain in his body in order that he may 'continue dead.'[3] The 'cause' here is taken to mean the 'thing' which was once a part of a set of things, and has clearly ceased to mean the sum of all the conditions. 'Most things,' he continues, once produced, remain as they are till something changes them. Other things require the continual presence of the agencies which produced them. But since all change, according to him, supposes a cause, it is clear that not only 'most things' but all things must remain as they are till something changes them. Persistence is implied in causation as much as change, for it is merely the other side of the

---

[1] *Logic*, p. 221 (bk. iii. ch. v. § 5).   [2] *Ibid.* p. 227 (bk. iii. ch. v. § 8).
[3] *Ibid.* p. 224 (bk. iii. ch. v. § 7).

same principle. Inertia is as much assumed in mechanics as mobility; for it is the same thing to say that a body remains in one place when there is no moving force, as to say that whenever it ceases to remain there is a moving force. The difference which Mill means to point out is that some changes alter permanent conditions of other changes, as when a man cuts his throat and all vital processes cease; while sometimes the change leaves permanent conditions unaffected, as when a man shaves himself, and his vital processes continue. But in no case is the effect produced, as he says, after the cause has ceased; it is always produced through the actually present conditions, which may have come into their present state through a change at some more or less remote period. Each link in a chain, according to the common metaphor, depends upon all the previous links and may be said to hang from them; but the distant link can only act through the intermediate links.

These slips imply a vagueness which leads to more serious results. Mill's aim is to construct a kind of logical machinery—a sieve, if I may say so, through which we pass all the phenomena of the universe in order to find out which are really loose and which are connected by the ties of causation. We are un-weaving the complex web of nature by discovering what is the hidden system of connections in virtue of which one event or thing is somehow fastened to another. Everything, we may say, which appears is called up by something else—the thunder by the lightning, the death by the poison, and so forth. In every case we can reduce a statement of causation to the form of an asser-

tion of sequence or coexistence. Here, as he observes,
we meet one difficulty. Everything is connected with
some other thing. But then it may or must be also connected with a third. The two connections may interfere,
and we have to consider how they can be disentangled.
This leads to a distinction to which he attaches, very
rightly, I think, the highest importance. In some cases,
the correct version of the facts can be obtained by simply
superposing the laws of simpler cases. A body moves
to the north under certain conditions ; but other conditions force it to move also east or south. We then
have only to combine the two ' laws,' and to say that it
is moving both north and east, that is, north-east, or
perhaps to interpret rest as an equal movement to both
north and south. This, as he remarks, represents the
general case in regard to mechanical phenomena. We
have simply to combine two rules to get what is called
in dynamics ' the composition of forces ' ; and, in accordance with this phase, he uses the general phrase, ' the
composition of causes.' [1] But, as he observes, this principle is in many cases not applicable. In chemical
combinations, in particular, we cannot infer the properties of the compound from the properties of the
components. The laws of simple substances will not
give us the laws of the product, and we can only learn
these derivative laws by experiment. This holds, still
more conspicuously, of organised bodies. From considering the properties of its chemical constituents
separately you cannot deduce the properties of the human
body. We thus come to a kind of knot in the web ;
we are at a deadlock, because the laws from which we

[1] *Logic*, p. 243 (bk. iii. ch. vi. § 1).

start are superseded by an entirely different set of laws.
Mill marks this by speaking of 'heteropathic laws.'[1]
Such laws are not analysable into simple laws.   He
thinks, indeed, that 'heteropathic laws' are—at least ' in
some cases may be — derived from the separate laws,
according to a fixed principle.'   The fact to which he
calls attention is undeniable.   We discover countless
laws as to the properties of bodies which it is impossible
at present either to resolve into simpler laws, or to deduce from the laws of the constituent elements.   Such
laws are properly 'empirical.'   The observation of the
facts asserted is the sole guarantee for our belief in their
truth; and they can be reduced under no more general
formula.   Is this, however, simply a challenge to the
man of science to inquire further, or does it oppose an
insuperable obstacle to further scientific researches?
Mill avowedly limits himself to 'our present state of
knowledge.'   He recognised that Grove, in his *Correla-
tion of Forces*,[2] made out a strong, though still only a
probable, case for believing that a 'heteropathic law'
may represent a complete transformation of one set of
forces into another.   Heat, light, and magnetism may
be all different manifestations of a single force—not so
much causes of one another as 'convertible into one
another.'[3]   Grove, as Mill adds, is not, as might be
supposed, deviating into ontology, but giving a strictly

---

[1] *Logic*, p. 245 (bk. iii. ch. vi. § 2).

[2] Grove's work was first published in 1846, *i.e.* after the first edition of the
Logic.

[3] *Logic*, fourth edition, p. 477 (bk. iii. ch. x. § 4).   In the eighth edition this
passage was suppressed, and Mill discusses the theory of 'conservation or persistence of force,' as he calls it, in an earlier section.—*Logic*, p. 228 (bk. iii. ch. v.
§ 10).

philosophical statement. Mill is here speaking of a great principle, imperfectly known at the time, which has been accepted by modern science, and he is quite ready to welcome it. It is, however, noticeable that he still guards himself against admitting any intrusion of 'necessity.' He will not allow that the dependence of the properties of compounds upon these elements must result in all cases 'according to a fixed principle.' The meaning of this may appear from his later assault upon the doctrine that 'like produces like.' This he reckons among the fallacies which he discovers in all manner of pestilent *a priori* philosophising. Descartes, Spinoza, Leibniz, and Coleridge have all been guilty of it in various forms.[1] We are therefore under no obligation to go further when we come to totally disparate phenomena in our series. We have unravelled our web sufficiently when we find laws disappearing and being superseded by a totally different set of laws, not describable even in the same language. That we may be forced to be content with such a result is undeniable. But it is equally true that one main end of scientific theorists is to get round this difficulty. Without inquiring in what sense the axiom that 'like produces like' may be fallacious, we must at least admit that to give a scientific law —that is, a rule by which one set of events is deducible from another—we must be able to express it in terms of some single measure. Till we can get such a statement, we have not the complete formula. There is a breach of continuity in our theories, which we try to remove by reducing all the forces to measures assignable in terms of space and number. The hypothesis of an ether and

---

[1] *Logic*, p. 501 (bk. v. ch. iii. § 8).

vibrating atoms enables us to regard phenomena as corresponding in some way to the laws which, as Mill says, can be compounded by simple superposition, without introducing heterogeneous terms. Though he does not condemn this hypothesis, Mill regards it with a certain suspicion as an attempt to wander into ontology, and the search for what is in its nature inaccessible.[1] At any rate, it does not appear to him that further inquiry is necessary when we come to an irreducible breach of continuity ; to a case in which one set of phenomena is simply superseded by another, instead of being transformable into it. If a compound is made of certain elements exclusively, a physicist would clearly infer that its properties *must* be a result of the properties of the elements according to ' some fixed principle.' Mill is only prepared to admit that this *may* be the case. The physicist, again, seeks for a mode of stating the principle in theorems capable of being combined and superposed, whereas Mill holds that our knowledge may have come to an ultimate insuperable end.

V. PLURALITY OF CAUSES

It is in the applications of this view that we come to what must be regarded as downright fallacies. If, as Mill holds, an effect may be something absolutely disparate from the cause—a new thing which starts into existence when its antecedent occurs—we are led to another result. There is, then, no apparent reason why the same thing should not spring up in answer to different summonses.

[1] See, for example, his criticism of a ' luminiferous ether ' in answer to Whewell, *Logic*, p. 328 (bk. iii. ch. xiv. § 6). He agrees here with Comte (*Phil. Positive*, ii. 639), whom he perhaps follows.

Not only is this possible, but, as Mill thinks, it constantly occurs. This is his doctrine of the 'Plurality of Causes.' A given cause, he holds, can only produce one effect. But a given effect may follow various causes. So long as the relation is merely one of arbitrary succession, not of continuity, this is obviously possible. The fully scientific view, I take it, would be that when we speak of 'cause and effect' we are really thinking of a single process regarded in different ways. We may analyse the process differently for different purposes, and infer the past from the future or the future from the past ; but we assume that, if we could perfectly understand the whole process, there would be thorough continuity, and no abrupt supersession of one thing or one set of 'laws' by another. This continuity is precisely what Mill systematically denies. A cause, he holds, means an absolute beginning of a new effect.[1] The process becomes a series of distinct terms—a set of 'links' in a chain, not a flow of a stream. One remarkable case is enough to illustrate the point. When Bacon's claims to have founded a truly scientific theory are considered, it is generally said that his guess as to the nature of heat is a point in his favour.[2] Mill, however, takes this particular case as an instance of Bacon's errors. Bacon, he says,[3] 'entirely overlooked the Plurality of Causes. All his rules imply the assumption, so contrary to what we now know of nature, that a phenomenon

[1] See especially the chapter on causation in the *Examination of Hamilton*.

[2] Tyndall, *e.g.*, in his *Heat as a Mode of Motion*, quotes Bacon's anticipation. It is summed up by Whewell (*Phil. Ind.* ii., *Sciences*, ii. 239) in the statement that the 'form of heat is an expansive, restrained motion, modified in certain ways, and exerted in the smaller particles of the body.'

[3] *Logic*, p. 500 (bk. v. ch. iii. § 7).

cannot have more than one cause.' Bacon was misguided enough to apply this to heat.   Now, as Mill had
already argued, heat may have several causes : the 'sun,'
or 'friction,' or 'percussion,' or 'electricity,' or 'chemical
action.'[1]   Consequently, the attempt to find a single
cause is doomed to failure.   We shall find, not that one
antecedent but, that one of several antecedents is always
present.   Clearly the 'sun' is not 'friction,' nor is 'percussion' 'electricity.'   Each of those phrases indicates
concrete facts involving various processes.   Heat, as a
'mode of motion,' occurs in them all, because all involve
particular phases of movement.   From the 'raw' fact, as
it presents itself—'This body is hot'—I cannot say
which of various laws represents the true antecedents in
that case.   The heat may have been caused by exposure
to fire or by friction.   In that sense, undoubtedly, one
effect may really have any number of 'causes.'   But
replace all the conditions, and it is evident that there
can be only one true analysis of the whole process.

Mill's insistence upon this imaginary 'plurality of
causes' is significant.   It indicates the precise stage in
the development of the idea of cause to which his doctrine corresponds.   Taking what we may call the popular
sense of causation, the 'plurality' expresses an obvious
truth ; and we can understand its plausibility.   We take,
in fact, two concrete events which follow each other, and
call them cause and effect.   We use a tool—a knife to
cut bread, for example ; we are forced to attend to the
fact that every difference in the knife will have an effect
on the result.   The work is better or worse, as the knife
is sharper or blunter.   If we did not recognise this in

[1] *Logic*, p. 288 (bk. iii. ch. x. § 3).

every purposeful action, all action would be intrinsically
uncertain.   We are, therefore, impressed with the necessity of admitting that the effect is determined by the
cause.   But, on the other hand, the knife is there.   It
may have been made by fifty different methods, and yet
be the same.   The handle may have been first made and
then the blade, or *vice versâ*, and so forth.   Therefore we
believe, and in this sense of cause believe correctly, that
one effect may be the product of any number of different
' causes.'   In order to reach the more scientific sense of
causation, we have to take into account all that we have
neglected.   The knife is one product of an indefinite
multitude of processes, and is therefore not the total
' effect ' of the concrete antecedent, but only a part of it
arbitrarily singled out.   We do not attend to all these
collateral results, because for us at the moment they have
no interest ; but when we systematically carry out the
' uniformity of nature ' principle, it is obvious that they
must be taken into account.   We then see that although
precisely similar products appear in an infinite variety
of concrete processes, they correspond only to a part
of those processes, and may always be analysed into
identical elements.   The effect can no more have two
causes than a cause two effects, for cause and effect are
distinguished by observing the same process in a different order.   It was just because men of science held
that the one effect must have one cause that they could
make a coherent theory of heat.   Mill, however, goes a
step further.   Bacon's error was the assumption that
there was only one ' form ' of heat.   Now it is specially
futile, says Mill, to seek for the causes of ' sensible
qualities of objects. . . . In regard to scarcely any of

them has it been found possible to trace any unity of cause.' Bacon, therefore, was seeking for ' what did not exist,' and to this Mill adds the surprising statement that ' the phenomenon of which he sought for the one cause has oftenest no cause at all, and, when it has, depends (as far as hitherto ascertained) on an unassignable variety of causes.' [1]

To explain this rather startling assertion we must take one more of Mill's theories. How from the doctrine, which he fully admits, that every event has a cause can he reach the conclusion that some things have ' no cause at all' ? Once more we have, I think, the misapplication of an undeniable truth. A ' law' of causation, taken by itself, will obviously not fully account for a single fact. It cannot lead to the conclusion : ' this fact must exist,' but only to the conclusion : this fact must exist if certain previous facts existed. We somewhere assume an initial stage. However far back we can go, we may still repeat the question. Given a single state of facts and the ' laws of causation,' we can go indefinitely backwards or forwards in time. Given the sun, the planets, and gravitation, we can trace the whole past and future history of the solar system ; but the facts at some period must be ' given.' We cannot say that they must, but only that they do exist. Mill himself puts this [2] with all desirable clearness. He expresses it by saying that

---

[1] *Logic*, p. 500 (bk. v. ch. iii. § 7). It may be noticed that Whewell (in 1847) equally regards Bacon's theory as a complete failure. He thinks more favourably of an ' imponderable fluid.' Mill, therefore, had good authority as to the failure. The modern doctrine, says Lord Kelvin (*Encycl. Britannica*), was established about 1851. See Huxley on the ' Progress of Science ' (*Essays*, i. 86) for Whewell's treatment of Bacon's guess.

[2] *Logic*, p. 226 (bk. iii. ch. v. § 7).

besides 'causation' there is 'collocation,' a word, he says, suggested by Chalmers.[1] To know the 'collocation,' therefore, is essential. A 'law' does not tell us that there 'must' be plums and suet, but only that if there are such things in certain 'collocations' a plum pudding 'must' be the result. All statements of fact have thus an empirical basis. This, however, takes a peculiar turn in his exposition, and one which is characteristic of a Utilitarian failing. He makes the distinction of relations correspond to a distinction of things. Instead of saying that both causation and collocation are implied in all phenomena, he speaks of some 'uniformities' as dependent upon causation and others as dependent upon collocation. He therefore writes a chapter on 'uniformities of coexistence not dependent on causation.'[2] This, however, is closely connected with, and must be explained by, another doctrine to which he attached the highest importance. After telling us how he was started afresh by Stewart's account of axioms, he adds that he came to 'inextricable difficulties' in regard to induction. He had come to the 'end of his tether,' and 'could make nothing satisfactory of the subject.' When, after five years' halt, he again set to work, he introduced his 'theory of kinds,' which, as he intimates, got round the difficulty. He felt, as we may conjecture, that he had now reduced all the facts to such purely empirical conjunctions that he did not see how to get any tie between them. Any cause, so far as we have gone, might lead to any effect; and even when we have

---

[1] *Logic*, p. 306 (bk. iii. ch. xii. § 2). See Chalmers's *Natural Theology*, bk. ii. ch. i.

[2] *Logic*, pp. 377-85 (bk. iii. ch. xxii.).

seen a case of conjunction, we can give no reason for its recurrence. Induction enables us to predicate attributes of a class; but a logical class is itself merely a bundle of attributes arbitrarily selected, and it remains to see why, from a thing's possession of some of the class attributes, we can infer that it has the others. Why should not the same set of attributes form part of different bundles? and if so, what is the justification for the primary logical procedure? From featherless bipedism we infer mortality. But why may not some class of featherless bipeds be immortal? If we admit the possibility, all induction becomes precarious. The 'theory of kinds' was, it seems, intended as an answer to these obvious difficulties.

VI. REAL KINDS

Mill's account of 'real kinds' corresponds, as he tells us, to the old logicians' distinction between genus and species. Though our classification may be arbitrary and nothing properly deducible from it, except the mere fact that we have chosen to give names to certain clusters of attributes, there is also a real difference. Some of our classes do not correspond to 'real kinds,' and are mistaken for them. Others, however, correspond to a real or natural kind. The difference is this: a 'real kind' has an 'indeterminate multitude of properties, not derivable from each other,' whereas an arbitrary or merely logical 'kind' may only differ in respect of the particular attribute assigned. Thus, to say that Newton is a man is to attribute to him the 'unknown multitude of properties' connoted by 'man.' To say that Newton is a Christian is only to attribute to him a particular belief and whatever consequences may follow from having that belief.[1]   One classification, as he says, 'answers to a much more radical distinction in the things themselves, than the other does'; and a man may thus fairly say, if he chooses, that one classification is made 'by Nature' and one 'by ourselves,' provided that he means no more than to express the distinction just drawn.   Now, it is easy to understand why Mill felt that this assertion entitled him to a 'real' bond which would keep phenomena together in a more satisfactory way. All things had become so loose and disconnected that it was difficult to explain any extension of knowledge even by induction.   Yet, whatever the reason, things do stick together in coherent and many-propertied clusters.   The bond seems to be real when it is stated 'objectively,' not 'subjectively'—as a property of the things observed, not of the classes made by the mind itself. I take the remark to be both true and important ; and, moreover, that Mill deserves credit for perceiving so clearly this weak joint in his armour.   His application, however, suggests, when he had hit upon an apparent escape from his 'inextricable' difficulties, he was too much relieved to work out its full effect upon his general theory.   The 'theory of kinds' is inserted rather than embodied in his philosophy, and makes rents in the attempt to fill a gap.   It plays, however, so important a part in the doctrine that it requires some further consideration.

A real kind, we see, has two characteristics ; it has innumerable properties, and those properties are not 'derivable' from the others.   In fact, a derivative

[1] *Logic*, pp. 79-81 (bk. i. ch. vii. § 4).

property would be merely a modification of a primitive property. A geometrical 'kind,' a curve of the
second order, for example, has innumerable properties,
but they are all derivative from the simple properties expressed in the axioms and definitions. They reciprocally imply each other. But can we say the same
of the properties of a thing—of a plant or of water
or of an atom? Here we have the distinction already
noticed. The so-called 'thing' may be merely a
collection of separate things, and we can discover the
'laws' applicable to all by combining the laws applicable
to each. From a given 'collocation' we can infer past
or future 'collocations,' and one set of results can be
added to or superposed upon the other. But when we
proceed to chemical or organic compounds, we have
'heteropathic' laws. The compound may be analysed
into elements, but we cannot derive the properties
of the compounds from the properties of the elements.
Hydrogen and oxygen can be combined into the form of
water; but we could not infer the properties of water
from the properties of the hydrogen and oxygen taken
apart. In organic compounds, the problem is still more
intricate. We have to consider a series of inter-related
changes taking place within the organism, and dependent
partly upon the 'environment' and partly upon the
complex constitution of the organism itself. It is a unit
in so far as all its properties manifest an organic law or
a system of organic laws. Individuals may differ from
external causes as plants, for example, in different soils,
and in that case we may regard the differences as simply
derivative. Differences which belong to the organic
law itself indicate differences of kind ; and these are

ultimate for us, so long as we cannot trace the way in which they are dependent upon differences of constitution. These, roughly stated, are the facts which Mill recognises. Now, in any case whatever, we can only 'explain' a fact by assuming both 'collocation' and 'causation'; or, in other words, we must have a statement of facts and of laws. Our analysis of the phenomena will in all cases come to showing how a given state results from, or results in, a previous or succeeding state. If new properties appear from the combination of simpler elements, we should infer that they result, though we may be quite unable in the existing state of knowledge to show how they result, from the properties of those elements. The properties do not manifest themselves, and are therefore not discoverable, till the combination is formed ; and are thus only known to us 'empirically.' No process of reasoning, that is, can be adduced to show that they must result from the combination. But, in the case supposed, we do not doubt that they do result, and we assume that the elements had certain latent properties not previously discoverable. This, however, is the point upon which Mill diverges, owing, as I think, to his imperfect view of causation.

The doctrine of 'kinds,' in fact, gives the answer to Mill's old problem, why a single instance is sometimes conclusive, whereas any number of instances may sometimes fail to give certainty. It is this reciprocal connection between the properties of a 'kind' which justifies the inference from one set of attributes to another attribute—the inference implied in all induction. But Mill's interpretation of the fact seems strangely inconsistent. His favourite instance is the black crow. I have seen a million black crows. Can I say that the million and oneth crow will be black? To answer this we must ask whether blackness is a property of 'kind.'[1] If the blackness be, 'as it were, an accident,' or not a property of kind, it must, he says, be a case of causation. If not a case of causation, it must be a property of kind. Hence we have the singular result, that if the coexistence be casual, it is caused, and if invariable, not caused. As 'causation' means according to him simply unconditional connection, the statement seems to be especially paradoxical. It is, however, explicable.

The blackness of the crow may be regarded as 'accidental,' if it is due to the external cause. The crow, perhaps, has fallen into a paint-pot. The blackness is 'caused,' then, by the properties of paint and by the 'accidental' collocation. It is an 'accident' in the crow, though caused in respect of the general arrangements of the universe. But why, if a property of 'kind,' should it be called 'not caused'? Here we have a curious result of Mill's view of causation. Our natural reply would be that the colour is still caused as everything else is caused.[2] We assume, that is, that 'crow' implies such a constitution that under a given environment crows will be black. Change something outside the crow and he may turn white. Or find a white crow in the same 'environment,' and we infer some difference in his constitution. There is

---

[1] *Logic*, pp. 377-86 (bk. iii. ch. xxii.).

[2] It has been suggested that upon Mill's principles the change of a lobster's colour to red is ' caused ' when he is boiled, but the colour before boiling uncaused. A case in the South Kensington Museum showing variously coloured crows is a tacit comment on Mill's illustration. The colour of crows is obviously considered by modern men of science as implying causal relations.

a relation, we assume, though we cannot specify its nature, which determines the colour, and as in all cases we have at once collocation and causation. Here is Mill's peculiar difficulty. Causation, as he is profoundly convinced, always means a beginning. It is only, as we have seen, concerned with changes, not with persistence. Therefore, if two things, like blackness and crowness, exist side by side, it is a case of collocation, and consequently, as he supposes, *not* a case of causation. He cannot recognise a reciprocal relation, although it is clear that if one thing is found always to accompany another, the argument is the same as though one always followed another. Indeed, his whole theory of induction implies the possibility of reasoning from one property or attribute to another. Make a change in one and the other must be changed. He sees this clearly in the case of organised bodies.[1] In that case, he says, there is a 'presumption' that the properties are 'derivable' and therefore 'caused,' because there we have sequences or one process following another. He thus seems to limit his 'natural kinds' chiefly to chemical compounds. There we have properties lying side by side and not 'derivable,' that is, not to be inferred by us from the properties of the elementary constituents. The very attempt to derive them is idle. As any event may cause any other, however unlike, so any set of properties may be simply stuck together. Bacon is again reproved[2] for assuming that 'every object has an invariable coexistent.' The ultimate properties, so far as we can conjecture, are 'inherently properties

[1] *Logic*, p. 382 (bk. iii. ch. xxii. § 6).
[2] *Ibid.* p. 381 (bk. iii. ch. xxii. § 4).

of many different kinds of things, not allied in any other respect.' They simply lie side by side, without reference to each other. Thus Mill pushes his empiricism to assuming not only that our knowledge of properties must rest upon direct observation, but that there is absolutely no connection or 'cause' to be known. The 'kind' after all, which was meant to be an essential bond, turns out to be itself a purely arbitrary collection of attributes, and we have to ask whether it does not lose all the significance which he attached to it. The 'collocation' means that the attributes simply lie side by side, and yet are always conjoined. The tie which combines them is undiscoverable, and therefore for us non-existent. It is, as he rightly insists, important that our classification should correspond to natural kinds. 'Kinds,' he says, are classes 'between which there is an impassable barrier'; the logical class is arbitrary, but the real class is an essential fact. His illustration is remarkable. He holds that the 'species of plants are not only real kinds, but are probably all of them real lowest kinds, *infimæ species*,' and that further subdivision would lead to no valuable results.[1] The doctrine that the species of botany must correspond to 'real kinds' is curious in a writer who was himself a botanist and familiar with the difficulty of making absolute divisions between kinds. The conflict with the conceptions implied in Darwinism is of the highest importance.[2] The distinction between 'kinds,' according to Darwin, is not absolute, for it is the product of gradual divergence from a single form. But,

---

[1] *Logic*, p. 470 (bk. iv. ch. vii. § 4). It is curious that this remains in the last edition, that is, after the first Darwinian controversies.

[2] See Sigwart's *Logik* (1889), ii. 456, etc.

on the other hand, the kinds existing at a given time are
discrete. There are gaps between them, as Mill remarks ;
though, in so far as they have a common origin, not
absolutely insuperable gaps.   This implies that the
organism does not correspond to a mere aggregate of
disconnected attributes, so that the difference of kinds
would be simply a difference of more or less, and each
type pass into the other by imperceptible gradations.
We are obliged to suppose a system of reciprocal
relations, so that any change in one organ involves
correlated changes in others ; and thus species diverge
along different lines instead of remaining constant or
simply adding on new properties.   Mill, it seems, has
to admit of kinds in order to account for the possibility of inference ; but then, as he wishes to avoid
' mystical bonds,' and inferences from ' definitions,' and
the scholastic beggings of the question, he declares
the relation between the attributes to be ' accidental '
or ' uncaused.'   Hence, though he sees the difficulty and
recognises the probability of 'causation' in organised
bodies, he really reduces the ' kind ' to be a mere
aggregate, and destroys the very organic bond of which
he is in need.

VII. UNIFORMITY OF NATURE

The effect of thus contra-distinguishing 'collocation' from causation, and admitting that 'uncaused
coexistences' cover a large part of all observable
phenomena, is to make the uniformity of nature
exceedingly precarious.   Indeed, Mill denies it to be
conclusively proved.   The chapter in which he sums
up 'the evidence of the law of universal causation'

leads to remarkable results. No one, he thinks, with a properly trained imagination will find any difficulty in conceiving that in remote parts of the universe 'events may succeed one another at random without any fixed law.' He concludes by asserting that it would be 'folly to affirm confidently' that the law does prevail in 'distant parts of the stellar regions.'[1] A truth which depends upon locality might, for anything one sees, break down in Australia and even at Paris as easily as at Sirius. Mill, accordingly, reaches a thoroughly sceptical conclusion,[2] and reduces the evidence for universal causation to an induction *per enumerationem simplicem*. The wider the generalisation, the greater the efficacy of such induction, upon which depends not only the law of causation but the principles of number and geometry. If the 'subject-matter of any generalisation' be so widely diffused that it can be tested at every time and place, and if it 'be never found otherwise than true, its truth cannot depend on any collocations, unless such as exist at all times and places, nor can it be frustrated by any counteracting agencies except such as never actually occur.'[3] Now no exception to the 'law of causation' has ever been found, and apparent exceptions have only confirmed it. It is no doubt true that if a law be universal, it will be confirmed by all our experiments; but it hardly follows that, because all our experiments have failed to detect an exception, it is true universally. All our experiments have covered but a small fragment of

---

[1] *Logic*, pp. 370-76 (bk. iii. ch. xxi. § 1, 4).
[2] *Ibid*. p. 372 (bk. iii. ch. xxi. § 2).
[3] *Ibid*. p. 373 (bk. iii. ch. xxi. § 3).

nature, and they do not justify us, as he expressly asserts, in reasoning about the stellar regions. It is difficult, moreover, to see how an ' exception ' could ever be proved, since, wherever we do not see a ' cause,' we can always suppose, and do in fact suppose, an invisible cause. Finally, the theory of ' natural kinds,' as it has now been interpreted, seems to fail us in our need. He takes it to indicate, indeed, that there are connections in nature, which, if known, would justify certain general inferences ; but it does not appear that we can know what are these connections, and as, moreover, we have been carefully told that they are ultimate or not ' derivative,' we have no right to be certain that they will recur. We do not know, for example, whether blackness be a property of kind. If we found a black crow among white ones, the property would be casual, and therefore ' caused.' If we found a race of white crows in Australia, we should simply say that there was a kind hitherto overlooked.[1] Such a discovery, he says, is not at all incredible. It might be proved by the evidence of a single credible witness. It merely supposes that there is a kind with a different set of attributes, and as the attributes are in no way ' derivative,' there is no improbability in this. The more general the rule, however, the greater the probability of its holding, because the greater the improbability of the exception being overlooked: We should easily believe in white crows, but not so easily in crows with a property ' at variance with any generally recognised universal property of birds,' and still less, if it were ' at variance with such a property of animals.'[2] We could hardly, that is, believe

[1] *Logic,* p. 382 (bk. iii. ch. xxii. § 5).   [2] *Ibid.* p. 384 (bk. iii. ch. xxii. § 8).

in crows with the stomachs of wolves, or in crows without stomachs at all. But the difficulty appears to depend
upon nothing else than the improbability that such animals,
had they existed, would have been unnoticed.

Without trying fully to unravel this logic, we may
notice one characteristic. Mill, trying to refer everything to 'experience,' has gone far to make experience
impossible. What has dropped out of this theory of
knowledge is the constructive part. He substitutes for
organisation combinations of disparate 'things.' He will
admit of no logic, except that of an external connection
of radically different objects. Attributes must be stuck
together without any reciprocal relations. All causation
becomes in his phrase 'collocation,' though he declares
causation and collocation to be not only different but
mutually exclusive. His one logical formula is the *nota
notæ est nota rei ipsius.*[1] Things are marks of each other,
not implied by each other. He forces this language even
upon mathematics. Even a geometrical 'kind,' if we
may use the word, an ellipse, or a curve of the second
order, is treated by the formula applicable to purely
empirical conjunctions. The equality of two straight
lines, it seems, is simply a 'mark' that if applied to
each other they would coincide; the fact that two things
are sums of equals is a 'mark' that they are equal, and
so forth.[2] He would apparently be inclined to say that
a thing's existence is a mark of its not being nothing.
Thus, even the 'natural kind' becomes merely a permanent combination. When the properties of a curve
are merely connected by 'marks,' it is no wonder that

[1] As he says in the *Examination of Hamilton,* ch. xix.
[2] *Logic,* p. 142 (bk. ii. ch. iv. § 4).

the properties of crows should be mere bundles. If it is only on such terms that we can thoroughly get rid of 'intuitions,' the advantage is doubtful.

I will venture to say another word upon the uniformity of Nature difficulty. It is easy, says Mill, to conceive of things happening at random. It is, indeed, in one sense perfectly easy. 'Raw' things, or unanalysed concrete events, do happen at random, that is, without uniform antecedents. Nothing is easier than to think of things without thinking of their causes. The primitive mind, and even the cultivated mind, may simply watch the series of events without trying to find any connection or indulging in any reasoning. But this is quite different from thinking of things as positively uncaused. A phenomenon suddenly intrudes without warning. I may accept it without asking whence it comes, or why. But there is no really positive meaning in the statement that it is caused by 'nothing.' It does not imply a contradiction, such as occurs when I put together the words crooked and straight, round and square; but it represents no intelligible meaning. It corresponds to a simple absence of thought. When I speak of the uniformity of Nature, I mean simply to indicate a condition of thinking about Nature at all. I may cease to reason or to think; but if I think, I must think coherently, and assume what has been called the 'Universal Postulate.'[1]

[1] Some writers, especially G. H. Lewes, have tried to maintain that the statement of the uniformity of Nature is an 'identical proposition.' The attempt is unsatisfactory, and certainly does not seem to have found favour with later writers; but, though I am unable to discuss the question, I will suggest that it seems to indicate the ideal result of reasoning. We assume that, if our knowledge were complete, we could state all the laws of action and reaction of any element as necessary consequences of its primitive consti-

The phrase seems to me to be inadequate; and at any rate it is a postulate with this peculiarity, that we cannot make any other. To deny it is to allow contradictory statements on the most intimate tissue of our reasoning. It is as impossible to do without it as to do without the principle of contradiction in pure logic. It helps us to no positive statement; but it is a warning that our statements must be coherent. Hence, we must allow the mind to have this modest capacity for working up its experience. If it starts from so unprejudiced a point of view as to admit contradictions, or allow of inconsistent statements about things, it will never be able to get anywhere, and when Mill has reduced all our knowledge to the relations between ideas in the mind, it is really quite inconsistent to allow the mind no power of putting ideas together. Without such a power it is difficult to say what is even meant by the perception of 'coexistences' and 'sequences.' The progress of knowledge, then, must be understood as corresponding to the process by which the chaos of impressions and ideas is gradually reduced to cosmos; and as starting from a position in which no cause has been yet discovered for great masses of facts, not from a position in which ' no cause' is an equally probable alternative with ' some cause.' To reason at all about facts is to arrange them in order of causation, and to suppose them as having certain time- and space-relations. To get behind that primitive germ of reasoning is really to

tution, as we can deduce all the properties of number and space from primary principles. Though we can never attain such a consummation, we can reject any theory which contradicts it, and, therefore, such doctrines as the 'plurality of causes,' which come to supposing that an identical process may be analysed in two inconsistent ways.

make logic impossible from the start. Mill's dread of *a priori* intuitions and necessary results thus led him into perfectly gratuitous difficulties. Granting the 'necessity' of arithmetic or geometry, it is still a hypothetical necessity. It can never take us beyond experience. Such theorems cannot tell us of the existence of a single thing or of its nature. They can only say that if we see things in space they will have certain relations which are deducible from the special confirmation. Without that power the universe would be undecipherable, but with it our knowledge still has throughout a completely empirical base. Not a single statement of fact can be made which is not derived from, and justified by, experience; nor can our experience ever get beyond saying that any given section of the whole is developed out of, and develops into, preceding and succeeding sections.

VIII. THE FOUR METHODS

I have dwelt upon these misconceptions to show why Mill was driven in defence of experience to assume the burthen of proving paradoxes which would be destructive to our very capacity for obtaining experience. Mill prided himself with some reason on his 'four methods.' Although they have been severely criticised,[1] they have, I take it, a genuine value; and, if we ask how they can be valuable in spite of his errors, a satisfactory

---

[1] *E.g.*, by Mr. F. H. Bradley in his *Principles of Logic* (1883), pp. 329-42. Dr. Venn, who is much more favourable to Mill, discusses them in his *Empirical or Inductive Logic* (1889), pp. 400-31, and shows very clearly how they assume what he calls the 'popular,' as distinguished from the 'rigidly scientific,' view of causation. Elsewhere (p. 58) he remarks that the popular might be called the 'Brown-Herschel-Mill view,' as those writers popularised the doctrine first clearly set forth by Hume. See also Sigwart's *Logik* (1889), ii. 469-500.

answer may perhaps be given. In the first place, his assumptions represent one genuine 'moment' in all reasoning about facts. The primitive intellect may be supposed to regard facts as simply conjoined, and to be guided by 'association of ideas.' The early generalisations of which Mill speaks—'fire burns,' 'water drowns,' and so forth—are really of this kind, and are apparently formed even by dogs and monkeys. Mill is quite right, moreover, in holding that a purely empirical element runs through the whole fabric of knowledge. The error, I think, is in his failure to allow for the way in which it is modified in scientific construction. The ultimate element out of which that construction is developed is always an observation of fact, but the fact means a definite relation of time and space. We start from a 'fact,' but it is not as a simple unanalysable unit, but as something which already is the base of a relation. The unit which corresponds to the final cell out of which tissue is composed is not properly a fact, but a 'truth.' We do not say simply 'this is,' but this is so and so, and has a certain order and configuration. This is gradually elaborated into physical science by the help of the geometrical and numerical relations already implied. Thus, causation, or the connection between phenomena, is not simple collocation, but supposes continuity. The unconditional sequence which Mill identifies with 'causation' does not, and cannot, give the 'cause,' though it does indicate 'causal connection.' So long as two things are entirely separate and distinguishable, we cannot say, in the full sense, that one is the cause of the other; but the connection, if proved, proves that there is a cause which may or may not be discoverable. Brown was right in thinking that something was still wanting, though his mode of filling the gap by an intuition was erroneous. Mill's answer that the 'intuition' was needless left the difficulty where Hume had put it. Two facts are supposed to be unrelated and yet always combined. That states a difficulty, and only pronounces it to be insoluble. It has, in fact, to be surmounted by scientific hypotheses. Thunder and lightning, for example, are causally connected, but not so that lightning can be properly called the cause of thunder. They are regarded as due to a common cause—to the processes which we call electric disturbance, and so forth. We cannot give the 'law' or state the casual connection adequately, but we regard them as indicating some common element, which is continuous and capable of being described in terms of pure number and geometry. Hence any observation, as soon as we begin to reason, may be regarded as a particular case of some general law, or rather, as being conceivably a case of an indefinite number of laws. Not only so, but any law under which it may be arranged is 'necessary' if all the conditions be restored. The process by which we select one of the possible formulæ, therefore, comes to eliminating all the formulæ which are incorrect when various conditions are altered. We all along assume that some coherent system of 'laws' is possible, or that the rule is there if only we can discover it. If lightning goes once with thunder, we are entitled to say not only that it may go with thunder hereafter, but that it must go with thunder under the same conditions. Therefore the simple inference from an empirical conjunction is justified by the 'law of causation' or the 'uniformity of nature.'

Now, Mill's 'four methods' are applicable to the
merely empirical conjunctions, which form a large part
of our knowledge, and are implied in every stage. The
methods do, in fact, I take it, form an approximately
accurate mode of dealing with such knowledge. His
cases are, for the most part, selected from the sciences,
chemistry in particular, where in point of fact our
knowledge is still purely empirical, and we can only
assert a collocation, or sequence, without bringing it
under a more general rule. He also observes, and the
remark must be remembered, that he is trying to give
a method of proof, rather than of discovery.[1] If the
scientific theory be true, these purely empirical truths will
hold good, although from them alone the theory might
not have been discoverable. The phenomenon which we
call the fall of a stone will be presented when an unsupported stone is near the earth, although the law of
gravitation requires an application of methods not
summed up by simple observation of conjoined phenomena. The most unsatisfactory part of the 'four
methods' results from this view.[2] The process of discovery is not sufficiently represented by the case of A
occurring with or without B. The sciences which have
risen to be quantitative advance by showing how a
variety of cases can be brought within some general and
precise formula, and every approximation to, or deviation
from, the law be exactly measured. Mill pays too little
attention to this essential characteristic, partly, perhaps,
because he considers mathematics as simply one part of
the 'inductive' or empirical sciences.

The final position may be shortly illustrated by Mill's

[1] *Logic*, p. 284 (bk. iii. ch. ix. § 6).   [2] Sigwart's *Logik* (1889), ii. 461.

relation to his contemporaries. It will show briefly
what were the alternatives between which he had to
choose, and that, if that which he chose leads to error,
there were at least equal errors on the other side. Mill
frankly states in his preface that but for Whewell's
History of the Inductive Sciences the corresponding part of
his own book 'would probably not have been written.'
He remarks with equal candour that Sir John Herschel,
in his *Discourse on the Study of Natural Philosophy*,[1] had
recognised the four methods. Herschel, however, was
his only predecessor, and a more distinct and articulate
exhibition of their nature was desirable. Herschel and
Whewell had graduated at Cambridge in 1813 and 1816.
Both of them were able mathematicians, and, with their
contemporary Babbage, had done much to introduce at
their university the methods of analysis developed on
the Continent. The university was gradually roused ;
Herschel won a great name in astronomy, and Whewell
took in earlier life a very active part in promoting
scientific studies in England.[2] Both of them had much

---

[1] Herschel's *Discourse* first appeared in 1830 as the first volume of Lardner's
Cabinet Cyclopædia. The 'four methods' are noticed, as Mill states, though
with comparative vagueness, in chap. vi. of the *Discourse*. Jevons prefers the
statement to Mill's. Whewell makes the obvious remark (*Philosophy of Discovery*, p. 284) that the four methods resemble some of Bacon's *Prærogativæ
Instantiarum*.

[2] For Whewell, see the *Writings* so described as to form a biography by
I. Todhunter (2 vols. 1876). The *Life and Correspondence*, by Mrs. Stair
Douglas, appeared in 1888. Whewell's chief philosophical works are : *His-
tory of the Inductive Sciences* (3 vols. 8vo, 1837 : second edition, 1840 ; third
edition, 1857) ; *Philosophy of the Inductive Sciences* (2 vols. 1840 : second
edition, 1847). This book was afterwards divided into three :—*History of
Scientific Ideas*, 2 vols. 1858 ; *Novum Organum Renovatum*, 1 vol. 1858 ; and
Philosophy of Discovery, 1 vol. 1860. Whewell also wrote a pamphlet *Of
Induction, with special reference to Mr. J. Stuart Mill's 'System of Logic.'*
This is republished as chap. xxii. of the *Philosophy of Discovery*.

closer acquaintance with the physical sciences than Mill, for whom they provided a useful store of materials. Herschel, though a friend of Whewell, approximates to Mill. A 'famous' review of Whewell's two books in the *Quarterly* of June 1841 [1] gives his position ; but although he seems to perceive the source of Whewell's weakness, he scarcely comes to close quarters. It is enough for my purpose to speak briefly of the points at issue between Mill and Whewell. Whewell, like his most eminent contemporaries at Cambridge, was becoming aware that German speculation could no longer be overlooked. Herschel was son of a German ; and Whewell's friends, Julius Hare (1795-1855) and Connop Thirlwall (1797-1875) were taking up the study of German. Their translation of Niebuhr's *History of Rome* (1828-1832) marked an epoch in English scholarship. Whewell meanwhile had read Kant, and been greatly impressed. Especially, as he says, he accepted Kant's theories of space, time, and, in some degree, causation, although he differed from Kant's doctrine as to other so-called 'fundamental ideas.' [2] He 'gladly acknowledges,' too, his obligations to the Scottish school. [3] In fact, it may be said that, like Sir W. Hamilton, he made a compromise between two modes of thought which very rapidly diverge from each other. Whewell begins his *Philosophy of the Inductive Sciences* by considering the fundamental antithesis of philosophy, which corresponds to the distinction between thoughts and things, necessity and experience, object and subject,

---

[1] Republished in Herschel's *Essays* (1857), pp. 142-256.
[2] *Scientific Ideas*, i. 88 (note added to this edition).
[3] *Philosophy of the Inductive Sciences* (1847), ii. 311.

and so forth. Time and space are, in his phrase, 'fundamental ideas,' upon which are founded the mathematical
sciences. But there are other 'fundamental ideas'—
'cause,' 'media,' 'polarity,' 'chemical affinity,' 'resemblance,' 'excitability,' and 'final cause'—which in succession become the foundation of various sciences.[1]

These fundamental ideas are, as he admits, something
like 'innate ideas,' except that they can be 'developed.'
They can somehow be 'superinduced upon facts,' and are
not 'generated by experience.' I shall not attempt to
explain a theory which seems to be radically incoherent,
and which made no converts. It will be quite enough
to notice two of the points of collision with Mill. Mill
and Whewell agree[2] that the 'first law of motion' which
asserts the uniform rectilinear motion of a body not
acted upon by a force was unknown till the time of
Galileo. Whewell admits further that, 'historically
speaking,' it was made 'by means of experiment.' We
have, however, attained a point of view in which we
see that it might have been certainly known to be true,
independently of experience. Mill naturally ridicules
this doctrine, according to which we burden ourselves
with 'truths independent of experience, and yet admit
that they were proved ' by (or ' by means of ') experiment.'
The history is admitted on both sides. It had been
observed that the motion of all bodies ceases unless they
receive a new impulse. The statement was true, though
vague, for all bodies upon the earth. But the progress
of astronomy and exact sciences required a more

---

[1] *Philosophy of the Inductive Sciences,* i. 80.

[2] Whewell's *Philosophy of Inductive Sciences,* i. 216-21 ; Mill's *Logic,*
pp. 160, 265 (bk. ii. ch. v. § 6, and bk. iii. ch. viii. § 7).

precise statement. Science has not simply to recognise
that motion declines, but to show at what rate, and
under what conditions it declines. Then, as we cannot
measure 'absolute motion,' or assign any fixed point
in space, we can obtain no rule as to absolute motion.
If we assume, however, that we have to account
not for motion but for change of motion, we can
get a consistent 'law' which at once gives a sufficient
account of many observed phenomena. We proceed to
define force as the cause of change in motion. Then
it becomes an identical proposition that all change of
motion implies force, or that bodies not acted upon continue to move uniformly. Thus the definition of force
takes the shape of an *a priori* axiom as to force. We
imagine that instead of simply co-ordinating our experience we are 'applying a fundamental idea' to it, the
idea, namely, of a 'cause' or 'force.'[1] The axiom is
not 'independent of experience.' Rightly understood,
the whole process is one of interpreting experience.
Mill, however, is hardly correct in saying that the law
was proved by experiment. We cannot observe a 'force'
apart from the moving body. Force is one of Bentham's
'fictitious entities,' a word which enables us to state the
relations of moving bodies accurately. It harmonises
our conceptions. The old belief that all motions stop
is not disproved by discovering cases in which force
is absent, but by postulating the presence of force
wherever we find change of motion. The real proof is

---

[1] Whewell, indeed, says that the 'necessary law' is that a change of
velocity must have a cause ; the 'empirical law' tells us that the time during
which it has been moving is not a cause.—*Philosophy of the Inductive Sciences,*
ii. 591. I need not go into this.

not in direct experiment but in the harmonising of an indefinite number of complex statements when once the principle is systematically applied. It can reveal no fact to us, for nothing but experience can show that there are such things as the planets fortunately are, bodies moving freely, so as to illustrate the law continuously. Mill puts the first law of motion on a level with the law that the period of the earth's rotation is uniform. Both 'inductions,' he says, are accurately true.[1] In fact, however, the earth's motion is not absolutely uniform, a truth which we discover by applying the laws of motion, though no direct experiment could exhibit the fact. The law of motion has the authority derived from its rendering possible a consistent interpretation of experiences, whereas the earth's rotation is simply a particular fact which might change if the conditions were altered. The 'law' implies, therefore, a reconstruction of experience not given by simple observation.

This applies to a controversy between Mill and Whewell as to Kepler's great discoveries. They both accept the familiar facts. Kepler's problem was to show how a simple configuration of the solar system would present the complex appearances which we directly observe. The old observations gave approximately correct statements of the movements of the planets, assuming the earth to be fixed, or, as we may say, neglecting the consideration of its motion. His theory shows how the apparent movements must result if we suppose the sun to be fixed, or rather (as the sun is not really fixed) if we measure from it as fixed. Whewell treats this as a case of 'induction.' It illustrates what he calls the 'colliga-

[1] *Logic*, p. 151 (bk. ii. ch. v. § 3).

tion of facts'—a happy phrase, accepted by Mill, for the
arrangement of facts in a new order, and the application
to the facts of the appropriate conceptions; in this case, of
the theorems of conic sections and solid geometry. The
argument takes the form of a discussion as to whether
this should be called induction or an operation subsidiary
to induction.[1] Kepler, as Mill urges, was simply describing facts. He discovered a fact in which all the
positions of the planet agreed—namely, that they were in
an ellipse. If he had been somewhere in space, or the
planet had left a visible track, he might have actually
seen it to be an ellipse. He had only to 'piece together'
his observations, as a man who sails round an island discovers its insularity. The only induction, then, was that
as Mars had been in an ellipse he would stay in an
ellipse. Apart from the verbal question whether the
process be rightly called induction or subsidiary to induction, the real issue is in Mill's complaint that Whewell
supposed a 'conception to be something added to the
facts.' The conception, Mill admits, is in the mind, but
it must be a conception of 'something in the facts.'
The ellipse was in the facts before Kepler saw it. He
did not put it, but found it there. Whether Kepler's
process was inductive or deductive or subsidiary, it was
an essential part of scientific investigation. The man
of science must, as Mill truly says, interpret the facts,
and nothing but the facts; he must also, as Whewell
truly replies, 'colligate' or arrange the facts in a new
order. The constructive process which justifies me in
saying this is an island, or this is an ellipse, is precisely
what makes scientific knowledge possible, and involves

[1] *Logic*, p. 190, etc. (bk. iii. ch. ii. § 3, 4); *Ibid.* p. 423 (bk. iv. ch. i. § 4).

something more than a mere putting together of raw fact. Every fact, as Whewell sees, may be regarded as a case of countless laws, each of which may be true under appropriate conditions. To eliminate the irrelevant, to organise the whole system of truths, so as to make the order of nature (as Mill forcibly says[1]) deducible from the smallest possible number of general propositions, is the aim of science; and Mill obscures this so far as he regards such operations as Kepler's as mere observations of fact, in such a sense as to omit the necessity of a new organisation of the data.

I have gone into some detail in order to show what was the essential characteristic of Mill's doctrine, which was itself, as I have said, an explicit statement of the principles implicitly assumed by his predecessors in the same school. To do him full justice, it would be necessary to show what was the alternative presented by his opponents. The Scottish writers and Whewell brought back 'innate ideas,' or endeavoured to connect knowledge by beliefs and intuitions arbitrarily inserted into the fabric as a kind of supernatural revelation. To explain these intuitive dogmas into effects of 'association' was the natural retort. Meanwhile the transcendental school was taking the bolder line of rejecting experience altogether, treating it with contempt as a mere rope of sand, and inferring that the universe itself is incarnate logic—a complex web woven out of dialectic, and capable of being evolved from mixing 'is' and 'is not.' To Mill this appeared rightly, as I should say, to be mysticism and ontology, or a chimerical attempt to get rid of the inevitable conditions of all knowledge

[1] *Logic*, p. 207 (bk. iii. ch. iv. § 1).

of reality. The real problem of metaphysics appears to be the discovery of the right method of statement, which will explain what appeared to be the insoluble antithesis between empiricism and intuitionism (to take Mill's phrase), and show that they are attempts to formulate correlative and essential truths.

IX. THE MORAL SCIENCES

Happily, philosophical theories are not really important solely as giving tenable and definitive results, but as indications of the intellectual temperament of different schools, and of the methods of reasoning which they find congenial. Without further disquisition, I shall conclude by indicating briefly Mill's application of his principles to the 'Moral Sciences.' This is the subject of the last book of his treatise, and represents, as we have seen, the purpose of the whole. As, however, the full application will appear hereafter, I may here confine myself to certain critical points. Mill begins of course by arguing that the 'Moral Sciences' are possible, and are to be created by applying the method of the physical sciences. This suggests the free will difficulty. The doctrine of 'philosophical necessity' had 'weighed on his existence like an incubus' during his early depression.[1] He escaped by the solution which now forms a chapter in the *Logic*. He discovered that the Hume and Brown theory removed the misleading associations with the word 'necessity.' It would be truer, he thinks, to say that matter is free than that mind is not free.[2] The supposed external 'tie' which binds things together is a

[1] *Autobiography*, pp. 168, 173. [2] *Logic*, p. 548 (bk. vi. ch. ii. § 2).

nonentity.   In practice, however, Owen and his like
had become fatalists rather than necessitarians.   Holding
that character is formed by circumstances, they had forgotten that our own desires are part of the 'circumstances,'
and therefore that the mind has the power to co-operate
in the 'formation of its own character.'   This, Mill
thinks, is the ennobling belief which is completely reconcilable with the admission that human actions are caused,
although the two doctrines had been on both sides
regarded as incompatible.   Upon this endless controversy
I can only suggest one hint.   Mill, I think, was right in
saying that the difficulty depends on the confusion of
'determinism' with 'fatalism'; that is, with the belief
that the will is coerced by some external force.   But he
does not see that his doctrine of causation always raises
the difficulty.   He orders us to think of the succession of
ideas as due simply to association, as in the external world
events are to be regarded as simply following each other ;
and in either case it is impossible to avoid the impression
that there must be some connecting link which binds
together entirely disparate phenomena.   We cannot help
asking why 'this' should always follow 'that,' and inferring that there is something more than a bare sequence.
The real line of escape is, I think, shown by an improved
view of causation.   If we hold that the theory of cause
and effect simply arises from the analysis of a single
process, we need no external force to act upon the will.
There is no 'coercion' involved.   Given the effect, there
must have been the cause ; as given the cause, the effect
must follow.   'All the universe must exist in order that
I must exist' is as true as that 'I must exist if all the
universe exists.'   There is not a man *plus* a law, but the

law is already implied in the man ; or the distinction of
cause and effect corresponds to a difference in our way
of regarding the facts, and implies no addition to the
facts. I must not, however, launch into this inquiry.   I
only note that Mill's view is connected with his favourite
principle of the indefinite modifiability of character.[1]   To
Mill, as to his father, this seemed to hold out hopes for
the 'unlimited possibility' of elevating the race. If J. S.
Mill denied 'the freedom of the will,' or, rather, the
existence of 'will' itself as a separate entity, actually
originating active principles, he admitted that the desires
erroneously hypostatised as 'will' could work wonders.
As the causal link between events is a figment, so, in the
sphere of mind, we are bound by no fixed mysterious tie.
He thus escapes from the painful sense of coercion by
holding that an infinite variety of results is made possible
by the infinite combinations of materials, though, in each
case, there is a necessary sequence. Association, in fact,
is omnipotent.   As it can make the so-called necessary
truths, it can transform the very essence of character.
Accordingly the foundation of the moral sciences is to be
found in the psychology, for an exposition of which he
refers to his father, to Mr. Bain, and to Mr. Herbert
Spencer.[2]   He thus drops, consciously or not, the claim
of treating metaphysical doctrine as common ground,
and assumes the truth of the association doctrine. To
pass from these principles to questions of actual conduct
requires a science not hitherto constructed—the science,
namely, of human character, for which he proposes the
name Ethology. This, as we have seen, occupied his
thoughts for some time, till it was ultimately dropped for

[1] *Autobiography*, p. 108.   [2] *Logic*, p. 557 (bk. vi. ch. iv. § 3).

political economy. The difficulty of forming such a science upon his terms is obvious. It holds an ambiguous place between 'psychology' and the 'sociology' which he afterwards accepts from Comte ; and as Professor Bain remarks, his doctrine would not fit easily to any such science. He has got rid of 'necessity' only too completely. In fact, his view of the indefinite power of association, and his strong desire to explain all differences, even those between the sexes, as due to outward circumstances, seem to make character too evanescent a phenomenon to be subjected to any definite laws.[1] Ethology, however, is taken by him to be the science which corresponds to the 'art of education,' taken in its widest sense, and would, if constructed, be a 'deductive science,' consisting of corollaries from psychology, the 'experimental science.'[2] The utility of such a science from his point of view is obvious. It would be a statement of the way in which society was actually to be built up out of the clusters of associated ideas, held together by the unit Man.

His method in 'moral science' follows the lines now laid down. All inference, as he has urged, consists of 'inductions' and 'the interpretation of inductions.'[3] Deduction is the application to new cases of the laws observed in previous cases. As our knowledge of such laws multiplies, science tends to become more deductive. But the deduction is still an induction ; and the true

[1] See his view that the difference of character between the sexes is due to external circumstances, and therefore removable.—*Logic*, p. 566 (bk. vi. ch. v. § 3).

[2] *Logic*, pp. 567, 569 (bk. vi. ch. v. § 4, 5). (Art is misprinted 'act' in the last edition.)

[3] *Ibid.* p. 185 (bk. iii. ch. i. § 1).

antithesis is not between deductive and inductive but
between 'deductive and experimental.'[1] Deductive
reasoning, that is, simply applies a previous induction ;
but reasoning becomes 'experimental' when we have to
interrogate nature for a fresh rule.   This has an important bearing upon the next step.   Social phenomena of
all kinds are so complex that we cannot apply his
four methods.   They belong to the region (in his
phraseology) of the 'intermixture of laws' and 'plurality
of causes ' ;[2] and though the phrases be inaccurate, the
example certainly illustrates their plausibility.   Experimental reasoning is thus impossible.   We have, therefore, to fall back upon the 'deductive' method, which,
indeed, would lead to mere 'conjecture' were it not for
the essential aid of Verification.[3]   The meaning of this
is explained in two chapters really directed against
Macaulay and James Mill, and giving the theory which
had been suggested by their controversy.[4]   Macaulay
used the 'chemical' method.   If men in society formed
a new product differing from the individual man, as
water from oxygen and hydrogen, or, in Mill's phrase,
if the social union afforded 'heteropathic' laws, we should
have to study social science apart from the science of
individual human nature.   But as men even in society
are still men, the social law is derivable from the
laws of individual nature.   It is a case of 'composition of causes.'   Now the purely empirical reasoner
neglects this obvious fact.   He reasons from immediate

---

[1] *Logic*, p. 144 (bk. ii. ch. iv. § 5).
[2] *Ibid.* pp. 576, 585 (bk. vi. ch. vii. § 4 ; bk. iv. ch. ix. § 2).
[3] *Ibid.* p. 303 (bk. iii. ch xi. § 3).
[4] *Autobiography*, p. 159.

experience without connecting his conclusions with psychology. He argues offhand that because the English have flourished under the old parliamentary system, therefore the old parliamentary system was perfect. That gives the crude empiricism preached by Macaulay in the name of Bacon. James Mill, on the contrary, represents the 'geometrical method.' He argued about politics as if all constitutional questions could be settled like a geometrical problem by appeals to a single axiom. Therefore a doctrine applicable to the immediate question of parliamentary reform was put forward as a general theory of government. Mill tells us in the *Autobiography*[1] that his reflection upon this controversy led to a critical point of his doctrine. Science must be deductive, when the effects are simply the sum of those due to the operating causes; inductive, when they are not the sum, that is, when 'heteropathic' laws appear. Hence, he inferred, politics must be treated deductively, though not as his father had done, geometrically.

Both the criticisms are much to the purpose. Here I need only remark one point which affects Mill's later conclusions. Was Mill's inference correct? Is it true that the social phenomena represent simply the sum of the individual actions? Undoubtedly, there is a good deal to be said for it. Society does not exist apart from the individuals of which it is constructed. Moreover, in a great many cases, if we know the average character of an individual, we can deduce the character of a number of individuals. The bulk of what is called knowledge of the world is made up from more or less

[1] *Autobiography*, p. 160.

shrewd conjectures as to the motives of the average man. If we know what the average man thinks, we can guess what will be the opinion of a majority of the House of Commons. There are, however, two points which are taken for granted. In the first place, if we are to deduce the social phenomena from the individual, we must know the individual, who is already a tolerably complex product. In Mill's language, we require an ethology ; and the name already indicates a difficulty. Can we consider the average man to be a constant ? or must we not take into account the fact that he is also a product of society, and varies upon our hands as society develops ? And beyond this there is the further question, whether, in so far as society can be properly regarded as an 'organism,' we can fully explain the laws of social combination by considering the laws of individual character. Are not the two sets of laws so intricately combined and blended that the analysis of a society into separate individuals becomes necessarily illusory ? Can we explain the reciprocal actions and reactions of a social body by simply adding together the laws of individual conduct? These questions will meet us in considering Mill's practical application of his theories. They amount to asking whether 'sociology' can be constituted from a purely 'individualist' basis, and Mill's view of sociology is a vital point in his doctrine. The name had already been invented by Comte, and Mill at this time was greatly influenced by Comte, and especially was kindled to enthusiasm by the last two volumes of the *Philosophie Positive*, containing a connected view of history. Although Mill had, as he says, worked out his theory of induction before reading Comte, he owed a great deal, as he fully acknowledges, to Comte's philosophy. The two lines of thought, however, could never completely coalesce, and the result appears in this part of Mill's book.

Admitting a deductive method to be necessary, Mill distinguishes the 'direct' and the 'inverse methods.'[1] The direct method is that of reasoning from one 'law of human nature,' considering, of course, the outward circumstances. This justifies the system of political economy, which considers men as acting solely from the desire of wealth. He points out that fallacies may here arise from applying to one state of society what is true of another ; but he also holds that one who knows the political economy of England, or even of Yorkshire, knows that of all nations, if he have good sense enough to modify his conclusions.[2] Mill admits fully that this method can only give us 'tendencies'—results which are true if certain conditions, never fully assignable, are actually secured ; and that it therefore requires to be constantly checked by verification, that is, by showing that the results are confirmed by direct observation. The admission, however, that such a method is in any case admissible separates him from Comte, who held that we must in all cases start from historical generalisations, not from independent 'laws of human nature.'[3] Comte, in fact, rejected Mill's psychology and political economy as pseudo-sciences, and the difference is really vital. Mill, however, was prepared to accept much of Comte's teaching, and in particular allows the legitimacy of the

[1] *Logic*, p. 583 (bk. vi. ch. ix. § 1).
[2] *Ibid*. p. 590 (bk. vi. ch. i. § 3).
[3] *Ibid*. p. 584 (bk. vi. ch. ix. § 1).

'historical method.' Upon this he writes a chapter,[1] which shows no want of appreciation of Comte or of the great French writers by whom, as his *Dissertations* show, he had been deeply impressed.[2] He complains of the English want of interest in such matters. They know nothing in French literature except the novels of Balzac and Eugène Sue, and are not aware that the French historians greatly surpass even the Germans.[3] He points out the importance of the conception of progress and of the great modifications of human character. Still, he charges the French with a misconception. History can never give us a 'law of nature,' only 'empirical laws,' which are not scientific till duly based upon psychology and 'ethology.' Comte alone has seen the necessity of a deeper foundation ; and he proceeds to give an admiring account of some of Comte's conclusions. Especially he insists upon the necessity of connecting the social phenomena with the intellectual development of mankind. This Comte alone has attempted systematically, and he ends by emphatically adhering to the doctrine of the three stages—theological, metaphysical, and positive. The essential difference, however, remains. Comte held that we must not explain humanity by man, but man by humanity.[4] To Mill, of course, this savoured of mysticism. In any case, it marks the divergence of the two : Mill is a thorough individualist. He thinks it absolutely necessary to base sociology upon 'ethology,'

[1] Bk. vi. ch. x.

[2] See especially the reviews of Tocqueville, Michelet, and Guizot in the *Dissertations*.

[3] *Dissertations*, ii. 121.

[4] *Lettres inédites de Mill à Comte* (1899), p. xxxv. Mill's letters to Comte upon his view of ethology are significant.

that is, a theory of the individual character, and this again must be based upon psychology. Sympathising with Comte's general purpose, and warmly admiring some of his results, Mill adheres to a doctrine which was sure to bring him into conflict with his master. To create the moral sciences, we must start from a scientific psychology. This means that we must work on the lines of Hartley, James Mill, and his own younger contemporaries, Professor Bain and Mr. Herbert Spencer. The corollary from psychology is ethology, or the science of character. This view does not conflict with the admission of the great importance of some historical method. At present, it needs only to be said that Mill accepts that method very cordially, subject to two conditions. First, he holds that some social sciences— political economy being, in fact, the only one to be clearly specified—can be deduced from ethology and psychology independently of history, though requiring verification from history. Secondly, he holds that the historical method cannot reveal true 'laws of nature' unless it is properly connected with psychological data. How far Mill really appreciated the significance of the historical method, or perceived its true relation to other departments of thought, must be left for consideration.

CHAPTER III

POLITICAL ECONOMY[1]

I. MILL'S STARTING-POINT

MILL's decision to abandon 'ethology' in favour of 'political economy' had one clear advantage. The function of a philosophical pioneer in the vast and vague region indicated by the new science was beset with difficulty. It was doubtful whether the proposed science could be constructed at all; and any conclusions attainable would certainly have belonged to a region remote from specific application to the questions of the day. Political economy offered a field for inquiry with a narrower aim of easier achievement. The greatest problems of the time were either economical or closely connected with economical principles. Mill had followed the political struggles with the keenest interest : he saw clearly their

---

[1] Mill's *Political Economy* reached a sixth edition in 1865. A popular edition was first reprinted in 1865 from this sixth edition. I quote from the popular edition of 1883 by chapter and section. This is applicable, with very slight exception, to all editions. The 'table of contents' is almost identical from the first to the last edition. Some sections were expanded by adding later information as to land-tenures and co-operation. The early chapter upon Ireland was altered on account of changes which, Mill thought, made it no longer appropriate. An addition was made to the chapter on 'International Values'; and book ii. chap. i. was rewritten in order to give a more favourable estimate of Socialism. On the whole, the changes were remarkably small.

connection with underlying social movements ; and he had thoroughly studied the science—or what he took to be the science—which must afford guidance for a satisfactory working out of the great problems. The philosophical Radicals were deserting the old cause and becoming insignificant as a party. But Mill had not lost his faith in the substantial soundness of their economic doctrines. He thought, therefore, that a clear and full exposition of their views might be of the highest use in the coming struggles. Hence arises one broad characteristic of his position. Mill was steeped from childhood in the principles of Malthus and Ricardo. In that capacity he had been a champion of their views against the followers of Owen. But he had come to sympathise with the aims, though he could not accept the theories, of the Owenites. Hence he was virtually asking how, given Ricardo's premises, are we to realise Owen's aspirations? The groundwork of argument, however, remained throughout. Though a more favourable estimate of Socialism was introduced in one chapter of his book, as I have already noticed, no corresponding changes were made in the remainder.

The *Political Economy* speedily acquired an authority unapproached by any work published since the *Wealth of Nations*. In spite of many attacks, it still holds a position among standard textbooks ; and in the case of textbooks, fifty years may be counted as remarkable longevity. During the first half of that period, a large school looked up to Mill as an almost infallible oracle. If in the later half that belief has vanished, we ought to recognise merits, sometimes overlooked by his assailants. The most undeniable is the singular skill of exposition. Mill had an admirable sense of proportion; each topic is taken up in intelligible order and treated with sufficient fulness; general principles are broadly laid down and clearly illustrated; and applications to actual cases are sufficiently indicated, without those superfluous digressions into minuter details which often entangle or break the main thread of an argument. The style is invariably lucid, and Mill, while free from arrogance and singularly courteous to opponents, wears his magisterial robes with the dignity of acknowledged authority. Whatever fallacies lie beneath the equable flow of didactic wisdom, we can understand what was the charm which concealed them from early readers. The book seemed to be a unique combination of scientific reasoning and practical knowledge, while the logical apparatus, so harshly creaking in the hands of Ricardo, not only worked smoothly but was in the hands of one whose opposition to 'sentimentalism' was plainly no cynical mask for coldness of heart.

Mill states his aim in the preface. He wished to expound the doctrine of Adam Smith with the 'latest improvements.' But he would take Smith for his model in combining economics with 'other branches of social philosophy.' Smith, he says, by never losing sight of this aim, succeeded in attracting both the general reader and the statesman. Mill certainly achieved a similar result. If he did not emulate Smith's wide researches into economic history, and had not Smith's curious felicity of illustration, he took a comprehensive view of the great issues of the time, and spared no pains in filling his mind with the necessary materials. His surprising power of assimilating knowledge had been strengthened by

official experience.   No one had a more vigorous digestion
for blue-books, or—what is perhaps rarer—less desire to
make a display by pouring out the raw material.

Although Mill's work upon 'pure political economy'
lies mainly beyond my province, it illustrates one important point.   Mill speaks as one expounding an
established system.   The speed with which the book
was written shows that it did not imply any revision
of first principles.   Mill is working in general upon
Ricardo's lines, in whose 'immortal *Principles*,' for
example, he finds the first philosophical account of
international trade.[1]   He assumes too easily that a
mere modification of old doctrines is needed, where
later writers have demanded a thoroughgoing reconstruction.   He has incurred some ridicule, for example,
by an utterance characteristic of his position.   He
says,[2] that 'there is nothing in the laws of Value
which remains for the present or any future writer
to clear up ; the theory of the subject is complete.'
The phrase was rash.   Apparently unassailable theories
have an uncomfortable trick of suddenly exploding.
Later economists often take this for a case in point.
They have, they think, made a specially successful
breach in this part of Mill's doctrine, and his confidence
was singularly infelicitous.   Mill's luckless boast was
suggested by his rectification of an ambiguity in the
terminology of the science.   How, he asked, could
there be a 'proportion' between two disparate things, a
'quantity' (supply) and a 'desire' (demand)?[3]   He

---

[1] See *Unsettled Questions* (1877), p. 1.

[2] *Political Economy*, p. 265 (bk. iii. ch. i. § 1).

[3] *Ibid.* p. 270 (bk. iii. ch. ii. § 3).

proceeds to remove the ambiguity by an account of the 'equation' between demand and supply, explaining the process by which values adjust themselves so that the quantity supplied at the current price will be equal to the quantity demanded at that price.   I take it that his account of the facts is substantially correct, and that, by removing certain inconsistencies of language, he had purified the theory from one set of fallacies.   But he himself seems to regard the improvement as merely one of terminology.   He thinks that his predecessors meant to state the same facts, and, indeed, that they must have seen the truth, though he could not find in them an express statement.   We may ask whether later improvements of Mill himself amount to a substantial change in the theory, or merely to a better mode of expression.   I do not doubt that modern economists have much improved the language in which the theory is expressed.   Nor, again, can it be doubted that the logic is rectified by rectifying the language.   The only question can be as to the importance of the improvement.   What strikes the sceptic is that, after all, when we approach any practical application of the theory, the old and the new theorists seem to be guided by pretty much the same reasoning.   The improvement in elegance and consistency of the language does not bring with it a corresponding improvement in the treatment of actual problems.   The obvious reason is that political economy has not reached, if it ever will reach, the stage at which the application of a refined logical method is possible or fruitful.   The power of using delicate scientific instruments presupposes a preliminary process.   We must have settled distinctly what are the data to be observed and measured ; and the use of mathematical formulæ is premature and illusory till we know precisely what we have to count and how to count it.   The data and the psychological assumptions of economists are still far too vague and disputable to admit of such methods, except by way of illustration.   Meanwhile rough and even inaccurate statements may be adequate to convey the knowledge which we can really apply.   We are really making use of facts admitted on all hands, and known with sufficient accuracy, though the principles upon which they depend have not been clearly defined.

II. CONTEMPORARY MOVEMENTS

To appreciate Mill's position, it is necessary briefly to notice the prejudices which he had to encounter and the sympathies upon which he could reckon.   Political economy had been exultant in the days of James Mill. He and his allies were entering the promised land.   They took the science to be in the same stage as astronomy just after the publication of Newton's *Principia*.   The main truths were established, though prejudice and sentiment still blinded the outside world to the clearest demonstration.   A narrow and unpopular circle naturally retorts dislike by fanaticism.   The Utilitarians were, and knew themselves to be, bitterly hated ; though they took the hatred to be an unconscious tribute to their real authority—the homage of the stupid to irresistible logic.   Richard Jones in the preface to his *Treatise on Rent* (1831), says, that the Ricardians had not only put forward 'startling and in some instances, unhappily, disgusting and most mischievous paradoxes,' but that they had thus alienated mankind and caused a distrust of political economy. When J. S. Mill's treatise appeared, this position was modified. The 'philosophical Radicals' had declined as a party; but the assault upon protectionism in which they had acted as forlorn hope had conquered a much wider circle. Their ideas had spread, whether by stress of argument or congeniality to the aspirations of the newly enfranchised classes. The conspicuous instance, of course, is the free trade movement. The triumph over the corn - laws seemed to establish the truth of the economic theory. Doctrines preached by professors and theorists had been accepted and applied by politicians on a grand scale. The result, as Cairnes, one of Mill's chief followers observes, was not altogether an advantage to the science.[1] The popular mind identified political economy with free trade, and thought that all difficulties could be solved by a free use of the sacred words 'supply and demand.' The strict economic doctrine had been, as Cairnes held, adulterated in order to suit the tastes of the exoteric audience. This remark suggests the problem, not strictly soluble, as to the causes of the free trade victory. Did it mark a triumph of logic, or was it due to the simple fact that the class which wanted cheap bread was politically stronger than the class which wanted dear bread? Cobden admitted fully that the free trade propaganda was a 'middle-class agitation.'[2] The genuine zealots were the manufacturers and merchants; and it was so far a trial of strength between the leaders of industry and the owners of the soil—a class struggle not between rich and poor, but

---

[1] *Logical Method of Political Economy* (1875), p. 4.
[2] See Morley's *Life of Cobden* (1881), ii. 249.

between the 'plutocracy' and the 'aristocracy.' Cobden was proud of the order to which he belonged, and held that the aristocracy represented blind prejudice. Some verses often quoted by popular orators declared that the landowners' motto was 'down with everything' (including health, wealth, and religion) 'and up with rent'; and Bright in 1842 told the workmen that 'the greatest enemy of the remorseless aristocracy of Britain must almost of necessity be their firmest friend.'[1] As usual in such cases, a legend arose which regarded the victory as due exclusively to the force of truth. Beyond all doubt, argument played its part as well as class prejudice. Cobden, though little interested in abstract theories, was an admirable, cogent, and clear reasoner. He was fully competent to assimilate so much political economy as was required for his purpose, and used it most effectively. Later history, however, has shown that in such matters pure reason cannot by itself win the battle against interested prejudice. For the time, the victory, taken by the winners to be a victory of reason, reflected glory upon the economists who from the days of Adam Smith had been labouring to indoctrinate the public mind. The triumph of the agitation was thus due to sheer force of argument and the consequent recognition of the principles of justice to the poor and goodwill to all mankind. Science and philanthropy had joined hands. The enthusiasm which soon afterwards greeted the Exhibition of 1851 showed the widespread conviction that the millennium of peace and liberty, of which the *Wealth of Nations* marked the dawn, was at last appearing in full daylight. And Mill was

[1] Prentice's *Anti-Corn Law League*, i. 77, 378.

regarded as the authorised representative in philosophy of the principles now at last fully applied to practice.

Mill himself did not fully share the optimistic exultation which helped to strengthen his authority ; nor was it accepted by the class most immediately affected. The 'big loaf' was a cry, it might be thought, which should appeal most strongly to the hungriest. Yet the Chartists, whose agitation was beginning when the Anti-Corn Law League was founded, were lukewarm or positively hostile. They interrupted free trade meetings and looked askance at the agitation.[1] The Chartists thought that the middle class, having got into power by their help, were throwing them over and monopolising all the fruits of victory. Their ablest leaders admitted, indeed, that free trade would be desirable, but desirable only on condition that the charter should first be conceded and democracy invested with political power to guard against misappropriation of the economic advantages. The employers, as they suspected, wanted cheap bread, because, as Lord Shaftesbury once put it, 'cheap bread means low wages.'[2] The freetraders, indeed, had constantly to meet this argument. Cobden constantly and earnestly denied the imputation. He desired free trade, as he asserted with unmistakable sincerity, above all in justice to workmen, and ridiculed the notion that wages sank with the price of corn.[3] Cobden, however, appeals rather to obvious

[1] Cobden's famous debate with Feargus O'Connor, the Chartist leader, took place on 5th August 1844. Cobden's victory is admitted even by the Chartist historian, who regards it as a proof of O'Connor's incapacity.—R. C. Gammage's *Chartist Movement* (1894), p. 254. Prentice has much to say of the perverseness of the Chartist leaders.

[2] Hodder's *Shaftesbury*, p. 341. This was in 1841. Shaftesbury afterwards accepted free trade.   [3] See, *e.g.*, Cobden's *Political Speeches*, i. 119, 197.

facts than to economic theorems; and Chartists who read Ricardo and M'Culloch might find some excuse for their opinion. If the 'iron law' held good, free trade in multiplying the labourers might only multiply the mass of misery. It might increase the aggregate wealth without raising the average welfare. The economical purists might reply that the poor would profit by the change on condition of also accepting the gospel according to Malthus. But the very name of Malthus stank in the nostrils of all Chartist leaders.

Another agitation gave special importance to this view. The credit which accrued to political economists from free trade was affected by their responsibility for the new poor-law. The passage of this measure in 1834 might be taken as a victory not merely of the economists in general, but specifically of the hated Malthus. He and his followers had denounced the old system most effectually, and had denounced it in the name of his principles. To Malthus and to Ricardo the only remedy seemed to be the ultimate abolition of the poor-laws. Their disciples were prominent in carrying the new law. Nassau Senior (already mentioned) had resolved when a young man to reform the poor-laws. He had lectured in 1828 on the Principles of Population as an adherent (with some modification) of Malthus. As an early member of the Political Economy Club he was at the very focus of sound doctrine. He was an active member of the commission of 1832, and is said to have drawn up the famous report upon which the new measure was founded.[1] The measure itself had therefore the highest credentials that strict political economists could desire.

[1] Reprinted in 1884.

Brougham as Lord Chancellor helped Miss Martineau, a most orthodox adherent of the school, and a personal friend of Malthus, to prepare the public mind by a continuation of her *Tales*.

The new poor-law, though placed to the credit of Malthusians, was by no means a pure and simple application of the Malthus theory. The gross abuses, rate-aided wages, and so forth, were suppressed in accordance with his views ; but the complete abolition of the poor-law, to which he had looked forward, was out of the question. The position was already critical. An experienced magistrate told the commission [1] that if the system went on for another ten years 'a fearful and bloody contest must ensue.' A generation of superfluous labourers, he said, had grown up demanding support. To maintain the system was dangerous, but simply to abolish it was to provoke a social war. The alternative was a cautious and gradual remodelling of the system ; and the transmutation of a demoralising into a disciplinary system. This meant so great a deviation from the extreme proposals that it might even tend to perpetuate the system by removing its abuses. Many of the evils resulted from the very fact which, in the eyes of Ricardo, was its chief palliation—the obligation of each parish to keep its own paupers. It had produced not economy but chaos. The commission recommend that the power of making regulations, now exercised 'by upwards of fifteen thousand unskilled and (practically) irresponsible authorities liable to be biased by sinister interests' (Bentham's sacred phrase) should ' now be confided to the central board of control, on which responsibility is most strongly concentrated,

[1] *Report of* 1834, p. 73.

and which will have the most extensive information.'[1] The competition between the parishes had produced the tangled laws of settlement, leading to endless litigation : the depopulation of some places, the overcrowding of others, the peculations and jobbery due to the ' sinister interests ' of petty local authorities, and the utter absence of any uniform or rational system.   To compel the fifteen thousand bodies to substitute co-operation for competition, to check their accounts, and to enforce general rules, it was necessary to create a central board with wide administrative authority.   For such a scheme, now obvious enough, the commissioners found their only precedent in a measure by which a barrister had been appointed to inspect savings banks and friendly societies.[2]

The new poor-law was thus a ' centralising ' measure, and marked a most important step in that direction.   It was denounced for that reason on both sides, and among the orthodox economists by M'Culloch.   J. S. Mill defended it warmly against this ' irrational clamour '; and but for certain restraining influences, especially the teaching of Tocqueville, would he thinks have gone into the opposite excess.[3]   It seems, however, that the Utilitarians generally accepted the law as a judicious application of Malthus, tempered by proper regard for circumstances. They were indeed bound in principle to be shy of the direct application of *a priori* formulæ.   Yet it may also be briefly noted that this was one of the cases on which the Utilitarians unconsciously forwarded a tendency to which they objected in general terms.   They wished to codify and simplify the poor-law, and found it necessary to introduce a central regulating body.   Though

[1] *Report of* 1834, p. 169.   [2] *Report*, p. 167.   [3] *Autobiography*, p. 193.

they meant to stimulate local activity, they were calling the central authority into fresh activity.

Meanwhile their opponents were equally ready to see nothing in it but Malthus, and to denounce it with corresponding bitterness. It was contrary to Christianity, to the rights of man, and to the good old laws of England. It was a part of the machinery by which cold-blooded economists were enslaving the poor. The operative, says the Chartist historian,[1] thought that it broke the last link in the chain of sympathy between rich and poor. Prison-like workhouses were rising to remind the poor of their 'coming doom.' They could expect nothing but 'misery in the present, and the Bastille in the future, in which they were to be immured when their rich oppressor no longer required their services.' The historian of the factory movement[2] confirms this statement. The poor man was to work or starve. Poverty, then, was to be treated as a crime. The parochial system was to be broken up, and the clergy thus separated from the poor. The whole system was anti-Christian : had not the commissioners put out a warning against almsgiving?[3] The commissioners again proposed the emigration of pauperised agricultural labourers into manufacturing districts, and were so playing into the hands of the capitalists.

[1] Gammage's *Chartist Movement*, p. 54.

[2] Alfred's *Factory Movement*, pp. 70-78. Alfred is a pseudonym for Samuel Kydd.

[3] Archbishop Whately is said to have thanked God that he had never given a penny to a beggar. The view suggests some confusion between the Political Economy Club and the Christian Church. In Newman's *Idea of a University* (1875, p. 88, etc.) there is an interesting passage upon the contrast between Christianity and the doctrine of the first professor of Political Economy at Oxford (Senior), that the accumulation of wealth was 'the great source of *moral* improvement.' The contrast was undeniable.

Cobbett's view gave the keynote to another version
of the case.   He saw as clearly as any one the evils of
pauperisation, but the old law at least admitted the poor
man's right to support.   In good old times he had been
supported by the church.   The great robbery at the
Reformation had been partly compensated by the poor-
law.   To abolish or restrict the old right was to consum-
mate the abominable robbery and to fleece the poor man
more thoroughly at the bidding of 'parson Malthus.'
Cobbett's view not only commended itself to his own class,
but was more or less that of the 'Young Englanders,'
who aspired to a reconstruction of the old social order.
The *Times* denounced the new law bitterly, and its proprietor, Walter, thought (as Kydd says), and no doubt
thought rightly, that the indignation roused by the
measure had done much to foster Chartism.[1]   Meanwhile, to Mill and his friends the whole of this declama-
tion came under the head of the later 'sentimentalism.'
They held with Malthus that an unlimited right to support meant an indefinite multiplication of poverty.   To
admit the right was to undertake an impossible task and
provoke a revolution on its inevitable failure.   Right
must be based upon fact ; and it is idle to neglect the
inevitable conditions of human life.   This position might
be logically unassailable ; and the measure supported on
the strength of it is now admitted to have been a vast
reform.   It came to be cited as one of the claims
to gratitude of the economists.   Their science had
arrested an evil which appeared to be almost incurable.

---

[1] Miss Martineau attributes the apostasy of the *Times* to the desire of the
proprietors to please the country justices.   See *History of the Peace* (1877),
ii. 508.

Sound reason had again triumphed over vague sentimentalism. The new law was, however, still given as an
illustration of the heartlessness of political economists.
Mill, who might claim justly that he was as anxious as
any one to raise the poor, had sorrowfully to admit that
the masses were too ignorant and their leaders too
sentimental to recognise his good intentions. They took
the surgeon for an assassin.

Among the enemies of the new poor-law were the
keenest agitators for factory legislation. The succession
of leaders in that movement is characteristic. The early
measures introduced by the first Sir Robert Peel and
supported by Owen had been tentative and of limited
application. As a demand arose for more drastic
measures, the first bill was introduced in 1831 by
John Cam Hobhouse (1786-1869), afterwards Lord
Broughton. Hobhouse's election for Westminster in
1820 had been a triumph for the Benthamites; and he
was afterwards one of the members through whom Place
tried to influence legislation. Hobhouse was too much
of the aristocrat to be up to Place's standard of Radicalism,
and on this point he was too much of an economist to
lead the movement. He declared the demands of the
agitators to be hopelessly unpractical; or, as Oastler put
it, gave in to ' the cold, calculating, but mistaken Scottish
philosophers,' who had an overwhelming influence on the
country.[1] The lead passed to Michael Thomas Sadler
(1780-1835). Sadler, a Tory and an evangelical, had
proposed to introduce the poor-law system into Ireland.
He had attacked Malthus (1830) in a book to be
presently noticed. He declared that Hobhouse had

---

[1] Alfred's *Factory Movement*, i. 138, 141.

surrendered to the economists, who were 'the pests of society and the persecutors of the poor.'[1] He now proposed a more stringent measure, which led to the appointment of a committee of the House of Commons in 1832. The report (presented 8th August 1832) startled and shocked the public. A royal commission was appointed in 1833 to collect further evidence. Sadler had meanwhile been defeated by Macaulay in a sharp contest for Leeds. His health soon afterwards broke down, under the strain of carrying on the agitation, and the lead fell to Lord Shaftesbury (then Lord Ashley). Shaftesbury, again, as an aristocrat and an evangelical, was a natural enemy of the Utilitarian. He was heartily approved by Southey, from the study of whose works he professed himself to have 'derived the greatest benefit.' He thought that the country was 'drooping under the chilly blasts of political economy,' and regarded the millowner as 'the common enemy of the operatives and the country-gentleman.'[2] Richard Oastler, the most effective and popular organiser of the agitation outside of parliament, was also a Tory, a churchman, and a protectionist. He had joined in the anti-slavery movement, and now thought that the factory system involved a worse slavery than that of the negro. He accepted the title of 'king of the factories,' given in ridicule by his enemies.[3] He became a martyr to his hatred of the new Poor-law by resigning his place as agent to an estate rather than enforce its provisions. He, too, hated the economists, and denounced 'the horrible Malthusian doctrine,' which

---

[1] See his life in *Dictionary of National Biography*.
[2] Hodder's *Shaftesbury*, i. 161, 339.
[3] Alfred's *Factory Movement*, i. 258.

he took to be that the ' Creator sent children into the
world without being able to find food for them.' [1]   John
Fielden, who became the parliamentary leader in 1846,
upon Shaftesbury's temporary retirement from the House,
had been brought up as a Quaker and a Tory.   He
became a Utilitarian and a Radical.   The typical Radical
for him was not Place but Cobbett, his colleague for
Oldham in the first reformed parliament.   ' Honest
John Fielden ' made a fortune by cotton-spinning, but
wrote a tract called the *Curse of the Factory System*, and
no doubt shared Cobbett's hatred of the Scottish ' philosophers ' and Parson Malthus.

These brief indications may be sufficient for one point.
The agitators on behalf of the factory movement took
the political economists, ' Malthusians,' and Utilitarians
to be their natural and their most dangerous enemies.
They assumed that the economist doctrine might be
condensed into the single maxim ' do nothing.'   Whether
it were a question of encouraging trade or supporting
the poor, or putting down ' white slavery ' in a factory,
government was to leave things alone or, in other words,
to leave them to the devil.   Chalmers, though an ultra-
Malthusian in some respects, approved the factory movement, because, as he said, it was a question between free
trade and Christianity.[2]   Christianity orders us to help
our neighbours, and political economy to let them alone.
Mill, of course, would have repudiated this doctrine.
Political economy, he would have replied, does not forbid
us to do good, or it would be opposed to Utilitarianism
as well as to Christianity.   It only shows us what will do
good by pointing out the consequences of our actions,

[1] Alfred's *Factory Movement*, i. 229.   [2] *Ibid.* ii. 251.

and Christianity can scarcely forbid us to disregard consequences.   Nor, in fact, was it true that the economists
unequivocally condemned the factory acts.   Malthus had
approved them, and M'Culloch wrote warmly to Shaftesbury to express his sympathy.

Undoubtedly, however, the opposition to the factory
legislation appealed to the principles accepted and most
vigorously enforced by the Utilitarians.   It came from
the free-traders, and from the inner circle of orthodox
theorists.   In the later debates, Bright and Cobden,
Villiers and Milner-Gibson, Bowring, Bentham's trusted
disciple, Roebuck, a wayward, though at first an eager,
follower, and the sturdy Joseph Hume were zealous
opponents.   The *Edinburgh* and the *Westminster Reviews*
rivalled each other in orthodoxy.[1]   The *Edinburgh* declared (July 1835) that Sadler's famous report was full
of false statements, if not wholly false ; and the *Westminster* (April 1833) thought that it was ' a stalking
horse ' to divert attention from the agitation against
the corn-laws and slavery.   *Fraser's Magazine*, on the
contrary, which was attacking the economists in a series
of articles, made a special point of the horrors revealed by
the report.   They might be summed up as ' child murder
by slow torture.'   The Tory organs, the *Quarterly* and
Blackwood, took the same side.   The manufacturers denied
the existence of the evils alleged, complained of spies and
unfair reports, and taunted the landowners with neglect
of the suffering agricultural labourers.   Shaftesbury

---

[1] See *Westminster Review* for April and October 1833; *Edinburgh Review*
for July 1835 and January 1844 ; *Blackwood's Magazine* for April 1833 ;
Fraser's Magazine for April 1833; and the *Quarterly Review* for December
1836.

says[1] that the argument most frequently used was a famous statement by Senior. That high authority had declared that all the profits of manufacturers were made in the last two hours of the twelve. Cut down the twelve to ten, and profits would disappear, and with them the manufacturing industry.[2] The same doctrine, in fact, worked into a variety of forms, sometimes fitted for practical men, and sometimes seeking the dignity of scientific formulation, was the main argument to be met. This is, in fact, typical of the economists' position. Some of them made concessions, and some of the Whigs shrank from the rigid doctrine.[3] But it was more in their way, at least, to supply ' chilling blasts ' of criticism than to give any warm support. One qualification must be noticed. The agitation began from the undeniable cruelty to children. The enthusiast's view was put into epigrammatic form by Michelet. The monster Pitt had bought the manufacturers' support by the awful phrase, ' take the children.'[4] In reality the employment of children had at first appeared desirable from a philanthropic point of view ; but it had developed so as to involve intolerable cruelty. The hideous stories of children worked to death, or to premature decrepitude, revealed by the commissions had made a profound impression. So far the Utilitarians as moralists were bound and willing to protest. They hated slavery, and to do nothing was to permit the most detestable slavery.

[1] Hansard, lxxiv. 911.

[2] The passage was quoted in full by Milner-Gibson, 15th March 1844.

[3] Macaulay's speech, 22nd May 1846 (in *Miscellaneous Works*, 1870, pp. 207-17), arguing that the moral question cannot be answered by pure economists, and defending the Ten Hours' Bill, is worth notice.

[4] See Alfred's *Factory Movement*, i. 2.

A child of tender years might be worked to death by brutal employers with the help of careless parents. This was fully admitted, for example, by Cobden, who said that he entirely approved of legislation for children, but held equally that adults should be encouraged to look for help to themselves and not to government.[1] Even the straitest economists seem to have admitted so much. The problem, however, remained as to the principle upon which the line must be drawn. If helpless children should be protected, have not women, or even working men in dependent positions, an equal right to protection ? Moreover, can interference in one case be practically carried out without involving interference in the whole system ?

The economic position was thus assailed on many points, though by enemies mutually opposed to each other. The general tendency of the economists was against government interference, and their most popular triumph on application of the do-nothing principle. In the free-trade agitation, their main opponents were the interested classes, the landowners, and the merely stupid Conservatives. Elsewhere they were opposed by a genuine, even if a misguided, philanthropy ; by Conservatives who wished to meet revolution not by simple obstruction, but by rousing the government to a sense of its duties. Southey's ' paternal government ' might be ridiculed by Macaulay and the Whigs ; Cobbett's good old times might be treated as the figment of an ignorant railer ; the Young Englanders who found their gospel in Disraeli's *Sibyl* might be taken to represent mere fanciful antiquarianism masquerading as serious politics ; and

[1] See Cobden's letter at the end of the first volume of Mr. Morley's *Life*.

Carlyle, with his fierce denunciations of the ' dismal science' in *Chartism* and the *Latter-Day Pamphlets* set down as an eccentric and impatient fanatic naturally at war with sound reason. The appropriate remedy, as Mill thought, was a calm, scientific exposition of sound principles. His adversaries, as he thought, reproduced in the main the old sentimentalism against which Bentham and James Mill had waged war, taking a new colouring from a silly romanticism and weak regrets for a picturesque past. But there was a perplexing fact. Churchmen and Tories were acting as leaders of the very classes to whom Radicals look for their own natural allies. Shaftesbury complained that he could not get the evangelicals to take up the factory movement.[1] They had been the mainstay of the anti-slavery movement, but they did not seem to be troubled about white slavery. The reason, no doubt, was obvious ; the evangelicals were mainly of the middle class, and class prejudices were too strong for the appeals to religious principles. On the other hand, the Radical artisans would accept men like Sadler or Shaftesbury for leaders as a drowning man may accept help from an enemy. The point of agreement was simply that something should be done, and that was enough to alienate the poor man from Whigs and Utilitarians, who were always proving that nothing should be done.

While these controversies were in the foreground the remarkable movement of which Mr. and Mrs. Sidney Webb[2] are the first historians, was developing itself.

[1] Hodder's *Shaftesbury*, i. 300, 325.
[2] *History of Trades-Unionism* (1894). See especially chaps. iii. and iv. (from 1829 to 1860).

Workmen were learning how to organise effective trades-unions, and co-operators were turning into a more practicable channel some of the aspirations of which Owen had been the prophet.   What Mill thought of such movements will appear presently.   Meanwhile it is enough to say that the economists generally confined themselves to throwing cold water upon what they held to be irrational schemes.   The working classes could not raise their position by combination, though they had an undeniable right to try fruitless experiments.   They were going astray after false prophets, and blind to the daylight of a true science.   The co-operative movement, indeed, received a warmer welcome when it came to be known. But the remarkable point is once more the wide gap between the 'philosophical Radicals' and the classes whom they aspired to lead.   The aspirations of the poorer class took a form condemned as simply absurd and illogical by the theories of their would-be leaders.[1]

III. MALTHUSIAN CONTROVERSY

Popular instinct recognised its natural enemy in Malthus.   'Malthusian' was a compendious phrase for anti-Christian, hard-hearted, grovelling, materialist, fatalistic. The formal controversy was dying out.   One of the last 'confutations' was by the enthusiastic Sadler, which provoked a slashing attack in the *Edinburgh* by the rising light Macaulay.[2]   Alison had prepared a ponderous

[1] For the view of the economists, especially Nassau Senior, and of a Whig government 'pledged to the doctrines of philosophical Radicalism,' see Mr. and Mrs. Sidney Webb's *Trades-Unionism*, pp. 123, etc., and the same writers' *Industrial Democracy*, p. 249.

[2] Sadler's *Law of Population*, 2 vols. 8vo, appeared in 1830, and was reviewed in the *Edinburgh* for July by Macaulay, who in the number for

treatise[1] by 1828, which, however, did not appear till
1840, when his popularity as a historian encouraged
its publication. Thomas Doubleday (1790-1870), an
amiable man and a sturdy reformer, published his *True
Law of Population* in 1841.[2] Sadler, the churchman
and philanthropist, Alison, the ponderous Tory, and
Doubleday, the Radical, are agreed upon one point.
They are all defending the beneficence of the deity, and
take Malthus to be a devil's advocate. Sadler, who was
a mathematician, devotes the greatest part of his book to
a discussion, helped by elaborate tables, of the famous
geometrical progression. Alison, of course, rambles over
all the articles of the Tory faith, defending the corn-
laws, protection, and slavery along with the factory
acts, the poor-law, and the allotment system, and expounding his simple philosophy of history and the inevitable currency question. The real difficulty is to assign
the precise point at issue. If Malthus is taken as asserting that, as a matter of fact, population actually and
invariably doubles every twenty-five years, or at any rate

January 1831 published a 'refutation' of Sadler's 'refutation.' The articles
were first collected in Macaulay's *Miscellaneous Works*.

[1] *Principles of Population and their Connection with Human Happiness*, 2 vols.
8vo, 1840.

[2] *The True Law of Population shown to be connected with the Good of the
People*, 1 vol. 8vo, 1841 (second edition, 1847). G. Poulett Scrope (1797-
1876), better known as a geologist than an economist, declares in his *Political
Economy* (1833) that if every nation were to be freed from all checks and 'to
start off breeding at the fastest possible rate,' very many generations would
pass 'before any necessary pressure *could* be felt' (p. 276). The doctrine
that there is an 'iron necessity' for resorting to inferior soils is in contradiction
to 'every known fact' (p. 266). Scrope was a sentimentalist who starts from
the 'natural rights' of man to freedom, the 'bounties of creation,' 'property,'
and 'good government.' Given these 'simple and obvious principles,' everything will go right.

always multiplies to starvation point, it is easy to ' confute' him ; but then he had himself repudiated any such
doctrine.   If, on the other hand, you only say that
over-population is in fact restrained by some means,
Malthus had said so himself.   It was common ground,
for example, that great towns were unfavourable to population ; and Macaulay could fairly tell Sadler that this was
admitted by Malthus, and was really a case of the famous
' positive checks.' [1] Alison takes similar ground in much
of his argumentation.   The difference seems to be that
Sadler and Doubleday assume a pre-established harmony
where Malthus traces the action of ' checks.'   Sadler,[2] for
example, agrees with the opinion of Muret, ridiculed by
Malthus, that God had made the force of life ' in inverse
ratio to fecundity.'   Sadler and Doubleday agree that
' fecundity' is diminished by comfort.   Men multiply
less as they become richer, instead of becoming richer as
they multiply less.   J. S. Mill says that Doubleday alone
among the Anti-Malthusians had some followers, but
thinks that this argument is sufficiently confuted by a
glance at the enormous families of the English upper
classes.[3]   Macaulay had taken more trouble to reply by
statistics drawn from the *Peerage.*   The one obvious
point is that none of the disputants could properly talk
of ' scientific laws.'   What Malthus had indicated was a
' tendency,' or a consequence of the elasticity of population which might arise under certain conditions, and to

---

[1] *Miscellaneous Works*, p. 193.   [2] Sadler's *Population*, ii. 387.

[3] *Political Economy*, bk. i. ch. x. § 3 *n.*   W. T. Thornton, in his *Over
Population* (p. 121), though a professed disciple of Malthus, agrees with
Doubleday.   Mr. Herbert Spencer criticises Doubleday in his *Biology*, chap. xii.
(§ 366 *n.*) in course of an elaborate discussion of the general question of
fertility.

which it was important to attend. But this gives no approach to a formula from which we can infer what will be the actual growth under given conditions. Macaulay showed clearly enough the futility of Sadler's reasoning. It was hopeless to compare areas, taken at random, large and small, heterogeneous or uniform, in different countries, climates, and social states, and attempt by a summary process to elicit a distinct 'law.' All manner of physiological, psychological, and sociological questions are involved ; not to be set aside by a hasty plunge into a wilderness of statistics. To discover a tenable 'law of population' we shall have to wait for the constitution of hitherto chaotic sciences.

Meanwhile, it may be noticed that the Whigs as represented by Macaulay were upon this matter as dogmatic as James Mill himself, whose dogmatism Macaulay had censured as roundly as he censured Sadler. Malthus, in fact, had triumphed ; and Mill's Malthusianism dominates his whole treatise. He had been brought up as an uncompromising Malthusian ; in youth he had become something of a martyr in the cause, and he never flinched from upholding the general principle. What was it ? In an early chapter [1] of his treatise he lays down the Malthusian propositions. 'Twenty or thirty years ago,' he says, they might have been in need of enforcement. The evidence is, however, so incontestable that they have steadily made way against all opposition, and may now be regarded as 'axiomatic.' This incontestable doctrine, as Mill here explains, is, firstly, that the human race can double itself in a generation ; and, secondly, that the obvious consequences can be avoided only by limiting

[1] Bk. i. ch. x.

this power through Malthus's positive or preventive checks—that is, by prudence on the one hand, and starvation and disease on the other.[1] This prudential restraint, then, is, if not the one thing necessary, the universal condition without which no other scheme of improvement can be satisfactory. It is the focus upon which his whole argument converges. Mill, however, gives a characteristic turn to the argument. The doctrine that the progress of society must 'end in shallows and in miseries'[2] was not, as had been thought, a 'wicked invention' of Malthus. Implicitly or explicitly, it was the doctrine of his 'most distinguished predecessors, and can only be successfully combated on his principles. The publication of his essay is the era from which better views of this subject must be dated.'[3] It gives the really fundamental principle. Mill agrees with Malthus that the root of social evil is not the inequality of property. Even an unjust distribution of wealth does not aggravate, but at most accelerates, the advent of misery. 'With the existing habits of the people' an equal division of property would only cause them to populate down to the former state.[4] And yet Mill here parts company from Malthus in the spirit, if not in the logic, of his argument. Malthus no doubt was thoroughly benevolent, and like many amiable country clergymen desired to see the spread of savings banks, friendly societies, and schools; but he was painfully conscious of the difficulty of infusing ideas into the sodden, sluggish labourers of his time, and

[1] *Political Economy*, p. 212 (bk. ii. ch. xi. § 3).

[2] One of Mill's rare quotations. See Shakespeare's *Julius Cæsar*, act iv. sc. iii.

[3] *Political Economy*, p. 452 (bk. iv. ch. vi. § 1).

[4] *Ibid.* p. 118 (bk. i. ch. xiii. § 2).

hoped rather for the diminution of abuses than for the regeneration of mankind. Mill, on the contrary, sympathised with the revolutionists who had alarmed Malthus. He tells them, indeed, with Malthus, that their schemes must conform to actual and inevitable conditions. But he also holds that the 'existing habits' of the 'people' can be materially modified ; and believes that a 'just distribution of wealth' would tend to modify them. Malthus emphasises the point that nothing can be done unless the standard of life be raised. Mill dwells on the other aspect : *if* the standard be raised, an indefinite improvement can be effected. What Malthus took to be a difficult though not impassable barrier Mill took to represent a difficulty which men might be trained to recognise and surmount. His sanguine belief in the educability of mankind enabled him to regard as a realisable hope what to Malthus in his early days had seemed a mere vision, and even in later days a remote ideal. The *vis medicatrix* is the same for Mill as for Malthus, but Mill has a far more vivid expectation of the probability of curing the patient.

IV. PEASANT-PROPRIETORSHIP

One of Mill's most characteristic doctrines shows conspicuously this relation. Malthus had found in Norway and Switzerland communities which flourished because they spontaneously practised his principles. 'It is worthy of remark,' says Mill,[1] 'that the two countries thus honourably distinguished are countries of small landed proprietors.' This coincidence was not acci-

---

[1] *Political Economy*, p. 99 (bk. i. ch. x. § 3).

dental ; and Mill's Malthusianism falls in with his admiration for peasant - proprietorship. He diverged in this respect from the orthodox economical tradition. The economists generally left it to sentimentalists to regret the British yeoman, and to weep musically with Goldsmith over the time 'when every rood of ground maintained its man.' Wordsworth had dwelt pathetically upon the homely virtues of the North-country statesman.[1] Cobbett had in his happiest passages dwelt fondly upon the old rural life, and denounced in his bitterest invectives the greedy landowners and farmers who had plundered and degraded the English peasant. The economists looked at the matter from the point of view represented by Arthur Young. Enclose commons; consolidate small holdings ; introduce machinery; give a free hand to enterprising landlords and substantial farmers, and agriculture will improve like commerce and manufactures. Small holders are as obsolete as handloom weavers ; competition, supply and demand, and perfect freedom of trade will sweep them away, new methods will be adopted, capital introduced, and the wages of the labourer be raised. M'Culloch, for example, took this view ;[2] denounced small holdings, and prophesied[3] that France would in fifty years become the greatest 'pauper-warren in Europe.' A remarkable advocate of a similar view was Richard Jones (1790-1855), who in 1835 succeeded Malthus at Haileybury.[4]

[1] See Mill's reference to Wordsworth, *Political Economy*, p. 155 (bk. ii. ch. vi. § 1 *n.*).

[2] See, *e.g.*, his note to the *Wealth of Nations*, p. 565 *seq.*

[3] As quoted by W. T. Thornton, *Plea for Peasant Proprietors* (1874), p. 133.

[4] Jones's *Essay on the Distribution of Wealth and on the Sources of Taxation* :

Jones admired Malthus and accepted with qualifications the account of rent given by Malthus and West. But he denounced Malthus's successors, Ricardo, James Mill, and M'Culloch for preferring 'anticipation' to 'induction,' and venturing to start with general maxims and deduce details from them. Jones deserves the credit of perceiving the importance of keeping historical facts well in view. He shows sufficiently that Ricardo's theory, if taken to be a historical statement of the actual progress of events, is not correct. He refuses to define rent, but treats historically of the various payments made in respect of land. After classifying these, he decides that rent of the Ricardian kind prevails over less than a hundredth part of the earth's surface. He considers it, however, as representing a necessary stage of progress. It is far superior to the early stages, because it supposes the growth of a class of capitalists, able to direct labour and introduce the best methods of cultivation. Hence Jones comes by a different route to an agreement with M'Culloch. He prophesies that peasant-proprietors will rapidly fall into want and their numbers be limited only by the physical impossibility of procuring food. They were precisely in the position least favourable to the action of prudential checks.[1]

Book I., *Rent*, appeared in 1831. Though constantly pressed by his intimate friend, Whewell, to complete the book, Jones never found time for the purpose. In 1859, Whewell published Jones's *Literary Remains*—chiefly notes for lectures—with a life.

[1] *Rent*, pp. 68, 146. Whewell in his preface to Jones's *Remains* (p. xvii.), seems to charge Mill with appropriating Jones's classification without due recognition of the merits. Mill used the book freely, and calls it a 'copious repertory of valuable facts' (*Political Economy*, bk. ii. ch. v. § 4). If he did not speak more strongly of the merits of Jones's classification (into 'labour,' 'métayer,' 'ryot,' and 'cottier' rents) it was probably because he thought Jones responsible for a fatal confusion between 'cottiers' and 'peasant-pro-

Mill upon this matter dissented most emphatically both from the 'classical' and the historical champion. The point is with him of vital importance. His French sympathies had prepared him to see the other side of the question. The most unequivocal triumph claimed, with whatever truth, for the French revolution was the elevation of the cultivators of the land. Mill, at any rate, held emphatically that the French revolution had 'extinguished extreme poverty for one whole generation,'[1] and had thereby enabled the French population to rise permanently to a higher level. Contemporary English history gave the other side. Poor-law controversies had brought into striking relief the degradation of the English agricultural labourer. The *Morning Chronicle* articles, to which he had devoted six months, combined with an advocacy of peasant-proprietorship an exposition of the inadequacy of poor-laws. The excellent W. T. Thornton (1813-1880) had been from 1836 Mill's colleague in the India House, and was one of the few friends who communicated freely with him during his seclusion.[2] In 1846 Thornton published a

prietors.' In the *Rent* this distinction is ignored. In the *Remains*, which Mill had not seen, Jones speaks (pp. 208, 217, 438, 522, 537) of 'peasant-proprietors' as an interesting class, but pronounces no definite judgment upon the system.

[1] *Political Economy*, p. 230 (bk. ii. ch. xiii. § 3).

[2] Bain speaks of Thornton as one of the friends who, like Sterling, maintained a close intimacy with Mill in spite of differences of opinion. These differences certainly did not prevent Thornton from speaking and writing of Mill in the tone of an ardent and reverential admirer. As little has been told of Thornton's private life, I will venture to say that, as a young man, I used often to see him, when he visited Fawcett and Fawcett's great friend, Mr. C. B. Clarke, at Cambridge. Thornton's extreme amiability, his placid and candid, if slightly long-winded, discussions of his favourite topics, won the affection of his young hearers, and has left a charming impression upon the survivors.

book upon *Over Population and its Remedy*, in which he declares himself to be a thoroughgoing Malthusian, and rebukes M'Culloch for saying that Malthus's work exemplified the 'abuse' of general principles. Thornton, like Mill, follows Malthus in thinking that over-population must be checked by preventing imprudent marriages;[1] but he makes a special point of the doctrine that misery is not only the effect but the 'principal promoter' of over-population.[2] Hence he is not content with Malthus's negative position. The evil will not die out of itself. His favourite remedy at this time was the 'allotment system.' From this Mill dissents.[3] They agree, however, upon the merits of peasant-proprietorship, upon which Thornton published a book in 1848, shortly before the appearance of Mill's treatise.[4] Mill says that this ought to be the standard treatise on that side 'of the question.'[5] Neither Mill nor Thornton had any first-hand knowledge of agriculture; but they forcibly attacked the assumptions then prevalent among English agriculturists. Thornton had been especially impressed by the prosperity of the Channel Islands—a rather limited base for a wide induction; but both he and Mill could refer to experience on a much larger scale throughout wide districts on the Continent. The pith of Mill's position is condensed in Michelet's picturesque passage, where the peasant is described as unable to tear himself away even on Sunday from the contemplation of his beloved plot of land. The three periods when the

---

[1] *Over Population*, p. 268.
[2] *Ibid.* p. 121.
[3] *Political Economy* (bk. ii. ch. xii. § 4).
[4] *Plea for Peasant Proprietors* (1874), p. 261 *n.*
[5] *Political Economy*, p. 223 (bk. ii. ch. vi. § 6).

peasant had been able to buy land were called the
'good King Louis xii.,' the 'good King Henry iv.'
and the revolution. Arthur Young's famous phrase
of the 'magic of property' which 'turns sand to gold'
was a still more effective testimony, because Young was
the Coryphæus of the modern 'English school of
agriculturists.'[1]

France, then, represented the good effects of
Malthusianism in action. The French peasantry, as
Thornton says after Lavergne,[2] had not read Malthus,
but they instinctively put his advice in practice. Mill
triumphantly quotes the figures which showed the slow
rate of increase of the French population.[3] The case of
Belgium, as he remarks, showed that peasant-proprietorship might be consistent with a rapid increase, but the
French case proved conclusively that this was not a
necessary result of the system. The 'pauper-warren'
theory at least is conclusively disproved. M'Culloch's
unfortunate prediction might be explained by his *a
priori* tendencies; but it is curious to find Mill confuting Jones, the advocate for a historical method, by
an appeal to experience and statistics. The possession
of the soundest method does not make a man infallible.
Jones and M'Culloch, as Mill said, had confounded two
essentially different things. They had argued simply as
to the economic advantages of production on a large and
small scale without reference to the moral effect upon
the cultivator. Their criterion is simply the greatness

[1] *Political Economy*, pp. 168, 171, 182 (bk. ii. ch. vi. § 67; vii. § 1, 5).
[2] *Peasant Proprietors* (1874), p. 159, referring to Lavergne's *Économie Rurale* (1860).
[3] *Political Economy*, p. 177 (bk. ii. ch. vii. § 4).

of the return to a given amount of capital on different systems. They had therefore treated the cases of France and Ireland as identical, whereas in one vital circumstance they are antithetical. France represented the observance of Malthus's true principle, because the peasant was moved by the 'magic of property'; he had absolute security in his little plot; and the *vis medicatrix* or desire to save was raised to its highest point. Ireland represents the defiance of Malthus, because the Irish cottiers, with no security, and therefore no motive for saving, multiplied recklessly and produced a true 'pauper-warren.' Mill accordingly reaches the conclusion that while peasant-proprietorship does not of necessity involve rude methods of cultivation, it is more favourable than any other existing system to intelligence and prudence, less favourable to 'improvident increase of numbers,' and therefore more favourable to moral and physical welfare.[1]

Jones would admit small culture as a natural stage towards the development of the English system. Mill considers it to be in advance of that system, but neither does he consider it to represent the absolutely best system. In a later passage he repudiates an opinion which, he says, might naturally be attributed to him by readers of the earlier chapters.[2] Though the French peasant is better off than the English labourer, he does not hold that we should adopt the French system, nor does he consider that system to be the ideal one. To cover the land with isolated families may secure their independence and promote their industry, but it is not

[1] *Political Economy*, p. 182 (bk. ii. ch. vii. § 5).
[2] *Ibid.* p. 460 (bk. iv. ch. vii. § 4).

conducive to public spirit or generous sentiment. To promote those qualities we must aim at 'association, not isolation, of interests.' This view is significant. Peasant-proprietorship, we are constantly told, is the great barrier against Socialism. It represents, in fact, 'individualism' in its highest degree. It stimulates the Malthusian virtues, prudence, industry, and self-help, and makes each man feel the necessity of trusting to his own energy. Yet Mill, with all his Malthusianism, thinks that such virtues might be stimulated too much; and, after preaching the merits of individualism, shows a leaning towards the antagonistic ideal of Socialism. He says little—perhaps it would hardly have been relevant to say much—of the historical aspect of the question. But there is a tacit implication of his argument of no little importance. According to him, the English labourer had been demoralised, and the whole Irish peasantry brought to the edge of starvation, while the French and other peasantries were prosperous and improving. To what historical causes was this vast difference due? The French revolution, however important, can only be understood through its antecedents. Systems of land-tenure, it is obvious, have been connected in the most intricate way with all manner of social, industrial, and political phenomena. Commerce and manufactures may seem in some sense a kind of natural growth—a set of processes at which government can look on from outside, enforcing at most certain simple rules about voluntary contracts. But, in the case of land, we have at every point to consider the action and reaction of the whole social structure and of the institutions which represent all the conflicts and combinations

of the great interests of the state.   Consequently neither
the results actually attained, nor those which we may hope
to attain, can be adequately regarded from the purely
industrial side alone.   Systems have not flourished purely
because of their economical merits, nor can they be
altered without affecting extra-economical interests.   To
do nothing is to leave agricultural institutions to be per-
verted by political or 'sinister' interests.   Mill was very
little inclined to do nothing.   He saw in the superiority
of the foreign to the British systems a proof of the
malign influence of the 'sinister interests' in our constitution.   The landed aristocracy were the concrete
embodiment of the evil principle.   The nobility and
the squirearchy represented the dead weight of dogged
obstructiveness.   They were responsible for the degradation of the labourer; and the Ricardian doctrine of rent
explained why their interests should be opposed to those
of all other classes.   Although Mill attributed enormous
blessings to the revolution in France, he was far too wise
to desire a violent revolution in England, and he was far
too just to attribute to individual members of the class
a deliberate intention to be unjust.   Yet he was prepared
to advocate very drastic remedies; and if there were
any human being of moderate cultivation from whom
he was divided by instinctive repulsion and total incapacity
to adopt the same point of view, it was certainly the
country squire.   The natural antipathy was quaintly
revealed when Mill found himself in the House of
Commons opposed to thick rows of squires clamouring
for protection against the cattle-plague.

So far Mill's position is an expansion or adaptation of
Malthus.   Obedience to Malthus makes the prosperous

French peasant ; disobedience, the pauperised English labourer. Malthus, as Mill interprets him, means that all social improvement depends upon a diminished rate of increase, relatively to subsistence [1] ; and to diminish that rate the prudential check must be strengthened. 'No remedies for low wages,' therefore, 'have the smallest chance of being efficacious which do not operate on and through the minds and habits of the people ' ; [2] and every scheme which has not for its foundation the diminution of the proportion of the people to the funds which support them, is 'for all permanent purposes a delusion.' [3] The two propositions taken together sum up Mill's doctrine. Social welfare can be brought about only by stimulating the *vis medicatrix* or sense of individual responsibility. Every reform which does not fulfil that condition is built upon sand. The application to England is a practical comment. The true remedies for low wages [4] are first an 'effective national education' so designed as to cultivate common-sense. This will affect the 'minds of the people' directly. Secondly, a 'great national measure of colonisation.' This will at once diminish numbers. Thirdly, a national system for 'raising a class of peasant-proprietors.' This will provide a premium to prudence and economy affecting the whole labouring class. Besides this, Mill approves of the new poor-law, which has shown that people can be protected against the 'extreme of want' without the

---

[1] *Political Economy*, p. 217 (bk. ii. ch. xi. § 6).

[2] *Ibid.* p. 225 (bk. ii. ch. xii. § 4).

[3] *Ibid.* p. 211 (bk. ii. ch. xi. § 3).

[4] *Ibid.* p. 230, etc. (bk. ii. ch. xiii. § 31, 34). Mill, in the later editions, observes that he has left this as it was written, although the rapid increase of means of communication has made the case 'no longer urgent.'

demoralising influence of the old system.[1] Mill here accepts, though he does not often insist upon, the doctrine upon which Thornton had dwelt in his *Over Population* : that poverty is self-propagating so far as it makes men reckless : education, as he remarks, is ' not compatible with extreme poverty.'[2]   Hence the remedies themselves require another condition to make them effective.   He declares emphatically that in these cases small means do not produce small effects, but no effect at all.[3]   Nothing will be accomplished, unless comfort can be made habitual to a whole generation. The race must be lifted to a distinctly higher plane, or it will rapidly fall back.   Mill, I fancy, would have been more consistent if he had admitted that great social changes must be gradual.   But in any case, he was far from   accepting the do-nothing principle.   Political economy, he says, would have ' a melancholy and a thankless task ' if it could only prove that nothing could be done.[4]   He holds that a huge dead lift is required to raise the labourers out of the slough of despond, and he demands therefore nothing less than great national schemes of education, of home and foreign colonisation. He speaks, too, with apparent approval of laws in restraint of improvident marriages.[5]   It is, indeed, true that upon his schemes government is to interfere in order to make the people independent of further interference.   Whether such a compromise be possible is another question.

---

[1] *Political Economy*, p. 221 (bk. ii. ch. xii. § 2).

[2] *Ibid.* p. 230 (bk. ii. ch. xiii. § 3).   [3] *Ibid.* p. 232 (bk. ii. ch. xiii. § 4).

[4] *Ibid.* p. 225 (bk. ii. ch. xiii. § 1).   [5] *Ibid.* p. 213 (bk. ii. ch. xi. § 4).

V. CAPITALISTS AND LABOURERS

Meanwhile a wider problem has to be considered. Unless some remedy can be found for the existing evils, he says, the industrial system of this country—the dependence, that is, of the whole labouring class upon the wages of hard labour—though regarded by many writers as the *ne plus ultra* of civilisation, must be 'irrevocably condemned.'[1]   The agricultural labourer can be taken out of that position.   By making him a proprietor he can be brought within the range of new motives.   The independent peasant has in visible form before his eyes the base from which he and his family must draw supplies. It requires no abstract reasoning to show him that, if he brings more mouths into existence, his fields will not therefore bear double crops.   But for the artisan who is a minute part of a vast organisation, whose wages come out of an indefinite, unexplored reservoir which may be affected by changes in commerce of the origin and exact nature of which he is completely ignorant, there is no such palpable limit.   The springs from which his subsistence flows may, for anything he sees, be inexhaustible. He is a unit in a large multitude, which, taken as a whole, must undoubtedly be somehow dependent upon the general resources of the nation.   But how to explain the intricate relations of the different classes is a problem puzzling to the best economists, and capable of all manner of fallacious solutions.   As an individual, the artisan might learn like other people to be prudent ; but to know what is prudent he must understand his position. Can the labourer rightfully demand or reasonably expect

---

[1] *Political Economy*, p. 229 (bk. ii. ch. xiii. § 2).

to get a larger share of the wealth which he produces, or must he confine himself to limiting his numbers, and trusting to supply and demand to bring his right share? Here the workman was misled by all manner of false lights; and it became incumbent upon Mill to explain the position.

A population entirely dependent on wages never, says Mill,[1] refrains from over-population unless from 'actual legal restraint,' or some 'custom' which 'insensibly moulds their conduct.' The English agricultural labourer seems to multiply just as far as he can.[2] All 'checks' have gone or are going. If the artisan is better off, it is due to the rapid expansion of our trade. Should the market for our manufactures—not actually fall off but—cease to expand as rapidly as it has done for fifty years, we may fall into the state of Ireland before 1846. He hopes, indeed, that the factory population may be intelligent enough to adapt itself to circumstances. The fact that so large a part of our population is composed of middle classes or skilled artisans is the only security for some restraint. Yet Mill's opinion even of the artisan was low. English experience confirms the evidence of Escher of Zürich.[3] The head of the English artisan is turned by the idea of equality. 'When he ceases to be servile, he becomes insolent.'[4] There is nowhere, he says elsewhere,[5] any friendly sentiment between labourers

---

[1] *Political Economy*, p. 213 (bk. ii. ch. xi. § 4).

[2] *Ibid.* pp. 213, 216 (bk. ii. ch. xi. § 3, 5).

[3] Quoted from the report of the Poor-law Commission in 1840.—*Political Economy* (bk. i. ch. vii. § 5).

[4] *Political Economy*, p. 68 (bk. i. ch. vii. § 5).

[5] *Ibid.* p. 460 (bk iv. ch. vii. § 4), where he speaks of the total want of fairness and justice on both sides.

and employers.   The artisan, swamped by the growing
multiplication of unskilled labour, will too probably, we
may infer, take a false view of the situation, and ascribe
his poverty not to his own neglect of Malthus, but to the
greed and hard-heartedness of the capitalist.   Such an
anticipation was likely enough to be realised.

This leads to the great problem of the true relation
between capital and labour.   The distinctive peculiarity
of England was the dependence of the masses upon
wages.   How, as Mill has asked, is this state of things
reconcilable with improvement?   He will assume, as his
predecessors had substantially done, that the capitalist
and labourers are separate classes, and that the labourer
derives his whole support from the capitalist.   Though
this is not everywhere true, it is for him the really
important case.   Moreover, he seems to think that the
rule derived from considering the classes separately will
not be altered when the two characters are united in
individuals.   The labourer, so far as he has 'funds in
hand,' is also a capitalist; and that part of his income
is still decided by the general law of profits.[1]   The
assumption of a complete separation, made for convenience of argument, might no doubt be confounded
with a statement of fact.   At any rate, it is merely an
explicit avowal of the tacit assumption of the orthodox
economists.

Here, then, we pass from Malthus to Ricardo.   Mill
adopts the Ricardian scheme, though trying to make it
more elastic.   Ricardo's doctrine of a 'minimum' rate
of wages to which the 'general rate' constantly approximates has enough truth for the 'purposes of abstract

[1] *Political Economy*, p. 252 (bk. ii. ch. xv. § 6).

science.'[1]   The rate indeed varies with the standard of living, and that, as we have seen, is a critical point. Yet the main outlines of the theory remain. As population presses upon the land, the landlord gets the benefit of his 'monopoly of the better soil,' and capitalist and labourer divide the remainder. Profits and wages, as Ricardo had said, vary inversely: a 'rise of general wages falls on profits; there is no possible alternative.'[2]   Here, indeed, an important modification must be made in Ricardo's words, in order to state what Ricardo 'really meant.'[3] Profit depends, not upon wages simply, but upon the 'cost of labour.'   The labourer is not a fixed quantity, representing so many 'foot-pounds' of energy; his efficiency, as Mill argued, may vary indefinitely with his moral and intellectual qualities;[4] it may be profitable to pay for the effective labour double the wages of the ineffective ; and, in point of fact, 'the cost of labour is frequently at its highest where wages are lowest.'[5]

Thus interpreted, Ricardo, like Malthus, admits of progress. By improving in efficiency, and by maintaining his standard of life, the labourer's position may be improved. Still, however, improvement supposes a due regard to the interests of the capitalists, who make all the advances and receive all the produce. Here we have the old doctrine of the 'tendency of profits to a minimum.'[6]   This theory, admitted though inade-

[1] *Political Economy*, p. 209 (bk. ii. ch. xi. § 2).
[2] *Ibid.* p. 418 (bk. iii. ch. xxvi. § 3).   [3] *Ibid.* p. 253 (bk. ii. ch. xv. § 7).
[4] *Ibid.* bk. i. ch. vii.   [5] *Ibid.* p. 254 (bk. ii. ch. xv. § 7).
[6] *Ibid.* bk. iv. ch. iv.   Cf. *Unsettled Questions*, pp. 105-6.   The article by Ellis, on the effect of improvements in machinery (*Westminster Review* for January 1826), though rather awkwardly stated, with the old capitalist and his quarters of corn illustration, puts the point clearly.

quately explained by Adam Smith, had been illustrated by E. G. Wakefield, and as Mill thinks, most scientifically treated by his friend Ellis. Another writer, to whom Mill refers with his usual generosity, was John Rae, whose *New Principles of Political Economy* had, he thinks, done in regard to accumulation of capital what Malthus had done in regard to population.[1] The necessity of resorting to inferior soils, which enriches the landowner, causes the difficulty of raising the labourer's 'real wages.' Profits are lowered not by the 'competition of capitalists,' but by the limitation of the national resources. As the difficulty of raising new supplies becomes more pressing, the 'cost of labour' rises, and the capitalist's profits diminish. Now, in every country, as Rae had shown, there is a certain 'effective desire of accumulation.'[2] It varies widely, and corresponds, we may say, to the principle which limits population—the 'effective desire' of propagation. There is a certain rate of profit which will induce men to save, and saving is the one source of capital. Hence, if the rate obtainable falls to this point, saving will cease, the capital which supports labour will not increase, and the country will be in the 'so-called stationary state.' Such a state, no doubt, is possible and often actual. Given a nation forced to draw its resources from a fixed area, and unable to improve its methods of cultivation, it is obvious that it may reach a point at which it can only just maintain its actual position. Mill holds not only that such a result is possible, but that it is always imminent. In an 'old country,' he says, 'the rate of profit is habitually within, as it were, a hair's-

[1] *Political Economy*, p. 102 (bk. i. ch. xi. § 2).
[2] *Ibid.* p. 103 (bk. i. ch. xi. § 3).

breadth of the minimum, and the country therefore on the very verge of the stationary state.'[1] He does not mean, he explains, that such a state is likely soon to be reached in Europe, but that, if accumulation continued and nothing occurred to raise the rate of profit, the stationary state would be very quickly reached. We have still the Malthusian view. We are always 'within a hair's-breadth' of the dead wall which will absolutely limit progress. Improvements are in fact constantly staving off the impending catastrophe. We are drifting, so to speak, towards a lee-shore, where, if not wrecked, we shall at least come to a standstill. Again and again we manage to make a little way, and by new devices to weather another dangerous point. By prudence, too, we may turn each new advantage to account, and improve our condition by refraining from increasing our numbers. But the danger is always threatening.

One noteworthy result is Mill's chapter upon the stationary state.[2] He has, it seems, been so impressed by the probability that he will find refuge from his fears by facing the worst. After all, are not the grapes sour? If we are unable to grow richer, is the loss of wealth so great a misfortune? He turns to think of the 'trampling, crushing, elbowing, and treading on each other's heels which form the existing type of human life.'[3] Is such a state desirable? In America, where all privileges are abolished, poverty unknown, and the six points of the Chartists accepted, the main result achieved is that 'the whole of one sex is devoted to dollar-hunting and

---

[1] *Political Economy*, p. 443 (bk. iv. ch. iv. § 4).

[2] *Ibid.* bk. iv. ch. vi.

[3] *Ibid.* p. 453 (bk. iv. ch. vi. § 2).

the whole of the other to breeding dollar-hunters.'[1]
Coarse stimuli are needed for coarse minds; but a better
ideal should be possible. We might aim at an order quite
compatible with the 'stationary state,' where labourers
should be comfortable, no enormous fortunes accumulated, and a much larger part of the population free
from mechanical toil and enabled to 'cultivate freely the
graces of life.' Nor is it desirable that cultivation should
spread to every corner of the world, every flowery waste
ploughed up and all wild animals extirpated. 'A world
from which solitude is extirpated is a very poor ideal.'

Mill agreed with Ruskin, though Ruskin did not
agree with Mill, and, indeed, called him a goose. A
stationary state of wealth need not, says Mill, imply a
stationary state of the 'art of living.' That art was
more likely to improve when we were not all engrossed
by the 'art of getting on.' How far that is true I do not
presume to say. It seems possible that in such a state
the struggle to be stationary might be as keen, though
advance would be hopeless. But, without criticising a
theory which represents rather a temporary protest than
a settled conviction, we may be content to notice how far
removed was this typical economist from the grovelling
tendencies often ascribed to his kind. Mill, as even
Carlyle would have admitted, was not a mere devotee of
'pig's-wash.'

This vision of a stationary state comes in the book in
which Mill passes from the 'statics,' as he calls it, to
the 'dynamics' of political economy. His purpose is

---

[1] *Political Economy* (1862), ii. 323. In the later editions this passage is
replaced by a reference to the civil war, which showed that the struggle for
wealth is not necessarily fatal to the 'heroic virtues.'

to trace the influence of industrial progress. His first chapter[1] notices the vast mechanical discoveries, the increased security of society and greater capacity for united action, which give reasons for hoping indefinite growth of aggregate wealth. There is, he thinks, 'not much reason to apprehend' that population will outrun, though we must sadly admit the possibility that it will keep up with, production and accumulation. This leads to the chapters in which he discusses the effect of progress upon the various classes concerned.[2] How does the 'progress of industry' affect the three classes—land-owners, capitalists, and labourers? Land is a fixed quantity; but population may increase, capital may increase, and the arts of production may improve by supposing each to increase separately and then together. A long and careful analysis gives us the general result. It is enough to notice the conclusion.[3]

Land represents the fixed 'environment' of the race. The proprietors of the land will be enriched by economical progress and the growing necessity for resort to inferior soils. The cost of raising the labourer's subsistence increases, and profits therefore tend to fall. The improvement of the arts of agricultural production acts as a 'counteracting force.' It relaxes the pressure and postpones the stationary state. For the moment the improvement may diminish (as Ricardo had argued), but in the long run must promote, the 'enrichment of landlords,' and, if population increases, will transfer to them the whole benefit. Mill, as we have seen, was fully alive to the enormous increase in past times of the

[1] *Political Economy*, bk. iv. ch. i.   [2] *Ibid.* bk. iv. ch. iii.
[3] *Ibid.* p. 439 (bk. iv. ch. iii. § 5).

general efficiency of labour and to the indefinite possibilities of the future. Yet the improvement seems here, again, to be regarded rather as checking the gravitation towards the stationary state, than as justifying any confident hopes of improvement. Meanwhile the elevation of the labouring classes depends essentially upon their taking advantage of such improvements to raise their standard, instead of treating an addition to their means 'simply as convertible into food for a greater number of children.'[1]

VI. THE WAGE-FUND

This doctrine led to one of the strangest of controversial catastrophes. In his chapter upon ' wages '[2] Mill had begun with an unlucky paragraph. He introduced the word ' wage-fund ' to describe the sums spent in ' the direct purchase of labour '; and stated that wages necessarily depended upon the proportion of this fund to the labouring population. This doctrine was assailed by Thornton in 1869.[3] Mill, reviewing Thornton, astonished the faithful by a complete recantation; and, though a disciple or two—especially Cairnes and Fawcett —continued to uphold the doctrine, or what they took to be the doctrine, political economists have ever since been confuting it, or treating it as too ridiculous for confutation. If we are to assume that the wage-fund was at once an essential proposition of the old ' classical ' economy and a palpable fallacy, the whole structure

---

[1] *Political Economy*, p. 436 (bk. iv. ch. iii. § 4).

[2] *Ibid.* p. 207 (bk. ii. ch. x. § 1).

[3] Thornton's *On Labour*; *its Wrongful Claims and Rightful Demands.* Another work generally mentioned in regard to this controversy is Longe, *Refutation of the Wages-Fund Theory* (1866).

collapses. The keystone of the arch has crumbled.
Nor, again, is it doubtful that this catastrophe marked
a critical change in the spirit and methods of political
economy. And yet, when the actual discussion is considered, it seems strange that it should have had such
importance. What was this ' wage-fund theory '? The
answer is generally given by quoting the passage already
mentioned from M'Culloch, a paragraph from Mill, and
Fawcett's reproduction of Mill. Mill's sentences, says
Professor Taussig, ' contain all that he ever said directly
and explicitly on the theory of the wage-fund.'[1] It is
strange that so vital a point should have been so briefly
indicated. Then Mill's ablest follower, Cairnes, declares
that though he had learned political economy from Mill,
he had never understood the wage-fund theory in the
sense which Thornton put upon it and which Mill
accepted.[2] But for Mill's admission, he says, he would
' have confidently asserted' that not only no economist
but ' no reasonable being' had ever asserted the doctrine.
We are left to doubt whether it be really a corner-stone
of the whole system or an accidental superstructure which
had really no great importance. At any rate it was
rather assumed than asserted ; and yet is so closely
connected with the system that I must try to indicate
the main issue.

In the first place, the ' wage-fund' is Mill's equivalent
for Adam Smith's ' fund which is destined for the main-

[1] Professor Taussig, *Wages and Capital* (1896), p. 23. Professor Taussig
gives a very thorough and candid discussion of the question, to which I am
glad to refer. To follow the many controversies which he notices would take
me into technicalities beyond the purpose of this book, and, I fear, beyond
my competence.

[2] Cairnes's *Leading Principles*, etc., p. 214.

tenance of servants';[1] and Mill, again, starts from a proposition inherited from Smith. 'Industry,' he says, 'is limited by capital'—a doctrine, as he adds, perfectly obvious though constantly neglected.[2] Undoubtedly an industrial army requires its commissariat : its food, clothes, and weapons. Its very existence presupposes an accumulation of such supplies in order to the discharge of its functions. A more doubtful assumption is stated by Adam Smith. 'The demand,' he says,[3] 'for those who live by wages naturally increases with the increase of national wealth, and cannot possibly increase without it.' The growth of the national wealth, that is, 'naturally' involves the growth of the wealth of every class. Machinery increases the efficiency of labour and therefore increases the power at least of supporting labourers. Moreover, in the long run, and generally at the moment, this power will certainly be exercised.[4] The interests of the capitalist will lead him to support more labourers. The identity of interest between the classes concerned might thus be taken for granted. Hence, we may trust to the spontaneous or 'natural' order of things to bring to all classes the benefit of improved industrial methods. This natural order, again, including the rate of wages, is understood to imply, at least, the absence of state interference. Political rulers must not tamper with the industrial mechanism. It will spontaneously work out

---

[1] *Wealth of Nations* (M'Culloch), p. 38. Ricardo (*Works*, p. 59) and Senior (*Political Economy*, p. 153) call it the 'fund for the maintenance of labour.'

[2] *Political Economy*, p. 39 (bk. i. ch. v. § 1).

[3] *Wealth of Nations* (M'Culloch), p. 31. I do not consider what was Adam Smith's general doctrine.

[4] This is the gist of Ellis's article (see above, p. 200 *n*).

the prosperity of the whole nation and of each class. Left
to itself the industrial organism generates those economic
harmonies upon which the optimist delighted to dwell.
'Natural' seems to take the sense of 'providential.'
The 'economic harmonies' are, like the harmonies perceived by Paley or the Bridgewater Treatise writers in
external nature, so many proofs of the divine benevolence; any attempt to interfere with them could only lead
to disaster. To show in detail the mischiefs involved, to
expose the charlatans whose schemes implied such interference, was the grand aim of most economists. Mill, as
we shall see, was very far from accepting this view without
qualification. He thought with the Utilitarians generally
that the 'sovereign' had enormous powers, and moreover
was bound to apply them for the redress of social evils.
Society, he held, was full of injustice. Laws aggravated
many evils and could suppress others. Still the normal
function of government is to prevent violence, see fairplay, and enforce voluntary contracts. When it exceeds
these functions, and tries by sheer force to obtain results
without considering the means, it may do infinite mischief.
It acts like an ignorant mechanic, who violently moves the
hands of the clock without regard to the mechanism.
Erroneous conceptions of the very nature of the machinery
had led to the pestilent fallacies which Smith and his successors had been labouring to confute. The freetraders[1]
had often to expose one sophistry which deluded the

---

[1] Mill scandalised the staunch freetraders by admitting an exception to the
doctrine in the case of new countries 'naturalising a foreign industry' by a
moderate duty (*Political Economy* bk. v. ch. x. § 1). Such incidental consequences are obviously possible. A prohibition to import a material of
industry might lead to the discovery of mines at home or to new methods of
manufacture. But such results seem to lie outside of pure political economy.

vulgar. Its essence is, as Mill puts it, that we attend
to one half of the phenomenon and overlook the other.[1]
The protectionist thinks of the producer and forgets the
consumer. Half the popular fallacies imply the failure
to take into account all the actions and reactions which
are implied by a given change. The processes by which
industry adapts itself to varying conditions—compensat-
ing for an ebb in one quarter by a flow in another—is
mistaken for a change in the whole volume. From the
neglect to trace out the more remote, though necessary
consequences, all manner of absurd doctrines had arisen.
The doctrine of 'gluts' and 'over-production' confounded the case of a production of the wrong things
with an excess of production in general. Improved
machinery was supposed not merely to displace one
class of labourers for a time, but to supersede 'labour'
in general. We should forbid the substitution of
power-looms and steam-ploughs for hand-weaving and
spades, or try to increase wealth by depriving workmen
of their tools. A strange confusion of ideas is involved.
People, said Whately,[2] ask for 'work' when what they
want is really 'wages.' They assume that because more
labour is required, more wages will be forthcoming.
The fire of London, as Mandeville observed, was an
excellent thing for the builders. If their wages had
simply dropped out of the skies, it might have been good
for everybody. So, again, Mill has to labour the point [3]
that society does not gain by unproductive expenditure,
that is, by the support of horses and hounds, but by

---

[1] *Political Economy*, p. 209 (bk. ii. ch. xi. § 2).

[2] As quoted by Cairnes's *Leading Principles*, p. 302.

[3] *Political Economy*, bk. i. ch. v. § 5.

'production'; that is, by expenditure on mines and
railways. He lays down a principle which, he says,
is most frequently overlooked, that 'demand for commodities is not demand for labour.' His doctrine has
been ridiculed and treated as paradoxical. It implies
at any rate an important distinction. It is intended to
draw the line between changes which merely mean that
a different employment is being found for labourers, and
changes which mean that a greater sum is being devoted
to the support of labourers in general.[1] The argument
against such fallacies might naturally be summed up by
saying that the real point to be considered was the effect of
any change upon the 'wage-fund.' The error, common to
all, is the confusion between the superficial and the more
fundamental—the functional, we may say, and the organic
changes. They are exposed by tracing the secondary
results, which have been overlooked in attending to the
more palpable but less conspicuous part of the phenomenon. Then we see that some changes imply not a
change in the quantity of labour supported; only a
redistribution of the particular energies. They do not
affect the 'wage-fund.' The phrase was useful as
emphasising this point; and useful, though it might be
in some sense a truism. Truisms are required so long
as self-contradictory propositions are accepted. But a
further problem is suggested. What, after all, is the
wage-fund? What determines its amount? If this
or that phenomenon does not imply a change in the
fund, what does imply a change, and what are its laws?

---

[1] Cairnes's *Leading Principles*, p. 222, explains the principle. Taussig (pp.
107 and 274) agrees with Brentano that Mill's doctrine is simply a corollary
from the theory that wages 'are paid out of capital.'

To this we get, in the first place, the old Malthusian answer. Whatever the fund may precisely be, the share of each man will be determined by the whole number depending upon it. This is obviously true, but does not answer the question, What actually fixes the sum to be divided? That problem seems to drop out of sight or to be taken as somehow implicitly answered. The answer should, however, be indicated by Mill's treatment of the most important cases.

The distribution problem, made prominent by Ricardo, was emphasised by controversies over the poor-law or the factory acts and trades-unionism. The economists had been constantly endeavouring to expose quack remedies for poverty. The old attempts to regulate wages by direct legislation had been too long discredited to be worth powder and shot. Mill, in discussing 'popular remedies for low wages,'[1] argues that competition 'distributes the whole wage-fund among the whole labouring population.' If wages were below the point at which this happens there would be 'unemployed capital'; capitalists would therefore compete and wages would be raised. If, on the other hand, law or 'opinion' fixes wages above the point, some labourers will be unemployed, or the 'wage-fund' must be forcibly increased. 'Popular sentiment,' however, claimed that 'reasonable wages' should be found for everybody. Nobody, he says, would support a proposal to this effect more strenuously than he himself, were the claim made on behalf of the existing generation.[2] But when the claim extends to all whom that generation or

[1] *Political Economy*, p. 219 (bk. ii. ch. xii. § 1).
[2] *Ibid.* p. 219 (bk. ii. ch. xii. § 2).

its descendants chooses 'to call into existence' the case
is altered.   The result would be that the poor-rate would
swallow up the whole national income, and the check to
population be annihilated.   Here, again, instead of hearing clearly why or how the wage-fund is fixed, we are at
once referred to Malthus.   The factory legislation suggests the same question.   The rigid economists had
maintained that here again the attempt to interfere must
be injurious.   It would hamper the growth of capital,
and therefore injure those dependent upon capital.   Mill
treats the case with remarkable brevity.   He apparently
regarded the whole movement as savouring of quackery.
But he discusses the question briefly from the moral
point of view.   Children, he says, should of course be
protected from overwork, for in their case 'freedom of
contract is but another word for freedom of coercion.'[1]
Women, he notes, are protected by the factory acts ;
but this is only excusable, if excusable at all, because,
as things now are, women are slaves.   If they were
free, it would be tyrannical to limit their labour.   The
old political economy still suffices.   Meanwhile the problem was coming up in other shapes.   The Utilitarians
have been active in procuring the repeal of the laws
against combination.   They had thought, indeed, that
the workmen, once set free, would find combination
needless, and would learn to act by means of individual
competition.   Trades-unionism, on the contrary, had
developed, and was producing long and obstinate
struggles with the capitalist.   Were these struggles
attempts to interfere with a 'natural' order ?   Were
they wasteful modes of attempting to secure a share

---

[1] *Political Economy*, p. 578 (bk. v. ch. xi. § 9).

of the 'wage-fund' which would come to them in
any case by the spontaneous play of the industrial
machinery? Socialists were beginning to declare that
instead of an identity there was a radical opposition of
interests. The answer made by orthodox economists
implies some wage-fund theory. They were never tired
of declaring that all attempts to raise wages by combination were fallacious. The struggle was always
costly, and, even if successful, could only benefit one
section of workmen at the expense of others. What
precise assumption might underlie this doctrine is
another question not so easily answered. It is taken
for granted that there is a definite fund, such that no
struggling can wring more from the capitalist; and all
the rugging and riving of labourers and unions can only
succeed in one body getting a larger share out of the
mouth of the others. Mill's final view seems to be given
in his discussion of erroneous methods of government
interference. Legislation against combinations to raise
wages is most vigorously condemned.[1] The desire to
keep wages down shows 'the infernal spirit of the slave-
master,' though the effort to raise them beyond a fixed
limit is doomed to failure. We ought to rejoice if combination could really raise the rate of wages ; and if all
workmen could combine such a result might be possible.
But even then they could not obtain higher wages than
the rate fixed by 'supply and demand'—the rate which
distributes the 'whole circulating capital of the country
among the labouring population.'[2] Combinations are
successful at times, but only for small bodies. The

[1] *Political Economy*, p. 563 (bk. v. ch. x. § 5).
[2] *Ibid.* p. 564 (bk. v. ch. x. § 5).

general rate of wages can be affected by nothing but the 'general requirements of the labouring people.' While these requirements (corresponding to the standard of living) remain constant, wages cannot long fall below or remain above the corresponding standard. The improvement, indeed, of even a small portion would be 'wholly a matter of satisfaction' if no general improvement could be expected. But as such improvement is now becoming possible, it is to be hoped that the better artisans will seek advantage in common with, or 'not to the exclusion of, their fellow labourers.' The trades-union movement, therefore, is taken to be equivalent to the formation of little monopolies through which particular classes of labourers benefit at the expense of others. Yet Mill is evidently anxious to make what concessions he can. Strikes, he thinks, have been the 'best teachers of the labouring classes' as to the 'relation between labour and the demand and supply of labour.' They should not be condemned absolutely—only when they are meant to raise wages above the 'demand and supply' limit; and, even then, he remembers that 'demand and supply' are not 'physical agencies'; that combinations are required to help poor labourers to get their rights (the 'demand and supply' rate) from rich employers; and, that trades-unions tend to advance the time when labourers will regularly 'participate in the profits derived from their labour.' Finally, it is desirable, as he characteristically adds, that 'all economical experiments, voluntarily undertaken, should have the fullest licence.'

Mill, unlike his rigid predecessors, is anxious to make out as good a case as he can for trades-unions. His sympathies are with them, if only the logic can be

coaxed into approval. To elevate the labouring class is
the one worthy object of political action. Yet he is
hampered by the inherited scheme. However modified,
it always involves the assumption of a fixed sum to be
distributed by 'supply and demand.' Limit the supply
of labour, and you raise the price. No other plan will
really go to the bottom of the problem. The rate of
wages is fixed by 'supply and demand'; and the phrase
seemed to imply that the rate of wages was fixed by a
bargain, like the price of corn or cloth at a given time
and place. Error, as Mill truly observes,[1] is often caused
by not 'looking directly at the realities of phenomena,
but attending only to the outward mechanism of buying
and selling.' Are we looking directly at realities when
we take for granted that 'labour' is bought and sold
like corn and cotton? Are we not coming in sight of
more fundamental changes, questions of the structure
as well as the functions of industrial organism, which
cannot be so summarily settled? Thornton argues as
though workmen secreted 'labour' as bees secrete honey,
and the value of the product were fixed by the proportion
between the quantity in the market and the quantity
which purchasers are prepared to take at the price.
He only tries to show that the price may still be
indeterminate. The 'equation' between supply and
demand of which Mill had spoken might be brought
about at varying rates of exchange. The whole supply
might conceivably be taken off either at a high or at a low
price. We need not go behind the immediate motives
which govern a set of buyers meeting a set of sellers at
an auction. Mill accepts the same assumptions. It is

[1] *Political Economy*, p. 56 (bk. i. ch. v. § 10).

quite true, he says, that in the case of wages various rates may satisfy the 'equation.' The whole labouring population may be forced to put up with starvation allowance or may be able to extort enough to raise their standard of life. This, he says, upsets the 'wage-fund' doctrine, hitherto taught by nearly all economists 'including myself.'[1] Moreover, the employer has the advantage in the 'higgling,' owing to what Adam Smith had already called 'the tacit combination of employers.'[2] This depressing influence can be resisted by a combination of the employed; and therefore the doctrine which declared the necessary incapacity of trades-unions to raise wages must be thrown aside.

Mill has received, and fully deserves, high praise for his candour in this recantation. We must, however, regret the facility with which he abandoned a disagreeable doctrine without sufficiently considering the effects of his admission upon his whole scheme.[3] To what, in fact, does the argument amount to which he thus yielded? He says that the capitalist starts with the 'whole of his accumulated means, all of which is potentially capital.' Out of this he pays both his labourers and his family expenses. No 'law of nature' makes it impossible for him to give to the labourer all 'beyond the necessaries of life,' which he had previously spent upon himself. The only limit to possible expenditure on wages is that he must not be ruined or driven out of business.[4]

---

[1] *Dissertations*, iv. 47 (reprint of article in *Fortnightly Review* of May 1869). [2] *Ibid.* iv. 67.

[3] Since no edition of the *Political Economy* appeared between this time and Mill's death, he had no opportunity of making alterations in his treatise. His review of Thornton, however, seems to indicate a failure to appreciate the full bearing of his concessions. [4] *Dissertations*, iv. 46.

This surely is obvious. No law of nature or of man forbids me from giving all that I have to my labourers, though I cannot give more than I have. If I have a balance at my bankers, I may pay my wage-bill by a cheque for any smaller sum, and live on the difference. Difficulties at once arise when we look at the 'realities' of the phenomena and turn from 'money wages' to 'real wages.' It is easy for an individual to give what he pleases, but not so easy to make such a change in the whole concrete industrial machinery as to apply it all to the production of labourers' commodities. What, in any case, was precisely the economical dogma inconsistent with Mill's statement? According to him, it was the doctrine that, at any given time, there is a certain fund in existence which is 'unconditionally devoted' to the payment of wages. This was taken to 'be at any given moment a predetermined amount.'[1] But how was it supposed to be predetermined? All events are predetermined by their causes, and to treat political economy as a possible science is to assume that wages, among other things, are somehow determinate. Mill means apparently to deny a determination by something in the nature of the capital itself. The capital might mean something which could not, even if everybody wished it, be applied in any other way. The circulating might bear to the fixed capital the same relation as wool, for example, to mutton. Save at all, and a certain part of your savings will be wages, as a certain part of the sheep will be wool. Unless you waste it, you will employ it on the only purpose for which it is adapted.

[1] *Dissertations*, iv. 43.

Such a 'predetermination' is of course a fiction. Was it ever taken for a fact?[1]   It was rather, I believe, an assumption which has slipped into their reasoning unawares.   Starting from the old proposition that 'industry is limited by capital,' and remarking that some capital did not go directly to wages, they simply amended the proposition by saying that wages depended on 'circulating' capital, and thought that the corrected formula would do as well as the old.   Perhaps they assumed roughly that 'circulating' must bear a fixed proportion to capital in general ; or that, at any rate, the proportion was somehow determined by general causes.   The doctrine thus understood tends to become a merely identical proposition : the 'wage-fund' means simply the wages, and the rate of wages is given by the total paid divided by the number of receivers.   The economists continued to lecture the labourers upon the futility of their aims with the airs of professors exploding the absurdity of schemes for perpetual motion.   It must, however, be observed that neither Mill nor his disciples held that the rate of wages was unalterable.   They had the strongest belief that it could be raised, and raised through the agency of trades-unions.   Mill's disciple, Fawcett, as Professor Taussig remarks,[2] lays down the old wage-fund formula, and yet proceeds to argue about strikes raising wages without reference to this supposed impossibility.   In an early article,[3] highly praised by Mill, Fawcett discussed strikes. He appeals to the wage-fund doctrine throughout, and

[1] See Taussig, pp. 211-45 for the vagueness of such writers as M'Culloch and Torrens.   'The point,' he says, 'was hardly ever raised in terms.'

[2] Taussig, p. 238.

[3] Article in *Fortnightly Review* for July 1860.   See Mill, *Political Economy*, p. 565 (bk. v. ch. x. § 5).

yet he approves of trades-unions, and only exhorts men to strike when trade is improving, instead of striking when it is falling off. It does not for a moment occur to him that 'supply and demand' or the wage-fund theory determine every particular case. Undoubtedly men, by combining and taking advantage of the 'conjuncture,' may get the best of a bargain. Fawcett holds, indeed, that the immediate advantage will be temporary or limited to one trade. Still combination will, for the time, enable the men to get an earlier share of the improved profits. Then, he argues, and it is of this that Mill approves, that such a system, by interesting the men in business and letting them perceive the conditions of success, will lead to the consummation most ardently desired by Mill and himself; to a perception of an ultimate identity of interests and a final acceptance of some system of co-operation. Thus, by listening to Malthus and raising the standard of life, the artisan will himself become a capitalist or a sharer in profits.

The wage-fund doctrine, so understood, included a reference not to the immediate bargain alone but to a more remote series of consequences. The 'predetermination' refers to the whole set of industrial forces which work gradually and tentatively. The ablest defender of the wage-fund, understood in this sense, was J. E. Cairnes (1823-1875),[1] who, like Thornton, was a personal friend of Mill; and, though an acute and independent thinker, was an admiring disciple. He met Mill's recantation by applying Mill's earlier faith. He does not believe in that 'economic will-o'-the-wisp,'[2] as Thornton calls

---

[1] See *Dictionary of National Biography* for a short notice.
[2] *On Labour*, p. 292.

it, the wage-fund, which supposes that in the bargain between men and masters there is a ' predetermined' amount which must be spent in wages. It is only pre-determined, he says, in so far as all men act from certain motives which, under given circumstances, must bring about certain results. Thornton, he says, has talked as if ' supply and demand' meant a power which forced men to act in a certain way, instead of being merely a general phrase indicating the normal operation of these motives. To determine the general rate of wages we have to look at the whole mechanism, not at the special bargain. To explain that action Cairnes starts again from the Ricardian scheme. On the one hand we have, of course, Malthus ; and on the other, the relation between wages and profits, the effective desire of accumulation, the necessity of resorting to inferior soils, with the conse-quent ' tendency of profits to a minimum' (for the proof of which he refers to Mill himself), and the accepted statement that profits are already within a hand's-breadth of the minimum.[1] Cairnes modifies the scheme in various ways, upon which I need not dwell : as by admitting ' non-competing industrial groups,' and arguing that the amount of the fixed and circulating capital is more or less determined by the direction of the national industries. Such conditions, he argues, determine the permanent rate of wages, though for a time oscillations within compara-tively narrow limits may of course take place. Mill, in his unregenerate days, had argued, as we have seen, that the whole ' wage-fund' must be distributed, without giving any precise reason for the necessity. He now held, with Thornton, that a 'conspiracy of employers' might retain

[1] *Leading Principles*, p. 257.

any part of it. Cairnes holds this conspiracy to be a fiction. It is not, as is often said, a question of rich men bargaining with poor men, but of rich men competing with each other. The competition of capitalists, as he holds, will always take place, not from any mysterious characteristic of 'circulating capital,' but because, as things are, they are always on the look-out for profitable employment of their capital. That process keeps wages up as the competition of labourers keeps them down, and, though it may act slowly, will inevitably keep wages approximating to an average.[1]

In this view Cairnes takes himself to be only expanding the doctrine which pervades Mill's whole treatise: in spite of the occasional *obiter dicta* about the wage-fund. He does not abandon—he declares that nobody ever held—the 'will-o'-the-wisp'—the absolute predetermination.[2] Certainly a doctrine which struck so thorough a student as one of which he had never even heard, and which appeared to him to be palpably absurd, could hardly have had the prominence usually assigned to it. When it has disappeared, the real point at issue is changed. Cairnes maintains that Thornton, though denouncing the sham doctrine, still virtually holds the old doctrine. Thornton said[3] that 'unionism could not keep up the rate (of wages) in one trade without keeping it down in others.' And this, as Cairnes says, implies some

---

[1] *Leading Principles*, p. 277.

[2] 'Historically,' says Professor Taussig (p. 242), 'there may be ground for that contention,' viz., that the wage-fund never meant more than Ricardo's doctrine that profits were the 'leaving of wages,' and that accumulation depended on profits. This, he adds, is held by many writers who reject the 'wage-fund' proper, that is, Thornton's 'will-o'-the-wisp.'

[3] *On Labour*, p. 288.

sort of 'predetermination,' though not the absolute
predetermination of the abandoned wage-fund.   The
main difference is that Cairnes holds that capitalists will
always compete ; whereas Thornton holds that they will
ultimately combine and then be certain of victory.[1]

This, I think, indicates the true underlying difficulty.
The 'natural' rate of wages, said the economists, is
fixed by 'supply and demand.'   'Supply and demand'
suggests the ordinary processes which level prices in
the market.   Thornton declares that 'labour' is bought
and sold like corn or cotton.   The analogy might be
denied.   Mr. Frederic Harrison observed that 'labour'
is not 'a thing' which can be bought and sold.
Thornton treats this as a purely verbal distinction,
and expects even his antagonist to admit that 'hiring'
is simply a case of 'buying,' and therefore governed
by the same laws.[2]   If so, we may apply formulæ
derived from the case of the market.   Then we tacitly
introduce the ordinary economic assumptions.   The proposition that wages are fixed by 'supply and demand'
is taken to mean that the rate can be deduced from
the simple process of bargaining.   The whole theory
of distribution can be worked out by considering the
fluctuations of the labour market : the value of labour
being fixed by the number of labourers, and the demand
for capital being represented by the rate of profit.   The
doctrine, it may be admitted, is approximately true at a
given time and place.   It simply generalises the arguments used in every strike.   Capital may be driven from
a trade if wages be excessive ; the influx or efflux of
capital will raise or lower wages in a given district, and

[1] *On Labour*, p. 274.   [2] *Ibid.* pp. 86, 87.

so forth. The facts may often be inaccurately stated by interested parties, but their relevance is undeniable. The forces of which Cairnes speaks, the competition of capitalists for profits, of labourers for wages, and their effect upon accumulation and population are undoubtedly the important factors. It was precisely because the economists recognised these obvious phenomena that they convinced themselves and persuaded others. They talked a great deal of undeniable common-sense. They could, again, fairly demand that some allowance should be made for 'friction'—for the fact, that is, that competition and the various changes which it implies do not take place so rapidly and automatically as they assumed. They took, it is true, considerable liberties ; they spoke as if capital could be changed by magic, and a thousand quarters of corn transformed into a steam-engine; or as if the population could instantaneously expand or contract in proportion to its means of support. They could forget at times that such phrases involve a kind of logical short-hand, and suppose a 'fluidity' of capital, a rapidity in the processes by which adaptations are carried out, which is unreal, and may cover important errors.

Still, with whatever allowances, we may accept the approximate truth of the assumptions, as describing the process by which immediate variations in wages are actually determined. The real difficulty comes at the next stage. Granting the approximate truth of the formulæ at any given time and place, can they give us a general theory of 'distribution'—formulæ which can be applied to determine generally what share of the total produce will go to labourers and what to capitalists? That is, in other words, can the purely economic formula become also a 'sociological' formula? Will it not only assign the conditions which govern the particular bargains, but enable us to determine the whole process by which the industrial mechanism is built up? That, as I take it, is the point at which the old economists broke down. Their doctrines, applicable and important within the appropriate sphere, become totally inadequate when they are supposed to give a complete theory of industrial development.

The unreality of the whole theory becomes obvious when we give it the wider interpretation. The excuse of 'friction' becomes insufficient. That may be applicable when the error is simply due to a permissible simplification of the data; not when the data are themselves wrongly stated. Ricardo, we have seen, had virtually made an assumption as to the social order. The labourers, we may say, are a structureless mass; a multitude of independent units, varying in numbers but otherwise of constant quality; the value of labour was thus dependent simply on the abundance or scarcity of the supply, and the labourers were assumed to be wholly dependent for support upon the capitalist. The formulæ applicable upon such a hypothesis might be correct so far as the data were correct. They would require a complete revision when we consider the actual and far more complex social state. Every difference of social structure will affect the play of competition; the degree in which population is stimulated or retarded; and the general efficiency of industry. A lowering of wages instead of producing an increase of profit and an accumulation of capital may lead to social degeneration, in which labour is less efficient and the whole organism is slack and

demoralised.   Conversely, rise of wages may lead to
a more than corresponding increase of production.
The effect, again, of accumulation of capital cannot be
expressed simply by the increased demand for labour.
That seems plausible only so long as capital is identified
with money.   It really implies an alteration of the industrial system and conditions under which the bargain is
made.   It may, again, be true that in any particular trade,
capital will be attracted or repelled by fluctuations in the
rate of profit; but it is by no means clear that we can infer
that a general rise or fall of profit will have the same
effect upon accumulation generally.   For such reasons,
as I take it, an investigation of the laws of distribution
would require us to go beyond the abstractions about
'supply and demand,' however appropriate they may be
to immediate oscillations or relatively superficial changes.
No such short cut is possible to a real sociological result.
'To follow out all the causes or conditions involved would
be,' as Professor Taussig says,[1] 'to write a book not only
on distribution but on social philosophy at large.'   Mill,
and especially Cairnes, were sensible of the need of
taking a wider set of considerations.   Still no satisfactory conclusion could be reached so long as it was
virtually attempted to solve the problem by bringing
it under the market formula, instead of admitting that
the play of market is itself determined by the structure
behind the market.   You have really assumed an
abnormally simple structure, and erroneously suppose
that you have avoided the necessity of considering the
structure at all.   The wage-fund controversy brought
out the inadequacy of the method.   One result has

[1] Taussig, p. 122.

perhaps been to encourage some writers to fall back into simple empiricism ; to assume that because the supposed laws were not rightly stated there are no laws at all ; that the justice of the peace can after all fix wages arbitrarily ; and that political economy should shrink back to be 'political arithmetic,' or a mere collection of statistics. The more desirable method, one must hope, would be to assign the proper sphere to the old method, and incorporate the sound elements in a wider system.

VII. SOCIALISM

Meanwhile, the over-confidence of the economists only encouraged Socialists to revolt against the whole doctrine. It might be a true account of actual facts ; but, if so, demonstrated that the existing social order was an abomination and a systematic exploitation of the poor by the rich. The 'iron necessity' was a necessity imposed by human law—not, that is, a legitimate development of social order, but something imposed by force and fraud. In some directions Mill sympathised with such doctrines. He professed to be in some sense a 'Socialist,' though he was not acquainted with some of the works published during his lifetime. He makes no reference to Marx or Lassalle and other German writers. Possibly a study of their writings might have led to modifications of his teaching. To him the name suggested Owen, Fourier, St. Simon, or his friend Louis Blanc.[1] Socialism, as understood by

---

[1] See the posthumous articles in the *Fortnightly Review* for February, March, and April 1879. They were obviously imperfect, and scarcely justified publication.

the early leaders, commended itself to Mill, because it proposed the formation of voluntary communities, like Fourier's Phalansteries or Owen's New Harmony. They are capable of being tried on a moderate scale, with no risk to any one but the triers.[1] They involve simply social experiments which could only injure those who tried them. But a different view was showing itself. Cairnes, commenting upon his master's so-called Socialism, says that the name now implies the direct interference of the state for the instant realisation of ' ideal schemes.'[2] He objects to this, and therefore, by anticipation, to 'state Socialism.' Here Mill's position is ambiguous. In the first place, while agreeing with the aims of the Socialists, he ' utterly dissents from the most conspicuous and vehement part of their teaching, their declamations against competition.'[3] 'Where competition is not,' he adds, 'monopoly is'; and monopoly means 'the taxation of the industrious for the support of indolence, if not of plunder.' Competition raises wages, if the supply of labourers is limited, and can never lower them, unless the supply is excessive. As Cobden is reported to have said, the real question is simply whether two masters are running after one man, or two men after one master. No one could speak more emphatically or forcibly upon this point, nor does he seem to have ever abandoned it. Both Mill and his disciples saw the only solution in a different direction. Co-operation is their panacea ; and they are never tired of appealing to the cases of its successful operation,

---

[1] *Political Economy*, p. 133 (bk. ii. ch. i. § 4).
[2] *Leading Principles*, p. 316.
[3] *Political Economy*, p. 476 (bk. iv. ch. vii. § 7).

beginning with M. Leclaire's experiment in France and the Rochdale pioneers in England. The pith of the doctrine was already given in the famous chapter[1] upon 'the probable futurity of the labouring class' due to Mrs. Mill's influence. His hope for them lay in co-operation, and later editions only differed from the first by recording new experiments. Cairnes deduces the same conclusion from his wage-fund. The labourer can only improve by ceasing to be a 'mere labourer'; profits must 'reinforce' the wage-fund; co-operation shows how this is to be done, and 'constitutes the one and only solution of our present problem.'[2] Thornton reaches the same conclusion, co-operation giving the only compromise which can end the internecine contest. He can only express his feelings in poetry, and his last chapter upon 'labour's Utopia' is written with creditable skill in the difficult *terza rima*. Fawcett fully shared this enthusiasm; and the reason is sufficiently obvious. Co-operation, in their sense, means simply the joint effort of independent individuals. Competition is assumed to remain in full force. All combinations, as Mill says of trades-unions, must be voluntary. That is an 'indispensable condition of tolerating them.'[3] The member of a co-operative society is as free to join or to leave as the shareholder in any commercial company. The societies compete with each other and with capitalists at every point. 'Supply and demand' regulate

---

[1] *Political Economy*, p. 476 (bk. iv. ch. vii.). Mill refers to Babbage's *Economy of Machinery and Manufacturers* for an incidental reference to applications of profit-sharing in Cornish mines, and a suggestion that it would be applicable elsewhere. Babbage gives little more than a passing suggestion.

[2] *Leading Principles*, pp. 339, 344.

[3] *Political Economy*, p. 566 (bk. v. ch. x. § 5).

every part of their transactions. The motive for joining is simply the desire of each member to invest his savings, and therefore the *vis medicatrix* is duly stimulated. Each man can thrive better by working in concert; but he resigns none of his rights as an individual. He has not enlisted in an army bound by discipline, but has joined in a voluntary expedition.

So far we have what seems to be the logical and consistent result of the individualist view. But Mill, though he remains an ' individualist' philosophically, is also led to conclusions very far from the ordinary individualist theory. The last part of his treatise is devoted to a discussion of the limits of government interference. He urges energetically that there should be some space in human ' existence entrenched round and sacred from authoritative intrusion,'[1] a doctrine inherited from his teachers and eloquently expanded in his *Liberty*. It marks the point of transition from his economic to his ethical and political teaching. After repeating the ordinary arguments against excessive interference by way of protection, usury laws and the like, he states as a general principle that the burden of proof is on the advocates of interference, and that ' letting alone should be the general practice.'[2] All coercion, as Bentham had said, is an evil, but, in certain cases, it is the least possible evil ; and Mill, as becomes an empiricist, declining to lay down an absolute rule, only asks what are the particular cases in which the evil is overbalanced by the good of interference. But, here, if we consider the list of exceptions, we must admit that the general

[1] *Political Economy*, p. 569 (bk. v. ch. xi. § 2).
[2] *Ibid.* p. 573 (bk. v. ch. xi. § 7).

principle is remarkably flexible. Some cases have been already noticed. Mill not only allowed but strongly advocated a national system of education.[1] He approved a great national scheme of emigration[2] and a scheme for home colonisation, and this expressly with a view to lifting the poor, not gradually but immediately into a higher level of comfort. He held that laws in restraint of imprudent marriage were not wrong in principle, though they might be inexpedient under many or most circumstances. He approved of measures tending to equalisation of wealth. He proposed that the right of bequest should be limited by forbidding any one to acquire more than a certain sum, and so counteracting the tendency to the accumulation of large fortunes.[3] He held that government should take measures for alleviating the sufferings of labourers displaced by new inventions or the excessive change of 'circulating' into 'fixed capital.'[4] He not only approved of measures for forming a peasant-proprietary, but, in his last years, became president of an association for altering the whole system of land tenure. He thought that government should retain a property in canals and railways, though the working should be leased to private companies. He approved, as I have said, of the poor-law in its new form. The factory legislation alone was still uncongenial to his principles, though on moral grounds he accepts the protection of children. Even in this direction he incidentally makes a remarkable concession. A point to

[1] He qualifies this to some extent in the *Liberty*. The state should enforce education and pay for it, but not provide schools. The line is hard to draw.

[2] See especially *Political Economy*, p. 585 (bk. v. ch. xi. § 14).

[3] *Political Economy*, p. 138 (bk. ii. ch. ii. § 4).

[4] *Ibid.* p. 61 (bk. i. ch. vi. § 3).

which political economists had not, he thinks, sufficiently attended is illustrated by the case of the ' Nine Hours Bill.'[1]   Assuming, though only for the sake of argument, that a reduction of labour hours from ten to nine would be to the advantage of the workmen, should the law, he asks, interfere to enforce reduction?   The do-nothing party would reply, No ; because if beneficial, the workmen would adopt the rule spontaneously.   This answer, says Mill, is inconclusive.   The interest of the individual would be opposed to the interest of the ' class collectively.'   Competition might enforce the longer hours ; and thus classes may need the assistance of the law ' to give effect to their deliberate collective opinion of their own interest.'   Here again Mill seems to be admitting as an ' exception' a principle which goes much further than he observed.   He is mainly interested by the ethical problem, Is it ever right to force a man to act against his own wishes in a matter primarily concerning himself alone ?   He concludes that it may be right, because each man may wish for a rule on condition that every one else obeys it.   In that case, the law only gives effect to the universal desire.   But the argument really involves an exception to the beneficent action of competition.   The case is one in which, upon his assumptions, free competition of individuals may lead to degeneration instead of a better development.   In such cases, it is possible that association, enforced by law, may lead to benefits unattainable by the independent units.   This admission would go far in the Socialist direction.   It would justify the principle of ' collective bargaining' to sanction the collective interests.   In the same way his

[1] *Political Economy*, p. 581 (bk. v. ch. xi. § 12).

justification of the factory acts in the case of children leads beyond the moral to economic grounds. Mill's view, so far as he goes, would fall in with the opinion that there was here a necessary conflict between Christian morality and political economy; or the admission that economic loss must be incurred for moral considerations. But, in the long run, the two views coincide; for practices which stint and degrade the breed must be ultimately fatal to economic efficiency. As was often said at the time, to forbid interference for economic reasons was to suppose that the country could only flourish by treating children as it might conceivably be necessary to treat them under stress of some deadly and imminent peril. When economists looked beyond the instantaneous advantage of the market, and remembered that children were made of flesh and blood, it was obvious that on the purest economic grounds, a system which implied the degradation of the labourer must be in the end pernicious to every interest. In this case, therefore, the interference of the law was desirable from the economic as well as from the moral point of view.

Nobody, of course, would have admitted this more cordially than Mill, and the admission would imply that we must here look beyond mere 'supply and demand' or individual competition. When we sum up these admissions, it appears that Mill was well on the way to state Socialism. Lange, the historian of materialism, praises him warmly upon this ground.[1] Lange is enthusiastic about Mill's *Liberty*, as well as about his *Political Economy*. He praises the *Economy* on the ground that

[1] J. S. Mill's *Ansichten über die Sociale Frage*, etc. (1866).

Mill's great aim is to humanise the science; and, especially, that in the various proposals which I have noticed Mill desires an active interference of government towards raising the moral level of society. Mill, in short, would have sympathised, had he come to know it, with the Socialism of the Chair, which was beginning at the time of his death to make a mark in Germany. Lange's appreciation was, I think, in great part correct; and suggests the question, How or how far was Mill consistent? Could a system essentially based upon Malthus and Ricardo be reconciled with modern Socialism?

Mill once more was an individualist in the philosophical sense. He assumes society to be formed of a number of independent units, bound together by laws enforced by 'sanctions.' The fundamental laws should be just; and justice presupposes equality; equality, at at least in this sense, that the position of each unit should depend upon his own qualities, and not upon mere outward accidents. In his articles upon Socialism Mill declared most emphatically that in the present state of society any idea of such justice was 'manifestly chimerical';[1] and that the main conditions of success were first birth, and secondly accident. In his first edition his discussion of Socialism ends by justifying 'private property.' The best scheme is that which lets every man's share of the produce depend on his own exertions. He complains, however, that the principle has 'never yet had a fair trial in any country.' Inequalities have been created and aggravated by the law.[2] This passage disappeared when he rewrote his views of Socialism.

[1] *Fortnightly Review* for February 1879.
[2] *Political Economy* (first edition) i. 252-53.

From the first, however, he asserts a principle for which
he gives the chief credit to his wife.[1] Laws of production, he says, are 'real laws of nature' ; methods of
distribution depend on the human will, or, as he says in
the *Political Economy*, 'the distribution of wealth depends
on the laws and customs of society.'[2] Can the laws
secure a just distribution?

Here, then, is a critical problem. As a Utilitarian he
would reply that government should make fair rules for
the general relations of individuals, and trust to the best
man winning in an open competition. Mill's point of
difference from the Socialists was precisely that he
believed in competition to the last, and was so far a
thorough 'individualist.' Yet, as a matter of fact, vast
inequalities of wealth and power had developed, and
exiled justice from the world—if, indeed, justice had
ever existed there. So far as this could be attributed to
laws, unjust because made by force and fraud, the
remedy might lie in reforming the laws. That case was
exemplified by land. 'Landed property,' he says, in
Europe, derives 'its origin from force.'[3] English land-
laws were first designed 'to prop up a ruling class.'[4]
By force, in fact, the landowners had secured the best
places at Malthus's feast, and were enabled to benefit by,
without contributing to, the growth of the national
wealth. Rent, says Cairnes, is 'a fund ever growing,
even while its proprietors sleep.'[5] Mill, of course,
admitted that part of rent is due to the application of

[1] *Autobiography*, p. 246.
[2] *Political Economy*, p. 123 (bk. ii. ch. i. § 1).
[3] *Dissertations*, iv. 59.   [4] *Ibid.* iv. 240.
[5] *Leading Principles*, p. 333.

capital; and he does not propose to confiscate the wealth of the actual proprietors who had acquired their rights fairly under the existing system. But he is convinced that land differs radically from movable property. Capital diminishes in value, as society advances; 'land alone . . . has the privilege of steadily rising in value from natural causes.'[1] Hence we have the famous proposal of taking the 'unearned increment.'[2] If the landowner was dissatisfied, he should be paid the selling price of the day. A good many landlords may regret that they had not this offer at the time that it was proposed (1873). Thus land was to be nationalised; the state was to become the national landlord, as in India,[3] and at any rate nothing was to be done by which more land could get into private hands. He seems, indeed, still to believe in a peasant-proprietary,[4] but does not ask how far the doctrine is compatible with nationalisation.

If, then, the forcible acquisition of land by its first owners be still a taint upon the existing title, is property in other wealth altogether just? Mill admits in his discussion of Thornton's book that something is to be said against capitalists. 'Movable property,' indeed, has, on the whole, a purer 'origin than landed property.' It represents industry, not simply force. There has, indeed, been a good deal of fraud, and many practices at which 'a person of delicate conscience' might scruple.[5] This is a gentle adumbration of the view of some recent

---

[1] *Dissertations*, iv. 263.   [2] *Ibid.* iv. 285.
[3] *Ibid.* iv. 274.   [4] *Ibid.* iv. 269.
[5] *Ibid.* iv. 60. The whole doctrine that the sanctity of property depends upon the mode of acquisition by remote proprietors seems to be scarcely reconcilable with sound Utilitarianism.

Socialists.   Is not capital, they would say, precisely the product of fraud, and stained through and through by cheating?   If Mill was far from the doctrine of Marx, and did not hold that capital was a mere name for the process of exploitation, he admitted at least that there was no such thing as justice in the actual industrial order. Wealth clearly represents something very different from a reward given in proportion to industry.   In the first place, it is inherited, and Mill, as I have said, proposed therefore to limit inheritances; and, in the next place, nobody can suppose that a poor man who grows rich, even by purely honourable means, gets a prize proportioned to his virtue or to his utility; while, finally, the poor man certainly does not start on equal terms with his richer rival.   He that hath not may not lose that which he hath; but he has small chances of climbing the ladder, and if he climbs, his success means devotion to his private interest.[1]   Mill's abandonment of the wage-fund, again, involved the acceptance of the 'tacit conspiracy.'   The poverty of the mass is not due to a 'law of nature'; and therefore it is due, partly at least, to the combination of capitalists, which enables them to bring their power to bear in keeping down the rate of wages to an indefinite extent.

The social injustice against which he protests exists under a system in which the laws are substantially equal. They no longer recognise class distinctions explicitly; they have ceased to forbid combinations or to fix the rate

[1] After giving Adam Smith's famous account of the causes of the varying rates of wages, Mill points out 'a class of considerations' too much neglected by his predecessors: cases, namely, in which unskilled labourers are insufficiently paid; and remarks that there is almost a 'hereditary distinction of caste.'—*Political Economy*, p. 238 (bk. ii. ch. xiv. § 2).

of wages; the paternal theory of government is gone, as he says, for ever, and the old relation of protector and protected supplanted by a system of equality before the law.[1] And yet monstrous inequalities and therefore injustices remain. What is the inference? Here we have the real inconsistency or, at least, failure to reconcile completely two diverging principles. Mill and all his disciples place their hopes in ' co-operation.' Co-operation can, they think, be reconciled with the ' liberty ' which they regarded both as desirable in itself and as equivalent to the absence of law. Co-operation, on this showing, implies first absolute freedom to join or to leave the co-operative body. The individual joins with other individuals, but does not sacrifice his individuality. The relation is still, so to speak, ' external,' and the various associations compete with each other as fully and unreservedly as the component individuals. And yet there is an obvious difficulty. Co-operation must involve a loss of ' liberty,' though the loss may be compensated. If I co-operate, I undertake obligations, enforcible by law, though not originally imposed by law. Mill throws out the conjecture that the choice between Socialism and individualism will ' depend mainly on one consideration, viz., which of the two systems is consistent with the greatest amount of human liberty and spontaneity.' [2] Now all association limits action in fact. When great companies take up an industrial function of any kind, they put a stress upon the individual, not necessarily the less forcible because not legally imposed. A great railway, for example, soon

---

[1] *Political Economy*, p. 456 (bk. iv. ch. vii. § 1).
[2] *Ibid.* p. 129 (bk. ii. ch. i. § 3).

destroys other private enterprises, and makes itself practically necessary. It is equally governed by a body in which most individual shareholders exercise as little influence as though they were appointed by the state. As the industrial machinery, human or material, is developed, it becomes as much a part of social order as if it were created by the legislature. The point upon which Mill insists, that all associations must be 'voluntary,' then becomes insignificant. I may be legally at liberty to stand aside; but, in fact, they become imperative conditions of life. That is to say, that the distinction drawn by the old individualism between the state institutions and those created by private action ceases to have the old significance. When a society once develops an elaborate and complex structure, it becomes almost pedantic to draw a profound distinction between a system which is practically indispensable and one which is legally imperative.

I will not inquire further whether Mill's position could be made logically coherent. One thing is pretty clear. If his views had been actually adopted; if the state educated, nationalised the land, supported the poor, restrained marriage, regulated labour where individual competition failed, and used its power to equalise wealth, it would very soon adopt state Socialism, and lose sight of Mill's reservations. Mill, as I believe, had been quite right when he insisted on the vast importance of stimulating the sense of individual responsibility. That is, and must always be, one essential moment of the argument. His misfortune was, that having absorbed an absolute system in his youth, and accepting its claims to scientific validity, he was unable when he saw its defects

to see the true line (if any one yet sees the true line) of
conciliation. His doctrine, therefore, contained fragments of opposite and inconsistent dogmas. While
fancying that he was developing the individualist theories,
he adopted not only Socialism, but even a version of
Socialism open to the objections on which he sometimes
forcibly insisted. Mill and the Socialist are both indi-
vidualists; only the Socialist makes right precede fact,
and Mill would make fact precede right. Every
individual, says the Socialist, has a right to support;
the consequences of granting the right must be left to
Providence. This, says Mill following Malthus, would
be fatal, because the individual would have no motive to
:upport himself. He must only have such a right as
i·⸱plies personal responsibility. But then, as facts also
show, many individuals may be unable to support themselves even if they wish it, and their responsibility
becomes a mockery. If we enforce duties on all, must
we not make the duty possible? Must not every one
be so trained and so placed that work will be sure
of reward? There is the problem, which he sees and
feels, though his answer seems to imply a doubtful
shifting between antagonistic theories.

VIII. LOGICAL METHOD

I must glance finally at the relation of Mill's method
to his general principles. In an early essay [1] he declares
that the method must be ' *a priori*,' that is, as he

---

[1] ' On the Definition of Political Economy, and on the Method of Investigation proper to it.' Reprinted in *Unsettled Questions*, and quoted in the
Logic, p. 388 (bk. vi. ch. ix. § 3).

explains, 'reasoning from an assumed hypothesis.'[1] In the *Logic* it is treated as a case of the 'direct deductive method.' This involves an important point in his system. He had derived from Comte, as he tells us,[2] only one 'leading conception' of a purely logical kind, the conception, namely, of the 'historical' or 'inverse deductive method.' This method, implied in Comte's sociology, starts, as Mill says, from the 'collation of specific experience.' Now Mill agrees that this 'historical' method was appropriate to sociology in general. He agrees, too, with Comte that it was not the method used by economists. But, whereas Comte had inferred that political economy must for that reason be a sham science,[3] Mill holds that economists were justified in using a different method. Comte, he thought, had failed to see that in certain cases the method of 'direct deduction' was applicable to sociological inquiry. One such case, though he will not undertake to decide what other instances there may be, is political economy.[4] He decides that the difficulties, regarded by Comte as insuperable, may be overcome. His early account is still valid; and he therefore explicitly rejects the 'historical' method.

I confess that the use of these technical phrases appears to me to be rather magniloquent, and to lead to some confusion. Setting them aside, Mill's view may be briefly stated. He argues, in the first place, that we cannot apply the ordinary method of experiment

---

[1] *Unsettled Questions*, p. 143.   [2] *Autobiography*, p. 210.

[3] See, *e.g.*, Comte's *Philosophie Positive*, iv. 266-78. The fourth volume of Comte disappointed Mill, as he says; and this probably explains one reason.

[4] *Logic*, p. 590 (bk. vi. ch. ix. § 4).

to economic problems. To settle by experience whether protection was good or bad, we should have to find two nations agreeing in everything except their tariffs; and that, of course, if not impossible, is exceedingly difficult.[1] It follows that if there be a true science of political economy, it must have a different method. We might indeed adopt Comte's answer: 'There is no such science'; a view for which there is much to be said. Mill, however, being confident that the science existed had to justify its methods. Political economy, he says, considers man solely as a wealth-desiring being; it predicts the 'phenomena of the social state' which take place in consequence; and makes abstraction of every other motive except the laziness or the desire of present enjoyment which 'antagonise' the desire of wealth. Hence it deduces various laws, though, as a fact, there is scarcely any action of a man's life in which other desires are not operative. Political economy still holds true wherever the desire of wealth is the main end. 'Other cases may be regarded as affected by disturbing causes'—comparable, of course, to the inevitable 'friction'—and it is only on account of them that we have an 'element of uncertainty' in political economy. Otherwise it is a demonstrable science, presupposing an 'arbitrary definition' of a man as geometry presupposes an 'arbitrary definition' of a straight line.'[2]

The relation of this doctrine to Mill's general views on logic is clear, but suggests some obvious criticisms. 'Desire for wealth,' for example, is not a simple but a highly complex desire, involving in different ways every

[1] *Unsettled Questions*, p. 148.
[2] *Ibid.* pp. 137-50.

human passion.[1]   To argue from it, as though its
definition were as unequivocal as that of a straight
line, is at least audacious.   Mill, no doubt, means to
express an undeniable truth.   Industry, in general,
implies desire for wealth, and the whole mechanism
supposes that men prefer a guinea to a pound.   The
fact is clear enough, and if proof be required can be
proved by observation.   We must again admit that
whatever psychological theorem is implied in the fact
must be assumed as true.   But it does not follow that
because we assume the 'desire for wealth' we can
deduce the phenomena from that assumption.   That
inference would confound different things.   If we were
accounting for the actions of an individual, we might
adopt the method.   In some actions a man is guided by
love of money, and in others by love of his neighbour.
We may 'deduce' his action in his counting-house from
his love of money, and consider an occasional fit of
benevolence as a mere 'disturbing cause' to be neglected
in general or treated as mere 'friction.'   A similar
principle might be applied to political economy if we
could regard it as the theory of particular classes of
actions.   But we have to consider other circumstances
to reach any general and tenable theory.   We have to
consider the whole social structure, the existence of a
market and all that it implies, and the division of
society into classes and their complex relations: the
distribution of functions among them and the creation
of the settled order which alone makes commerce possible.
We cannot argue to the action without understanding
the structure of which the agent is a constituent part,

[1] Mill makes this remark himself in writing to Comte about phrenology.

and which determines all the details of his action. The building up of society implies the influence not of any single desire, but of all the desires, modes of thought, and affections of human beings. If, therefore, a comprehension of existing institutions be necessary to political economy, the deductive method is clearly unequal to the task which he, partly following Comte, regards as implied in 'sociology' generally. To deduce, not the social structure at large, but any social organ, from such an abstraction is hopeless, because every organ is affected through and through by its dependence upon other organs. Mill virtually supposes that because the particular function can be understood by abstracting from accidental influences, the organ of which it is a function can be understood by abstracting from its essential relations to the organism.

Here, in fact, is the error which I take to be implied in Mill's individualism. Given the social structure as it is, you may fairly make some such abstraction as the postulates. You may consider large classes of actions, exchange of wealth, and all the normal play of commercial forces, as corresponding to the rather vague 'desire for wealth,' and ask how an individual or a number of individuals will act when under the influence of that dominant motive. That is legitimate, and applies to what is called 'pure political economy' —the relatively superficial study of the actual working of the machinery without considering how the machinery came to have its actual structure. But directly you get beyond this, to problems involving organic change, you get to 'sociology,' and can only proceed—if progress be possible—by the 'historical method,' or, in other words, by studying the growth of the institutions of which we form a part, and of which we may be considered as the product. This again means that the general conception of the Utilitarians, which recognises nothing but the individual as an ultimate unit, though capable of combining and grouping in various ways, omits one essential element in the problem. It regards all social structures as on the same plane, temporary and indefinitely alterable arrangements; and involves a neglect of the historical or general point of view which is essential not only to an understanding of society, but also of the individuals whose whole nature and character is moulded by it. I have tried to show the results upon the legal and political conceptions of Mill's teachers. We now see how the conception of political economy as a 'deductive' or *a priori* science naturally misled the school. When they mistook their rough generalisations for definitive science, they brought discredit upon the theory, and played into the hands of their enemies, the sentimentalists, who, finding that the science was not infallible, resolved to trust to instincts and defy 'laws of nature' in general. Read as common-sense considerations upon social questions, the writings of Mill and his followers were generally to the point and often conclusive. When read as scientific statements, they fail from their obvious inadequacy, and the vague terminology which takes the airs of clearly defined conceptions. Yet it is impossible to conclude without noticing two admirable characteristics of Mill and his disciples. The first is the deep and thorough conviction that the elevation of the poorer classes is the main end of all social inquiries. The second and the rarer is the resolution to speak the plain truth, and to denounce all sophists who, professing the same end, would reach it by illusory means. Mill's sympathies never blinded him to the duty of telling the whole truth as he saw it.

CHAPTER IV

POLITICS AND ETHICS

I. MILL'S PROBLEM

In the *Political Economy* Mill had touched upon certain ethical and political questions.   These are explicitly treated in a later group of works.   The first and most important was the essay upon *Liberty* (1859).   I have already spoken of the elaborate composition of this, his most carefully written treatise.[1]   The book, welcomed by many even of his opponents, contains also the clearest statement of his most characteristic doctrine.   The treatises on *Representative Government* (1861), upon the *Subjection of Women* (written at the same time, but not published till 1869), and upon *Utilitarianism* (in *Fraser's Magazine*, 1861, and as a book in 1863), are closely connected with the *Liberty*, and together give what may

---

[1] *Autobiography*, p. 50.   The most elaborate attack upon the *Liberty* is contained in *Liberty, Equality, Fraternity* (1873), by my brother, Sir James FitzJames Stephen, in whose life I have given an account of the book.   I shall not here go into the controversy.   I am content to say that, though I cannot agree with my brother, I think that he strikes very forcibly at some weak points in Mill's scheme.   The most remarkable point is that the book is substantially a criticism of Mill's from the older Utilitarian point of view.   It shows, therefore, how Mill diverged from Bentham.

be called his theory of conduct.[1] I shall try to bring
out their leading principles.

The *Liberty*, says Mill, could have no claim to
originality except in so far as thoughts which are
already common property receive a special impress
when uttered by a thoughtful mind. Hymns to liberty,
indeed, have been sung so long and so persistently that
the subject ought to have been exhausted. The admission that liberty can be in any case an evil is generally
evaded by a device of touching simplicity. Liberty,
when bad, is not called liberty. 'Licence, they mean,'
as Milton puts it, 'when they cry liberty.' Bentham
exposes the sophistry very neatly as a case of 'sham-
distinctions' in the book of 'Fallacies.'[2]

The general sentiment is perfectly intelligible from the
Jacobin point of view. At a time when legislators were
supposed to have created constitutions, and priests to
have invented religions, history was taken as a record of
the struggle of mankind against fraud and force. War
is simply murder on a large scale, and government force
organised to support tyrants. All political evils can be
attributed to kings, and superstition to priests, without
blaming subjects for slavishness and stupidity. Such
language took the tone of a new gospel during the great
revolutionary movements of the eighteenth century.
Men who were sweeping away the effete institutions
upheld by privileged classes assumed 'Liberty' to be an
absolute and ultimate principle. The Utilitarians,
though political allies, were opposed in theory to this

[1] I refer for the *Liberty* and the *Representative Government* to the People's
Editions of 1867.

[2] *Works,* ii. 451.

method of argument.   Liberty, like everything else, must be judged by its effects upon happiness. Society, according to them, is held together by the sovereign. His existence, therefore, is essentially necessary, and his power almost unlimited. The greater was the importance of deciding when and where it should be used. Bentham and James Mill assumed that all ends would be secured by making the sovereign the servant of the people, and therefore certain to aim at the greatest happiness. They reached the same conclusions, therefore, as those who reached them by a rather shorter cut, and their doctrine differed little in its absolute and *a priori* tendency. Thorough democracy would give the panacea.   J. S. Mill had become heretical.   I have noticed in his life how he had been alarmed by the brutality and ignorance of the lowest classes, and had come to doubt whether 'liberty,' as understood by his masters, would not mean the despotic rule of the ignorant.   The doubts which he felt were shared by many who had set out with the same political creed.

Here we come once more to the essentially false position in which the philosophical radicals found themselves.   The means which they heartily approved led to ends which they entirely repudiated. They not only approved, but were most active in advocating, the adoption of democratic measures. They demanded, in the name of liberty, that men should have a share in making the laws by which they were bound.   The responsibility of rulers was, according to James Mill, the one real principle of politics; and it followed that, to use the sacred phrase, the 'sinister interests' which distract them should be destroyed.   The legislation which followed the Reform Bill gave an approximate sanction to their doctrine. The abolition of rotten-boroughs destroyed the sinister interest of the land-owners ; the reform of municipalities, the sinister interest of the self-elected corporations ; the new poor-law, the sinister interest of the parish vestries ; and the ecclesiastical reforms showed that great prelates and ancient cathedrals were not too sacred to be remodelled and made responsible. The process inevitably smoothed the way for centralisation. The state, one may say, was beginning to come to life. The powers which, in a centralised government, are exercised by an administrative hierarchy, had been treated under the category of private property. To introduce responsibility was to remove the obstacles to uniform machinery. Vigorous action by a central authority had been impossible so long as power had been parcelled out among a number of different centres, each regarding its privileges as invested with all the sanctity of private property. The duke, who claimed that he ' might do as he would with his own '—including his boroughs—had surrendered that part of his property to the new voters. They enjoyed their rights not as a personal attribute, but in virtue of satisfying some uniform condition. For the time, indeed, the condition included, not simply a ripe age and masculine sex, but ' ten-pound householdership.' Power held by men as members of a class is, at any rate, no longer private property, but something belonging to the class in general, and naturally used in the interests of the class collectively. The legislature could make general rules where it used rather to confirm a set of distinct bargains made with each proprietor of ultimate authority.   So far, the generalising and centralising process was both inevitable and approved by the Utilitarians.   Nor could they, as prominent advocates of codification and law-reform generally, object to the increased vigour of legislation no longer trammelled by the multitude of little semi-independent centres.   But a further implication often escaped their notice.   'Liberty' is increased by destroying privilege in the sense that the individual acquires more influence upon the laws that bind him.   But it does not follow that he will be 'freer' in the sense of having fewer laws to bind him.   The contrary was the case.   The objection to the privileges was precisely that the possessors retained them without discharging the correlative functions.   The nobles and the corporations had not been too active, but too indolent.   They had left things undone, or left them to be done after a haphazard fashion by individual energy.   The much-lauded 'self-government' implied an absence of government, or precisely the state of things which was no longer possible when the old privileges were upset.   The newly organised municipalities had to undertake duties which had been neglected by the close corporations, and others which had been clumsily discharged by individuals.   The result was that the philosophical radicals found that they were creating a Frankenstein.   They were not limiting the sphere of government in general, only giving power to a new class which would in many ways use it more energetically. The difference came out in the economic matters where the doctrine of non-interference had been most actively preached.   The Chartists and their allies claimed their 'rights' as indisputable possessions, whatever might be the consequences. To the Utilitarians this meant that the Chartists were prepared in the name of *a priori* principles to attack the most necessary institutions, and fly in the face of 'laws of nature.' The old system had tended to keep the poor man down. The Chartist system would help him to plunder the rich. The right principle was to leave everything to 'supply and demand.' As the contrast became clearer, some of the philosophical radicals subsided into Whiggism, and others sank into actual Tories. Mill remained faithful, but with modified views. He had seen in the hostility of the lower classes to sound economy an illustration of the ignorance, selfishness, and brutality of the still uneducated mass.[1] But he drew a moral of his own. The impression made upon him by Tocqueville's *Democracy in America* is characteristic. That remarkable book led him to aim at a philosophical view of the whole question. It was an impartial study of the whole question of the social and political tendencies summed up in the phrase, 'democracy.' The general result was to open Mill's eyes to both the good and evil sides of democracy, to regard democracy in some shape as inevitable instead of making it a religion or denouncing it as diabolical; and to consider how the evils might be corrected while free play might be allowed to the beneficial tendencies. It enlightened him, he says, more especially on the great question of centralisation, and freed him from the 'unreasoning prejudices' which led some of the radicals to oppose even such measures as the new Poor Law.[2] So much may indicate Mill's general attitude; and, if his

---

[1] *Autobiography*, p. 231.
[2] *Ibid.* pp. 191-95.

conclusions were questionable, the main purpose was so far eminently philosophical.

Mill begins his *Liberty* by insisting upon the danger to which his attention had been roused by the course of events. The conflict between liberty and authority led to the demand that rulers should become responsible to their subjects ; and when this result was secured, a new evil appeared. The tyranny of the majority might supplant the tyranny of rulers ; and, if less formidable politically, might be even worse spiritually. 'Social tyranny' may be more penetrative than political, and enslave the soul itself.[1] In England the 'yoke of law' may be lighter, but the 'yoke of opinion' is perhaps heavier than elsewhere in Europe. When the masses have learned their power, they will probably be as tyrannical in legislation as in public opinion.[2] The purpose of his essay is to assert 'one very simple principle' by which this tendency may be restrained. That principle is (briefly) that the sole end which warrants interference with individual action is 'self-protection.' He will argue not from 'abstract rights,' but from 'utility' understood in its largest sense, and corresponding 'to the interests of a man as a progressive being.'

II. INTELLECTUAL LIBERTY

The principle thus formulated is applicable both in the sphere of speculation and in the sphere of conduct. Mill first considers 'liberty of thought and discussion.' He has here the advantage of starting from a generally admitted principle. Every one now admits, in words at

[1] *Liberty* (People's Edition, 1867), p. 3.   [2] *Ibid.* p. 5.

least, the doctrine of toleration.   Mill might have adduced
a catena of authorities beginning with the seventeenth
century writers who, having themselves suffered persecution, were slowly perceiving that persecution even of
error was objectionable.   It is a proof of his ability that
he could give fresh interest to so old a topic.   In the
previous generation indeed it had still been a practical
question.   The early Utilitarians had to attack the
disqualifications imposed upon dissenters, and had re-
monstrated against the persecution of Carlile.   That
incident had started Mill's literary career.   Moreover,
as he points out, the prosecutions of Pooley, Truelove,
and Mr. Holyoake showed that the old spirit was not
extinct in 1857.[1]   Still, these were but 'rags and remnants
of persecution.'   In denouncing them Mill was going
with the tide.   The ground upon which he plants his
argument is more significant.   The older writers had
chiefly insisted upon the question of right.   It cannot
be just to punish a man for acting rightly, and it must
surely be right for me to speak what I conscientiously
believe to be true.   One of James Mill's articles in the
Westminster took this ground.   Samuel Bailey had
argued that a man cannot be responsible to men for
his beliefs, inasmuch as they are beyond his own control.
He may be foolish, but he cannot be immoral—a thesis
which James Mill defended against certain theological
opponents.[2]   J. S. Mill, taking the ground of 'utility,'
is led to wider considerations.   He argues in substance
that the suppression of opinions or of their free utterance

---

[1] *Liberty*, 17 *n.*   The Bradlaugh case showed that the old spirit was not
extinct twenty-five years later.

[2] See Bain's *James Mill*, p. 304.

is always opposed to the most vital interests of society. Hence the question as to liberty of thought connects itself with the whole question as to liberty of conduct. It comes under his general principle as to the rightful provinces of collective and individual action. His general conclusion upon freedom of dismission is summed up in four propositions.[1] The opinions suppressed may, in the first place, be true. To deny that possibility is to assume infallibility. Secondly, if not wholly, they may be partly, true ; and to suppress them is to prevent necessary corrections of the accepted beliefs. Thirdly, even a true opinion which refuses to be tested by controversy will be imperfectly understood. And fourthly, an opinion so held will become a dead formula, and only ' cumber the ground,' preventing the growth of real and heartfelt convictions.

The general validity of the arguments is unimpeachable, and the vigour of statement deserves all commendation. Mill puts victoriously the case for the entire freedom of thought and discussion. The real generosity of sentiment, and the obvious sincerity which comes from preaching what he had practised, gives new force to well-worn topics. The interest of the race not only requires the fullest possible liberty to form and to communicate our own opinions, but rather makes the practice a duty. Though Mill gives the essential reasons, his presentation of the case has significant peculiarities. Even if an opinion be true, he says, it ought to be open to discussion. He proceeds to urge the more doubtful point, that contradiction, even when the truth is contradicted, is desirable in itself. Free discussion not only destroys

[1] *Liberty*, pp. 30, 31.

error, but invigorates truth. It preserves a wholesome intellectual atmosphere, which kills the weeds and stimulates the healthy growths. In mathematical reasoning, indeed, the evidence is all on one side. There are no objections, and no answers to objections. But as soon as we reach any question of the truths even of physical, and still more of the moral, sciences, truth must be attained by balancing 'two sets of conflicting reasons.'[1] The doctrine, true or false, which is not contradicted, comes to be held as a 'dead belief.' An objector is supposed to observe that on this showing, the existence of error is necessary to the vitality of truth, and that a belief must perish just because it is unanimously accepted. Mill 'affirms no such thing.' He admits 'that the stock of accepted truths must increase.' But the growth of unanimity, though 'inevitable and indispensable,' has its drawbacks. It would be desirable to encourage contradiction even by artificial contrivances. The Socratic dialectics and the school disputations more or less supplied a want which we have now no means of satisfying.[2] By systematic discussion of first principles, men are forced to understand the full bearing and the true grounds of their professed beliefs. This doctrine is illustrated, and no doubt was derived in part from the early discussions in which Mill had trained his logical powers. It suggests a valuable mode of mental

---

[1] *Liberty*, p. 21. The excellent Abraham Tucker remarks that if he met 'a person of credit, candour, and understanding,' who denied that two and two made four, he would give him a hearing.—*Light of Nature* (1834), p. 125.

[2] *Liberty*, pp. 25, 26. 'To become properly acquainted with a truth,' says Novalis (quoted in Carlyle's essay upon him), 'we must first have disbelieved and disputed against it.' But Novalis also observed that 'my faith gains infinitely the moment I see it shared by some one else.'

discipline; but as a statement of the conditions of belief, it seems to confuse the accident with the essence. The bare fact of sincere contradiction surely tends to weaken belief; and resistance to contradiction, though it measures the strength of belief, is not the cause of its strength. No doubt a truth may be strengthened in passing through the ordeal of contradiction, so far as we are thus forced to realise its meaning. The same result may be produced by other means, and, above all, by applying belief to practice. We believe in arithmetical truths, partly because the oftener we have to count the more we realise the truth that two and two make four. Whatever the original source of our beliefs, the way to make them vivid is to act upon them. Mill himself incidentally observes that men have a living belief in religious doctrines, 'just up to the point to which it is usual to act upon them.'[1] That, I take it, hits the point. The doctrine, for example, that we should turn the second cheek is practically superseded, not because it is never contradicted, but because it does not correspond to our genuine passions or actions. Beliefs, true or erroneous, preserve their vitality so long as they are put into practice, and not the less because they are held unanimously. What is true is that they are then rather instincts than opinions. Beliefs do not die when unchallenged, but are the more likely to be 'dormant' or held implicitly without conscious formulation.

This leads to a further result. As Mill insists in the *Logic*, 'verification' is an essential part of proof. To act upon a belief is one way of verifying. The fact that we apply a theory successfully is also a valid proof that

---

[1] *Liberty*, p. 24.

it is true in the great mass of everyday knowledge.   But a religious belief is not verified in the same sense.   The fact that I act upon it, and am satisfied with my action, proves that it is in harmony with my emotions, not that it is a true statement about facts.   The persuasive force often remains, though the logic has become unsatisfactory.   This suggests the question as to the nature of a satisfactory 'verification.'   We clearly hold innumerable beliefs which we have not fully tested for ourselves. Mill supposes his opponent to urge that simple people must take many things on trust.[1]   We might rather say that even the wisest has to take nine-tenths of his beliefs on trust.   We may rightly believe many truths which we are incompetent either to discover or to prove directly because we can verify them indirectly.   We can accept whole systems of truth, though we are unable to follow the direct proofs.   A belief in astronomical theories, for example, is justified for the vast majority, not because they can understand the arguments of Laplace or Newton, but because they may know how elaborately and minutely the conclusions of astronomers are daily verified.   The question is not whether we should take things on trust; we cannot help it; but upon what conditions our trust becomes rational.   Authority cannot simply justify itself; but it is reasonable to trust an authority which challenges constant examination of its credentials and thorough verification of its conclusions.

Mill's tendency is not, of course, to deny, but to treat this too slightly.   He is inclined to regard 'authority' as something logically opposed to reason, or, in other words, to accept the old Protestant version of the 'right of

[1] *Liberty*, p. 22.

private judgment'; or to speak as if every man had to build up his whole structure of belief from the very foundations. There is, he would admit, a structure of knowledge erected by the convergence of competent inquirers, and tested by free discussion and careful verification at every point of its growth. New theories give and receive strength from their 'solidarity' with established theories; and 'authority' is derived from the reciprocal considerations of various results of investigation. Mill is apt to speak as if each thinker and each opinion were isolated. The 'real advantage which truth has, consists,' he says, 'in this, that though a true opinion may be often suppressed, it will be generally rediscovered, and may be rediscovered at a favourable moment, when it will escape persecution and grow strong enough to defend itself.'[1] Persecution may succeed and often has succeeded. The doctrine that it cannot succeed is a 'pleasant falsehood' which has become commonplace by repetition. The statement is surely incomplete. Errors, like truths, may be 'rediscovered' or revived. There are 'idols of the tribe'—fallacies dependent upon permanent weaknesses of the intellect itself, which appear at all ages and may gain strength under favourable circumstances. Truth becomes definitively established when it is capable of fitting in with a nucleus of verified and undeniable truth. Mill seems to have in mind such a truth as the discovery of a particular fact. If the existence of America had been forgotten, it would be rediscovered by the next Columbus. If the dream of an Atlantis had once vanished, we need never dream it again. But the statement is inadequate when the truth

[1] *Liberty*, p. 17.

discovered is some new law which not merely adds to our knowledge, but helps to systematise and to affect our whole method of reasoning.

This position affects Mill's view of the efficacy of persecution. He argues, rather oddly, from the suppression of Lollards, Hussites, and Protestants. Mill certainly did not hold that the suppressed opinions were true; and he does not attempt to prove that they would not have died out of themselves. If Protestantism was suppressed in Spain, the reason may have been that it was so little congenial to the Spanish people, that the persecutions were on the side of the really dominant tendencies of the majority. That a tree without roots may fall the quicker when the wind blows needs no proof; but is not conclusive as to the effect upon a living tree. The true view, I venture to think, is different.[1] Opinions are not a set of separate dogmas which can be caught and stamped out by themselves. So long as thought is active it works by methods too subtle to be met by such coarse weapons. It allows the dogma to persist, but evacuates it of meaning. The whole structure becomes honeycombed and rotten, as when in France sceptics had learned to say everything without overtly saying anything. Persecution directed against this or that separate theory only embitters and poisons a process which is inevitable if people are to think at all; and persecution can only succeed, either where it is superfluous, or where it is so systematic and vigorous as to suppress all intellectual

---

[1] Note in *Liberty* Mill's theory that the impulse given at 'three periods'—the Reformation, the last half of the eighteenth century, and the 'Goethean and Fichtean' period in Germany—have made Europe what it is. Yet each 'period' is only the product of the preceding periods. Has Europe owed nothing to the seventeenth century?

activity. In either case the result is most lamentable, and the admission only strengthens the case against persecuting. Persecution can only succeed by paralysing the whole intellectual movement.

I think, then, that Mill, though essentially in the right, has an inadequate perception of one aspect of the question. Elsewhere [1] he complains that we have substituted an apotheosis of instinct for an apotheosis of reason, and so fallen into an infinitely more 'degrading idolatry.' Here, he seems inclined to attack all beliefs not due to the individual reason acting independently. He accentuates too decidedly the absolute value, not of freedom, but of its incidental result, contradiction. He seems to hold that opposition to an established opinion is good in itself. He would approve of circle-squarers and perpetual-motion makers because they oppose established scientific doctrines. He admires 'originality' even when it implies stupidity. Intelligence shows itself as much in recognising a valid proof as in rejecting a fallacy; and the progress of thought is as dependent upon co-operation and the acceptance of rational authority as upon rejecting errors and declining to submit to arbitrary authority. A man after all ought to realise the improbability of his being right against a consensus of great thinkers. Mill himself remarks, when criticising Bentham, that even originality is not 'a more necessary part of the philosophical character than a thoughtful regard for previous thinkers and for the collective mind of the human race.' [2]

[1] *Subjection of Women*, p. 6.
[2] *Dissertations*, p. 351. So in *Subjection of Women* (second edition, 1869, p. 129) he remarks that originality generally presupposes 'elaborate discipline,' and agrees with F. D. Maurice that the most original thinkers are those who know most thoroughly what has been done by their predecessors.

That, I take it, is perfectly true, but is apt to pass out of sight in his argument. The ideal state is not one of perpetual contradiction of first principles, but one in which contradiction has led to the establishment of a rational authority.

III. THE DECAY OF INDIVIDUALITY

I have insisted upon this chiefly because a similar error seems to intrude into the more difficult problems which follow. The real difficulty of toleration arises when we have to draw the line between speculation and action. Is it possible to discriminate absolutely? to give absolute freedom to thought and yet to maintain institutions which presuppose agreement upon at least some general principles? If men, as Mill asks, should be free to form and to utter opinions, should they not be free to act upon their opinions—to carry them out, so long at least as it is 'at their own risk and peril'—in their lives?[1] How does the principle present itself in this case? Mill has declined[2] to take advantage of any assumption of absolute right. He wishes to give a positive ground; to show that the liberty which he demands corresponds in point of fact to a necessary factor of human progress. His own doctrine is that the 'development of individuality is one of the leading essentials of wellbeing'; and he adopts as identical the doctrine of Wilhelm von Humboldt,[3] that the right end of man is 'the highest and most harmonious development

[1] *Liberty*, p. 32.   [2] *Ibid.* p. 7.
[3] Humboldt's *Sphere and Duties of Government* was translated by Joseph Coulthard in 1854. Though originally written in 1791 it did not appear in a complete form till published in the collected edition of his works by his brother

of his powers to a complete and consistent whole.'
Humboldt considers this end to be 'prescribed by the
eternal or immutable dictates of reason.' Mill would
prefer, we may suppose, to have regarded it as the
uniform teaching of experience. In either case, it is a
broad and elevated doctrine which few thinkers would
deny in general terms. It is, moreover, eminently
characteristic of Mill in his best mood. He never wrote
more forcibly than in his exposition of this doctrine.
He is now stimulated by the belief that he is preaching in
painfully deaf ears. In advocating freedom of thought
or denouncing despotism he was enforcing the doctrines
most certain of popular applause. But nobody cared
much for 'individuality' or objected to the subtler forms
of moral tyranny. The masses are satisfied with their
own ways ; and even 'moral and social reformers' want
as a rule to suppress all morality but their own. Mill is
uttering forebodings common to the most cultivated class.
The fear lest the growth of democracy should imply a
crushing out of all the higher culture has been uttered in
innumerable forms by some of our most eloquent writers
and keenest thinkers. The course of events since Mill's
death has certainly not weakened such fears. The
problem is still with us, and certainly not solved. Mill's
view is eminently characteristic of his whole doctrine.
How, starting as a democrat, he had been led to a strong

Alexander in 1852. The book shows the influence of Kant and Rousseau.
Humboldt was at the time a kind of philosophical antinomian objecting to all
external law as injurious to spontaneous spiritual development. Marriage
should be left to individual contract, because 'where law has imposed no fetters
morality most surely binds.' In Bentham's phrase 'external sanctions' weaken
the internal. The state should provide 'security,' and leave religion and
morality to themselves. Humboldt's philosophy is not Mill's, though on most
points the practical application coincides.

sense of the possible evils of democracy, I have already tried to show. I have now to inquire into the relation of this view to his general theory.

'Custom' in conduct corresponds to tradition in opinion. So far as you make it your guide, you need no faculty but that of 'ape-like imitation.'[1] You cultivate neither your reason nor your will when you let the world choose your plan of life. You become at best a useful automaton—not a valuable human being ; and of all the works of man, which should be perfected and beautified, the first in importance is surely man himself. Obedience to custom implies condemnation of 'strong impulses' as a snare and a peril. And yet strong impulses are but a name for energy, and may be the source of the 'most passionate love of virtue and the sternest self-control.' Individual energy was once perhaps too strong for the 'social principle.' Now 'society' has fairly got the better of individuality. We live in dread of the omnipresent censorship of our neighbours, desire only to do what others do, bow even our minds to the yoke, shun 'eccentricity' as a crime, and allow our human capacities to be starved and withered. Calvinism, he says, preaches explicitly that self-will is the 'one great offence of men.' Such a creed generates 'a pinched and hidebound type of human nature.' Men are cramped and dwarfed, as trees are clipped into pollards. It has lost sight of qualities belonging to a different type of excellence. 'It may be better to be a John Knox than an Alcibiades ; but it is better to be a Pericles than either.'

[1] It would be curious to compare Mill's theory with the very interesting books in which M. Tarde has shown the vast importance of 'imitation' in sociology.

Clipping and cramping means loss of 'individuality,' and 'individuality' may be identified with 'development.' This, he says, might close the argument; but he desires to give further reasons to prove to those who do not desire liberty for themselves that it should be conceded to others. His main point is the vast importance of genius, which can only exist in an atmosphere of freedom. The 'initiation of all wise and noble things comes, and must come, from individuals.' He is not such a 'hero-worshipper' as to desire a heroic tyrant, but he ardently desires a heroic leader; and where eccentricity is a reproach, genius will never be able to expand. Press all people into the same mould, condemn tastes which are not the tastes of the majority, and every deviation from the beaten path becomes impossible. Yet public opinion tends to become more stifling. 'Its ideal of character is to be without character.' 'Already energetic characters on any large scale are becoming merely traditional.' The greatness of England is now all collective. We are individually small, and capable of great things only by our 'habit of combining.' 'Men of another stamp made England what it has been, and men of another stamp will be needed to prevent its decline.' The evil is summed up in the 'despotism of custom.' China is a standing warning. It had the 'rare good fortune' of possessing a particularly good set of customs. But the customs have become stereotyped, the people all cast into the same mould, and China therefore is what England is tending to become.

Hitherto European progress has been due to the diversity of character and culture of the various nations. It is losing that advantage. Nations are assimilated; ranks

and professions are losing their distinctive characters ;
we all read the same books, listen (not quite all of us?)
to the same sermons, and have the same ends.   The
process is accelerated by all the past changes.   The
extension of education, the extension of means of communication, the extension of manufactures, and, above
all, the supremacy of public opinion, are all in its favour.
With 'so great a mass of influences hostile to individuality' it is 'not easy to see how it can stand its
ground.'

When Mill, as a young man, suddenly reflected that,
if all his principles were adopted, he should still be un-
happy, he did not doubt their truth.   But now he seems
to be emphatically asserting that the victory of all the
principles for which he and his friends had contended
would be itself disastrous.   'Progress' meant precisely
the set of changes which he now pronounces to lead to
stagnation.   Democracy in full activity will extinguish
the very principle of social vitality.   And yet, when at
a later period Mill became a politician, he gave his vote
as heartily as the blindest enthusiast for measures which
inaugurated a great step towards democracy.   His
sincerity in both cases is beyond a doubt, and gives
emphasis to the problem, how his practical political
doctrine can be reconciled with his doctrine of development.

The first question provoked by such assertions is the
question whether this is a correct, still more, whether
it is an exhaustive, diagnosis of the social disease?
May not Mill be emphasising one aspect of a complex
problem, and seeing the extinction of that 'individuality'
which is really an element of welfare, in the extinction

of such an 'individualism' as is incompatible with social improvement? His general aim is unimpeachable. The harmonious development of all our faculties represents a worthy ideal. The first or most essential of all human virtues, as Humboldt had said, is energy; for the greater the vitality, the more rich and various the type which can be evolved by cultivation. Yet it may be doubted whether the two aims suggested will always coincide. Energy certainly may go with narrowness, with implicit faith and limited purpose. The stream flows more forcibly in a defined channel. If Knox was inferior to Pericles or, say, the Jew to the Greek, the inferiority was not in energy or endurance. The efflorescence of Greek culture was short lived, it has been said, because there was too much Alcibiades and too little of Moses.[1] Culture tends to effeminacy unless guarded by 'renunciation' and regulated by concentration upon distinct purpose. As in the question of toleration, Mill overestimates the value of mere contradiction, so in questions of conduct he seems to overestimate mere eccentricity. Yet eccentricity is surely bad so far as it is energy wasted; expended upon trifles or devoted to purposes which a wider knowledge shows to be chimerical. To balance and correlate the various activities, to direct energy to the best purposes, and to minimise a needless antagonism is as essential to development as to give free play to the greatest variety of healthy activities.

Mill's doctrine may thus be taken as implying a historical generalisation. Historical generalisations are wrong as

[1] Mill, in his *Representative Government* (p. 17), argues that the Hebrew prophets discharged the functions of modern liberty of the press; and that the Jews were therefore the 'most progressive people of antiquity' after the Greeks. Still, their 'culture' was hardly so wide.

a rule; and one defect in this seems to be evident. Are energetic characters really rarer than of old? We may dismiss the illusion which personified whole processes of slow evolution in the name of some great prophet or legislator. It may still be true that the importance of the individual has really been greater in former epochs. The personal qualities of William the Conqueror or of Hildebrand may have affected history more than the personal qualities of Bismarck or of Pius IX. The action of great men, indeed, at all periods whatever, is essentially dependent upon their social environment; but personal idiosyncrasies may count for more in the total result at one period than another. The fortunes of a rude tribe may be, not only more obviously but more really, dependent upon the character of its chief than the fortunes of a civilised nation upon the character of its prime minister. And, therefore, it may be, the individual as a more important factor in the result, seems to represent greater individual energy. Yet the energy of the old feudal baron, who could ride roughshod over his weaker neighbours or coerce them with fire and sword, is not necessarily greater than the energy of the modern statesman, who has by gentler means slowly to weld together alliances of nations, to combine and inspirit parties, to direct public opinion, and to act therefore with constant reference to the national or cosmopolitan order.

Mill's[1] lamentation over the pettiness of modern English statesmen is familiar. What is really implied? England, as Mill the democrat would have said, was once a country of castes: the priest, the noble, the

[1] *Liberty*, p. 41.

merchant, the peasant, represented distinct types. Each class was bound by an unalterable custom and conforms to inherited traditions ; each, again, discharged some simple or general function now distributed among many minor classes. In later phrase, modern England has been made by processes of 'differentiation' and 'integration.' The old class lines have disappeared, the barriers of custom have been broken down, the old functions have been specialised, and instead of independent individual action, the whole system of life depends upon the elaborate and indefinitely ramified systems of co-operation, deliberate or unconscious. The obvious result is a growth of organic unity, accompanied by an equal development of diversity. Each unit can be assigned to a more special function, because other functions are assigned to co-operating units, and greater mutual dependence is implied in the greater variety of careers and activities. In his democratic phase, Mill blesses this process altogether ; he approves the destruction of privilege and caste distinctions ; he approves the 'division of labour,' the increased diversity of occupation, and the consequent growth of co-operation; he desires the fuller responsibility of the ruling class or the closer dependence of government upon the people. But in the later phase, when he emphasises the evils of democracy, does he not condemn what is a necessary implication in the very process which he approves? The division of labour, he now observes, narrows a man's life and interests; the necessity of co-operation narrows the sphere of 'individuality'; and the process which gives diversity to society as a whole implies certain uniformities in the social atoms. The less the variety in the units, the greater is the facility of arranging them in different configurations. The eccentric man is a cross-grained piece of timber which cannot be worked into the state. 'Individuality' is so far a hindrance to the power of entering into an indefinite number of combinations. And yet so far as 'individuality' diminishes, the responsibility of government means the subordination of rulers to the average commonplace stupidity. What, then, is the 'individuality' which may be called unconditionally good? How are we to define the danger so as to avoid condemning the conformity which is a necessary implication of progress? How are we to manage 'differentiation' at the expense of 'integration'; to exalt such 'individuality' as is incompatible with 'sociality'; and to regard 'eccentricity' and 'antagonism' and contradiction as valuable in themselves instead of accidental results in particular cases of originality which in some sense is priceless? Here, I think, is the real difficulty. Have we to deal with forces necessarily 'counteracting' each other, in Mill's phrase, or with forces which can be combined in a healthy organism? Mill undoubtedly supposes that some conciliation is possible. The historical view has shown the evil. We have now to consider the remedy to be applied to the various forms in which it affects economic, political, and ethical conditions. The general principle has been given. 'Self-protection' is the only justification for the interference of society with the individual. Although absolute liberty would mean anarchy, we may still demand a maximum of liberty, and suppress such a use of liberty by one man as would in fact restrain the liberty of another. Mill, like Bentham, holds to the purely empirical view. Interference is bad when the harm caused by the coercion is not counterbalanced by the good.

Bentham's doctrine is not only plausible but, within a certain sphere, points to one of the most obvious and essential conditions of useful legislation. The Utilitarians were always affected by the legal principles from which they started. In the case of criminal law, Mill's principle marks the obvious minimum of interference. A state must suppress violence. If I claim liberty to break your head, the policeman is bound to interfere. If you and I claim the same loaf, the state, even if it be a communistic state, must either settle which is to eat it, or leave us to fight for it. And, again, if the principle does not fix the maximum of legislation, it points to the most obvious limiting considerations. The state means the judge and the policeman, who cannot look into the heart, and must classify criminal action by its definable external characteristics. It can reach the murderer but not the malevolent man, who would murder if he could. It is therefore incompetent to punish wickedness except so far as wickedness is manifested by overt acts. If it went further it would be unjust, because acting blindly, as well as intolerably inquisitorial. Nor can it generally punish actions which produce no assignable injury to individuals. To punish a man for neglecting definite duties is necessary ; but to try to punish the idleness which may have caused the neglect would be monstrous. The state would have to be omniscient and omnipresent, and at most would favour hypocrisy instead of virtue. Briefly, the law is far too coarse an instrument for the function of enforcing morality in general. It must generally confine itself to cases where injury is inflicted

upon an assignable person and by conduct defined by
definite outward manifestations. This had been clearly
stated by Bentham. Mill, in his chapter on the 'limits
of the authority of society upon the individual,' insists
upon objections obvious in the legal case. Can we deduce from these legal limits a general principle defining
the relation between society and its units? I notice
first the difficulty already suggested by the *Political
Economy*.

IV. ECONOMIC APPLICATION

How, as Mill had asked, in speaking of the economic
aspects of government interference, are we to mark out
the space which is to be sacred from 'authoritative
intrusion'? So long as the social state is simple, the
application is easy. When one savage catches the deer,
and another the salmon, each may be forbidden to take
the other's game by force. Each man has a right to
the fruits of his own labour. In the actual state of
things there is not this charming simplicity. A man's
wealth is not a definable material object, but a bundle of
rights of the most complex kind ; and rights to various
parts of the whole national income, which are the product of whole systems of previous compacts. The
possessor has not even in the vaguest sense 'created'
his wealth ; he has more or less contributed the labour
of brains and hands to the adaptation of things to use,
or enjoys his rights in virtue of an indefinite number of
transactions, bargains made by himself, or bequests trans-
ferring the rights to new generations. To protect his
property is to protect a multifarious system of rights
accruing in all manner of ways, and to sanction the

voluntary contracts in virtue of which the whole elaborate network of rights corresponds to the complex social
order.   The tacit assumption of the economists was
that this order was in some sense 'natural' and law
an artificial or extra-natural compulsion.   Can the line
be drawn?   The legal regulation has been an essential
though a subordinate part of the whole process.   Law,
at an early stage, is an undistinguishable part of customs,
which has become differentiated from mere custom as
settled governments have been evolved and certain
definite functions assigned to the sovereign power.
We cannot say that one set of institutions is due to
law and another to customs or to voluntary contracts.
The laws which regulate property in land or inheritance
or any form of association have affected every stage of
the process and have not affected it as conditions imposed from without, but as a part of the whole elaboration.   The principle that 'self-protection' is the only
justification of interference then becomes hard of application.   I am to do what I like with my own.   That
may be granted, for 'my own' is that with which I
may do what I like.   But if I am allowed in virtue of
this doctrine to make any contracts or to dispose of my
property in any way that I please, it follows that the
same sanctity is transferred to the whole system which
has grown up by voluntary action at every point, and
which is therefore regarded as the 'natural' or spontaneous order.   Now the actual course of events, as
Mill maintains, produced a society with vast inequalities
of wealth—a society which, as he declares, does not even
show an approximation to justice, or in which a man's
fortunes are determined not by his merits but by accident.

On this interpretation of the principle of non-interference, it follows that in the name of legal 'liberty' you approve a process destructive of 'liberty' in fact. Every man is allowed no doubt by the laws to act as circumstances admit ; but the circumstances may permit some people to enjoy every conceivable pleasure and to develop every faculty, while they condemn others to find their only pleasure in gin, and to have such development as can be acquired in 'London slums.' A famous judge pointed out ironically that the laws of England were the same for the rich and the poor ; that is, the same price was charged for justice whether the applicants could afford it or not. Is it not a mockery to tell a man that he is free to do as he pleases, if it only means that he may choose between starvation and the poorhouse? Mill had himself been inclined to remedy the evils by invoking an omnipotent legislature to undertake very drastic measures of reform. Equal laws will produce equal results when, in point of fact, they apply to men under equal conditions. If a society consists of mutually independent and self-supporting individuals, the principle of non-interference may work smoothly. Each man has actually his own secret sphere, and the law only affects the exchange of superfluous advantages among independent units. But that is to say that to make your rule work, you must prevent all that process of development which is implied in civilisation. Society must be forced to be 'individualistic' in order that the formula may be applicable. Self-protection means the protection of existing rights. If they are satisfactory, the result of protecting them will be satisfactory. But if the actual order, however produced, is essentially unjust, the test becomes illusory. Yet, if the laws are to interfere to prevent the growth of inequality, what becomes of the sacred sphere of individuality?

Here we have the often-noted conflict between equality and liberty. Leave men free, and inequalities must arise. Enforce equality and individuality is cramped or suppressed. And yet inequality certainly means a pressure upon the weaker which may lead to virtual slavery. We must admit that neither liberty nor equality can be laid down as absolute principles. The attempt to treat any formula in this fashion leads to the perplexities exemplified in Mill's treatment of the 'liberty' problem. His doctrines cannot be made to fit accurately the complexities of the social order. 'Equality' and 'liberty' define essential 'moments' in the argument, though neither can be made to support an absolute conclusion.

The difficulty was indicated in Bentham's treatment of 'security' and 'equality.' Both, he said, were desirable, but when there was a conflict 'equality' must give way to 'security.' Here we come to another closely allied doctrine. 'Security' implies 'responsibility.' A man must be secure that he may be industrious. He will not labour unless he is sure to enjoy the fruit of his labour. This gives the Malthusian *vis medicatrix*. But, stated absolutely, it implies pure self-interest. Robinson Crusoe was responsible in the sense that if he did not work he would starve. And, if we could, in fact, mark off each man's separate sphere, or regard society as a collection of Robinson Crusoes, the principle might be applied. Each man should have a right to what he has himself 'created.' But when a man 'creates' nothing; when his 'environment' is not a desert island but an organised society, the principle must be differently stated. 'Responsibility,' indeed, always implies liberty—the existence of a sphere within which a man's fortunes depend upon his personal character, and his character should determine his fortune. But, as Mill can most clearly recognise, social responsibility means something more. One most 'certain incident' of social progress is the growth of co-operation, and that involves, as he says, the 'subordination of individual caprice' to a 'preconceived determination' and the performance of parts allotted in a 'combined undertaking.'[1] The individual, then, is part of an organisation, in which every individual should play his part. The over-centralisation which would crush him into an automaton is not more fatal than the individual independence which would be incompatible with organisation. The desirable 're-sponsibility' is not that of a Robinson Crusoe but that of the soldier in an army. It should be enforced by other motives than mere self-interest, for it affects the interests of the whole body corporate. Now Mill, believing even to excess in the power of education, included in education the whole discipline of life due to the relations of the individual to his social environment; and it is his essential principle that this force should be directed to enforcing a sense of 'responsibility' in the widest acceptation of the word.

V. POLITICAL APPLICATION

A similar doctrine is implied in his political writings, of which the *Representative Government* is the most explicit. The book is hardly on a level with his best work. Treatises of 'political philosophy' are generally

---

[1] *Political Economy*, bk. iv. ch. i. § 2.

disappointing. The difficulty lies, I suppose, in combining the practical with the general point of view. In
some treatises, the 'philosophy' is made up of such
scraps about the social contract or mixture of the three
forms of government as excited Bentham's contempt in
Blackstone's treatise. They are a mere juggle of abstractions fit only for schoolboys. Others, like James Mill's,
are really party pamphlets, masquerading as philosophy,
and importing obvious principles into the likeness of
geometrical axioms. A good deal of wisdom no doubt
lurks in the speeches of statesmen ; but it is not often
easy to extricate it from the mass of personal and
practical remarks. Mill's treatise might suggest some
such criticism ; and yet it is interesting as an indication
of his leading principles. Some passages show how long
experience in a public office affects a philosophic thinker.
Mill's exposition, for example, of the defects of the
House of Commons in administrative legislation,[1] his
discussion of the fact (as he takes it to be) that governments remarkable for sustained vigour and ability have
generally been aristocratic,[2] and his panegyric upon the
East India Company,[3] record the genuine impressions of
his long administrative career, and are refreshing in the
midst of more abstract discussions. I have, however,
only to notice a general principle which runs through
the book.

Mill starts by emphasising the distinction applied in
the *Political Economy* between the natural and the
artificial. Political institutions are the work of men and
created by the will. The doctrine that governments

[1] See chap. v.   [2] *Representative Government*, p. 45.
[3] *Ibid.* p. 104.

'are not made, but grow,' would lead to 'political fatalism' if it were regarded as true exclusively of the other. In fact, we might reply, there is no real opposition at all. 'Making' is but one kind of 'growing.' Growing by conscious forethought is still growing, and the antithesis put absolutely is deceptive. Mill is striving to enlarge the sphere of voluntary action. He wishes to prove that he can take the ground generally supposed to imply the doctrine of 'freewill.' Institutions, he fully admits, presuppose certain qualities in the people; but, given those qualities, they are 'a matter of choice.'[1] In politics, as in machinery, we are turning existing powers to account; but we do not say that, because rivers will not run uphill, 'water-mills are not made but grow.' The political theorist can invent constitutions as the engineer can invent machinery, which will materially alter the results; and to inquire which is the best form of government 'in the abstract' is 'not a chimerical but a highly practical employment of the scientific intellect.' The illustration is difficult to apply if the 'river' means the whole society, and the 'water-mill' is itself, therefore, one part of the 'river.' The legislator is not an external force but an integral part of internal forces.

In the next place, Mill rejects a distinction made by Comte[2] between order and progress. Comte had made a distinction between 'statics' and 'dynamics' in sociology, which are to each other like anatomy and physiology. The conditions of existence, and the conditions of continuous movement of a society correspond to

---

[1] *Representative Government*, p. 5.

[2] Coleridge, he observes, had also distinguished 'permanence' and 'progression.'—*Representative Government*, p. 8.

'order and progress.'[1] Mill replies that 'progress' includes 'order,' and that the two conditions cannot give independent criteria of the merits of the institutions. Comte, in any case, regarding sociology as a science, considers the dependence of political institutions upon social structure to be much closer than Mill would admit. The power of the legislator to alter society is strictly subordinate and dependent throughout upon its relation to the existing organism. In his study of Comte,[2] Mill declares emphatically that Comte's work has made it necessary for all later thinkers to start from a 'connected view of the great facts of history.' He speaks with enthusiasm of Comte's great survey of history, and fully accepts the principle. Yet, in fact, he scarcely applies the method in his political system, and accepts a doctrine really inconsistent with it. His anxiety to give a far wider sphere to the possibilities of modifying, leads him to regard institutions as the ultimate causes of change, instead of factors themselves strictly dependent upon deeper causes. Hence he substitutes a different distinction. We are to judge of institutions by their efficiency as educating agencies, on the one hand, and as the means of carrying on 'public business' on the other. Institutions should do their work well, and turn the workers into good citizens.[3]

The educative influence of government is thus his characteristic point. The 'ideally best form of government,' as Mill of course admits, is not one applicable 'at all stages of civilisation.'[4] We have to suppose certain

---

[1] See *Philosophie Positive*, iv. 318, etc.

[2] *Auguste Comte and Positivism* (reprinted from the *Westminster Review*, 1865), p. 36.

[3] *Representative Government*, p. 14.   [4] *Ibid.* p. 22.

conditions, and he takes pain to show in what cases his ideal would be inapplicable.[1] But, given the stage reached in modern times (as he practically assumes), there is 'no difficulty in showing' the ideal form to be the representative system ; that in which 'sovereignty is vested in the entire aggregate of the community,' every citizen having a voice and taking at least an occasional part in discharging the functions of government.[2] This applies the doctrine already expounded in the *Liberty*. Citizens should be 'self-protecting and self-protective';[3] the 'active,' not the 'passive' type of character should be encouraged. The striving, go-ahead character of Anglo-Saxons is only objectionable so far as it is directed to petty ends ; the Englishman says naturally, 'What a shame!' when the Frenchman says, '*Il faut de la patience!*' and the institutions which encourage this energetic character by giving a vote to all, by permitting freedom of speech, and by permitting all men to discharge small duties (to act on juries for example) are the best. I will only note that this tends to beg the important question, Are the institutions really the cause or the effect? Has the energy of the English race made their institutions free? or have the free institutions made them energetic? or are the institutions and the character collateral effects of a great variety of causes? When so much stress is laid upon the educational effect — of serving upon a jury, for instance—we are impelled to ask what is the ultimate cause. Are people so much morally improved by serving on juries? If the institution like the 'water-mill'

---

[1] *Representative Government*, ch. iv.　　[2] *Ibid.* p. 21.
[3] *Ibid.* p. 22.

only directs certain instincts already existing, we must not speak as if the mill made the water-power ; and Mill's arguments suggest a liability to this fallacy. It becomes important at the next stage.

The ideal form of government has its infirmities, as Mill insists. Two are conspicuous : the difficulty of inducing a democracy to intrust work which requires skill to those who possess skill ;[1] and the old difficulty —the 'tyranny of the majority.' Mill's contention that the 'Demos' may be stupid, mistake its own interests, and impress its mistaken views upon the legislation, needs no exposition. We are thus brought to the question how the ideal government is to be so constituted that the interests of a section—even if it be the majority —may not be so powerful as to overwhelm the other sections even when backed by 'truth and justice.'[2] Danger of popular stupidity and danger of class legislation indicate two great evils to be abated as far as possible by 'human contrivance.'[3] A sufficient 'contrivance' was in fact revealed at the right moment. A discovery of surpassing value had been announced by one of his friends. Hare's scheme of representation, says Mill with characteristic enthusiasm, has the 'almost unparalleled merit' of securing its special aim in almost 'ideal perfection,' while incidentally attaining others of almost equal importance. He places it among the very greatest 'improvements yet made in the theory and practice of government.'[4] It would, for example, be almost a 'specific' against the tendency of republics to ostracise their ablest men.[5] And it would

---

[1] *Representative Government*, p. 47.   [2] *Ibid.* p. 52.   [3] *Ibid.* p. 53.
[4] *Ibid.* p. 57.   [5] *Ibid.* p. 59.

be the appropriate organ of the great function of 'antagonism'[1] which now takes the place of contradiction in intellectual development. There will always be some body to oppose the supreme power, and thus to prevent the stagnation, followed by decay, which has always resulted from a complete victory.

Is not the 'water-mill' here expected to work the river? The faith in a bit of mechanism of 'human contrivance' becomes sublime. Hare's scheme may have great conveniences under many circumstances. But that Hare's scheme or any scheme should regenerate politics seems to be a visionary belief, unworthy of Mill's higher moods. He seems to fall into the error too common among legislative theorists, of assuming that an institution will be worked for the ends of the contriver, instead of asking to what ends it may be distorted by the ingenuity of all who can turn it to account for their own purposes. There is a more vital difficulty. If Hare's scheme worked as Mill expected it to work, one result would be necessarily implied. The House of Commons would reflect accurately all the opinions of the country. Whatever opinion had a majority in the country would have a majority in the House. Labourers, as he suggests when showing the dangers of democracy, may be in favour of protection, or of fixing the rate of wages. Now in this scheme the majority in the country may enforce whatever laws approve themselves to the ignorant. I do not say that this would actually be the result; for I think that, in point of fact, the change of mere machinery would be of comparatively little importance. The power of

[1] *Representative Government*, p. 60.

the rich and the educated does not really depend upon the system of voting, or the ostensible theory of the constitution, but upon the countless ways in which wealth, education, and the whole social system affect the working of institutions. Mill can fully admit the fact at times. But here he is taking for granted that the effect of the scheme will be to secure a perfectly correct miniature of the opinions of all separate persons. The wise minority will therefore be a minority in the land. It will be able to make speeches. But the speeches, however able, are but an insignificant trickle in the great current of talk which forms what is called 'public opinion.' The necessary result upon his showing would be, that legislation would follow the opinions of the majority, or, in other words, facilitate the 'tyranny of the majority.'

This suggests one vital point. Mill, as I have said, has endeavoured to enlarge as much as possible the sphere of operation of the freewill—of the power of individuals or of deliberate conscious legislation. The result is to exaggerate the influence of institutions and to neglect the forces, intellectual and moral, which must always lie behind institutions. We can admit to the full the importance of the educational influence of political institutions, and the surpassing value of energy, self-reliance, and individual responsibility. The sentiment is altogether noble, and Mill expresses it with admirable vigour. But the more decidedly we hold his view of the disease, the more utterly inadequate and inappropriate appears his remedy. The tendency to levelling and vulgarising, so far as it exists, can certainly not be cured by ingenious arrangements of one part of the political machinery. I take this to mark Mill's weakest side. The truth was divined by the instinct of his democratic allies. So long as he voted for extending the suffrage, they could leave him to save his conscience by amusing himself with these harmless fancies.

VI. WOMEN'S RIGHTS

Mill's *Subjection of Women* brings out more clearly some of the fundamental Utilitarian tenets. None of his writings is more emphatically marked by generosity and love of justice. A certain shrillness of tone marks the recluse too little able to appreciate the animal nature of mankind. Yet in any case, he made a most effective protest against the prejudices which stunted the development and limited the careers of women. Mill declares at starting, that till recently the 'law of force' has been 'the avowed rule of general conduct.' Only of late has there been even a pretence of regulating 'the affairs of society in general according to any moral law.'[1] That moral considerations have been too little regarded as between different societies or different classes is painfully obvious. But 'force' in any intelligible sense is itself only made applicable by the social instincts, which bind men together. No society could ever be welded into a whole by 'force' alone. This is the Utilitarian fallacy of explaining law by 'sanctions,' and leaving the 'sanctions' to explain themselves. But the argument encourages Mill to treat of all inequality as unjust because imposed by force. The 'only school of genuine moral senti-

[1] *Subjection of Women* (1869), p. 16.

ment,' he says, ' is society between equals.' Let us
rather say that inequalities are unjust which rest upon
force alone. Every school of morality or of thought
implies subordination, but a subordination desirable only
when based upon real superiority. The question then
becomes whether the existing relations of the sexes correspond to some essential difference or are created by sheer
force.

Here we have assumptions characteristic of Mill's
whole logical method ; and, especially, the curious oscil-
lation between absolute laws and indefinite modifiability.
His doctrine of ' natural kinds ' supposed that two races
were either divided by an impassable gulf, or were divided
only by accidental or superficial differences. He protests
against the explanation of national differences by race characteristics. To say that the Irish are naturally lazy, or
the Negroes naturally stupid, is to make a short apology
for oppression and for slavery. Undoubtedly it is wrong,
as it is contrary to all empirical reasoning, to assume a
fundamental difference ; and morally wrong to found
upon the assumption an apology for maintaining caste and
privilege. But neither is it legitimate to assume that the
differences are negligible. The ' accident of colour ' has
been made a pretext for an abominable institution. But
we have no right to the *a priori* assumption that colour
is a mere accident. It may upon Mill's own method be
an indication of radical and far-reaching differences. How
far the Negro differs from the white man, whether he is
intellectually equal or on a wholly lower plane, is a question of fact to be decided by experience. Mill's refusal
to accept one doctrine passes imperceptibly into an equally
unfounded acceptance of its contradictory. The process

is shown by the doctrine to which, as we have seen, he attached so much importance, that political science must be deductive, because the effect of the conjoined causes is the sum of the effects of the separate causes. When two men act together, the effect may be inferred from putting together the motives of each. 'All phenomena of society,' he infers, 'are phenomena of human nature generated by the action of outward circumstances upon masses of human beings.'[1] We can therefore deduce scientific laws in sociology as in astronomy. This tacitly assumes that man, like molecule, represents a constant unit, and thus introduces the *de facto* equality of human beings, from which it is an inevitable step to the equality of rights. The sound doctrine that we can only learn by experience what are the differences between men becomes the doctrine that all differences are superficial, and therefore the man always the same. The doctrine becomes audacious when 'man' is taken to include 'woman.' He speaks of the 'accident of sex' and the 'accident of colour' as equally unjust grounds for political distinctions.[2] The difference between men and women, Whites and Negroes, is 'accidental,' that is, apparently removable by some change of 'outward circumstances.'

Mill, indeed, does not admit that he is begging the question. He guards himself carefully against begging the question either way,[3] though he thinks apparently that the burthen of proof is upon those who assert a natural difference. Accordingly he urges that the so-

[1] *Logic*, p. 572 (bk. vi. ch. vi. § 2).
[2] *Representative Government*, p. 76. Cf. *Political Economy*, p. 493 (bk. iv. ch. vii. § 2).
[3] *Subjection of Women*, pp. 41, 104.

called 'nature of women' is 'an eminently artificial thing'; a result of 'hothouse cultivation' carried on for the benefit of their masters.[1] He afterwards[2] endeavours to show that even the 'least contestable differences' between the sexes are such as may 'very well have been produced merely by circumstances without any differences of natural capacity.' What, one asks, can the 'circumstances' mean? Pyschology, as he truly says, can tell us little; but physiology certainly seems to suggest a difference implied in the whole organisation and affecting every mental and physical characteristic. It is not, apparently, a case of two otherwise equal beings upon which different qualities have been superimposed, but of a radical distinction, totally inconsistent with any presumption of equality.[3] When we are told that the legal inequality is an 'isolated fact'—a 'solitary breach of what has become a fundamental law of human institutions'[4]—the reply is obvious. The distinction of the sexes is surely an 'isolated fact,' so radical or 'natural' that it is no wonder that it should have unique recognition in all human institutions. Mill has, indeed, a further answer. If nature disqualifies women for certain functions, why disqualify them by law? Leave everything to free competition, and each man or woman will go where he or she is most fitted. Abolish, briefly, all

---

[1] *Subjection of Women*, pp. 48-9.

[2] *Ibid.* p. 105. In one of the letters to Carlyle Mill asks whether the highest masculine, are not identical with the highest feminine, qualities. I should like to see Carlyle's answer.

[3] This argument is put by Comte in his correspondence with Mill. So far, Comte seems to have the best of it; and Mill's inability to appreciate the doctrine is characteristic. At this time Mill seems to have been undecided upon the question of divorce. See the discussion in the *Letters*, pp. 208-73.

[4] *Subjection of Women*, p. 36.

political and social distinctions, and things will right themselves. If 'inequality' is due to 'force,' and the difference between men and women be 'artificial,' the argument is plausible. But if the difference be, as surely it is, 'natural,' and 'force' in the sense of mere muscular strength, only one factor in the growth of institutions, the removal of inequalities may imply neglect of essential facts. He is attacking the most fundamental condition of the existing social order. The really vital point is the bearing of Mill's argument upon marriage and the family. He thinks[1] that the full question of divorce is 'foreign to his purpose'; and, in fact, seems to be a little shy of what is really the critical point. He holds, indeed, that the family is a 'school of despotism,'[2] or would be so, if men were not generally better than their laws. Admitting that the law retains traces of the barbarism which regarded wives as slaves, the question remains whether the institution itself is to be condemned as dependent upon 'force.' Would not the 'equality' between persons naturally unequal lead to greater instead of less despotism? If, as a matter of fact, women are weaker than men, might not liberty mean more power to the strongest? Permission to the husband to desert the wife at will might be to make her more dependent in fact though freer in law. Whatever the origin of the institution of marriage, it may now involve, not the bondage but an essential protection of the weakest party. This is the side of the argument to which Mill turns a deaf ear. We are to neglect the most conspicuous of facts because it may be 'artificial' or due to 'circum-

---

[1] *Subjection of Women*, p. 59. Cf. *Liberty*, p. 61.
[2] *Subjection of Women*, p. 81.

stances,' and assume that free competition will be an
infallible substitute for a system which affects the most
vital part of the whole social organism. To assume existing differences to be incapable of modification is doubtless wrong ; but to treat them at once as non-existent is
at least audacious. Finally, the old difficulty recurs in a
startling shape. If differences are to disappear and the
characteristics of men and women to become indistinguishable, should we not be encouraging a 'levelling'
more thoroughgoing than any which can result from
political democracy?

VII. THE SELF-PROTECTION PRINCIPLE

These special applications raise the question : What
is the interpretation of his general principle? 'Self-
protection' is the only justification for social interference. Where a man's conduct affects himself alone
society should not 'interfere'[1] by legislation. Does
this imply that we must not interfere by the pressure
of public opinion? We may, as Mill replies, approve
or disapprove, but so long as a man does not in-
fringe our rights, we must leave him to the 'natural
and, as it were, the spontaneous consequences of
his faults.' We may dislike and even abhor anti-social
' dispositions '—cruelty and treachery—but self-regarding
faults and the corresponding dispositions are not subjects
of ' moral reprobation.' A man is not accountable to his
fellow creatures for prudence or 'self-respect.'[2] Mill
anticipates the obvious objection. No conduct is simply
' self-regarding.' 'No one is an entirely isolated being';

[1] *Liberty*, p. 44.   [2] *Ibid.* p. 46.

and injuries to myself disqualify me for service to others. ' Self-regarding ' vices, as his opponent is supposed to urge, are also socially mischievous ; and we must surely be entitled to assume that the experience of the race has established some moral rules sufficiently to act upon them, however desirous we may be to allow of ' new and original experiments in living.' [1] Mill's reply is that we should punish not the fault itself but the injuries to others which result. We hang George Barnwell for murdering his uncle, whether he did it to get money for his mistress or to set up in business. We should not punish him, it is implied, for keeping a mistress ; but we should punish the murder, whatever the motive. The criminal lawyer, no doubt, treats Barnwell upon this principle. But can it be morally applicable ? Mill admits fully that self-regarding qualities may be rightfully praised and blamed. We may think a man a fool, a lazy, useless, sensual wretch : we may, and are even bound to, tell him so frankly, avoid his society, and warn others to avoid him. My judgment of a man is not a judgment of his separate qualities but of the whole human being. I disapprove of George Barnwell himself, not simply his greediness or his vicious propensities. I think a man bad in different degrees if he is ready to murder his uncle, whether from lust or greed or even with a view to a charitable use of the plunder. The hateful thing is the character itself which, under certain conditions, leads to murder. As including prudence, it may be simply neutral or respectable ; as implying vice, disgusting ; and as implying cruelty, hateful. Still, I do not condemn the abstract qualities—interest in oneself,

[1] *Liberty*, p. 47.

or sexual passion or even antipathy—each of which may
be desirable in the right place—but the way in which they
are combined in the concrete Barnwell.   No quality,
therefore, can be taken as simply self-regarding, for it
is precisely the whole character which is the object of my
moral judgment of the individual.   I have spoken of
the inadequate recognition of this truth by Bentham and
James Mill.   It makes J. S. Mill's criterion inapplicable
to the question of moral interference.   If, as he argues,
we are to impress our moral standard upon others, we
cannot make the distinction ; for our standard implies
essentially an estimate of the balance of all the man's
qualities, those which primarily affect himself as much as
those which primarily affect others.   Here is the vital distinction between the legal and the moral question, and
the characteristic defect of the external view of morality.
Keeping, however, to the purely legal question, where
the criterion is comparatively plain, we have other
difficulties.   We are only to punish Barnwell as an
actual, not as a potential, murderer.   We should let a
man try any 'experiment in living' so long as its failure
will affect himself only, or, rather, himself primarily, for
no action is really 'isolated.'   We are, says Mill, to
put up with 'contingent' or 'constructive' injury for
the sake of 'the greater good of human freedom.'[1]
'Society,' he urges, cannot complain of errors for which
it is responsible.   It has 'absolute power' over all its
members in their infancy, and could always make the
next generation a little better than the last.   Why, then,
interfere by the coarse methods of punishment to suppress what is not directly injurious to itself?   The

[1] *Liberty*, p. 48.

strongest, however, of all reasons against interference, according to him, is that it generally interferes wrongly and in the wrong place. In proof of this he refers to various cases of religious persecution : to Puritanical laws against harmless recreation : to Socialist laws against the freedom to labour : to laws against intemperance and on behalf of Sunday observance : and, generally, to laws embodying the 'tyranny of the majority.' We may admit the badness of such legislation ; but what is the criterion by which we are to decide its badness or goodness ? Is it that in such cases the legislator is usurping the province of the moralist ? that he is trying to suppress symptoms when the causes are beyond his power, and enforcing not virtue but hypocrisy ? Or is it that he really ought to be indifferent in regard to the moral rules which are primarily self-regarding—to leave prudence, for example, to take care of itself or to be impressed by purely natural penalties ; and to be indifferent to vice, drunkenness, or sexual irregularities, except by suppressing the crimes which incidentally result ? Mill endeavours to adhere to his criterion, but has some difficulty in reconciling it to his practical conclusions.

Mill holds 'society' to be omnipotent over the young. It has no right to complain of the characters which it has itself concurred in producing. If this be so, can it be indifferent to morality ? Indeed, Mill distinguishes himself from others of his school precisely by emphasising the educational efficiency of the state. Institutions, according to him, are the tools by which the human will—the will of the sovereign— moulds the character of the race. Mill's whole aim in economic questions is to encourage prudence, self-reliance, and energy. He wishes the state to interfere to strengthen and enlighten ; and to promote an equality of property which will raise the standard of life and discourage wasteful luxury. What is this but to stimulate certain moral creeds and to discourage certain ' experiments in living '? How can so powerful an agency affect character without affecting morals—self-regarding or extra-regarding ? The difficulty comes out curiously in his last chapter. He has recourse to a dexterous casuistry to justify measures which have an obvious moral significance. Are we to legislate with a view to diminishing drunkenness? No : but we may put drunkards under special restrictions when they have once been led to violence. We should not tax stimulants simply in order to suppress drunkenness ; but, as we have to tax in any case, we may so arrange taxation as to discourage the consumption of injurious commodities. May we suppress gambling or fornication? No : but we may perhaps see our way to suppressing public gambling-houses or brothels, because we may forbid solicitations to that which we think evil, though we are not so clear of the evil as to suppress the conduct itself. We may enforce universal education, though he makes the condition that the state is only to pay for the children of the poor, not to provide the schools. And, once more, we are not forbidden by his principle to legislate against imprudent marriages ; for the marriage clearly affects the offspring, and, moreover, affects all labourers in an over-populated country. Yet, what interference with private conduct could be more stringent or more directly affect morality ?

A principle requiring such delicate handling is not well

suited to guide practical legislation. This timid admission
of moral considerations by a back-door is the more
curious because Mill not only wishes to have a moral
influence, but has the special merit, in economical and
in purely political questions, of steadily and constantly
insisting upon their moral aspect. He holds, and is
justified in holding, that the ultimate end of the state
should be to encourage energy, culture, and a strong
sense of responsibility. It is true that, though he
exaggerates the influence of institutions, he insists chiefly
upon the negative side, upon that kind of 'education'
which consists in leaving a man to teach himself. Yet
his political theory implies a wider educational influence.
Every citizen is to have a share both in the legislative
and administrative functions of the government. Such
an education must have a strong influence upon the
moral characteristics. It may promote or discourage
one morality or another, but it cannot be indifferent.
And this impresses itself upon Mill himself. The
principles of 'contradiction' in speculation and of
'antagonism' in politics; the doctrines that each man
is to form his own opinions and regulate his own life,
imply a society of approximately equal and, as far as
possible, independent units. This, if it means 'liberty,'
also means a most effective 'educational' process.
One lesson taught may be that 'any one man is as
good as any other.' Mill sees this clearly, and declares
that this 'false creed' is held in America and 'nearly
connected' with some American defects.[1] He persuades
himself that it may be remedied by Hare's scheme, and
by devices for giving more votes to educated persons.

[1] *Representative Government*, p. 74.

One can only reply, *sancta simplicitas!* In fact, the 'educational' influence which implies levelling and equalising is not less effective than that which maintains ranks or a traditional order. It only acts in a different direction. Here, once more, Mill's argument seems to recoil upon his own position. When, in the *Liberty*, he sums up the influences hostile to individuality, including all the social and intellectual movements of the day, he is describing the forces which will drive his political machinery. The political changes which are to break up the old structure, to make society an aggregate of units approximately equal in wealth and power, will inevitably facilitate the deeper and wider influences of the social changes. If, in fact, 'individuality' in a good sense is being crushed by the whole democratic movement—where democracy means the whole social change—it will certainly not be protected by the political changes to be made in the name of liberty. Each man is to have his own little sphere; but each man will be so infinitesimal a power that he will be more than ever moulded by the average opinions. In the *Liberty*[1] Mill puts his whole hope in the possibility that the 'intelligent part of the public' may be led to feel the force of his argument. To believe that a tendency fostered by every social change can be checked by the judicious reasoning of Utilitarian theorists, implies a touching faith in the power of philosophy.

Mill's doctrines, I believe, aim at most important truths. 'Energy' is, let us agree, a cardinal virtue and essential condition of progress. It requires, undoubtedly, a sphere of individual freedom. Without freedom, a man is a tool

[1] *Liberty*, p. 41.

—transmitting force mechanically, not himself co-operating intelligently or originating spontaneously. Every citizen should be encouraged to be an active as well as a passive instrument. Freedom of opinion is absolutely essential to progress, social as well as intellectual, and therefore thought should be able to play freely upon the sway of irrational custom. The tyranny of the commonplace, of a mental atmosphere which stifles genius and originality, is a danger to social welfare. That Mill held such convictions strongly was the source of his power. That he held to them, even when they condemned some party dogma, was honourable to his sincerity. That he failed to make them into a satisfactory or consistent whole was due to preconceptions imbibed from his teachers. Perhaps it is truer to say that he could not accurately formulate his beliefs in the old dialect than that his beliefs were intrinsically erroneous.

Upon his terms a clear demarcation of the sphere of free action is impossible. Mill, as an 'individualist,' took society to be an 'aggregate' instead of an 'organism.' To Mill such phrases as 'organic' savoured of 'mysticism'; they treated a class name as meaning something more than the individuals, and therefore meant mere abstractions parading as realities,[1] and encouraged the fallacies current among Intuitionists and Transcendentalists. And yet they point at truths which are

---

[1] See in *Representative Government*, p. 62, his argument against the objection to Hare's scheme that it would destroy the local character of representation. The objectors think, he says, that 'a nation does not consist of persons but of artificial units, the creation of geography and statistics'; that 'Liverpool and Exeter are the proper objects of a legislator's care in contradistinction to the population of those places.' This, he thinks, is 'a curious specimen of delusion produced by words.' The local interests and affections which bind neighbours and townsmen together may thus be simply set aside.

anything but mystical. It is a plain fact that society is a complex structure upon which every man is dependent in his whole life ; and that he is a product, moulded through and through by instincts inherited or derived from his social position. Conversely it is true that the society is throughout dependent upon the character or the convictions and instincts of its constituent members. To overlook the reciprocal action and reaction, and the structure which corresponds to them, is necessarily to make arbitrary and inaccurate assumptions and to regard factors in a single process as independent entities. The tendency of the Utilitarian was to regard society as a number of independent beings, simply bound together by the legal or quasi-legal sanctions. Morality itself was treated as a case of external 'law.' The individual, again, was a bundle of ideas, bound together by 'associations which could be indefinitely modified.' In both cases, the unity was imposed by a force in some sense 'external,' and therefore the whole social structure of individual character became in some sense 'artificial.' It is the acceptance of such assumptions which hinders Mill in his attempt to mark out the individual sphere.

We have seen the difficulties. In morality, it is impossible to divide the 'extra-regarding' from the 'self-regarding' qualities, because morality is a function of the whole character considered as a unit. Mill, therefore, has to concede a considerable sphere to moral pressure. The fact that in positive law it is not only possible but necessary to distinguish 'self-regarding' actions from 'extra-regarding' actions marks the sphere within which legislation can work efficiently. But the same fact proves also that the direct legal coercion is only a subordinate element in the whole social process. Though it is only called into play to suppress certain overt actions, it indirectly affects the whole character : it may help to stimulate all the qualities, 'self-regarding' or otherwise, which form a good citizen ; and to argue that it should be indifferent to these broader results is to omit a reference to the wider 'utility' which is identical with morality. Mill is thus driven to awkward casuistry by trying to exclude the moral considerations where they are obviously essential, or to admit them under some ingenious pretext. In economic problems the difficulty is more conspicuous ; for we have there to do with the whole industrial structure, which is affected throughout by institutions created or confirmed by law. It is, again, impossible to distinguish the spheres of the 'natural' and the 'artificial'—or of individual and state action. The industrial structure is a product of both. Consider all state action to be bad because 'artificial,' and you are led to such an isolation of the 'individual' as reduces all responsibility to a name for selfishness. You are to teach men to be prudent simply by leaving the imprudent to starvation. Mill, revolted by this consequence, admits that the state must have regard to the injustice for which it is, at least indirectly, responsible. He then inclines to exaggerate the power of the 'artificial' factor because it embodies human 'volition' and leans towards the crude Socialism which assumes that all institutions can be arbitrarily reconstructed by legislative interference. Hence when we come to the political problem, to the organ by which the legal bond is constructed, Mill exaggerates the power of 'making' as contradistinguished from the 'growing.' He seems to assume that institutions can 'create' the instincts by which they are worked: or to forget that they primarily transmit instead of originating power, though indirectly they foster or hinder the development of certain tendencies. Mill would guard against the abuse of political power by dividing it among the separate individuals. He then perceives that he is only redistributing this tremendous power instead of diminishing its intensity. By isolating the 'individual' he has condemned him to narrow views and petty ideals, but has not prevented him from impressing them upon the mass of homogeneous units. Hence, he is alarmed by the inevitable 'tyranny of the majority.' He has put a tremendous power into the hands of Demos, and can only suggest that it should not be exercised.

It is, if I am right, the acceptance of this antithesis, put absolutely, the 'individual,' as something natural on one side, and law, on the other side, as a bond imposed upon the society, which at every step hampers Mill's statement of any vital truths. He cannot upon these terms draw a satisfactory distinction between the individual and the society. When man is taken for a ready-made product, while his social relation can be 'made' offhand by the sovereign, it is impossible to give a satisfactory account of the slow processes of evolution in which making and growing are inextricably united, and the individual and the society are slowly modified by the growth of instincts and customs under constant action and reaction. The difficulty of course is not solved by recognising its existence. No one has yet laid down a satisfactory criterion of the proper limits of individual responsibility. The problem is too vast and complex to admit of any offhand solution ; and Mill's error lies chiefly in underestimating the difficulty.

The contrast to Comte is significant. The inventor of 'sociology' had seen in the 'individualism' of the revolutionary school a transitory and negative stage of thought, which was to lead to a reconstruction of intellectual and social authority. Mill could see in Comte's final Utopia nothing but the restoration of a spiritual despotism in a form more crushing and all-embracing than that of the mediæval church. They went together up to a certain point. Comte held that 'contradiction' and 'antagonism' were not ultimate ends, though they may be inseparable incidents of progress. In the intellectual sphere we should hope for the emergence of a rational instead of an arbitrary authority, and a settlement of first principles, not a permanent conflict of opinion. The hope of achieving some permanent conciliation is the justification of scepticism in speculation and revolutions in politics. Comte supposed that such a result might be achieved in sociology. If that science were constituted, its professors might have such an authority as now possessed by astronomers and teachers of physical sciences. Society might then be reconstructed on sound principles which would secure the responsibility of rulers to subjects, and the confidence of the subjects in rulers. Mill in his early enthusiasm had admitted the necessity of a 'spiritual power' to be founded on free discussion.[1] He had, with Comte, condemned the merely critical attitude of the revolutionary school. When he saw Comte devising an elaborate hierarchy to govern speculation, and even depreciating the reason in com-

[1] See *Correspondence with Comte*, p. 414.

parison with the 'heart,' he revolted. Comte was a
great thinker, greater, even, he thought, than Descartes
or Leibniz,[1] but had plunged into absurdities suggestive
of brain disease. The absurdities were, indeed, flagrant,
yet Mill still sympathises with much of Comte's doctrine;
with the positivist religion; and the general social conceptions. Even a 'spiritual authority' is, he thinks, desirable. But it must be developed through free discussion
and the gradual approximation of independent thinkers,
not by premature organisation and minute systematisa-
tion.[2] The regeneration of society requires a moral and
intellectual transformation, which can only be regarded
as a distant ideal. We may dream of a state of things
in which even political authority shall be founded upon
reason: in which statesmanship shall really mean an
application of scientific principles, and rulers be recognised as devoted servants of the state. Even an
approximation to such a Utopia would imply a change
in moral instincts, and in the corresponding social structure, to be worked out slowly and tentatively. Yet
Mill is equally over-sanguine in his own way. He puts
an excessive faith in human 'contrivances,' representation
of minorities, and the forces of 'antagonism' and 'individuality.' If Comte's scheme really amounts, as Mill
thought, to a suppression of individual energy, Mill's
doctrine tends to let energy waste itself in mere eccentricity. As originality of intellect is useful when it
accepts established results, so energy of character is
fruitful when it is backed by sympathy. The degree
of both may be measured by their power of meeting
opposition; but the positive stimulus comes from co-

---

[1] *Auguste Comte*, p. 200.   [2] *Ibid.* pp. 94-100.

operation. The great patriots and founders of religion have opposed tyrants and bigots because they felt themselves to be the mouthpiece of a nation or a whole social movement. And, therefore, superlative as may be the value of energy, it is not generated in a chaos where every man's hand is against his neighbour, but in a social order, where vigorous effort may be sure of a sufficient backing. When the individual is regarded as an isolated being, and state action as necessarily antagonistic, this side of the problem is insufficiently taken into account, and the question made to lie between simple antagonism and enforced unity.

VIII. ETHICS

The problem must be left to posterity. Mill's doctrine, if I am right, is vitiated rather by an excessive emphasis upon one aspect of facts than by positive error. He seems often to be struggling to express half-recognised truths, and to be hampered by an inadequate dialect. I have already touched upon the morality more or less involved in his political and economic views. His ethical doctrine shows the source of some of his perplexities and apparent inconsistencies. His position is given in the little book upon *Utilitarianism*, which is scarcely more, however, than an occasional utterance.[1] In a more systematic treatise some difficulties would have been more carefully treated, and assumptions more

---

[1] I refer to the second edition (1864). Mill's *Utilitarianism*, and some other parts of his writings referring to the same subject, have been republished in 1897 by Mr. Charles Douglas as *The Ethics of John Stuart Mill*. He has prefixed some interesting 'Introductory Essays.' Mr. Douglas had previously published *John Stuart Mill; a Study of his Philosophy*, 1895. Both are valuable studies of Mill.

explicitly justified. The main lines, however, of Mill's Utilitarianism are plain enough. The book is substantially a protest against the assertion that Utilitarian morality is inferior to its rivals. 'Utilitarians,' he says, 'should never cease to claim the morality of self-devotion as a possession which belongs by as good a right to them as to the Stoic or to the Transcendentalist.'[1] The Utilitarian standard is 'not the agent's own happiness, but the happiness of all concerned.' The Utilitarian must be 'as strictly impartial as a disinterested and benevolent spectator' in determining his course of action. The spirit of his ethics is expressed in 'the golden rule of Jesus of Nazareth.' Mill insists as strongly as possible upon the paramount importance of the social aspect of morality. Society must be founded throughout upon justice and sympathy. Every step in civilisation generates in each individual 'a feeling of unity with all the rest.'[2] Characteristically he refers to Comte's *Politique Positive* in illustration. Though he has the 'strongest objections' to the system of morals and politics there set forth, he thinks that Comte has 'superabundantly shown the possibility of giving to the service of humanity, even without the aid of belief in a Providence, both the psychical power and the social efficacy of a religion.' Nay, it may 'colour all thought, feeling, and action, in a manner of which the greatest ascendency ever exercised by any religion may be but a type or foretaste.' The danger is that the ascendency may be so marked as to suppress 'human freedom and individuality.' The love of the right is to become an all-absorbing passion, and selfish motives admitted only so far as subordinated to

---

[1] *Utilitarianism*, p. 24.   [2] *Ibid.* p. 48.

desire for the welfare of the social body. Clearly this is a
loftier line than Bentham's attempt to evade the difficulty
by ignoring the possibility of a conflict between private and
public interest. The only question, then, is as to the logic.
Can Mill's conclusions be deduced from his premises?

We must first observe that Mill's argument is governed
by his antipathy to the 'intuitionist.' The intuitionist
was partly represented by his old antagonist Whewell,
who in a ponderous treatise had set forth a theory of
morality intended not only to give first principles but
to elaborate a complete moral code. Mill attacked him
with unusual severity in an article in the *Westminster
Review*.[1] Whewell, in truth, appears at one time to
be founding morality upon positive law—a doctrine
which is at best a strange perversion of a theory of
experience; and yet he denounces Utilitarians by the
old arguments, and brings in such an 'intuitionism'
as always roused Mill's combative propensities. Mill
defends Bentham against Whewell, and his *Utilitarianism*
starts essentially from Bentham's famous saying, 'Nature
has placed mankind under the governance of two sovereign
masters, pain and pleasure.' Happiness, says Mill, is the
'sole end of human action'; to 'desire' is to find a
thing pleasant; to be averse from a thing is to think of
it as painful; and, as happiness gives the criterion of
all conduct, it must give 'the standard of morality.'[2]
To 'prove' the first principle may be impossible; one
can only appeal to self-consciousness in general; but it
seems to him so obvious that it will 'hardly be disputed.'[3] It still requires explicate statement in order to

[1] October 1852, reprinted in *Dissertations*, ii. 450, etc.
[2] *Utilitarianism*, pp. 17, 58.   [3] *Ibid.* p. 59.

exclude a doctrine held by many philosophers. Mill[1] refers to Kant, whose formula that you are to act so that the rule on which you act may be law for all rational beings, is the most famous version of the doctrine which would deduce morality from reason. It really proves at most, as Mill says, the formal truth that laws must be consistent, but it fails 'almost grotesquely' in showing which consistent laws are right. Absolute selfishness or absolute benevolence would equally satisfy the formula. For Mill, then, all conduct depends on pain and pleasure ; every theory of conduct must therefore be based upon psychology, or consequently upon experience, not upon abstract logic. Every attempt to twist morality out of pure reason is foredoomed to failure ; logical contradiction corresponds to the impossible, not to the immoral, which is only too possible. That is a first principle, which seems to me, I confess, to be unassailable.

It follows, in the next place, that Mill's argument is substantially an interpretation of facts, a sketch of a scientific theory of certain social phenomena. We find that certain rules of conduct are as a matter of fact generally approved ; and we have to show that those rules are deducible from the assumed criterion. The rule, 'act for the greatest happiness of the greatest number,' coincides with the conduct approved in the recognised morality, and we need and can ask for no further explanation of the 'criterion.' Mill answers the usual objections. The criterion, it is said, can only justify the 'expedient' not the 'right.' The Utilitarian must act from a calculation of 'consequences,' and consequences are so uncertain that no general rule can be

---

[1] *Utilitarianism*, p. 5.

framed. To this, as urged by Whewell, Mill replied that his adversary had proved too much.[1] The argument would destroy 'prudence' as well as morality. We can make general rules about the interests of the greatest number as easily as about our own personal interests. And, if it be urged that such general rules always admit of exceptions, all moralists have had to admit exceptions to moral rules. Exceptions, however, as James Mill had said, can only be admitted in morality, when the exception itself expresses a general rule. All moralists admit of lying in some extreme cases, but only where the obligation to speak truth conflicts with some higher obligation. If something be wanting in this defence, it may perhaps be supplied from Mill himself. The importance of cultivating a sensitive love of truth is, he says, so great as to possess a 'transcendent expediency'[2] not to be violated by temporary considerations. When discussing the question of justice Mill insists upon the importance of the confidence in our fellow-creatures as corresponding to the 'very groundwork of our existence.' The general rule, that is, corresponds to an individual quality which is essential to the social union. A strong sense of veracity is unconditionally good, though circumstances may require exceptions to any rule when stated in terms of outward conduct. Lying may be necessary, but should always be painful. This is familiar ground on which it is needless to dwell. But another criticism of the 'criterion' is more important and leads to one of Mill's most characteristic arguments. The greatest happiness criterion, it is often said, will be interpreted differently as men form different judgments of

[1] *Dissertations*, ii. 474.   [2] *Utilitarianism*, p. 33.

what constitutes happiness. The 'felicific calculus' will give different results for the philosopher and the clown .ne sensualist and the ascetic, the savage and the civilised man ; and it is part of the empiricist contention that in fact the standard has varied widely. Mill himself observes, and he is only following Locke [1] and Hume, 'that morality has varied widely; has in some cases sanctioned practices the most revolting' to others, and that the ' universal will of mankind is universal only in its discordance.' [2] It is indeed precisely for that reason that the Utilitarian has declined to accept the authority of the 'moral sense' and appealed to facts. The belief that our feeling is right, simply because it is ours, is the 'mental infirmity which Bentham's philosophy tends to correct and Dr. Whewell's to perpetuate.' [3] That is to say, Bentham can lay down an 'objective criterion' because he calculates actual pains and pleasures. But will not this criterion be after all ' subjective ' because our estimate of pains and pleasures is so discordant? Mill tries to meet this by a famous distinction between the qualities of pleasures. Bentham had insisted that one pleasure was as good as another. 'Quantity of pleasure being equal, push-pin is as good as poetry.' [4] Mill now declares that it is quite compatible with the principle of utility to recognise the fact that some kinds of pleasure are more desirable and more valuable than others.' We must consider 'quality' as well as 'quantity.' [5] The 'only competent judges,' he argues,

[1] See Locke's *Essay* (bk. i. ch. iii. § 9) upon the ' Caribbees ' and 'Tououpinambos.'

[2] *Dissertations*, ii. 198.   [3] *Ibid.* ii. 389.   [4] *Ibid.* ii. 389.

[5] *Utilitarianism*, p. 12. It is rather odd to find Mr. Ruskin making the same remark.—*Fors Clavigera*, xiv. 8.

are those who have known both. Now, it is an 'un-
questionable fact' that those who have this advantage
prefer the higher or intellectual to the lower or sensual
pleasures. It is better to be a Socrates dissatisfied than
a fool satisfied. If the fool or the pig dissents it is
because he only knows his own side of the question.[1]

Answers are only too obvious. What is 'quantity' as
distinguished from 'quality' of pleasure? The statement, 'A cubic foot of water weighs less than a cubic
foot of lead' is intelligible ; but what is the corresponding proposition about pleasure? Can we ask, How much
benevolence is equal to how much hunger? The 'how
much' is strictly meaningless. Moreover, are not both
Socrates and the pig right in their judgment? Pig's-wash
is surely better for the pig than dialogue ; and dialogue
may be better for Socrates than pig's-wash. If 'desirable'
means that pleasure which each desires, each may be right.
If it means some quality independent of the agent, we
have the old fallacy which in political economy makes
'value' something 'objective.' All 'value' must depend
upon the man as well as upon the thing. And this
again suggests that neither Socrates nor a Christian saint
would really make the supposed assertion. It is not
true absolutely that 'intellectual' pleasures are simply
'better' than sensual. Each is better in certain circumstances. There are times when even the saint prefers a
glass of water to religious musings ; and moments when
even a fool may at times find such intellectual pleasures
as he can enjoy better than a glass of wine. This seems
to be so obvious that we must suspect Mill of hastily

[1] *Utilitarianism*, p. 14. The argument is virtually Plato's. See *Republic*,
book ix. (581-83).

stopping a gap in his argument without duly working out the implications. Indeed, he seems to be making room for something very like an intuition. He assumes the proposition, doubtful in itself and apparently inconsistent with his own position, that all competent people agree, and then makes this agreement decisive of a disputable question.

Bentham, from his own point of view, was, I think, perfectly right in his statement. To calculate pleasures, the only question must be which are the greatest pleasures, and the only answer, those which, as a fact, attract people most. If a man is more attracted by 'push-pin' than by poetry, the presumption is that push-pin gives him most pleasure. We are simply investigating facts ; and cannot overlook the obvious fact that estimates of pleasure vary indefinitely. Some things are pleasant to the refined alone, while others are more or less pleasant to everybody, and others, again, cease to be pleasant or become disgusting as men advance. To introduce the moral valuation in an estimate of facts—to change the 'desirable' as 'that which is desired' into the 'desirable' as 'that which ought to be desired' is to beg the question or to argue in circle.

Yet Mill was aiming at an obvious truth. As men advance intellectually, intellectual pleasures will clearly fill a larger space in their ideal of life. The purely sensual pleasures will have their value as long as men have bodies and appetites ; but they will come to have a subordinate place in defining the whole ends of human conduct. The morality of the higher being will include higher aspirations. We have then to inquire, In what sense is a 'felicific calculus' possible or required? The moral rule

is, as Mill holds, a statement of certain fundamental conditions of social life, giving, as he puts it, the 'groundwork' upon which all social relations are built up. This
again supposes essentially a society made of the most
varying elements, poets and men of science, philosophers
and fools, nay, according to him, including both Socrates
and the pig. In criticising Whewell, for example, he
quotes[1] with most emphatical approval that 'admirable
passage' in which Bentham includes animal happiness in
his criterion. We are to promote the pig's happiness
so far as the pig is 'sentient,' little as he may care for
a Socratic dialogue. But if so, the 'greatest happiness'
rule must have for its end the conditions under which
the most varying types of happiness may be promoted
and each kind of happiness promoted according to the
character of the subject.   And in point of fact, the
actual moral rules, 'Love your neighbour as yourself,'
be truthful, honest, and so forth, do not as such define
any special type of happiness as good.   They assume
rather that happiness, as happiness, is so far good ; and
that we ought to promote the happiness of others if
our action be not objectionable upon some other ground.
This indicates a really weak point of the old Utilitarianism,
which Mill was trying to remedy.   If, as Bentham would
seem to imply, we are to form our estimate of happiness
simply by accepting average estimates of existing human
beings, we shall be tempted to approve conduct conducive
to the lower kinds of happiness alone.   I should reply
that this is to misunderstand the true nature of morality.
If morality, as Mill would admit, corresponds essentially
to the primary relations of social life, it is defined

1 *Dissertations*, ii. 482.

not by any average estimates of happiness, but by a statement of the conditions of the welfare of the social organism. It states the fundamental terms upon which men can best associate. It gives the fundamental 'social compact' (if we may accept the phrase without its fallacious connotation) implied in an ordered system of society. The happiness of each is good, so far as it does not imply anti-social characteristics. But morality leaves room for the existence of the most varied types of character from 'the saint to the pig, and aims at producing happiness—not by taking the existing average man as an ultimate unalterable type, but—by leaving room for such a development of men themselves as will alter their character and therefore their views of happiness. As the society progresses the individual will himself be altered, and the type which implies a greater development of intellect, sympathy, and energy come to prevail over the lower, more sensual, selfish, and feeble type. Though happiness is still the ultimate base, the morality applies immediately to the social bond, which contemplates a general development of the whole man and a modification of the elements of happiness itself. Mill, perceiving that something was wanted, makes the unfortunate attempt at supplying the gap by his assumption of an imaginary consensus of all the better minds. What is true is that all men may consent to conditions of society which leave a free play to the higher influences : that is, are favourable to the more advanced type with greater force of intellect and richness of emotional power.

Here we return to the old Utilitarian problem: What is the 'sanction' of morality? The 'sanction' can be

nothing else than the sum of all the motives which induce men to act morally. What, then, are they? The
Utilitarians, starting from the juridical point of view,
had a ready answer in the case of positive law. The
sanction, briefly, is the gallows. Law means coercion, and
as everybody (with very insignificant exceptions) objects
to being hanged, the gallows may be regarded as a sanction
of universal efficacy. If the moral law be taken in the
same way as implying a rule of conduct to be enforced
by an external sanction, the correlative to the gallows was
hell-fire. This satisfied Paley, but as the Utilitarians
had abolished hell, they were at some loss for a substitute.

Here Mill accepts the principles laid down by his
father. He defends the Utilitarians upon the ground
that they 'had gone beyond all others in affirming that
the motive has nothing to do with the morality of the
action, though much with the morality of the agent.'[1]
They based morality upon 'consequences,' and the consequences of an action are no doubt independent of the
motive. If I burn a man for heresy, the 'consequences'
to him are the same whether my motive be love of
his soul or the hatred of a bigot for a free-thinker.
To estimate the goodness or badness of an action, we
must consider all that it implies. We must inquire
whether a society in which heretics are repressed by
the stake is better or worse than one in which they are
left at liberty; and that cannot be settled by simply
asking whether the persecutor is benevolent or male-

[1] *Utilitarianism*, p. 26. Mill is answering the criticism that Utilitarianism
puts the standard of morality too high if it assumes that every man is to be
prompted by desire for the 'greatest happiness of the greatest number.'
I have spoken of this in considering James Mill's ethical position.

volent. The purest benevolence may be misguided if it is directed by erroneous belief. The 'sentimentalism,' denounced by Utilitarians, implied refusal to look at consequences, and the justification, for example, of corrupting charity on the ground that it was pleasant to the sympathy of the corrupter. Their especial function was to warn philanthropists that misguided philanthropy might stimulate the greatest evils. But to infer from this the general principle that the 'motive' was indifferent involves the characteristic fallacy. The true inference is that sound morality has an intellectual as well as an emotional basis; it supposes a just foresight of consequences as well as a desire for happiness. Conduct depends throughout upon character; it cannot be altered without altering character, though the alteration may imply enlightenment of the intellect rather than development of the feelings. When we come to the moral 'sanction' the motive becomes all important. The legislator may be contented if he can induce a bad man to act like a good man or to refrain from murder in the presence of the policeman. He can take the policeman and the gallows for granted; and assume the existence of the fundamental social instincts upon which the judicial machinery depends. But it is precisely with those instincts that the moralist is concerned. He has to ask what are the forces which work the machinery and cannot be indifferent to the question of 'motive.' Mill only half recognises the point when he admits that the 'motive' has much to do with the 'morality of the agent.' If 'motive' be interpreted widely enough it constitutes the agent's morality. An action is moral in so far as it implies a character thoroughly 'moralised' or fitted to play the right part in society. The distinction between the morality of the conduct and the morality of the agent vanishes. A good act is that which a good man would perform. If a bad man, under compulsion, acts in the same way, he acts from fear, and his act is therefore morally neutral, and to call him good on account of his action is therefore a mistake. He simply shows that he is a man, and dislikes hanging even more than he hates his fellow-men.

An 'external sanction' really means a motive for acting as though you were good even if you are not good. That such sanctions are essential to society, that they provide a shelter under which true morality may or must grow up, is obvious. It is true, also, that in early stages the distinction between the law which rests upon force and that which rests upon the character is not manifest. But ultimately morality means nothing but the expression of the character itself. Hence to find a universal 'sanction' for morality is chimerical. Such a sanction would be 'a motive' which would apply to all men good or bad; that is, it would not be a moral motive. Fear of hell or the gallows may indirectly help (or hinder) the development of a moral character; but in itself the fear is neither good nor bad. The very attempt, therefore, to find such a 'sanction' implies the 'external' or essentially inadequate view of morality, into which the Utilitarians with their legal prepossessions were too apt to fall. The law, resting upon external sanctions, may be useful or prejudicial to morals, but must always be subordinate; for its application depends upon instincts by which it is guided and which it cannot create.

Mill recognises this, virtually, though not explicitly, in his discussion of the 'Utilitarian sanction.' He declares in rather awkward phrase that the 'ultimate sanction of all morality (external motives apart)' is 'a subjective feeling in our own minds.' (Where else can such a feeling be, and what is 'an objective feeling'?) These feelings exist, as he argues, equally for the Utilitarian and the 'Transcendentalist,' though the 'Transcendentalists' think that their existence ' *in* the mind' implies that they have a 'root out of the mind.'[1] The 'conscience,' that is, pain in breaking the moral law, exists as a fact, whatever its origin. If 'innate' it can still be opposed, and the question, 'Why should I obey it?' is equally difficult to answer. Even if innate, again, it may be an innate regard for other men's pains and pleasures, and so coincide with the Utilitarian view. He argues accordingly, that, in point of fact, we may acquire that 'feeling of unity' with others which gives the really 'ultimate sanction' to the 'Happiness morality.'[2] With this result I at least can have no quarrel. I hold it to be perfectly correct and as good an account of morality as can be given. The fault is in placing the 'external sanction' on the same level with the 'internal' and failing to see that it is not properly 'moral' at all. But here, once more, it is necessary to look at the difficulty of deriving his conclusion from the premises inherited from his teachers. The essential difficulty lies in the psychological analysis and the theory of association. We are again at James Mill's point of view. Conduct is determined by pain and pleasure. An action supposes an end, and that 'end' must be a pleasure. If we ask,

[1] *Utilitarianism*, p. 42.   [2] *Ibid.* p. 48.

pleasure to whom ? the answer must be, pleasure to the agent. All conduct, it would seem, must be directly or indirectly self-regarding, for the 'end' must always be my own pleasure. Mill maintains that 'virtue' may, for the Utilitarian as well as for others, be a 'thing desirable in itself.'[1] That is a 'psychological fact,' independently of the explanation. But at this point he lapses into the old doctrine. Virtue, he admits, is not 'naturally and originally part of the end.' Virtue was once desired simply 'for its conduciveness to pleasure' and especially 'to protection from pain.' It becomes a good in itself. This is enforced by the familiar illustration of the 'love of money' and of the love of power or fame. Each passion aimed originally at a further end, which has dropped out while the desire for means has become original. The moral feelings, as he says in answer to Whewell,[2] are 'eminently artificial and the product of culture.' We may grow corn, or we may as easily grow hemlocks or thistles. Yet, as he declares in the *Utilitarianism*,[3] 'moral feelings' are not 'the less natural' because 'acquired.' The 'moral faculty' is a 'natural outgrowth' of our nature. The antithesis of 'natural' and 'artificial' is generally ambiguous ; but Mill's view is clear enough upon the main point. Virtue is the product of the great force 'indissoluble association.' Now 'artificial associations' are dissolved 'as intellectual culture goes on.' But the association between virtue and utility is indissoluble, because there is a 'natural basis of sentiment' which strengthens it—that basis being 'our desire to be in unity with our fellow-creatures.'[4] One further

---

[1] *Utilitarianism*, p. 54.
[3] *Utilitarianism*, p. 45
[2] *Dissertations*, ii. 472.
[4] *Ibid.* p. 46.

corollary deserves notice. To become virtuous, it is necessary to acquire virtuous habits. We 'will' at first simply because we desire. Afterwards we come to desire a thing because we will it. 'Will is the child of desire, and passes out of the dominion of its parent only to come under that of habit.'[1] Thus, as he had said in the *Logic*,[2] we learn to will a thing 'without reference to its being pleasurable'—a fact illustrated by the habit of 'hurtful excess' and equally by moral heroism. It would surely be more consistent to say that habit is a modification of character which alters our pains and pleasures but does not enable us to act against our judgment of pains and pleasures. He is trying to escape from an awkward consequence; but the mode of evasion will hardly bear inspection.

Mill's arguments imply his thorough adherence to the 'association psychology.' They really indicate, I think, an attempt to reach a right conclusion from defective premises. The error is implied in the analysis of 'ends' of action. When a man acts with a view to an 'end' the true account is that his immediate action is affected by all the consequences which he foresees. This or that motive conquers because it includes a perception of more or less remote results. But what determines conduct is not a calculation of some future pains or pleasures, but the actual painfulness or pleasurableness of the whole action at the moment. I shrink from the pain of a wound or from the pain of giving a wound to another person. Both are equally my immediate feelings; and it is an error to analyse the sympathetic pain into two different factors, one the immediate action and the other

---

[1] *Utilitarianism*, p. 60.   [2] *Logic*, bk. vi. ch. iii. § 4.

the anticipated reaction. It is one indissoluble motive,
just as natural or original as the dislike to the unpleasant
sensation of my own wound. To distinguish it into
two facts and make one subordinate and a product of
association is a fallacy. We can hardly believe that
'association' accounts even for 'love of money' or
'fame.' Avarice and vanity mean an exaggerated fear
of poverty or regard to other people's opinions. They
do not imply any forgetfulness of end for means, but an
erroneous estimate of the proportion of means to ends.
The really noticeable point, again, has already met us in
James Mill's ethics. When Mill speaks of 'virtue' as
'artificial' or derivative, he is asserting a truth not to
be denied by an evolutionist. Undoubtedly the social
sentiments have been slowly developed; and undoubtedly
they have grown up under the protection of external
'sanctions.' The primitive society did not distinguish
between law and morality ; the pressure of external
circumstances upon character and the influence of the
character itself upon the society. A difficulty arises
from the defective view which forces Mill to regard
the whole process as taking place within the life of the
individual. The unit is then a being without moral
instincts at all, and they have to be inserted by the
help of the association machinery. Sympathy is not
an intrinsic part of human nature in its more advanced
stages, but something artificial stuck on by indissoluble
association. Mill, himself, when discussing the virtue
of justice in his last chapter, substantially adopts a line
of argument which, if not satisfactory in details, sufficiently recognises this point of view. And, if he still
fails to explain morality sufficiently, it is in the main

because he never freed himself from the unsatisfactory assumptions of the old psychology. Here, as in so many other cases, he sees the inadequacy of the old conclusions, but persuades himself that a better result can be reached without the thorough revision which was really necessary.

CHAPTER V

HISTORICAL METHOD

I. JOHN AUSTIN

I HAVE spoken more than once of the paradox implied in the Utilitarian combination of appeals to 'experience,' with indifference to history. The importance of historical methods already recognised by Mill has become more obvious in later years. It was, as he saw, clearly desirable that the Utilitarians should annex this field of inquiry and apply appropriate methods. I have said something of Mill's view of the problems thus suggested ; but the attitude of the Utilitarians in regard to them may be more fully indicated by the writings of some of his allies.

John Austin (1790-1859)[1] was accepted as the heir-apparent to Bentham in the special department of jurisprudence. Five years' service in the army was a unique apprenticeship for a Benthamite ; and, as his widow tells us, helped to develop his chivalrous sense of honour. It may also help to explain a want of sympathy for the democratic zeal of most of his comrades. In any case, it did not suppress a delight in intellectual activity. Austin left the army, and in 1818 was called to the bar, but ill-health compelled him to retire in 1825. He was

[1] See Memoir by Mrs. Austin prefixed to the edition of his *Lectures*, edited by Mr. R. Campbell (1869).

thus qualified to be a jurist by some knowledge of practice, and forced to turn his knowledge to theoretical application. Upon the foundation of the London University he became the first professor of jurisprudence. With the true scholar's instinct for thorough preparation, he went to Bonn, studied the great German writers upon jurisprudence, and made the acquaintance of eminent living professors. The insular narrowness of Bentham and James Mill was thus to be corrected by cosmopolitan culture. Austin returned amidst the highest expectations. A clear voice, a perfect delivery, and a courteous and dignified manner were suited to give effect to his teaching ; and unanimous tradition tells us that his powers in conversation were unsurpassed. Why did he not acquire such an intellectual leadership in London as Dugald Stewart had enjoyed in Edinburgh ? Some reasons are obvious. English barristers and law students were serenely indifferent to the 'philosophy of law.' They had quite enough to do in acquiring familiarity with the technicalities of English practice. The University itself turned out to be chiefly a high school for boys not yet ripe for legal studies. Though J. S. Mill attended his lectures and took elaborate notes, few men had Mill's thirst for knowledge. Moreover, Austin thought it a duty to be as dry as Bentham, and discharged that duty scrupulously. The audiences dwindled, and the salary, derived from the fees, dwindled with it. Austin, a poor man, could not go on discoursing gratuitously to empty benches, and gave his last lecture in 1832.

Admiring friends did their best to find a sphere for his talents. Brougham placed him on the Criminal Law Commission, where he soon found that there was no serious chance of being employed, as he desired, in active codification. A course of lectures promoted by the sound Utilitarian, Henry Bickersteth (Lord Langdale), at the Inner Temple fell as flat as the former. Austin retired to France, saying that he was born out of time and place, and should have been a ' schoolman of the twelfth century or a German professor.' He was afterwards on a Commission at Malta, with his friend Sir. G. Cornewall Lewis for a colleague. A change of government brought this employment to an end. Austin gave up active work. He passed some years in Germany and France in the enjoyment of intellectual society. After the revolution of 1848 he returned to England, and led a quiet country life at Weybridge. His sole later publication was a pamphlet against parliamentary reform in 1859. He died in the following December. Weak health and a fastidious temperament partly account for his silence. After publishing his early lectures he could never be induced to bring out a second edition. He suffered from scholar's paralysis—preference of doing nothing to doing anything short of the ideal standard. He had not strength to satisfy the demands of German professors, and cared nothing for the applause of the British public. His ' estimate of men was low,' says Mrs. Austin, ' and his solicitude for their approbation was consequently small.' His want of success did not embitter, though it discouraged him ; and he was constantly, we are told, ' meditating on the sublimest themes that can occupy the mind of man.' He kept the results for his own circle of hearers. Utilitarian zeal for democracy was impossible for him. He had the scholar's contempt for the vulgar, and dreaded political changes which could increase the power of the masses. It is the more remarkable that Austin's Utilitarianism is of the most rigid orthodoxy. A thorough Benthamite training gave absolute immunity to even the germs of transcendental philosophy. He speaks with the profoundest respect of the great German professors, especially of Savigny. He cordially admires their learning and acuteness. But when they deviate into philosophy he denounces their 'jargon' as roundly as Bentham or James Mill. Austin became the typical expounder of Benthamite jurisprudence. His lectures long enjoyed a high reputation : partly, I cannot help guessing, because, good or bad, they had the field to themselves ; partly, also, because their dry, logical articulation fits them admirably for examination purposes ; and partly, I do not doubt, because they represent some rare qualities of mind. Their fame declined upon the rise of the 'historical school.' Austin's star set as Maine's rose. Yet Austin himself claimed that his was the really historical method. The historical school, he says,[1] is the school which appeals to 'experience,' and holds that a 'body of law cannot be spun out of a few general principles, considered *a priori*.' Bentham clearly falls under the definition, for Bentham considered the reports of English decisions to be 'an invaluable mine of experience for the legislator.' If this be an adequate criterion, how does Bentham differ from the school which claimed the historical method as its distinctive characteristic? Austin aims at giving a 'philosophy of law.' The phrase at once indicates two correlative lines of inquiry. A 'law' supposes a law-giver

[1] *Jurisprudence*, p. 701.

—an authority which lays down or enforces the law. We may then inquire what is implied by the existence of this authority, or what is its origin, growth, and constitution ? That is a problem of 'social dynamics.' We may, again, take the existence of the state for granted; inquire what are the actual laws; how they can be classified and simplified; and what are the consequent relations between the state and the individual. That is a problem of 'social statics,' and corresponds to the ordinary legal point of view. The conception of 'law' is common to both, though it may be approached from opposite directions, and may require modification so as to bring the results of the two lines of inquiry into harmony. The problems, and therefore the methods of inquiry, must be distinct, but each may be elucidated by the other.

Austin's position is given by his definition of law. It implies what has been called the 'Austinian analysis,' and is considered by his followers to dissolve all manner of sophistries. It is already implied in Hobbes.[1] A law, briefly, is the command of a sovereign enforced by a sanction. The definition gives the obvious meaning for the lawyer. Murder is punishable by death. That is the law of England. To prove that is the law, we need only go to the statute-book. The statute rests upon the absolute authority of the legislature. It assumes the existence, then, of a sovereign; an ultimate authority behind which the lawyer never goes. It is for him infallible. The English lawyer accepts an act of parliament as a man of science accepts a law of nature. If

[1] For Austin's admiration of Hobbes see especially the long note in *Jurisprudence*, p. 286, etc.

there be any law which has not these marks it is for him no law. Conduct is illegal when the state machinery can be put in force to suppress it. Therefore the sphere of law is precisely marked out by the conception of the sovereign and the sanction.

The definition, then, may be true and relevant for all the lawyer's purposes. But a definition, as J. S. Mill would point out, is not a sufficient foundation for a philosophy. It may provisionally mark out some province for investigation ; but we must always be prepared to ask how far the definition corresponds to an important difference. Now Austin's definition has important implications. It excludes as well as includes. Having defined a law, he argues that many other things which pass by that name are only ' metaphorically ' or ' analogically ' laws ; and this raises the question, whether the fact that they do not conform to his definition corresponds to a vital difference in their real nature ? Is he simply saying, ' I do not call them laws,' or really pointing out an essential and relevant difference of ' kind ' ? An important point is suggested by one exclusion. We are not to confound the so-called laws proper with the ' laws of nature ' of scientific phraseology. Such a law of nature is simply a statement of a general fact. The astronomer asserts that the motion of bodies may be described by a certain formula. In saying so, he does not assert, even if he believes the inference to be legitimate, that their motion is caused by a divine command or enforced by a sanction. The actual uniformity is all that concerns him. The uniformity produced by law proper led, as Austin holds, to a confusion between different conceptions. Austin was clearly right in pointing out the difference ;

and scientific thinkers, before and since his time, have
had to struggle with a fallacy, singularly tenacious of
life. A 'law of nature' in the scientific sense is not
a law in the jurist's sense. The difference may be
regarded in another way. The two senses of law differ
as a 'command' differs from a proposition ; the imperative
from the indicative mood. The command, 'Do not
murder,' is not a simple proposition. It belongs rather
to action than to belief. It utters a volition and therefore
creates a fact, instead of simply expressing a truth. Yet
a command is also a fact, and may be regarded as part
of the general system of fact. The command, 'Do not
murder,' implies the fact, ' murder is forbidden.' We
might show that in certain social conditions murder
becomes punishable by death. That is a property of
society at certain stages. If the social machinery worked
with perfect accuracy, it would be as much a law of
nature that a society kills murderers as that a wolf kills
lambs or that fire burns straw. From this point of
view, then, a 'law proper' falls under the conception of
a 'law of nature,' though a law of nature is not a 'law
proper.' It is a law of nature in the making, or a law of
nature which is only fulfilled when a number of complex
conditions of human conduct are satisfied. Austin,
denying that free-will means a really arbitrary element,
would no doubt have admitted that the 'law proper'
was a product of the general laws (in the scientific sense)
of human nature. This aspect of the case, however,
passes out of sight. The law is something created ; 'set,'
as he calls it, or laid down by the sovereign at his own
will, and is thus perfectly arbitrary. That is the ultimate
fact, and makes a radical difference. We stop at the

'command,' and do not ask how the command itself comes into existence. This corresponds to J. S. Mill's distinction between 'making' and 'growing.' Law belongs to the region of 'making.' It originates in the will of the sovereign. Whatever he wills and 'sanctions,' and nothing else, is therefore law in the proper sense of the term.

Another class of 'laws' is excluded by the definition. A 'custom' is not a law proper. I obey many rules, which are not 'commands' and not enforced by legal sanctions. I conform to countless rules of conduct, though no assignable person has ever made them, and though the sovereign will not punish me for breaking them. In such rules the disapproval of society may act in the same way as a sanction, though not annexed by a sovereign. The resemblance may pass into identity. Customs become laws, as they receive the sanction of the legislator or of the courts. This includes Bentham's 'judge-made' law; and Austin diverges from Bentham by recognising this as a legitimate mode of legislation. The question then arises whether the distinction between laws and customs is essential or superficial—a real distinction of kinds or only important in our classification. From the lawyer's point of view, again, the importance is obvious. He always wishes to know precisely at what point the law can be brought to bear; whether a rule will be enforced by the courts, or generally under what circumstances a custom will be accepted as a law. The answer necessarily leads to much legal subtlety. The custom may be treated as constructively a law. The sovereign has not actually made nor 'sanctioned' it; but virtue has somehow gone out of him by

implication, and his recognition is equivalent to imposi-
tion of the rule. Though the ' sovereign ' has not
really ' made ' the law, he may be considered as having
made it by a metaphysical fiction. In this direction
Austin becomes the twelfth century schoolman, and
has to split hairs to force his definition upon the facts.
The inquiry, though necessary from the lawyer's point
of view, becomes irrelevant from the sociologist's. The
social action is the same, whether the rule obeyed
be a custom or a law strictly so called. Confusion
therefore follows when the question of legal validity
is substituted for the question of real efficacy. Primitive societies obey implicitly a variety of elaborate
' laws ' or ' customs,' though they have no conception of
legislation. The obedience to the rule is instinctive,
and the rule regarded as absolutely unalterable. Are
such rules ' laws '—though not made by a sovereign—
or mere ' customs,' though obeyed as strictly as the most
effective ' laws ' ? Austin answers consistently that they
are not laws at all. There are people, he says, in ' a state
of nature,'[1] such as the savages in New Holland or
North America. Their life, in Hobbes's famous phrase,
is ' solitary, poor, nasty, brutish, and short.' Their laws
correspond to mere ' positive morality or the law set by
public opinion,' which is necessarily so uncertain that it
cannot serve as a complete guide of conduct, nor can
it be sufficiently minute or detailed.[2] Savages, it seems,
form herds not societies, and may be simply left out of
consideration by the philosophical jurist. Austin, of
course, could not be expected to anticipate more recent
investigations into archaic institutions ; but he was un-

---

[1] *Jurisprudence*, p. 238.   [2] *Ibid.* p. 791.

lucky in thus summarily condemning them by anticipation. In any case the position indicates an important gap in his system. What was the legal bond which converted the herds into political societies? The problem of the formation of society had been solved not by historical inquiry but by the 'social contract theory.' Austin follows Bentham and Hume. They had shown conclusively not only that the contract was a figment historically, but that it could not supply what was wanted. It professed to add the sanctity of a promise to the social bond, whereas the sanctity of a promise itself requires explanation. The theory simply amounted, as Bentham had urged, to a roundabout way of introducing utility. Any sort of contract, as Austin urges,[1] presupposes a formed political society. Clearly it cannot otherwise be a contract in his sense—an obligation enforced by a sanction—when it is itself to be the foundation of sovereignty or sanctions. Austin therefore rejects contemptuously the doctrine of natural law accepted by his German teachers. The theory that there is somehow or other a body of law, deducible by the pure reason, and yet capable of overriding or determining the 'law proper,' is his great example of ontological 'jargon' and 'fustian.' Austin's disciples hold[2] that his main service to the philosophy of law was precisely his exposure of the fallacy. The 'Natur-Recht' is 'jargon.' It is most desirable to discuss ideal law as meaning the law which it would be useful to adopt; but to speak as if it had already some transcendental reality is to confuse 'ought' with 'is' or, as Austin would say, the question of utility with the question of actual existence. The

---

[1] *Jurisprudence*, p. 336.   [2] Cp. Mill's *Dissertations*, iii. 237, etc.

' natural law ' corresponds to the legal fictions denounced by Bentham, under which, when really making law, judges pretended to be only applying an existing law ; and to the theories attacked in the *Anarchical Fallacies*, according to which this ideal law could override the actual law. Austin's polemic was no doubt directed against a theory fertile in confusion and fallacies.

Still the social contract, though exploded, leaves a problem for solution. Somehow or other the social organism has been put together, or, in Austin's phrase, the sovereign has come into existence. To explain this is the sociological problem. Austin recognises a difficulty. Generally speaking, he says, ' the constitution of the supreme society has grown.' [1] It should then, we might expect, be studied like other growths, as the physiologist studies the growth of plants and animals and tries to formulate the processes. Austin, however, protests by anticipation. He does not use the ' fustian but current phrase,' Growth, to cover anything mysterious. He only means that governments have in fact been put together by unsystematic processes ;—' by a long series of ' authors' and ' successive sovereigns.' They did not, that is, spring ready-made from the hand of a supernatural legislator, but they were made by a series of patchings and cobblings carried out by ignorant and short-sighted rulers. The ' growing,' then, was really ' making,' however blundering and imperfect. Thus we have no ' mystical' social bond. Society has been constructed all along by the same method. The ultimate cause has always been ' the perception of the utility of political government, or the preference by the bulk of the com-

[1] *Jurisprudence*, p. 330.

munity of any government to anarchy.'[1]   The theory thus appears to be that men in fact made such an agreement as the social contract supposes, though the agreement had not the force of a contract.   Men have always seen, as they see now, that government is useful ; and thus ' perception of utility' (not utility simply) is the sole force which holds society together and supports the sovereign and the sanctions.

A practical lawyer has little concern with savages and the origin of civil society.   Austin's principles, however, apply to the modern society also.   Law, as he seems to think, excludes or supersedes custom, so that the whole fabric of the state is entirely dependent upon the ' sovereign,' and the social union upon the ' perception of utility.'   As a rule, one might observe, the question hardly arises.   Men accept the social constitution into which they are born, because they can't help it.   They never ask whether it is useful because they have no alternative of joining or separating.   I may ask whether I shall belong to this or that club ; but no one can choose whether he shall or shall not be a member of society. This leads to the point already noticed under Bentham. Custom is not really the creature of law, but law the product of custom.   The growth of a society does not imply the disappearance of instinct, but implies on the contrary that certain fundamental instincts and the corresponding modes of action have become so thoroughly settled and organised that the society is capable of combining to modify particular regulations.   When the English people passed the Reform Bill and the Americans

---

[1] *Jurisprudence*, p. 303.   Austin makes certain qualifications which I need not notice.

accepted the constitution of the United States they altered very important laws, but it was precisely because they had been so thoroughly imbued with certain habits of combined action, involving the acceptance of complex legislative processes, that they were able to make changes in the less essential parts of the constitution. The ' sanction ' no doubt determines the conduct of the individual. But when we ask upon what then does the sovereign power depend, we must go behind the law, and ask what are the complex instincts, beliefs, and passions which in fact bind men together and constitute the society as a moral organism.

The weak side of the 'Austinian analysis' is this transference of a legal conception to a sociological problem. Distinctions valid and important in their own sphere become irrelevant and lead to idle subtleties beyond that sphere. What, in fact, is the sovereign ? He stands for an undeniable fact. Law presupposes a state and political unity. Political order implies some supreme and definite authority which can be invoked in all controversies as to what is or is not the law. The simplest case would be an irresponsible despot who could command whatever he pleased, and whose commands would be implicitly obeyed. If he does not exist he must be invented, as Voltaire said of the Deity. He is a ' fictitious entity,' or the incarnation of legal authority. This corresponds to the truth implied in the Utilitarian polemic against the supposed balance of powers and the mixture of the three abstract forms, monarchy, aristocracy, and democracy. The existence of the state implies unity of authority and the agreement that the validity of laws shall depend upon their elaboration by definite constitutional processes. But then we have to ask, Who precisely is the sovereign? The answer would be simple in the case of the individual despot. When the sovereign is not a single man but an organised body of men, such phrases as 'will' and 'command' become metaphorical. The will is not one will, but the product of multitudinous wills acting in complex though definable ways. The sovereign is not an entity distinct from the subjects, but is composed of the subjects themselves, or some fraction of them, according to a definite set of regulations. Can the state be treated as the embodiment of an external force? Austin is greatly puzzled to say who, in a given case, is the sovereign? Is parliament, or the House of Commons, or the electoral body the ultimate sovereign of England? Who is the true sovereign in a federal government such as the United States, where sovereign powers are distributed in complex ways? The legal question, What are the recognised forms by which valid laws are nominally constructed? is again confounded with the question of fact, What are the real forces which, in fact, produce obedience? The British Constitution has been steadily altering from remote times as a certain understanding has been developed. The centre of power has imperceptibly shifted without definite legislation; and the legal theory has remained unaltered, or has only conformed to customs already established. The question, therefore, what forms must be observed in conformity to precedent or explicit legislation, is entirely different from the question, What are the really dominant forces? The crown can undoubtedly veto an act of parliament in the legal sense of 'can'; whether it 'can' do so in the practical sense is a question only to be solved by saying what are the real forces which lie beneath the constitutional machinery.

I have already noticed the tendency of the Utilitarians to confuse the legal doctrine of the sovereign's omnipotence with the doctrine of his omnipotence in fact. Macaulay had sufficiently pointed out to Mill that the sovereign was limited : limited by his own character and by the impossibility of enforcing laws not congenial to the public sentiment. Austin illustrates a further result. Customs are legally invalid till recognised and sanctioned by the sovereign. That is important for the lawyer. But interpreted as a law of ' social dynamics,' it leads to the inversion by which custom is supposed to be created by the law, and the sovereign made the ultimate source of power, instead of being himself the product of a long and intricate process of development of custom. Here, therefore, is the point at which the Utilitarian view becomes antithetic to the historical. It seeks to explain the first state of society by the last, instead of explaining the last by the first. We can see, too, the main reason for this mode of conceiving the case. To Austin the reference to the underlying forces by which political society is built up seemed to be ' mysticism.' A fully developed ' law ' is intelligible : the customs which grow up in the twilight before the full light of day has appeared are too incoherent and shadowy for scientific treatment. The mode of analysing all phenomena into independent and uniform atoms leads to this result. Causation itself had been reduced to mere sequence to get rid of a ' mystic bond,' and the same method is applied to social phenomena.[1] We have the difficulty which occurs so

[1] Austin refers his readers to Brown's essay on ' Cause and Effect '; and

often in the Utilitarian theories. They desire on the
one hand to be scientific, and on the other hand to be
thoroughly empirical. The result is to divide the two
spheres : to enlarge as much as possible the variability of
human society in order to be 'empirical'; and to regard
the constituent atoms as unchangeable. Hence they
have always a difficulty of conceiving of growth or
'evolution,' in which variation is supposed to be compatible with the existence of law, or to combine the
two aspects of change and uniformity. That always
appears to them to be 'mystical.' Though they deny
'freewill,' they give the widest possible range to the
sphere of voluntary action. 'Making' is radically distinguished from 'growing,' instead of being simply growth
directed by conscious foresight. There is nothing really
more 'mystical,' though there is something much more
complex, in the growth of a society than in the growth
of a natural species. But as it supposes a change due to
something in the constitution of the man himself, not to
merely 'external circumstances,' it has to be rejected as
much as possible. Hence we get our omnipotent
sovereign creating laws and customs and to be taken as
an ultimate fact.

I need not point out at length the relation of these
views to Utilitarianism in general, and to the belief in
the indefinite modifiability of human nature and the
transcendent importance of political machinery. It is
enough to note that Austin's position involves one
assumption remarkable in a Utilitarian. The empiricism
of the Utilitarians is interpreted to mean that everything

takes Brown to have proved 'beyond controversy' that the faculty called the
'will' is just nothing at all.—*Jurisprudence*, pp. 424-25.

must be explained by circumstances, and conduct therefore by 'external' sanctions. Austin feels that, after all,
some bond must be required to hold men together. The
legislative sanctions cannot be quite ultimate. In fact, we
want 'morality'; and he therefore includes the 'laws
of God' among the laws which are really, not metaphorically, laws. He thus accepts the Paley view, though
with a certain reserve. 'Utility' is the sole criterion or
'index,' as he calls it, to the moral law. Still, the law
requires a sanction. The sanction is left in judicious
vagueness; but we are told that God must be benevolent,
and must therefore be held to approve the conduct
which promotes the happiness of his creatures. This, it
would seem, is essential to Austin's position.[1] Whether
he was practising some 'economy,' and what his fellow-
Utilitarians would have thought of it, and how precisely
he would have justified his position logically, are questions
which I cannot discuss.

The application of Austin's principles to the purely
legal sphere lies beyond my purpose. His aim is to
analyse the primary conceptions of jurisprudence in
accordance with his principles, and to obtain a rational
classification of law in general. Whether the result was
satisfactory, or how far satisfactory, I cannot inquire.
The lectures were reviewed in the *Edinburgh* both by
J. F. Stephen[2] and by J. S. Mill.[3] Both of them
speak warmly of the merits of Sir Henry Maine, then
beginning to be famous, and both regard the two

---

[1] Mill touches this point characteristically in his review of Austin, but
does not discuss the validity of the logic.

[2] *Edinburgh Review*, October 1861.

[3] Mill's *Dissertations*, iii. 206-74, from *Edin. Rev.* of Oct. 1863.

methods as correlative rather than antagonistic. That they ought to be correlative is clear. A sound theory of origins and growth should be perfectly compatible with a sound theory of the actual order. But whether the two systems actually present that harmony is another question.

The political application of Austin's principles might be illustrated from the writings of his friend and disciple, Sir George Cornewall Lewis (1806-1863).[1] Strong sense, unflagging industry, and the highest integrity won for Lewis high authority in parliament. A boundless thirst for knowledge, supported by a remarkable memory, enabled him to discuss many topics of historical criticism. He was intimate with Grote, who accepted his suggestions upon Greek history respectfully; and his intellect was of the true Utilitarian type. His writings are as dry as the most thoroughgoing Utilitarian could desire. He will not give his readers credit for understanding the simplest argument till it is set down at full length in plain black and white. He was sceptical, and practical experience had impressed him, even to excess, with the worthlessness of human testimony. In politics scepticism naturally becomes empiricism ; and as a thoroughgoing empiricist he rejects altogether James Mill's absolute methods. He is as convinced as Macaulay that political theories must be based upon observation, and is entirely free from the error of supposing that a constitution can be devised without reference to time, place, and circumstance. Yet he could write a dialogue

---

[1] For Lewis see especially the very interesting article in Bagehot's *Works* (by Forrest Morgan), 1891, iii. 222-68. His chief political treatise is *A Treatise on Methods of Reasoning and Observation in Politics* (1852).

upon the best form of government, which seems to imply that some real meaning can be given to the problem without reference to the stage of social development, that is, to the one condition which makes the problem intelligible.

One reason is that Lewis was a practical man, and he shows very clearly why the practical man was inclined to Utilitarianism. A chancellor of the exchequer knows that the fate of a budget depends upon him, and refuses to regard himself as a mere tool of fate. A scientific treatment of history would lead, he thinks, to fatalism.[1] Everything is intrinsically uncertain where the human will is concerned.[2] Such events as the French revolution, therefore, must be regarded as controllable by statesmanship, and not, with some historians, declared to have been 'inevitable.' When we have got to the statesman or to the sovereign we have the ultimate cause, and need not ask whether he be not himself a product. Thus all laws, constitutional or otherwise, may be compared to machinery,[3] and suppose contrivance or design. All institutions have been made, and he assumes that even polygamy and slavery were 'dictated by unsound practical arguments.'[4] The tendency of such a doctrine is clear. All institutions, from the most organic to the most superficial, are regarded as equally a product of conscious manufacture. Their relation to the processes of social growth is tacitly disregarded, and the whole organism can be modified by a simple shuffling of the cards. We can therefore attack the problem ·of the best form of government

[1] *Methods of Observation*, etc., i. 448. [2] *Ibid.* i. 357.
[3] *Ibid.* ii. 356. [4] *Ibid.* ii. 370.

without emphasising the necessary reference to historical conditions. Lewis's wide reading supplied him with any number of judicious remarks, drawn from all authorities between Aristotle and Comte. Undoubtedly such remarks deserve respect ; they are apt to be commonplace, but are not therefore useless. Only, to apply them to any purpose, it is necessary to have a more definite understanding of the processes of social development which limit and define their value at any given stage. Empiricism, thus understood, really makes scientific method, as well as any definite scientific conclusion, impossible. Even in the purely practical sphere, the most important of all problems for a statesman is to know what are the limits of his powers, and to recognise what is really 'inevitable' in the great changes. Otherwise, he is in the position of Mrs. Partington fighting the Atlantic. Lewis became a Whig instead of a Utilitarian Radical ; but it may be doubtful whether Whig 'opportunism' was not the most natural development of the Utilitarian empiricism.

II. GEORGE GROTE

The great representative of Utilitarian history is George Grote (1794-1871).[1] In some respects he was the most typical Utilitarian. Grote had been introduced to James Mill by Ricardo in 1817. He had yielded after some struggle to Mill's personal influence ; and, though a

---

[1] Mrs. Grote's *Personal History of George Grote* is neither adequate nor quite accurate. Compare a very useful life by G. Croom Robertson in *Dictionary of National Biography*, and the article in the *Encyclopædia Britannica* by William Smith.

student of Kant, had become an unhesitating proselyte. He had edited *Philip Beauchamp*, had defended radical reform against Mackintosh in 1821, and had joined J. S. Mill and other young friends in their systematic logical discussions. He fully sympathised with J. S. Mill's philosophy, and, as Professor Bain tells us,[1] hardly any man 'conned and thumbed' the *Logic* as he did. He was more of a Millite than Mill. Their friendship survived in spite of Mill's seclusion, and of certain doubts in Grote's mind of his friend's orthodoxy. The articles upon Coleridge and Bentham, marking Mill's sentimental backslidings, alarmed the more rigid adherent of the faith. During the political career of the 'philosophical Radicals' Grote was the faithful Abdiel. He defended their pet nostrum, the ballot, until the party became a vanishing quantity. 'You and I,' said Charles Buller to him in 1836, 'will be left to "tell" Molesworth.'[2] On the fall of the Melbourne ministry he gave up parliament, and in 1843 retired from the bank in which he had been a partner. His continued interest in the old Utilitarian principles was shown by his lifelong activity in the management of University College and the University of London. Happily, he could occupy himself in a more productive enterprise. He had been long interested in Greek history, and his great work appeared at intervals from 1846 to 1856. His study of *Plato* appeared in 1865, and he was still labouring upon *Aristotle* at the time of his death.

Of the substantial merits of Grote's History I shall not presume to speak. It took its place at once, and

[1] Bain's *J. S. Mill*, p. 83.
[2] Mrs. Grote's *Philosophical Radicals of* 1832 (1866), p. 28.

gives a conclusive proof that the Utilitarian position was no disqualification for writing history. It seems, indeed, to prove a good deal more ; namely, that the Utilitarian who was faithful to his most vital principles was especially qualified to be a historian.

The true position may perhaps be suggested by a remark in a recent book [1] by MM. Langlois and Seignobos. In laying down the conception of history as now accepted by the best writers, they remark that Grote ' produced the first model of a history ' in the class to which it belongs. The principle illustrated is significant. ' The aim of history,' we are told, ' should now be not to please, nor to give practical maxims of conduct, nor to arouse the emotions, but [to give] knowledge pure and simple.' History should be a descriptive science. Historians must be content to give political facts as a writer upon a natural science gives the ascertained facts about physiology or chemistry. Nothing, it may be said, could be more in accordance with Utilitarian doctrine. It was their very first principle to rely upon fact pure and simple, and to make it precede speculation and to minimise ' sentiment,' ' vague generalities,' and *a priori* theories. If Grote wrote a model history, it was because he thoroughly embodied the Utilitarian spirit. He studied the evidence with immense knowledge, unflagging industry, and thorough impartiality. He resembled an ideal judge investigating evidence in a trial. That was the method which, upon their own showing, the Utilitarians were bound to apply to all subjects, and Grote applied it to Greece with triumphant success.

[1] *Introduction to the Study of History* (English translation, 1898), p. 310.

The Utilitarian principle, again, was opposed to the errors most seductive to earlier historians. The classical histories were meant to be works of art. The artistic aim is incompatible with scientific history, so far as it interferes with the primary aim of giving the unadulterated facts. To give a clear, coherent, and distinct narrative of a complex series of events requires, indeed, powers of literary expression even of the highest order. The artistic purpose must be strictly subordinate rather than absent. A writer must not disguise or embellish or omit with a view to artistic effect of the whole ; and must often sacrifice the impressive to the truthful. Sometimes, indeed, the historian must be dull — but that is a condition against which neither Grote nor the Utilitarians generally protested. It had been the aim of a different school to avoid dulness and to rival the *Waverley Novels* in making past history live. The errors of such men as Thierry and Michelet, or Carlyle, Macaulay and Froude, show the dangers of the method. The severe historian may perhaps forgive them in consideration of the interest which they excited in their studies. May he not also admit that the aim is, in some sort, legitimate ? The people, after all, were once alive, and that truth has some bearing upon their history. If imagination means a faculty of generating illusions, as the Utilitarians generally thought, it is no doubt mischievous. But even for the bare purpose of judging evidence and perceiving truth the imagination is essential. The error of transposing modern standards of thought into previous epochs is too obvious to require illustration ; but it is really the fault less of an excess than of a defect of imagination. The writer must be able, at every turn, to put himself in the place of his heroes, and of their contemporaries, if he would understand the meaning of their actions, or even judge the weight to be attributed to the evidence. That requires a trained and duly subordinate faculty of imagination. Even for mere annals—simple statements of hard facts—imagination is required, and it is required the more as we endeavour to rise from annals to history, or to make history more than an 'old calendar.'

A sound Utilitarian might be expected to make the proper compromise. No one could be more on his guard against the error of subordinating truth to poetic fancy. But he would not deny the importance of so much imaginative sympathy as is implied in a clear apprehension of the mental and moral condition of past epochs. He might find a sufficient substitute for the dangerous faculty of picturesque imagination in the more sober faculty which Grote possessed—massive common-sense; the 'knowledge of human nature,' as it is called, which corresponds not to poetic imagination or to a set of established formulæ, but to the practical insight acquired by intimate acquaintance with actual affairs. If Grote was able to rival or to surpass German professors on their own ground, it was because his want of some of their special training was more than counter-balanced by his experience of business and public life. In Threadneedle Street and at Westminster he had acquired an instinctive perception which served him in describing the political and economical conditions of Athenian life. When joined with an ardour for research that power gave a value to his judgments of fact which enabled him to write a model history.

The 'graphic' or 'artistic' type of history may be

objectionable ; is not the philosophical worse? Nothing
distorts facts so much as theory ; and a scientific historian
should be on his guard against the philosopher of all
men. But how to draw the line? Stick to bare fact and
you can only write annals. History proper begins as you
introduce causation, and the mere series is transformed into
a process. It is impossible to get a bare fact without
some admixture of theory. The Utilitarian principle,
again, suggests the right aim. It excludes the mischievous
didacticism of older historians. The question of fact must
everywhere precede the question of right. In politics,
economics and ethics Bentham and Malthus and the Mills
had in various relations applied the principle which applies
equally to history. The historian may adopt Spinoza's
great saying. His business is to understand, not to
approve or denounce. A historian treats of some great
event such as the French revolution. His one legitimate
and dominant purpose should be to explain its causes,
and he should inquire with absolute impartiality how it
came to pass, not whether it was right or wrong. The
old method of writing history attributed events to
individuals, and consistently applied a moral estimate. If
the action of this or that man, Mirabeau or Robespierre,
was the ultimate cause of the events, we may ask whether
the action was good or bad, and infer that the event
ought or ought not to have happened. The scientific
view fixes attention simply on the causes. What were
the conditions which determined the event? We must
inquire as impartially as a pathologist examining the
causes of a disease. The category of causation is the sole
category relevant. Ethical judgments may follow : we
may decide that certain processes implied progress or

decay ; we may go on to judge of the individuals, making
allowance for their motives after estimating what view of
the facts was possible for them, and we shall generally
find that there were good men and bad men on both sides,
and that it is out of place to apply such words as right or
wrong to the events themselves. The moral question
is transferred to another sphere, and human conduct is
treated as a case of natural causation. This method
is implied in the very conception of scientific history and
was fully in accordance with Utilitarianism. Men had been
complaining of the inadequacy of the old history, which
dealt exclusively with political intrigues and the military
incidents. As history became more scientific the necessity
of attending to social conditions was daily more evident,
though the extent of the change implied is scarcely even
yet realised. The history, for example, of political or
religious changes cannot be fully written without reference
to the economic conditions of the country, and whole
systems of investigation are requisite before those
conditions can be tolerably understood. Nothing could
be more in accordance with Utilitarianism than a thorough
acceptance of this view. Nor, again, should any men have
been more free from the temptation of allowing *a priori*
theories and hasty generalisations to colour their view of
facts. The true attitude of the historical inquirer should
be that which was illustrated in science by Darwin. On
the one side, he must collect as large as possible a store of
facts, observed as impartially and accurately as possible.
On the other side, he must be constantly but cautiously
generalising ; endeavouring to fit the facts in their true
order ; to discover what formulæ serve to 'colligate'
them satisfactorily ; and always to assign causes which are

both real and adequate, such that their existence can be verified, and that, if they exist, they will fit into a reasoned theory. But his theories must be tentative and liable to constant revision. They may be suggestive even if not established, but in so complex an inquiry they must be regarded as being only a relative or approximate truth.

Briefly, then, the historian should aim at providing materials for a ' sociology,' but be on his guard against supposing for a moment that such a science now exists or can ever be raised to a level with the fully developed sciences. The word corresponds to an ideal aim, not to an established fact. It is important to regard history scientifically, though we cannot hope for a complete science of history. It simply means that we must regard the history of man as the history of the gradual development of the individual and of society by forces dimly perceived, not capable of accurate measurement, but yet working regularly and involving no abrupt or discontinuous intervention.

If Grote's history be really a ' model,' it was because he virtually accepted such limitations. Historians should admit that they are still in the stage of collecting the facts upon which any wide generalisations are still premature. Grote was a student of philosophy ; he had, like Mill, been impressed by Comte, though he never, like Mill, took Comte for a prophet. He discussed early beliefs and institutions, and he certainly supposed his history to have important political implications. But a cautious intellect and a desire for a solid groundwork of fact restrained him from excessive theorising, and prevented his prejudices from overpowering his candour. So far, he represented the best Utilitarian spirit, and obeyed what was, or at least should have been, their essential canon : to make sure of your facts before you lay down your theories. They wished to apply scientific methods to history, as to law, political economy, ethics, and psychology : and, upon their view, the first condition of success was a sufficient accumulation of facts. Yet, as has abundantly appeared, they had been little disposed to confine themselves to this preliminary stage. They were too ready to assume that the sciences could be constituted offhand, and to accept convenient postulates as absolute truths. They had not only pointed out, but taken possession of, the promised land. Their premature dogmatism showed the weakness of their trusting their assumptions. The result to philosophy of history may be illustrated from the remarkable writer, who, in the period of Mill's philosophic supremacy, attempted to lay its foundation.

III. HENRY THOMAS BUCKLE

Henry Thomas Buckle (1821-1862) represents this aspiration by his *History of Civilization in England.*

Buckle[1] had some qualifications of the rarest kind.

---

[1] Buckle's *Life*, by Alfred Henry Huth, appeared in 1880. I have also to call attention to the very able and learned work, *Buckle and his Critics*, by John Mackinnon Robertson (1895). Mr. Robertson passes a severe judgment upon a criticism of Buckle which I contributed to the *Fortnightly Review* for May 1880, and takes the opportunity of pointing out some of my manifold shortcomings. Though his tone is not such as to make an apology easy, I must state my position frankly. Mr. Robertson points out the measureless inferiority of a book of mine upon the eighteenth century to Buckle's great performance. He thinks, too, that my attack was 'unchivalrous,' considering the pathetic circumstances of Buckle's death, and the fact that his work 'seemed to be sufficiently discredited already.' Now I can quite agree upon

He had been prevented by delicate health from coming into contact with contemporaries at school and college, and his intellectual tastes made him abandon a business career. He had from an early age devoted himself to a life of study. He absorbed enormous masses of knowledge, learned many languages, and had ranged over the most varied fields of literature. A most retentive memory

one point. It never entered my head to compare my own abilities to Buckle's. I could no more have rivalled his history than have encountered him at chess. It is impossible to speak more strongly. Why, then, did I presume to criticise? Because I was not giving my own unaided opinion. I had been interested by a problem. Like all young men of my time I had been impressed by the controversial storm which followed the publication of Buckle's book, and by that which soon afterwards was roused by the publication of Darwin's *Origin of Species*. Many years later, when Buckle's *Life* appeared, I was struck by a contrast. Darwin's speculations had affected every department of thought, and his influence was still spreading. Buckle's, on the other hand, had lost much of their interest—what was the reason? Briefly, as I thought, and as I still think, that Darwin had supplied a fruitful suggestion suited to the general movement of thought; and that Buckle, for want of it, had struck into a wrong path. I tried in my article to point out the nature of his error. Mr. Robertson's book confirms the truth of my impression as to facts. Had Buckle continued to interest the leaders of thought, Mr. Robertson would not have given so prominent a position to an old review article never republished, and which, so far as I know, had never attracted any particular attention. Mr. Robertson's elaborate survey of recent sociology shows that while some distinguished writers more or less coincide with Buckle, they scarcely recognise any indebtedness. That is, I think, because there was little to recognise. Buckle, in short, as it appeared to me, had not produced an effect at all comparable to those produced by Darwin or by Mr. Herbert Spencer; and I cannot think that Mr. Robertson accounts for the fact. My own explanation may of course have been wrong; but I do not see that there was anything 'unchivalrous' in trying to explain why a man of genius has not produced an effect proportionate to his powers. Nor can I see that Buckle's pathetic death made it necessary for me to modify my language in discussing his philosophy. Upon re-reading my article I recognise faults which may partly justify Mr. Robertson's resentment. I should certainly have avoided anything savouring of contempt. I did recognise Buckle's extraordinary powers, but I forgot clearly to distinguish condemnation of his opinions from depreciation of the power displayed. Substantially my view is not changed.

and methodic habits of work gave him a full command of
his materials, and the consciousness of intellectual force
suggested a daring ambition. He proposed to write a
general history of civilisation, though his scheme, as he
gradually became aware of the vastness of his task,
narrowed itself to a history of civilisation in England, with
preliminary surveys of other civilisations. Buckle had
been educated in the religious and political atmosphere of
the average middle-class type. Foreign travel and wide
reading had sapped his prejudices, and he had become
a Liberal in the days when J. S. Mill's influence was
culminating. Buckle shared the enthusiasm of the period
in which the triumph of Free Trade and the application of
Adam Smith's principles seemed to be introducing a new
era of peace and prosperity and the final extinction of
antiquated prejudice. He cannot be reckoned as a simple
Utilitarian, but he represents the more exoteric and independent allies of the chief Utilitarian thinker. He
accepts the general principles of Mill's *Logic*, though his
language upon metaphysical problems implies that his
intellect had never been fully brought to bear upon such
questions. The general sympathy with the Utilitarians
is, in any case, unmistakable, and the most characteristic
tenets of the Mill school of speculation are assumed or
defended in his writings. Buckle was thus fitted to
interpret the dominant tendencies of the day, and his
literary ability was fully adequate to the office. He has
much of the clearness and unflagging vivacity of Macaulay,
and whatever defects may be discoverable in his style, no
writer was better qualified to interest readers outside the
narrow circle of professed philosophers. The book was
accepted by many readers as an authoritative manifesto of

the scientific spirit which was to transform the whole intellectual world.

Buckle's aim is to fill the gap in the Utilitarian scheme by placing historical science upon a basis as firm as that of the physical sciences. Statistics, he argues, reveal regularities of conduct as marked as those which are revealed by the observation of natural phenomena. He gives a fatalistic turn to this statement by speaking as though the 'laws' somehow 'overrode' the individual volitions, instead of simply expressing the uniformity of the volitions themselves. Fate, it seemed, went round and compelled a certain number of people every year to commit suicide or post undirected letters in spite of themselves. Without asking how far this language, which not unnaturally startled his readers, might be corrected into a legitimate sense, we may pass to a further application. The laws by which human conduct is governed may, he says, be either 'physical' or 'mental,' the physical having more influence in the early, and the mental in the later, stages of development. This corresponds to the distinction, now familiar, between the 'organism' and the 'environment,' and requires an obvious correction. The two sets of laws refer to two factors present at every stage of human development. The 'organism' is, from first to last, dependent upon its 'environment,' but the action of the environment depends also upon the constitution of the organism. The 'mental' and 'physical,' therefore, do not act separately, but as parts of a single process. Buckle's language, however, expresses an obvious truth. As civilisation advances, the importance of the 'mental' laws in explaining the phenomena increases. The difference between two savage races may be explained simply by the difference of their surroundings ; but the civilised man may vary indefinitely, while his dwelling-place remains constant. The earlier stages are those which, in Buckle's language, are under the predominant influence of physical laws. Climate, food, and soil on the one hand, and the 'general aspects of nature' on the other hand, represent these influences. To show their action at the dawn of civilisation, Buckle points to India, Egypt, and the ancient empires in America. In those regions arose great governments, displaying remarkable coincidences of structure, and thus suggesting the operation of some ascertainable causes. If we possessed a complete ' sociology,' these phenomena would clearly illustrate important laws, working with great uniformity, though in complete independence, and therefore, it may be inferred, revealing some general principles upon the origin of governments. Nothing can present a more legitimate field of inquiry. A great despotism implies an abundant population, and therefore certain physical conditions, geographical and climatic—as the existence of a whale implies an open sea and plenty of food. The problem, then, is how do the conditions lead to the observed phenomenon ? How do the physical conditions lead to the formation of these early civilisations ? Here Buckle makes a remarkable assumption. He finds a solution in the teaching of the economists. An increase of population means a lowering of wages ; or, as he puts it, the question of wages is, ' in the long run,' a question of population.[1] Now, in cold countries more food is required, and the food is harder to procure than in the hot.[2] Hence population will

---

[1] *Civilisation*, i. 49. Note the 'wage fund' in the next page.　　[2] *Ibid.* i. 58.

increase faster in hot countries, and wages will in them tend to be low. The case of Ireland confirms or extends the theory. There, cheap food does what general fertility does in India. The potato, more than the 'scandalous misgovernment,' is the most active cause of Irish poverty. Cheap food, then, means low wages. The result, startling for an enthusiastic freetrader, suggests a confusion. An increase of population on a given area may lower wages; but it does not follow that a larger population must be worse off when the area is more productive. He ought to show that the Indian population must be in greater excess; he has only shown that it may be positively greater. There is no proof that it will increase at all when the 'checks' are once operative, or increase in a greater ratio to its support. What is the real relation of cause and effect? Did Irishmen become poor because they had cheap food, or take to cheap food because they were poor? The food enabled them, no doubt, to support a larger number of poor, and in a more precarious position. When the potato failed they could not substitute wheat. That is enough to confute the hasty assumption that cheap food is a panacea for poverty, but does not prove that plenty necessarily causes poverty. There is another step to be taken. Ricardo now supplements Malthus. He had shown that the whole wealth of a country must be divided into wages, rent, profit, and interest, while interest is proportional to profit. Now, in India, interest and rent have been enormously high; therefore wages are low and profits high.[1] A high rate of interest, however, may show that capital is scarce and payment precarious. The

---

[1] *Civilisation*, p. 69.

moneylender may extort high interest from the peasant, and yet the aggregate of profits may be small, and the whole country miserably poor. Ricardo's doctrine assumes that the wages of the labourer are advanced by the capitalist. It does not apply to a population of village communities, where the differentiation of classes has not yet taken place.[1]

Buckle, however, does not trouble himself with such difficulties. The great empires are supposed to have arisen from the growth of a rich class, whose wealth has enabled them to gain political power. No doubt the despots had great wealth in poor countries; but it does not appear that they owed it to the development of a great class of rich capitalists, or even that such a class existed. The objection to Buckle's method is apparent. In the first place, it takes for granted the existence of a complex industrial organisation as an antecedent to the growth of the despotism. The system under which the capitalist, the labourer, and the landowner share profits, wages, and rent, the whole machinery of exchange and

[1] Mr. Robertson holds that Buckle's 'generalisation' is not, as I 'strangely' represent it, an 'arbitrary application of the Ricardian law of rent to the society of Ancient India, but constitutes an elevation of Ricardo's other law of the subsistence of labour into a broad historic principle.' He points out, too, that Buckle supposed a previous stage of development, and thinks that he had appreciated Jones's correction of Ricardo, in regard to Indian rent (Buckle and his Critics, pp. 49, 59, and see p. 138). I can only say that I adhere to my statement. Buckle expressly quotes Ricardo, and makes the origin of the civilisations depend upon the threefold division. That I hold to be unjustifiable, and to be false in fact. The 'broad historic principle' seems to be simply the fact that great empires rose where physical conditions, including, of course, fertility, were favourable. Buckle may deserve credit for dwelling upon the fact. I only say that his explanation does not explain; and that it is impossible to lay down as unconditionally true that cheap food involves cheap wages. If one is to have a theory, why should we not say that empires were made by conquerors instead of by capitalists?

competition, is postulated as though it represented a
necessary state, even in the early stages of civilisation.
That was a natural application of the necessary assumption
of the orthodox political economy.   It professed to
deduce its conclusions from the laws of human nature
common to all men in all ages.   They were therefore as
valid in the earliest as in the latest time, and explain the
causes as well as the consequences of social development ;
and hence it follows that the 'mental laws' can be excluded.   Since the organism is constant, all differences
are due to differences of environment, or, in Buckle's
language, to the 'physical laws.'   'In India,' he says,
'slavery, abject slavery, was the natural state of the
great body of the people ; it was the state to which they
were doomed by physical laws utterly impossible to
resist.'[1]   In Europe, as he elsewhere puts it,[2] man is
stronger than nature ; out of Europe nature is stronger
than man.   Man is in one case the slave, and in the
other the master of the physical forces.   That is to say,
that in the earlier stages we may argue directly from the
'environment' to the 'organism.'   The hopeless slavery
to which so many millions have been doomed is a direct
and inevitable result of the 'physical laws,' that is, of the
climate, soil, and food.   We are therefore dispensed
from any inquiry into the character of the organism
itself and the 'mental' laws implied in its constitution ;
or we take for granted that the laws which regulate the
more developed organism are absolute and permanent,
and may therefore explain the earliest stages of growth.[3]

---

[1] *Civilisation*, i. 73.   [2] *Ibid.* i. 222.

[3] Buckle, I may notice, thinks Brown's essay upon Causation one of the
greatest works of the century and a statement of the principles, derived ulti-

Thus the inquiry into the nature of the social organisation, into the primitive institutions out of which the empires have grown, is virtually set aside. Because the 'mental laws' work so uniformly they may be neglected. We are left with the bare result that great empires have grown up under appropriate physical conditions, and they are all lumped together as 'despotisms.' That is to emphasise a remarkable set of facts, but not to make them more intelligible. The facts, that is, reveal a remarkable uniformity in the social organism ; but that does not show what is the nature of its organisation. If we know that, we shall be able to understand the differences and the way in which similar forces have worked under varying conditions. Buckle's leap at a generalisation so far distracts attention from the most fruitful line of inquiry. Malthus and Ricardo will solve the problem offhand. The simple coincidence of despotism and fertility entitles us to set them down as cause and effect, without further analysis of the precise mode of operation.

Buckle's next step illustrates the same point. The 'physical' laws have thus determined the distribution. They also influence religion, art, and literature by the action of 'aspects of nature' upon the imagination. The powers of nature, as he oddly puts it,[1] 'have worked

---

mately from Hume, upon which the 'best inquirers into these matters take their stand ' (*Civilisation*, ii. 460 *n*). This, I take it, explains his tendency to take a simple statement of fact for a 'law.' The most curious instance of the confusion is the remark (*Civilisation*, i. 155) that physiologists have never been able to discover the cause of the equality in the number of male and female births. Statisticians have now answered the question by showing that the proportion is 20 to 21. Obviously they have not answered the question at all. They have only ascertained the facts. Buckle partly admits this ; and yet he seems to think that the statement somehow indicates a new method of historical inquiry.   [1] *Civilisation*, i. 136.

immense mischief.' They generate superstition on one side, as they generated slavery on the other. Here Buckle's doctrine is connected with Comte's. He accepted, as he says elsewhere,[1] Comte's conclusions as to the earliest stage of the human mind. The man ignorant of scientific laws attributes all phenomena to 'supernatural causes.' Comte was only putting into a compact formula a theory more or less assumed by his predecessors. Superstition represents a necessary stage in the intellectual development of the race. It embodies the crude hypotheses of an early stage which have been falsified by later experience. They continue to exist, however, when they have long been untenable to educated minds ; and Buckle's remarks may help to explain their vitality. The 'aspects of nature' represent the impression made by apparently irregular phenomena. Superstition thrives where men's lives are at the mercy of events which cannot be foreseen. One special and characteristic instance is the influence of earthquakes. Spain, Portugal, and Italy are the European countries in which earthquakes are most frequent, and are also the countries in which superstition has been most rife. The excessive stimulus to the imagination has led to the collateral result that while these countries have produced all the greatest artists, they have (with the partial exception of Italy) produced no great names in science.[2] The principle that superstition is fostered by such conditions may well be illustrated by these facts. Hume had remarked that the events which to good reasoners were the 'chief difficulties in admitting a supreme intelligence' were to the

---

[1] *Civilisation*, i. 342 *n.*   [2] *Ibid.* i. 112.

vulgar 'the sole arguments for it.'[1]   Buckle might
well extend the argument.   But to say that earthquakes
'cause' Spanish superstition is a bold generalisation.   It
is an application of Mill's canon of simple agreement.
Earthquakes and superstition coexist in two or three
districts; therefore earthquakes are the cause of superstition.[2]   On Buckle's own showing, earthquakes are
only one of countless conditions which may produce
superstition.   Why is this special condition to be isolated?
If Spain is now superstitious, must not that be due to
the concurrence of innumerable causes?   Have not
other countries been steeped in the profoundest superstition though they had no earthquakes?   How, indeed, is
the amount of superstition in a country to be measured?   If
we were to explain a particular superstition by the apparent
irregularity of the phenomena concerned—the belief in an

---

[1] *Natural History of Religion*, sec. vi.   Mr. Robertson attacks me for my
criticisms of Buckle's assertions of the deductive character of Scottish philosophers.   I cannot go into the question, but I make one remark.   He quotes
the first sentence of Hume's *Natural History* to prove that Hume was a deist
when he wrote it, and says that this is implied through the whole essay.
Now Hume's most serious attack upon theology, the *Dialogues*, was written
by 1751, though posthumously published.   The *Natural History* appeared in
1757.   The deistic phrases obviated the necessity for leaving it also for
posthumous publication.

[2] A curious illustration is given by Mr. Robertson (p. 140).   The Japanese,
it had been said, are less superstitious than their neighbours, and yet more
exposed to earthquakes.   If Buckle's theory means that superstition necessarily
follows earthquakes, the fact seems to contradict the theory.   So Mr. Robertson seems to take it, for he gives an explanation.   The Japanese do not suffer
from earthquakes because they build slighter houses.   If so, earthquakes, it
surely might be urged, do not produce superstition, but rational precautions.
If, on the other hand, the Spaniards have not modified their architecture, that
would surely prove that they have not been much impressed by earthquakes.
The case seems to me to prove simply the rashness of any such hasty guesses.
Buckle's early critics were misguided enough to deny the facts alleged, and
so gave him a triumph.

earth-shaking deity, for example—the explanation might
be adequate. The objection rises when it is presented
as a general scientific formula. Since 'superstition' is a
universal incident of early stages of human thought, it
is clearly not explicable by the phenomena of special
districts. That may be an instructive example, but
cannot give the general law. It is illegitimate to single
out the particular condition as if it were the sole cause.
The main point, however, is again the mode of arguing
from the environment to the organism. The argument
from the environment to the organism, from the earthquakes to superstition, has then an obvious limit. The
constant condition can only explain the constant qualities.
The palpable fact is that the same country has been
occupied by races of most different characters. Free-
thinking flourishes where there was once abject superstition, and therefore the country cannot by itself explain
the superstition. When, for example, Buckle explains the
artistic temperament of Greeks or Italians by the physical
characteristics, he is no doubt assigning a real cause, but
obviously a cause insufficient to explain the singular
changes, the efflorescence and the decay of artistic production in either country. One result is characteristic. The
differences are often explained by 'heredity' or the inheritance by races of qualities not developed by their present
environment, and essentially dependent upon the previous
social evolution. Buckle fully admits that the question
of 'heredity' is not settled by scientific inquiry.[1] He
infers, and I suppose rightly, that we cannot assume
that there is any organic difference between an infant
born in the most civilised country and one born in the

[1] *Civilisation*, i. 161.

most barbarous region. Still, he ' cordially subscribes '
to Mill's protest against explaining differences of character by race.[1] So far as this excludes all the influences
by which a society is moulded through inherited beliefs
and customs, it sanctions an erroneous inference. Because
race differences are not ultimate, or indicative of absolute
organic distinctions, they are altogether cast out of
account. The existing differences have to be attributed
entirely to the physical surroundings ; and the influence of ' aspects of nature ' is summarily adduced to
explain much that is really explicable only through the
history of the organism itself.[2]

How far this may have led Buckle to exaggerate the

[1] *Civilisation*, i. 37 *n.*

[2] Mr. Robertson reproves me for not quoting the passage in which Buckle
says that the question of hereditary influence is still unsettled. Probably I
should have recognised this more clearly. I did, however, say that Buckle
held that the superiority of the civilised to the barbarian infant was 'not
proved.' I said also that I thought that Buckle was justified for his purposes
in neglecting the possibility of a superiority. He says, in the passage quoted
above, that we have no right to assume such a change as an increase of
brain capacity. I took it that for any historical period we may assume
equality. The brain of a modern Englishman is not presumably superior
to the brain of an Athenian. Evolution of that kind may be neglected
by the historian of civilisation. The evolution, which I did take him to
neglect, was the moral or social evolution, which is compatible with approximate identity of the brain or the innate faculties. Buckle, I said, shared the
error of the Utilitarians who assumed moral progress to consist, not in a
changed estimate of happiness, but simply in a better knowledge of the
means of attaining it. Buckle's identification of progress with increase of
knowledge involved, I said, the same error. The change is regarded as
superficial or ' external.' Meanwhile my argument, which Mr. Robertson
attacks, about the fallacy of arguing from the fixed environment to the
varying organism applied to such cases as the inference from earthquakes to
superstition or from climate to æsthetic tendencies. Such a generalisation, taken
as an explanation of superstition, generally implies, as I held, an inadequate
appreciation of the social or moral evolution. Perhaps I did not put the point
clearly or accurately, and, if so, I regret it.

direct efficacy of mere physical surroundings I cannot further inquire. At any rate, his whole purpose is to explain the growth of civilisation, which must, as he perceives, be done by introducing a variable element. Here, therefore, we have to consider the state in which the 'mental' become more influential than the physical laws. Buckle begins by expounding a doctrine of critical importance. In general terms, he holds that progress depends upon the intellectual factor. A similar doctrine had been emphatically asserted by Comte, and was, indeed, implied as a fundamental conception in his whole work. Ideas, he says, govern the world : 'Tout le mécanisme social repose sur les opinions.'[1] The law of the 'three stages' is a systematic application of this doctrine. The doctrine, again, recognises an undeniable truth. Man is dependent throughout upon his environment. That, in a sense, remains constant. The savage lives in the same world as the civilised man. But every step of knowledge implies a change in the man's relations to the world. His position is determined not simply by the 'physical laws,' but by his knowledge of the laws. The discovery of iron or of electricity makes his world, if not the world, different ; and the whole system of knowledge corresponds to an ultimate condition of his life. His knowledge, therefore, is an essential factor in the problem. The rationalism of the eighteenth century and the later progress of science had of course emphasised this truth. The natural sciences represent the intellectual framework, which steadily grows and at every stage gives a final determinant of all human activity. Superstitions and theology in general correspond to the

[1] *Philosophie Positive*, 1852, i. 44, and cp. *Ibid.* iv. 648, etc.

erroneous theories which are gradually dispelled as we construct a definitive and verifiable base of solid knowledge. But is the scientific progress not only the ultimate but the sole factor in all social development? Man is a complex being, with an emotional as well as an intellectual nature, which, proximately at any rate, determines his conduct. How are we to allow for this factor of the inquiry?[1]

Buckle's version of the principle is significant. He begins by distinguishing 'progress' into 'moral' and 'intellectual.'[2] Which of these is the important element? Do men progress in the moral or in the intellectual element? Since, as we have seen, we cannot assume an improvement in the individual, the later differences must be ascribed to the 'external advantages'—to the opinions and so forth of the society in which the child is educated. In the next place, the opinions are constantly varying, whereas the 'moral motives' are singularly constant.[3] A 'stationary element,' when surrounding circumstances are unchanged, can only produce a stationary effect, and hence we must explain civilisation by the variable agent. Buckle argues that the moral code recognised has remained unaltered since distant times. The same general rules are accepted, and no additional articles have been inserted. Then the great stages of progress—especially the growth of religious toleration and of peace—have been due to intellectual, not to moral

[1] Mr. Herbert Spencer raises this question in a criticism of Comte, contained in a pamphlet upon the 'Classification of the Sciences.' See Mill's remarks upon this in his *Auguste Comte and Positivism*, pp. 34, 43, 102, 114. The controversy between Mr. Spencer and Comte lies beyond my province.

[2] *Civilisation*, p. 152.   [3] *Ibid.* pp. 160-63.

changes; and, finally, as he thinks, the average man remains pretty much the same. Some men are good and some bad; but the good and the bad actions neutralise each other. Their effects are temporary, while the 'discoveries of great men' are 'immortal,' and contain the 'eternal truths which survive the shock of empires, outlive the struggles of rival creeds, and witness the decay of successive religions.'[1] Buckle, that is, reserves for the 'eternal truths' of scientific discovery the enthusiasm which others had lavished upon the eternal truths of the great religious teachers. The doctrine agrees with the Utilitarian theories in one respect. Man is supposed to remain on the whole constant, in his natural capacities and in his moral qualities. On the other hand, Buckle dwells more emphatically than Mill upon the spontaneous growth of scientific ideas as the sole but sufficient force which moulds the destinies of mankind. From Mill's constant insistence upon the power of association and the empirical character of all knowledge, it might be inferred that even scientific progress is precarious and unstable. To Buckle the development of scientific knowledge seems to be inevitable, if only the mind is allowed to work freely. The most conspicuous facts of the day gave force to his conviction. The enormous changes in the whole constitution of society were due to the advance of mechanical discoveries and to the triumph of freetraders. Watt and Adam Smith, not the religious preachers, represent the real transforming force. The steam-engine has altered the whole position of the human race. The sermons of Methodists and Catholics have left the

[1] *Civilisation*, p. 206.

average man just where he was. Napoleon was a great criminal, and Wilberforce, perhaps, a great philanthropist. Their influence has been transitory, while the scientific inventors have set up changes which will continue to gather force as the ages roll.

The truth contained in this, again, seems to be undeniable. Modify the 'environment' and your organism is modified throughout. Alter the climate, the soil, the amount of fertile land, and the whole state of mankind will be altered. That, again, has been virtually achieved by modern discoveries. Though the natural forces may be the same, our relation to them has been altered ; and, if more fertile soil has not been brought into existence, the fertile soil has been brought, we may say, nearer to our doors. Moreover, the change has been primarily due to scientific discovery and not to any moral change ; or the moral changes, whatever they may be, have been the consequence, not the cause. So far as Buckle emphasised this aspect, he was clearly insisting upon a truth which requires recognition. The question is what bearing this has upon the philosophy of history, and whether it justifies us in discarding the influence of the 'moral' element in building up the social structure.

The general doctrine leads to the conclusion that the essential difference between two stages of history is the difference between the quantity of knowledge possessed and its diffusion throughout all classes. That is really Buckle's contention, from which all his conclusions are deducible. The 'totality of human actions,' as he says, is 'governed by the totality of human knowledge ; [1] or, as he elsewhere puts it, [2] the history of every 'civilised

[1] *Civilisation*, p. 209.   [2] *Ibid.* p. 354.

country is the history of its intellectual development.'
If early societies are governed by the 'physical laws,'
later societies are governed by the action of those laws
upon our minds, and the action is thus profoundly
modified as our knowledge of the laws extends. The
'environment' has a different relation to us, but remains
the ultimate and independent determinant. If this be
the whole truth, it would follow that we might write the
history of mankind by writing the history of science.
All other phenomena would be simply deducible as
corollaries from the state of knowledge. Comte had
suggested that history might be written without mention-
ing the names of individuals. On Buckle's assumption,
history may deal simply with the growth of scientific
ideas; and, therefore, we need not take into account the
moral ideas or all the complex system of actions which
come under the head of the will and the emotions in
psychological treatises.

Is it possible to write a history upon such terms?
Granting that knowledge defines the base upon which the
whole structure must repose, can we abstract from all
this considerations of the way in which men's beliefs are
brought to bear upon the constitution of society? The
difficulty becomes obvious as soon as Buckle turns from
his general principle to the historical application. Mark
Pattison,[1] in his review of the History on its first
appearance, puts the point. Buckle, he says, after
insisting upon the utter inadequacy of the old historical
and metaphysical methods, proceeds to 'exemplify the
very method of writing history which he had con-

---

[1] *Essays* (1889), ii. 422. (Essay on Buckle, reprinted from *Westminster Review* of 1857.)

demned.' His account of French society is, as Pattison says, a 'masterly sketch,' unequalled in breadth and comprehensiveness of view by any English writer. But, then, it brings in precisely the elements of individual influence, and so forth, which Buckle expressly professed to exclude. I will add nothing to the commendation possessing a higher authority than my own. Buckle's surveys, not only of French, but of English, Spanish, and Scottish, I believe, may fully justify the opinion that his abilities, rightly directed, might have produced a history surpassing the achievement of any of his rivals. But the only question with which I am concerned is the relation of the history to the philosophy. Buckle, if he had simply written a history of England, might have eclipsed Hallam or Macaulay in their own line. Did he really inaugurate a better method of writing history in general? or, if not, what caused the failure of a man possessed of such singular qualifications?

A difficulty is suggested even in regard to the purely scientific development. Buckle speaks with the warmest enthusiasm of great men, such as Descartes, whose scientific discoveries revolutionised thought, or Adam Smith,[1] who, by publishing a single work, contributed more to human happiness than all the statesmen and legislators of whom we have an authentic record. How can this be reconciled with the insignificance of the individual? A great discovery is necessarily the work of an individual. No combination of second-rate men could have supplied the place of a single Newton. It therefore occurs to Buckle that, after all, the individual has to be taken into account. If Descartes and Smith

[1] *Civilisation*, i. 197.

had died of the measles in infancy, progress would have been arrested. To escape this conclusion, he refers to the 'spirit of the age,' which would have made the discovery fruitless at a different period. What is covered by that phrase ? The social influence does not supersede the necessity for individual genius. Everything that is done must of course be done by individuals. The 'spirit of the age' must mean such a social order as fosters discovery ; an order, for example, in which so many men are devoted to scientific inquiry that discovery becomes certain. The man of genius is still first in the race ; but he is first of many competitors, who, even if he were to die, would achieve the same result a little later. The individual is still required, but the importance of any particular individual is so far diminished. The growth of science cannot be explained, in the historical sense, without reference to the social order which leads to the cultivation of science. It is not something which grows of its own accord outside of society, but supposes the whole social structure and the moral factor which we are endeavouring to discard.

The difficulty affects Buckle's mode of dealing with the great historical problems. Since progress depends absolutely upon the growth of science, the one essential is the spirit of inquiry, or, as he calls it, 'scepticism.' Its natural antagonist is the 'protective' spirit, which implies servile submission to authority in matters of opinion or practice. The disastrous effects of such a spirit are traced in Spain and Scotland. The 'inquisition' and the tyranny of Puritan ministers are its natural fruits. No one, of course, will deny the evils due to a suppression of intellectual activity. To exhibit and to denounce those

evils is a task which Buckle performs with admirable
vigour. But, so far, he is merely writing an effective
pamphlet on a large scale. He is denouncing the protective spirit as the Whig historian denounces Toryism,
or rival religious historians find the evil principle in
Protestantism or Popery. The protective spirit is an
abstraction which means a quality of the whole society
considered from one point of view ; its relation, namely,
to scientific progress. It cannot be an ultimate cause—
a power in itself—but is a product of many complex
conditions. To consider it impartially, to form an accurate diagnosis of the disease is the problem for the
scientific historian. He should discover the uniform
laws whose working is manifest in the morbid condition,
and, in the case of Spain, render the intellectual paralysis
permanent and incurable. Here Buckle's method becomes that of the ordinary historian. He refers to the
earthquakes and various physical conditions which apply
to the case of Spanish superstition. We now learn, however, that these physical influences are 'interwoven with a
long chain of other and still more influential events,' which
enable us to trace the steps of decline with 'unerring
certainty.'[1] We go back, therefore, both in Spain and
Scotland to the political history ; to the play of party and
class-interests, which have forced a priesthood at one
time to ally itself with despots, and at another to throw
itself upon the people. The history may be accurate and
the facts alleged are no doubt relevant ; but they leave
the difficult problems unsolved. Why, for example, was
the Spanish people at the head of European races in the
sixteenth century, and why did it then suddenly sink into

[1] *Civilisation*, ii. 9.

decay? Why did Scotland, sunk in superstition in the seventeenth century, become, though still the most superstitious country in Europe, the most energetic and progressive part of the British empire? To attack such problems it would, I take it, be necessary to study impartially a vast variety of social and of what Buckle calls moral questions; to give weight to a number of 'interwoven' causes, determining the history of the two races. The facts—the intellectual stagnation of Spain and the intolerance of Scottish Puritanism—imply, as Buckle urges, some general causes. The history shows them at work, and Buckle's survey brings out many significant facts. Still, when the protective spirit is hypostatised and made a kind of independent cause, determining and not determined by the general social state, we miss the most interesting problem, or take the solution for granted. What, after all, is the true secret of this mysterious power? Whence came its vitality? The evil principle appears like the supernatural sovereign in 'Philip Beauchamp' or the Demogorgon of Shelley's *Prometheus,* a cruel tyrant enforcing false belief—even so, he requires to be explained as well as denounced, and we are at least tempted to ask whether the church and the king must not have discharged some useful social function; and the creed have embodied some element of thought and emotion congenial to human nature. That is the aspect neglected by Buckle.

One or two conspicuous examples of the result may be indicated. Buckle has to deal with the French revolution.[1] Nobody has been more emphatic in insisting that

---

[1] On this point Mr. Robertson virtually agrees with me, though he attaches less importance to it.

history should deal with the facts which illustrate the state
of the people instead of confining itself to court intrigues.
Nor could any one speak more strongly of the misery
of the French population before the revolution.   Yet the
whole explanation has to be sought in the purely intellectual causes.   The social causes are simply dropped out
of account.   The revolution was due to the French
philosophers.   Intellectual activity had been entirely suppressed by the despotism of Louis xiv.   The philosophers, he holds, learned the new doctrine from England.
The persecution of the freethinkers by the later rulers
and a servile priesthood forced the philosophers to attack
both the despots, and (unfortunately, as Buckle holds) to
attack Christianity as well.   Hence both the achievements
and the incidental evils caused by the final outbreak.
The theory, though strangely inadequate, is a natural
corollary from the doctrine that the history of a nation is
the history of its intellectual development.   Voltaire's
study of Locke becomes the efficient cause of a gigantic
social change..   A single characteristic, itself the product
of many factors, is made to account for the whole complex
process.   Still more significant is his account of the
decreasing influence of the warlike spirit.   That, too,
must be a product of purely intellectual causes.   Divines
have done nothing by preaching, but intellectual movement has operated in 'three leading ways.'[1]   The discoveries of gunpowder, of free trade principles, and of
the application of steam to travelling have produced the
peaceable tendencies, which, in Buckle's day, were apparently so near a final triumph.   Let us fully grant what I
hope is true, that this corresponds to a truth ; that the

[1] *Civilisation*, i. 185.

various forces which have brought men together may ultimately conduce to peace ; and, moreover, that the discoveries of science are among the ultimate conditions of the most desirable of all changes. Does this enable us to abstract from the social movement ? Gunpowder, according to Buckle, facilitated the differentiation of the military from the other classes. That already assumes a process only intelligible through the social history. Buckle tells us that ' divines ' have done nothing. If he means that they have not persuaded nations, or not even tried to persuade them, to turn the second cheek, he is unanswerable. Religion, as he says elsewhere,[1] is an ' effect,' not a cause of human improvement. It can, in fact, be an original cause only on the hypothesis of a supernatural intervention. It must be an ' effect ' in the sense that it is a product of human nature under all the conditions. If by religion is meant simply the belief in fictitious beings, it may be considered as simply an obstruction to scientific advance ; and the priesthood, as Buckle generally seems to hold, is the gang of impostors who turn it to account. In any case, the ' moral ' teaching of priests cannot be the ultimate cause of moral improvement. Yet no one, it might be supposed, could explain the history of the warlike sentiment in Europe without taking into account the influence embodied in the church. That the Catholic church represented a great principle of cohesion ; that it was an organisation which enabled the men of intellect to exercise an influence over semi-barbarous warriors, are admitted facts which the historian is at least bound to consider. At whatever period the body may have become corrupt, it is an essential fact in

[1] *Civilisation*, p. 235.

the social processes which preceded the invention of gunpowder, and certainly the discoveries of Watt and Adam
Smith.   Buckle, as a rule, treats the church simply as an
upholder of superstition.   He ridicules the historians who
believed in absurd miracles in ' what are rightly termed
the dark ages,' [1] and declares summarily that ' until doubt
began, progress was impossible.'   Yet Buckle would certainly have admitted that there was some progress between
the heptarchy and the reformation.

The truth which his method compels him to neglect
seems to be obvious.   The movement of religious thought
represents forces not to be measured by the quantity of
effete superstitions which it contains.   The religion
corresponds to the development of the instincts which
determine the whole social structure.   The general moral
axioms—love your neighbour, and so forth—may, as
Buckle urges, remain unaltered ; but the change in the
ideals of life and the whole attitude of men to each other
takes place in the religious sphere.   If Christianity does
not correspond to a force imposed from without, it may
still correspond to the processes of thought by which
sympathy has extended and men been drawn into comparative unity and harmony.   To treat the power of
religion as simply a product of ignorant superstition is to
be unable to understand the history of the world.   So
much Buckle might have learned from Comte in spite of
the later vagaries of positivism.

Another collateral conclusion marks Buckle's position.
As a historian of political progress he is constantly
dwelling upon the importance of individual action.   The

---

[1] *Civilisation*, pp. 248, 283, 289, 306.   He occasionally admits that the
church protected the poor and was useful in its time.   *Ibid.* pp. 462, 559.

tolerant policy of Richelieu, the despotic system of Louis
XIV., and so forth, are the great aids or impediments to
human progress. How is this reconcilable with the
doctrines that individual action is nothing and the spontaneous growth of knowledge everything? In answer
we are referred to the great general causes, or to the
protective spirit or the spirit of the age, which really
govern the whole process in spite of superficial and transitory causes. What precisely is meant by these abstractions? To what does the protective spirit in politics owe
its malign persistence? What, in short, is the source and
true nature of the power of government? The answer
is, that to Buckle, as to the Utilitarians, government
represents a kind of external force; something imposed
upon the people from without; a 'sovereign,' in Austin's
sense, who can never originate or impel, though he can
coerce and suppress. He chooses the history of England
for his subject, as he tells us, because England has been
'less affected than any other country by the two main
sources of interference, namely, the authority of government and the influence of foreigners.'[1] Both are treated
as 'interferences' from without, which distort the natural
development. English history is interesting not because
its political constitution is a most characteristic outgrowth
of its social state, but because all government is simply
an interference, and in England has had a minimum
influence. Consistently with this, he attacks the opinion
that progress has ever been due to government. Government is, of course, necessary to punish crime and prevent anarchy;[2] but even its successful efforts are
'altogether negative'; and, even where its intentions have

[1] *Civilisation*, i. 213.   [2] *Ibid.* i. 257.

been good, it has been generally injurious. Briefly, government is powerful for evil, and the one principle is that rulers should have a 'very little' power and exercise it 'very sparingly.'[1]　At times he is inclined to deny all influence to government. Speaking of Scotland, he remarks that though bad government can be extremely injurious for a time, it can 'produce no permanent mischief.'[2]　'So long as the people are sound,' he says, 'there is life and will be reaction. . . . But if the people are unsound all hope is gone and the nation perishes.' What, then, makes the people 'sound'? Is not this a tacit admission of the importance of the moral factor? Has not the religion of a nation some influence, and sometimes perhaps an influence for good, upon its morality? Puritanism in Scotland was associated with gross superstition ; was it not also an expression of the moral convictions which preserved the 'soundness' of the race? Catholicism in Spain is still, according to Buckle, associated with a high moral standard ; but this has 'availed the Spaniards' nothing,[3] because it has suppressed intellectual progress.　It has surely been of some use if it has preserved their virtue.　But, in any case, what is the explanation of the power of government which can thus destroy the 'soundness' or morality and ruin the fortunes of a people? Buckle's theory might apply to the case of a nation conquered by a foreign tyrant. He denounces conquerors in the old tone as pests and destroyers of men, who pass their whole lives in increasing human misery.[4] Yet conquest has been a factor in the development of all nations, and Buckle

---

[1] *Civilisation*, i. 264.　　　　[2] *Ibid*. ii. 274.
[3] *Ibid*. ii. 145, 146.　　　　[4] *Ibid*. i. 729.

himself argues that the Norman conquest was an essential step in establishing the liberties of Englishmen.[1] It is still more difficult to suppose that a government which is the growth of a people's own requirements can be simply mischievous. Without trying to solve such puzzles, we may say that the whole doctrine seems to imply a misconception of the relations between the political and the social and moral constitution of a nation. No satisfactory theory can be formed, when it is assumed that the function of government is simply to keep the peace instead of inquiring historically what functions it has actually discharged. When Buckle regards government like the 'physical laws' as the cause of pure mischief, he ceases to be scientific and becomes after a fashion a moralist, denouncing instead of explaining.

The connection of this with the do-nothing doctrine which Buckle accepts in its fullest form is obvious. The less government the better is the natural formula for a disciple of Adam Smith. What is here important is the connection of the doctrine with Buckle's first principles. The political order cannot be thus treated as if it were an independent power impinging from without upon a natural order ; it is a product of the whole organism, and to denounce it as simply bad is really meaningless. It is part of the essential structure, and therefore we cannot properly abstract from the other parts of the system. This or that regulation, or this or that wheel of the political machinery may be superfluous or mischievous ; but the question can only be decided by regarding the system as a whole, and not by treating the ruling power as something separable. Its interference

---

[1] *Civilisation*, i. 563.

has to be treated as abnormal or as simply mischievous, and yet as of vital importance in history. It becomes a mystery simply because we do not investigate its nature with due reference to its functions in the body politic. In other words, Buckle becomes incoherent because his method induces him from the start to neglect what is implied when society is described as organic. IIe was speaking an indisputable truth when he said that society depends throughout upon the 'environment' in the physical laws. It is not less true to say that as the intellectual progress developed, the recognition of those laws supplies an ultimate and unchangeable condition of the whole process of social growth. All civilisation depends absolutely, as he asserts, upon the corresponding state of knowledge. The error is in the assumption that we can therefore omit the consideration of the complex laws which govern the growth of the organism itself. The individualism which he shares with the Utilitarians makes him blind to the importance of the line of inquiry which was to show its power in the following period. If the primitive despotisms are set down simply as a necessary result of 'physical laws,' it is superfluous to inquire into the real nature of the institutions which they imply, or to gain any light upon the working of similar principles elsewhere. When the whole ecclesiastical and political constitution of later ages is set down simply as a relic of barbarism, and the religious and social instincts which are elaborated through them as simply products of ignorance, the process becomes unintelligible. If, therefore, Buckle was recognising a real condition of sound investigation, he condemned in advance the very kind of inquiry which has proved most fruitful. If he did more in his purely historical inquiries it was because he then forgot his philosophy and had to take into account the considerations which he had pronounced to be irrelevant. That, I believe, is the reason why Buckle, in spite of his surpassing abilities, did not make any corresponding mark upon later investigations. He was trying to frame a philosophy of history upon principles which really make the formation of a coherent philosophy impossible. Briefly, then, Buckle shared the ambition of the Utilitarians to make all the moral sciences scientific. So far as his writing strengthened the leaning to a scientific tendency he was working in the right direction. Unfortunately he also shared their crude assumptions: the 'individualism' which ignores the social factor, and deduces all institutions from an abstract 'man'; the tendency to explain the earlier from the later stages; and the impression that 'laws of nature' are to be unravelled by a summary method of discovering co-existences of concrete phenomena; and was therefore led to substitute hasty generalisations for that elaborate study of the growth of institutions and beliefs which has been the most marked tendency of sociological inquiry during the last generation. So far he shares and illustrates the real weakness of the Utilitarians, the premature attempt to constitute a science when we can only be labouring effectually by trying to determine the data.

Here I may try to indicate, though I cannot develop, a general conclusion. What was the true significance of the Utilitarian paradox—the indifference to history combined with the appeal to experience? History in the narrower sense is a particular case of evolution; and if it could be made scientific, would formulate the laws by which the existing institutions, political, ecclesiastical, and industrial, have grown out of earlier states. The importance of taking into account the 'genetic' point of view, of inquiring into the growth as well as the actual constitution of things, is obvious in all the sciences which are concerned with organic life. Though we cannot analyse the organism into its ultimate constituent factors, we can learn something by tracing its development from simpler forms. The method is applicable to biology as well as to sociology; and as sciences extended, its importance became manifest. Some theory of evolution was required in every direction, and must obviously be necessary if we are to carry out systematically the principles of the uniformity and continuity of nature. The difficulty of the Utilitarians was all along that theories of evolution appeared to them to involve something mystical and transcendental. They proposed to analyse everything till they could get to single aggregations of facts, or in their sense ideal, that is, to a thoroughgoing atomism. This leads to the paradox indicated by Hume's phrase. The atoms, things and thoughts, must be completely separate and yet invariably conjoined. Causation becomes mere sequence or conjunction, and 'experience' ceases to offer any ground for anticipation. I have tried to show how this affected the Utilitarians in every subject; in their philosophical, legal, ethical, and economical speculations; and how they always seem to be in need of, and yet always to reject by anticipation, some theory of evolution. To appeal to 'experience' they have to make the whole universe incoherent, while to get general laws they have to treat variable units as absolutely constant. 'External circumstances' must account for all variation, though it is difficult to see how everything can be 'external.' The difficulty has now appeared in history proper, and the attempt to base a sociology upon a purely individualist assumption. This may help to explain the great influence of the Darwinian theories. They marked the point at which a doctrine of evolution could be allied with an appeal to experience. Darwin appealed to no mystical bond, but simply to verifiable experience. He postulated the continuance of processes known by observation, and aimed at showing that they would sufficiently explain the present as continuous with the past. There was nothing mystical to alarm empiricists, and their consequent adoption of Darwinism implied a radical change in their methods and assumptions. The crude empiricism was transformed into evolutionism. The change marked an approximation to the conceptions of the opposite school when duly modified, and therefore in some degree a reconciliation. 'Intuitions' no longer looked formidable when they could be regarded as developed by the race instead of mysteriously implanted in the individual mind. The organic correlations were admissible when they were taken to imply growth instead of supernatural interference, and it was no longer possible to regard 'natural kinds' as mere aggregates of arbitrarily connected properties. I need not ask which side really gained by the change, whether Darwinism inevitably leads to some more subtle form of atomism, or whether the acceptance of any evolution does not lead to idealism—to a belief in a higher teleology than Paley's—and the admission that mind or 'spirit' must be the ultimate reality. Such problems may be treated by the philosopher of the future. Without anticipating his verdict, I must try to indicate the final outcome of what passed for philosophy with the Utilitarians.

CHAPTER VI

PHILOSOPHY

I. MILL'S OPPONENTS

MILL's logic embodies the cardinal principles of his philosophy. The principles implied that little of what is called philosophy could be valid. Mill necessarily held that many of the most pretentious speculations were, in reality, nothing but words ; cobwebs of the brain to be swept into the dustbin, finally, though politely, by the genuine thinkers. His view of the consequences to theology and religion could for a long time be inferred only from incidental remarks. Gradually he came to think that the reticence was undesirable, and had given his final conclusions in the *Essays*, which were published after his death. The philosophical position which underlies them is most clearly exhibited in his *Examination* of Hamilton (1865).[1] This included a criticism of Mansel's application of Hamilton's metaphysical doctrines to theology. Mansel's doctrine, stated in the

---

[1] Mill's *Examination of Sir William Hamilton's Philosophy and of the Principal Philosophical Questions discussed in his Writings* was first published in 1865. I refer to the fourth edition (1872). The book was more changed than any of Mill's other writings in consequence of the insertion of replies to various criticisms. A list of these replies is given in the preface to the third and fourth editions. The essays on 'Religion' appeared in 1874.

Bampton Lectures of 1858, had provoked some sharp
and many-sided controversies. He defended himself
against Mill's criticism. Other writers joined the fray,
and in one way or other a perplexing set of intellectual
encounters resulted. The leading champions were Mill,
representing the pure Utilitarian tradition, Mansel, who
represented the final outcome of what Mill called ' intuitionism,' and F. D. Maurice, who may be briefly called
the intellectual heir of Coleridge ; while another line of
inference was represented by Mr. Herbert Spencer's *First
Principles*. Many of the arguments have already a
strangely obsolete sound ; but they may serve to illustrate the direction of the main currents of opinion.

The writings of Sir William Hamilton provided the
ostensible battle-ground. Mill had seen in Hamilton
certain symptoms of a hopeful leaning towards the true
faith. Upon taking up the study more seriously, he
discovered that Hamilton was really an intuitionist at
bottom, and even a ' chief pillar ' of the erroneous philosophy. I shall therefore inquire, in the first place, into
the true nature of this version of the evil principle. It
has been so often ' lucidly expounded ' that it is hard to
say what it really means.

Hamilton,[1] born 8th March 1788, was grandnephew,
grandson, and son of three successive professors of
anatomy at Glasgow. While still an infant, he lost his
father, and was ever afterwards on terms of the tenderest
affection with his mother, who died in 1827. After
studying at Glasgow, he went to Balliol as a Snell
exhibitioner in 1807, and there startled his examiners by

---

[1] See Veitch's *Life of Hamilton* (1869), and an article by Hamilton's daughter
in the *Encyclopædia Britannica*.

his portentous knowledge of Aristotle.[1]   After some
medical study, he decided to join the Scottish bar.   He
took, however, more interest in the antiquarian than in
the practical branches of the laws ; and spent a great deal
of time and labour on abstruse genealogical researches to
establish his claim to a baronetcy.   He had to show that
he was heir to a Sir Robert Hamilton, who died in 1701,
through a common ancestor who died before 1552.   His
love of obscure researches, or his want of aptitude for
speaking, together with his adherence to Whig principles,
kept him out of the road to professional success.   He
was known, however, as a 'monster of erudition.'   He
visited Germany with his college friend J. G. Lockhart
in 1817, and on a second visit in 1820 began a systematic
study of the language.

In 1820 Hamilton was a candidate for the chair of
Moral Philosophy at Edinburgh, vacant by the death
of Thomas Brown.   To the scandal of philosophers, it
was given to Wilson, or 'Christopher North,' mainly on
political grounds.   Probably it was also held that anybody
could talk Moral Philosophy.   Hamilton was appointed to
a small professorship in 1821, but the salary, payable from
a duty on beer, was stopped and he ceased to lecture.

In 1829, Macvey Napier, upon succeeding Jeffrey as
editor of the *Edinburgh Review*, applied to his friend

[1] A letter from Hamilton to Dr. Parr in 1820 (Parr's *Works*, vii. 194-
202), on occasion of the contest at Edinburgh, gives an account of his studies.
He was personally unknown to Dugald Stewart, to whom he desires Parr to
write a letter upon the advantages of studying ancient philosophy, to be shown
to the Town Council (who then elected the professor).   Hamilton says that
he took up nearly all Aristotle, most of Plato, and of Cicero's philosophical
works ; that he had read many Greek commentators upon Plato and Aristotle,
and that many of his books were declared to be too metaphysical for the schools
and were forbidden to be taken up again.   Veitch gives a similar account.

Hamilton for an article. The result was the review of Cousin, which appeared in the number for October 1829. Jeffrey was rather scandalised by this novelty in his old organ ; the writer showed an unholy familiarity with the Absolute and the Infinite and the jargon of German metaphysics ; he could not, said Jeffrey, be a ' very clever man,' and the article was the 'most unreadable thing that had ever appeared in the *Review*.' [1] The average reader, however, was awed if not interested ; and a select few, including Cousin, were greatly impressed. Hamilton's reputation was made ; he wrote other articles which confirmed the impression, and in 1836 was appointed to the Edinburgh professorship of ' Logic and Metaphysics.' He was at length in his proper place ; and many students of that generation became ardent disciples. For the next twenty years he was regarded with an enthusiasm like that which had surrounded Dugald Stewart in the previous period and Reid at an earlier date. His impressive appearance and force of character contributed to increase the respect due to his vast reading and tone of rightful authority. He was unmistakably upright, a lover of speculation for its own sake, and a man of warm and pure affections. No one could be happier in domestic life. In 1828, after his mother's death, he married his cousin, Janet Marshall, by whom he had four children. He is described as gentle and kindly in his family ; joining in childish games, writing in the general room, and amusing himself with extravagant romances. He possessed great physical strength till, in 1844, his imprudent habits of study brought on a paralytic stroke. He recovered partially, but became weaker and died on 6th May 1856.

[1] Napier's *Correspondence*, p. 70.

With all Hamilton's claims to respect, there was a very weak side to his character. A queer vein of pedantry ran through the man. A philosopher ought surely not to spend two years unearthing a baronetcy. Hamilton stickled for his rights in other cases in a way which one feels to have been scarcely worthy of him. His real magnanimity was combined with a mental rigidity which made him incapable of compromise. He is undeniably candid and always speaks generously of his opponents; but his own logic always appears to him to be infallible, and neither in practical matters nor in argument would he yield a jot or a tittle of his case. His self-confidence was unfailing, and he speaks even in his first article with the air of an intellectual dictator. He was resolved, it seems, to justify his position by knowing everything that had ever been written upon philosophy. Like Browning's old grammarian, he would 'know all,' both text and comment, and when the 'little touch' of paralysis came, he was still preparing and accumulating. He had read a vast mass of obscure literature and helped a powerful memory by elaborate commonplace books. His passion for imbibing knowledge, indeed, was out of proportion to his giving out results. He has left comparatively little, and much of that is fragmentary. His writings are all included in the *Discussions* (from the *Edinburgh Review* and elsewhere), the often elaborate notes to his edition of Reid, and the *Lectures*. The two first volumes of these lectures (on Metaphysics), as we are told by the editors, were written in the course of five months for his first session. They were repeated for twenty years without serious alteration. The lectures upon logic, filling two volumes more, were written in the same way for the second session. Writing in such haste, Hamilton naturally eked out his work by making very free use of his commonplace book, and, in the course upon logic, by long quotations from previous textbooks. The notes to Reid consist in part of long chains of quotations. They show one palpable weakness. The extracts, detached from their context, lose their true significance. He gives a list of 101 authorities from Hesiod to Lamennais, with quotations, in which an appeal of some kind is made to 'common-sense.' He might have collected a thousand; but instead of showing approval of the special Scottish doctrine, they really show that the phrase may be used more or less freely by holders of every doctrine. He seems to share the opinion of old writers that every statement in a printed book is an 'authority.' The results are sometimes grotesque. It was natural enough that Hamilton should note an unfavourable opinion of mathematical study expressed by Horace Walpole ; but a grave citation of Horace Walpole as an authority upon mathematical studies would have amused nobody more than Walpole himself. On such a method the fuel too often puts out the fire, and Hamilton's direct expositions are few and his opinions often to be inferred from fragmentary criticisms. They naturally vary as he places himself at different points of view ; and we are left to guess how he would have tried to combine them.

Henry Longueville Mansel (1820-1871),[1] Hamilton's most noteworthy interpreter, was a typical Oxford don, as became his birth. He was the descendant of an old

[1] Notice by Lord Carnarvon prefixed to *Gnostic Heresies* (1875), and Burgon's *Twelve Good Men*.

family of country-gentlemen, the younger members of which had entered the army or navy or held the family living. He had been a brilliant schoolboy, had distinguished himself in Oxford examinations, and became known as a wit in common-rooms, a writer of vivacious squibs, and a sound Tory and high Churchman. He had a clear intellect, a forcible style, and had studied theology and German metaphysics with remarkable energy. He apparently began as a Kantian; but he was greatly impressed by Sir William Hamilton, with whom he had no personal relations; and he adopted from Hamilton the peculiar theory which was to enlist Kant in the service of the church of England. His Bampton Lectures in 1858 made him famous as a champion of orthodoxy. In 1868 he was appointed to the deanery of St. Paul's; but his labours had been too much for his brain, and he died suddenly in 1871.

Hamilton started under the double influence of the Scottish philosophy and of Aristotle. Formal logic was to him the most congenial of studies. He would have been thoroughly in his element in the mediæval schools, syllogising to the death. According to an enthusiastic pupil, he laid the top stone on the fabric founded by the 'master hand of the Stagirite.'[1] He was in his element when dividing, subdividing, and cross-dividing all manner of philosophical tenets. The aim was admirable. To have all opinions properly articulated and correlated would be the final result of a history of philosophy and a step to further progress. The danger of accepting such a classification prematurely is equally obvious. The technical terms of metaphysics have the most provoking

[1] See Mill's *Examination of Hamilton*, p. 496.

habit of shifting their meaning ; they shade off imperceptibly into each other, and sometimes even change places ; they represent aspects of truth caught from a particular point of view, which become inapplicable or carry different implications as the point of view imperceptibly shifts.   What appear to be contradictory utterances may be merely qualifications of each other, or may mean the same thing in different dialects.   A system built of such unsubstantial and slippery materials is apt to crumble into mere chaos without extreme care and penetration.   Hamilton, most fully aware of this in general terms, was nevertheless not sufficiently on his guard.   He always seems to fancy that he can avoid all ambiguities by a definition, and does not remember that the words by which he defines are as shifting in their sense as the word defined.   The consideration is especially important because it is Hamilton's main purpose to mediate between conflicting opinions.   He starts from Reid's 'common-sense,' and has to show how the position can be protected against scepticism on the one side and mysticism on the other.

Cousin, as a disciple of the Scottish philosophers, represented one line of deviation from the judicious mean. Beginning with Reid, he had become, with certain reserves, a follower or developer of Schelling.   Coleridge's 'genial coincidence' with Schelling had led to no very tangible result ; but Cousin's systematic development showed the philosophy diverging into a false track, and wasting itself upon the pursuit of utterly chimerical aims. Hamilton, therefore, endeavoured to expose the fallacies involved in the whole procedure.   He agreed, as we shall see, with an important part of Kant's doctrine ; but thought that by certain oversights Kant had opened the door to Schelling's empty speculations. There was an opposite danger to which Hamilton was equally awake. He insisted upon it in an article published October 1830 upon the 'Philosophy of Perception.' This is, in the main, a fierce attack upon Brown— the one philosophical writer of whom he cannot speak without betraying prejudice. Hamilton's antipathy has been already explained. Brown shows Scottish philosophy lapsing into mere empiricism and 'inductive psychology.' Hamilton never mentions him without accusing him of blunders and of crass ignorance.

Hamilton thus stands up for the orthodox common-sense theory of Reid, and resents backslidings into transcendentalism on the right hand and sensationalism on the left. Like the excellent David Deans, he would keep the 'ridge of the hill, where wind and water shears.' When, however, he set about the edition of Reid's works, he began to discover inconsistencies. He doubted whether Reid had really taught the true faith; and he was led to restate more articulately his own view. To the end of his life, however, Hamilton called himself a Natural Realist; and held, though with increasing qualifications, that Reid's doctrine was an approximate statement of the same doctrine. What Natural Realism may be is another question.

The two essays just mentioned[1] give the pith of Hamilton's philosophical theories. His other writings on philosophy are mainly remodelled versions of the same views, or classifications of other solutions of the

[1] Reprinted as the first two chapters in the *Discussions* on the 'Philosophy of the Unconditioned' and the 'Philosophy of Perception.'

problems. His speculations in logic, whatever their
value, belong to a sphere which fortunately lies outside
my province. In treating of perception, Hamilton gives
the rationale of our belief in the external world ; and in
treating of the 'Unconditioned' the rationale of our
belief in a deity. The results are in both cases
remarkable.

II. HAMILTON ON PERCEPTION

What is the relation between the world of matter and
the world of mind? That had been Reid's problem,
and Hamilton starts from the acceptance of Reid's
common-sense reply. We have to steer between opposing difficulties. Give too much to the mind and
you will drift into mysticism, idealism, or ultimately
to 'nihilism.' Give too much to matter and you will
become a materialist or a mere sensationalist. Common-
sense gives the true answer. Reid was in the right path
when he declared himself to be on the side of the
'vulgar.'[1] Things are just what they seem to be. It
is the philosophers who, in Berkeley's famous phrase,
have raised a dust, and complain that they cannot see.
This doctrine gives the principle of an elaborate classification of philosophers generally, and supplies the test
of their soundness.[2] The truth lies with the 'Natural
Realists' or 'Natural Dualists,' who do justice to both
sides. They believe both in mind and matter 'in
absolute co-equality'; in a 'duality' which presents the
elements of consciousness in 'equal counterpoise and

---

[1] Reid's *Works*, p. 823.
[2] See in *Discussions*, p. 55 ; *Lectures*, i. 295, etc.; Reid's *Works*, p. 817 (the
most elaborate).

independence.'[1] Unluckily, there is a mock dualism which virtually makes the true position untenable. It surrenders the real key of the position. This is the unfortunate case of the 'Cosmothetic Idealists,' whose theory represents an illogical compromise. They assert that the mind perceives—not matter but—something which 'represents' matter. It is conscious only of its own 'ideas.' These form the visible imagery, an unreal screen, somehow 'representing' a real world behind. The sceptic, then, had only to point out that the world behind was a superfluity, and our whole world turns out to be illusion. Reid had answered Hume by sweeping away all this superfluous machinery, and proving (or at least asserting) that what we see is itself real. Reid's analysis of consciousness, when duly corrected, showing that 'we have, as we believe we have, an immediate knowledge of the material world, accomplished everything at once.'[2] 'Natural Realism' and 'Absolute Idealism' are the only systems worthy of a philosopher.[3] The Cosmothetic Idealist occupies a position from which he can be driven at any moment by the more thoroughgoing idealist. Yet, as Hamilton declares, Cosmothetic Idealism has been held in various forms by the immense majority of philosophers,[4] indeed, by almost all who have not been driven by its absurdity into materialism or scepticism. A few 'stray speculators'[5] alone have found the narrow way. The list is apparently exhausted by the names of Peter Poiret, Reid, and Sir William Hamilton,[6] and even

---

[1] *Lectures,* i. 292.   [2] *Discussions,* p. 93.   [3] Reid's *Works,* p. 817 *n.*
[4] *Discussions,* p. 56.   [5] *Ibid.* p. 192.
[6] *Lectures,* i. 230, 293. Peter Poiret corresponds to 'Johnny Dodds of Farthingsacre,' the one orthodox friend of Davie Deans.

Reid may be said with much plausibility to have held a version of the creed which would make his whole philosophy 'one mighty blunder.'[1] What has caused this universal apostasy?

The answer is remarkable. It is due to a 'crotchet of philosophers'[2]—a crotchet, moreover, not only unsupported by, but opposed to, all the evidence. It appeared first with Empedocles; it produced the 'gnostic reasons' of the Platonists; the 'pre-existing species' of Avicenna; the common intellect of Themistius and Averroes; the 'intentional species' of the schools; the 'occasional causes' of the Cartesians; the predetermined harmony of Leibniz; the plastic medium of Cudworth and the phenomena of Kant. When so many masters of thought have invented theories it is unhappily easy to believe that they have all gone wrong; but one would at least infer that there was some difficulty to be solved. And yet all these fabrics of sham philosophy are founded upon a 'baseless fancy,' which Reid alone was too independent to take for granted. That 'fancy' was that the 'relation of knowledge inferred an analogy of existence.'[3] Norris of Bemerton had urged that a direct perception of matter was impossible because 'material objects' are removed from the mind 'by the whole diameter of Being.' Reid, with 'an ignorance wiser than knowledge,' confessed his inability to understand this argument. Seeing no difficulty in supposing an immediate perception of a totally disparate thing, he did not make an 'irrational attempt to explain what is in itself inexplicable.'[4] We can no more know how the mind is conscious of itself

---

[1] *Lectures*, i. 331.
[2] *Discussions*, p. 61.
[3] *Discussions*, p. 61; *Lectures*, i. 225.
[4] *Discussions*, i. 62.

than how it is percipient of its contrary. The whole
puzzle, then, is gratuitous ;—which is a consoling result
for ordinary common-sense.

Philosophers had thus bewildered themselves by refusing to admit a plain, though ultimate, fact. There is
a gulf between mind and matter over which no bridge
can be thrown, but no bridge is wanted. The attempt to
construct one is superfluous. Yet in a different form
the question is still prominent, and modern science has
invested it with fresh interest. How are we to conceive
of the relation between the mental and the material
spheres ? How, after all, do we draw the line between
things and thoughts, object and subject, ego and non-
ego ? Where do we reach the impassable gulf, and
what, therefore, is the precise sense in which we must
pronounce all attempt at bridging it to be preposterous?
Hamilton's first position is that we are bound to stand
by ' consciousness.' The ' watchword ' of the Natural
Realist is ' the facts of consciousness, the whole facts and
nothing but the facts.'[1] He constantly appeals to the
' deliverance of consciousness,' and assures us again and
again that unless we can believe this deliverance, we must
suppose man to have been formed only to ' become the
dupe and victim of a perfidious creator.'[2] The error of
the Cosmothetic Idealists consisted precisely in the arbitrary
rejection of a truth given by the testimony of consciousness. An original conviction is to be distinguished from
derivative knowledge, as he tells us, by various characteristics, among which is especially its ' necessity.' We
cannot really resist it.[3] If a disbelief in consciousness
be impossible, why argue against it ? If not impossible,

---

[1] *Discussions*, p. 64.   [2] Reid's *Works*, p. 745.   [3] *Ibid.* p. 754.

how can you assert that the belief is necessary? You have only to state the belief and, on your showing, it will prove itself. To this Hamilton answers that 'necessity' may be of two kinds. We cannot believe a self-contradictory statement; and we are therefore sufficiently guarded by logic against errors which are in this sense impossible. But there are other assertions which may be denied without self-contradiction, and of which, notwithstanding this, the denial would lead to universal scepticism. This corresponds apparently to the difference between a statement of fact and a statement of judgment. A false statement of facts may be as consistent as a true statement, and can only be met by somehow appealing to experience.[1] So far, then, as consciousness assures us of a fact, we may deny it without contradicting ourselves ; but yet, by denying it, we 'make God a deceiver and the root of our nature a lie.'[2] We may thus say without self-contradiction, that memory in general is an illusion, and the world a mere dream or bundle of baseless appearances;[3] but we cannot say so without denying the primary deliverance of consciousness, and striking at the base of all knowledge. Certain truths, though not logically self-supporting, so run through the whole fabric of belief, as to be essential to its existence. If I am conscious, I cannot really doubt the fact of consciousness. The knowledge of the fact and the fact become identical. The possibility of error begins with judgment, or with the interpretation of the fact. It is undeniable, again,

---

[1] Hamilton admits the distinction between 'primary truths of fact' and 'primary truths of intelligence,' but says that as their sources are not different, he will not give them different names.—Reid's *Works*, p. 743 *n.*

[2] Reid's *Works*, p. 743.   [3] *Lectures*, i. 294.

that, in some sense or other, I believe in an external world. Every philosopher, as Hamilton says, admits this to be a fact, and Berkeley appeals to the common sense of mankind when denying, as confidently as Reid when affirming, the existence of matter. We must inquire, then, what precisely is this ultimate deliverance. Does consciousness testify merely to the fact of the belief, or also to the truth of the belief; and, in either case, of what belief? This is what Hamilton has to answer, before summoning us to admit the truth on penalty of making God a liar.

The highwater mark of his opinion seems to be given in a passage of the *Lectures*. He there tells us that, though it is a strange, it is a correct, expression to say, ' I am conscious '—not merely of perceiving the inkstand but—' of the inkstand.' [1] Reid's blunder—which, if he really made it, would convert his whole philosophy into one mighty blunder—lay in misunderstanding this. Reid had been startled at his own boldness in asserting the immediacy ' of our knowledge of external things ' ; [2] and therefore weakly admitted that we are conscious of perceiving the rose, not conscious of the rose itself. This comes of distinguishing ' consciousness ' from perception, and would end in philosophical suicide. It would seem, then, that according to this doctrine we are bound either to assert that the rose—the visible, coloured, scented object, is revealed in consciousness as part of the ' material world ' and therefore exists independently of us, or to admit that God is a liar. It is ' palpably impossible that we can be conscious of an act without being conscious of the object to which the act is relative.' [3]

[1] *Lectures*, i. 228.   [2] *Ibid.* i. 224.   [3] *Ibid.* i. 212.

To carry out this theory is the central aim of Hamilton's 'Natural Realism.' Reid's statement might seem to be not a blunder, but a truism. 'I am conscious of the rose' means precisely 'I have certain sensations which I regard as implying the existence of a permanent external reality.' But this is to interpret perception as involving an 'inference,' and therefore, according to Hamilton, is to abandon the essential doctrine of Natural Realism.[1] It may seem strange, he admits, but it is true, 'that the simple and primary act of intelligence should be a judgment, which philosophers in general have received as a compound and derivative operation.'[2] 'Knowing' and 'knowing that we know' are the same thing; as conceiving the sides and angles of a triangle are the same process, distinguishable in thought, but 'in nature, one and indivisible.'[3] What, then, is this essential judgment? In an act of sensible perception, says Hamilton, I am conscious of myself and of something different from myself.[4] This might seem to define the distinction between 'consciousness' and 'perception.' The object of my thought may, as Hamilton remarks, be a 'mode of mind' as well as a 'mode of matter.'[5] Consciousness of self, we should infer, differs from consciousness of the notself, and it is just the presence of the notself which distinguishes perception from simple consciousness. Hamilton, however, argues that perception is simple consciousness; or that the distinction, for his purpose, is irrelevant. There is a 'logical' but not a 'psychological' difference.[6] Every act of conscious-

---

[1] Reid's *Works*, p. 822.   [2] *Lectures*, i. 204.   [3] *Ibid.* i. 194.
[4] Reid's *Works*, p. 744.   [5] *Ibid.* p. 806.
[6] *Discussions*, p. 50, etc.; *Lectures*, i. 225, etc.

ness implies a conception of the ego. But 'the science of opposites is one.' Therefore consciousness of the ego involves consciousness of the non-ego, or, in the simplest possible act of intelligence I must be taken to affirm the existence both of an ego and a non-ego.

If I cannot even think about myself without affirming the existence of an external world, it would be superfluous to look about for further proofs of its existence. But here occurs a singular difficulty. Hamilton has to guard against the transcendentalist as well as against the sceptic. He is therefore not only a 'realist,' but with equal emphasis a 'relativist.' That our knowledge is essentially relative is one of the points upon which he insists most emphatically, and confirms as usual by a catena of authorities. It is, he says, the truth 'most harmoniously re-echoed by every philosopher of every school, except the modern Germans.'[1] The phrase relativity has more than one meaning; but according to Hamilton means at least this : 'our whole knowledge of mind and matter is relative—conditioned—relatively conditioned.' Of mind and matter 'in themselves' we only know that they are 'incognisable.' 'All that we know is therefore phenomenal—phenomenal of the unknown.' This, then, is a cardinal doctrine. How is it compatible with the doctrine that the ego and non-ego are given in every act of consciousness? Mind and matter, as we have seen, are separated 'by the whole

---

[1] *Discussions*, p. 639. This is the passage welcomed by Mill. Hamilton, as Mr. Stirling notices, applies to the Cosmothetical Idealist Virgil's *Rerumque ignarus, imagine gaudet*, and elsewhere uses the same words to give the position of the true philosopher (*Discussions*, pp. 57, 640 ; *Lectures*, i. 138). The inability to get beyond the phenomenon is ridiculed in one case and accepted in the other.

diameter of being.' They express 'two series of phenomena, known less' (? not) 'in themselves than' (? but)
'in contradistinction from each other.'[1] What is given
is not two facts, the ego and the non-ego, but the
'relation.' Somehow, the conscious act implies the
presence of two factors, unknowable in themselves.
The 'science of opposites' may be 'the same,' but, if I
know neither opposite, there can be very little science.
Strangely, Hamilton seems to confuse the difference
between knowing a relation and knowing the two things
related. He tells us as a rough illustration, that if we
consider the perception of a book to be made up of
twelve parts, four may be given by the book, four by the
sight, and four by 'all that intervenes.'[2] He infers,
presently, that the 'great problem of philosophy' is to
'distinguish what elements are contributed by the knowing subject, what elements by the object known.'[3]
Between these statements we have a renewed and emphatic
assertion of the 'relativity of knowledge.' Hamilton,
that is, speaks as if from the fact that life supposes
breathing we could infer how far life depends upon the
lungs and how far upon the air. From a relation between
two things, unknowable in themselves, we can surely
learn nothing as to the things separately. Equality of
two quantities is compatible with indefinite variation in
the equal quantities.[4] The difficulty is increased when we
ask how the line is actually drawn. The distinction between
subjective and objective corresponds to the distinction
between the primary and secondary qualities of which
Berkeley had denied the validity. Both, he held,

[1] *Lectures*, i. 225.   [2] *Ibid.* i. 147; ii. 129.   [3] *Ibid.* i. 160.
[4] Mill puts this in the *Examination*, p. 35.

are on the same plane, and exist only 'in our minds.'
Hamilton holds that the so-called 'secondary qualities'
are only 'subjective affections.' They are not properly
qualities of Body at all, but sensations produced in the
mind by the action of bodies on the nervous system.[1]
The opinion that these secondary qualities belong to the
non-ego is the 'vulgar or undeveloped form of natural
realism.' Hence, when we say that we are conscious of
the 'rose' or the 'inkstand,' we ought to regard the
colour, fragrance, temperature, and so on, as affections of
the ego. To the non-ego belong the primary qualities
alone ; and these are substantially nothing but extension
and solidity.[2] In other words, the rose belongs to the non-
ego as space-filling ; to the ego, as coloured and fragrant.
Upon this, it is easy to remark with Mill, that as the
vulgar admittedly consider the whole rose to belong
to the non-ego, and the distinction to have been first
drawn by philosophers, we at once admit an illusion in
what, on Hamilton's principles, is apparently a 'deliverance of consciousness.' Why are we forbidden to make
the same hypothesis as to the primary qualities ? 'Falsus
in uno,' as Hamilton somewhere says, 'falsus in omnibus.'
If my judgment of colour be illusory, why not my judgment of extension? The veracity of the Creator is
equally concerned in both cases.

But, in the next place, we now reach a more serious
difficulty. The non-ego, we see, corresponds simply to
the qualities fully assignable in terms of space. But

---

[1] Reid's *Works*, pp. 854, 857.

[2] *Lectures*, ii. 112. In the more elaborate discussion in Reid's *Works*,
Note D, he concludes (p. 857) that the primary 'may be roundly characterised
as mathematical, the secundo primary as mechanical, the secondary as
physiological.'

Hamilton has read Kant, and moreover been convinced by him. Kant has proved beyond 'the possibility of doubt,'[1] the truth that space is a 'fundamental condition' of thought, and therefore belongs to the ego. This at once throws us back into idealism. The whole rose has become a thought, not a thing. So long as he roundly asserts that mind perceives matter, that matter means solid space, and that this truth is implied by the very simplest act of intelligence, we may wonder at his audacity, but we may admit his consistency. But to combine this with the most positive assertions of the 'relativity' of knowledge, that is, of our inability to know either mind or matter, and then to accept as conclusive Kant's theory that space is a mental form, is to land us in a hopelessly inconsistent position. What Kant precisely meant, or whether he had not various and inconsistent meanings, is happily a question beyond my purpose. Hamilton's view of Kant is clear. 'The distinctive peculiarity' of Kant's doctrine, he says, is 'its special demonstration of the absolute subjectivity of space, and in general of primary attributes of matter.'[2] He argues that if Reid virtually held the same view, he abandoned the principle of Natural Realism.[3] If, then, Kant's theory was conclusively proved, was not Hamilton bound to give up his essential principle? He tells us that the primary qualities are 'unambiguously objective (object—objects),' whereas the secondary are 'unambiguously subjective (subject—objects).'[4] Yet, he admits that Kant proves the primary to be absolutely subjective. 'I have frequently asserted,' he says again, that in 'perception we are conscious of the external

---

[1] *Lectures*, ii. 113, 114.
[2] Reid's *Works*, p. 845.
[3] *Ibid.* p. 820.
[4] *Ibid.* p. 858.

object immediately and in itself. This is the doctrine of Natural Realism.' But he explains that by speaking of a thing 'known in itself' he does not mean known 'out of relation to us,' but known 'as the necessary correlative of an internal quality of which I am conscious.'[1] That is, apparently, knowing a thing 'in itself' is knowing it 'not in itself,' but only in its effect; which again is to abandon 'Natural Realism.'

Hamilton finds a way out of these apparent contradictions which satisfies himself. Both theories, he suggests, may be true. We have clearly an *a priori* knowledge of space 'considered as a form or fundamental law of thought,' but also an empirical knowledge of what, in this relation, may be called 'extension.'[2] He agrees, he says, with Kant that an '*a priori* imagination' of space is a 'necessary condition of the possibility of thought'; but differs from Kant by holding that we have an '*a posteriori* percept' of space 'as contingently apprehended in this or that actual complexus of associations.'[3] It is most natural to interpret this as a virtual acceptance of Kant's doctrine. It falls in with what he says elsewhere : 'the notion of space is *a priori*, the notion of what space contains, adventitious or *a posteriori*. Of this latter class is that of Body or Matter.'[4] If I merely fill up space by the sense of resistance, as he thinks, that is a subordinate operation, in no way affecting the subjective character of space generally. If, on the other hand, I can acquire an empirical notion of space independently, it seems impossible to see why I should admit the *a priori* notion. Hamilton starts from the assertion that we

[1] Reid's *Works*, p. 866 *n.*   [2] *Lectures*, ii. 114.
[3] Reid's *Works*, p. 882.   [4] *Ibid.* p. 846.

actually perceive facts, and comes to admit that we simply organise sensations.[1]

Finally, Hamilton turns to yet another theory. His essential point is the necessity of believing consciousness. When we inquire what is the sphere within which consciousness is infallible, we have to accept something very like the condemned 'crotchet' of the Cosmothetic Idealists. The infallibility of consciousness has, after all, to be limited. The summary assertion that the mind can leap the gulf which separates it from matter insists upon some explanation. Consciousness is infallible when it is its own object. But it is plain, as Hamilton agrees, that this primary, direct, or presentative knowledge is only, as it were, the limiting case of knowledge. Accordingly he condemns Reid for speaking of memory as an 'immediate knowledge of the past.'[2] The 'object' in this case is not the past event, but some picture of the past event ; not (in his illustration) George IV. landing at Leith, but a mental image of the landing, 'including a conviction' that it somehow represents a past reality. It is natural, then, to inquire whether my belief in an external world may not be a consciousness of a modification of myself, including a conviction that it merely 'represents' an external world,[3] and is not in direct contact with the 'non-ego.' Immediate knowledge of the past

[1] Mr. Hutchison Stirling, in a severe examination of Hamilton's *Philosophy of Perception* (1865, p. 79 *n.*), thinks that Hamilton never understood that, according to Kant, space was a 'perception,' not a 'conception'; and infers that he knew little of Kant except from the 'literature of the subject.'

[2] *Lectures*, i. 218.

[3] Mill's argument about this in the *Examination* (ch. x.) is entangled in the question about the opinions of Thomas Brown and 'Cosmothetic Idealists,' which perhaps lays him open to a reply made by Veitch. I cannot go into this, which illustrates one confusion in the controversy.

is ' a contradiction in terms.' And this, he adds, applies equally to an 'immediate knowledge of the distant.'[1] It is false to say with Reid that ten men all see the same sun. Each sees a different object, because each sees a different set of rays from which he infers the object.[2] We perceive only modifications of light, or, as he has said before, the 'rays of light in relation to and in contact with the retina.'[3] There is, as he adds, no greater marvel in our perception of the external world than in the admitted fact that mind is connected with body. Therefore, in his final statement,[4] it is laid down as an essential principle that consciousness is a 'knowledge solely of what is now and here present to the mind.' What is meant by the 'here'? 'It is the condition of intuitive perception,' he says, that a sensation is actually felt 'there where it is felt to be.' To suppose that a pain in the toe is felt really in 'the brain is conformable only to a theory of representationism.'[5] If the mind is not itself extended or in any way a subject of space-relations, does this not imply that the whole external world is somehow outside the sphere of immediate knowledge—a construction, not a mode of consciousness? To this Hamilton replies that the 'nervous organism . . . in contrast to all exterior to itself, appertains to the concrete human ego, and is in this respect *subjective, internal*; whereas in contrast to the abstract, immaterial ego, the pure mind, it belongs to the non-ego, and in this respect is *objective, external.*'[6] This

---

[1] *Lectures*, i. 218 and 221 *n*.   [2] *Ibid.* ii. 153.   [3] *Ibid.* ii. 130.

[4] Reid's *Works*, Note B, p. 810.   [5] Reid's *Works*, p. 821.

[6] Reid's *Works*, p. 858 *n*.; cf. p. 880 *n*. The ' organism ' is ' at once objective and subjective,' ' at once ego and non-ego.' Unless we admit this we must be materialists or idealists.

view leads him into pure physiology. He asks whether the mind is conscious of sensations at the periphery of the nerves, or at a 'central extremity in an extended *sensorium commune*.' He declares, lest such language may appear suspicious, that the question of materialism is not raised by this assumption.[1] Anyhow, since the body is now in some sense part of the concrete human ego, our consciousness of the primary qualities is in this sense part of our consciousness of ourselves. They are given as existing in our own organism, or, in other words, as we occupy space, we have an 'immediate' knowledge of space.[2] I only note the peculiar interpretation now put upon the deliverance of consciousness. I fancy myself to perceive the sun ; what I really ' perceive ' is the action of rays of light on my retina. Yet it is obvious that I only learn of the existence of 'rays' or 'retina' long after the perception. Nobody's 'consciousness,' we may be sure, ever told him that he perceived not the sun but the action of rays of light on his eye. Hamilton has diverged from a consideration of the consciousness itself to a consideration of the physical conditions of consciousness. Having started with Reid, he next admits Kant to be conclusive, and ends by escaping to what is only expressible in terms of materialism. The deliverance of consciousness has come to be a statement that my fingers are different from my toes, and

[1] Reid's *Works,* p. 862.

[2] Mr. Stirling (pp. 80-110) thinks this ' exceedingly ingenious,' though really fallacious. Mansel accepts it in his *Metaphysics* (1860), p. 114; and in the *Philosophy of the Conditioned* (pp. 72, 75, 83) tries to reconcile it with other phrases. He talks of matter being 'in contact with mind,' and the object of perception being ' partly mental and partly material.' The composition is like the chemical fusion of an acid and an alkali.

that, as I am fingers and toes, I am aware of the fact.
I will not ask whether it is possible by any interpretation
to put a tenable construction upon Hamilton's language.
Hamilton begins by discarding the philosopher's crotchet
that the difference between mind and matter prevents
them from affecting each other ; and now he seems to
admit its force so fully that he conceives of the nervous
organism as a kind of amalgam of mind and matter.[1]

I have followed Hamilton so far in order to illustrate
the way in which, by superposing instead of reconciling
two different sets of dogma, he became hopelessly confused. The old Scottish doctrine really becomes bank-
rupt in his version. Hamilton is still struggling with
Reid's old problem, and attacking the 'cosmothetic
idealism' as Reid attacked the ideal system. How are
we to cross the gulf between mind and matter, especially
when we know nothing about either mind or matter
taken apart from matter or mind? The problem is insoluble on these terms because it is really meaningless.
The answer suggested by Kant was effective precisely—as
I take it—because it drew the line differently, and therefore altered the whole question. Kant did not provide
a new bridge, but pointed out that the chasm was not
rightly conceived. To try to settle whether the 'primary
qualities' belong to 'things external to the mind' is idle.
It leads to the inevitable dilemma. If the 'primary qualities' belong to the things or the object, geometry
becomes empirical and deducible only from particular

---

[1] Veitch tries to make a coherent doctrine from these utterances. All that
Hamilton requires, he thinks, is that the object perceived has the 'quality of
a non-ego.'—Veitch's *Hamilton*, p. 191. As the non-ego is a merely negative
conception, this tends to coincide with the doctrines of Tracy and Brown.

experiments, like other physical sciences. Then we cannot account for its unique character and its at least apparent ' necessity.' If, on the other hand, the primary qualities belong to the mind, we can understand how the mind evolves or constructs, but it is at the cost of admitting them to be after all unreal, because ' subjective,' or deriving knowledge of fact from a simple analysis of thought. But the dilemma is really illusory. We cannot say that the truths of geometry refer either to things ' out of the mind ' or to things ' in the mind.' They are ' subjective ' in the sense that they are constructed by the mind in the very act of experiencing. They are not subjective in the sense of varying from one experience to another or from one mind to another. They belong to perception as perception, or to the perceiver as perceiving. It is, therefore, meaningless to ask whether they are ' objective ' or ' subjective,' if that is to be answered by deciding, as Hamilton would decide, what part is due to the subject and what part to the object. That feat could only be performed if we could get outside of our minds, which we always carry about with us, or outside of the universe to which we are strictly confined. Then we might perhaps understand what each factor is, considered apart from the other. As it is, we can only say that the truths are universal as belonging to experience in general, and necessary as corresponding to identical modes of combining our experience. But we must abandon the fruitless attempt to separate object from subject, and then to construct a bridge to cross the gulf we have made.

III. MILL ON THE EXTERNAL WORLD

Upon this I have spoken sufficiently in considering Mill's *Logic*. Mill's failure to appreciate the change in the real issues made by the Kantian doctrine in this and other questions is a source of perplexity in his criticism of Hamilton.[1] His straightforward statement of his own view is a relief after Hamilton's complex and tortuous mode of forcibly combining inconsistent dogmas. He is able, moreover, to expose very thoroughly some of Hamilton's inconsistencies. But though he can hit particular errors very hard, he has not a sufficient clue to the labyrinth. Metaphysicians for him are still divided into two great schools—intuitionists and empiricists, or, as he here says, the ' introspective ' and the ' psychological ' school.[2] The Scottish and the Kantian doctrines are still lumped together, and therefore more or less misunderstood. Hence in treating of our belief in an external world he is still in the old position. Kant, according to him, supposes the mind not to perceive but itself to ' create ' attributes, and then by a natural illusion to ascribe them to outward things.[3] The mind, on this version, does not simply organise but adds to, or overrides, experience. Consequently the external world would become subjective or unreal ; and unless we admit a quasi-miraculous intuition, we are under a necessary

[1] Mill had by this time read Kant, and makes frequent references to him. He may perhaps be excused for not appreciating the Kantian view by Kant's own inconsistencies and obscurities. This is a very ticklish point, which I cannot discuss, but which, as I think, does not really affect the argument.

[2] *Examination*, etc., p. 176. Mill here uses 'introspective,' which might be applied to psychology, as equivalent rather to logical ; or to the *a priori* method which attempts to discover fact by analysis of pure reasoning.

[3] *Examination*, etc., p. 456 ; cf. p. 194.

illusion. Mill substantially starts from Berkeley's position.
The distinction between the primary and secondary
qualities is, he holds, illusory. We know nothing of
'object' or 'subject,' 'mind' or 'matter' in themselves.[1] Our knowledge is therefore 'subjective.' Our
whole provision of material is necessarily drawn from
sensations. The problem occurs, how from mere
sensations we make an (at least) apparently external
world. Mill endeavours to show that this is possible,
though he thinks that Berkeley's attempt was inadequate.[2] We can leap the gulf without the help of
any special machinery invented for the purpose, such as
Reid's 'intuitions' or Kant's forms of perception. He
offers his own theory as an 'antagonist doctrine to that
of Sir William Hamilton and the Scottish school,'[3] and
it certainly has the advantage of simplicity.

Mill lays down at starting[4] the postulates from which
he is to reason. Here, of course, we appeal to association. Association, he tells us, links together the thoughts
of phenomena which are like each other, or which have
been contiguous or successive ; the link strengthens as
the association is repeated, and after a time becomes
'inseparable.' Now belief in an external world means
the belief that things exist when we do not think of
them ; that they would exist if we were annihilated ;
and further, that things exist which have never been
perceived by us or by others. This belief is explicable
by the known laws of association. For at any moment a

---

[1] *Examination*, etc., p. 266.

[2] Cf. Mill's interesting article upon Berkeley.—*Dissertations*, vol. iv. pp.
154-87.   [3] *Examination*, p. 248.

[4] *Ibid.* p. 225.

given sensation calls up 'a countless variety of possibilities of sensation.' They are regarded, that is, as sensations which I might experience if circumstances were altered. Again, these possibilities of sensation (which, he adds, are 'conditional certainties') are permanent, because they may be called up by any of the fleeting sensations. This permanence is one of the characteristics of the outside world ; and we thus have always in the background, or as a 'kind of permanent substratum,' whole groups of 'permanent possibilities' suggested by the passing sensations. These become further consolidated when fixed orders of succession have suggested the ideas of cause and effect—themselves a product of association. Hence, we get our external world, and can define Matter to be a 'Permanent Possibility of sensation.' The phrase became famous.

This involves the metaphysical question which was reserved or evaded in the *Logic*. His whole purpose there is to show that thoughts should conform to things. But how things differ from thoughts was never made clear. 'Attributes,' we were then told, were the same as 'sensations.' The sensations somehow cohere in clusters. But what makes them cohere in different forms? When a sensation is not accompanied by the sensation previously associated, why is not the association simply weakened or destroyed instead of suggesting a 'conditional certainty'? I learn that fire is hot because the sensations of brightness and heat have occurred together; but when I see the brightness without feeling the heat, why does not the association simply become fainter? Why should I interpret the experience to mean, 'If I were nearer I should feel the heat'?

Does not the interpretation imply that I have already some system of combining my impressions and a need of making the two experiences consistent instead of contradictory? Upon the single assumption of sensations occurring together or successively, and related in time alone, there seems to be no need for any external world whatever. The hypothesis would be exemplified in the case of an animal which, though capable of sensations, had no capacity for arranging them so as to represent space at all. And, again, the statement suggests no distinct reference to any criterion of truth or falsehood. It accounts for illusions as well as for true beliefs. What is the difference? The fact that certain sensations adhere in clusters is not the same thing as the belief in their regular recurrence; and considering the vast variety and intricacy of our sensations, the question which I have mentioned in connection with James Mill arises again : Why should any two people have the same clusters or (on this showing) the same belief—or how one association can be said to be (not real but) true, and another (not unreal but) false?

This difficulty shows itself when Mill proceeds to investigate the 'primary qualities.' They are to be simply 'attributes' co-ordinate with other attributes. With the help of Professor Bain and Mr. Herbert Spencer, in whose then recent writings he saw a most encouraging development of his father's principles, Mill makes out a case to show how the perception of space may be developed. The problem discussed by those authorities and their successors is clearly a legitimate part of psychology; their investigations, though still on the threshold of a vast and difficult inquiry, are at least valuable beginnings; and when the experts have all agreed, we shall be ready to accept their conclusions. There is, however, a difficulty which exposes Mill to another criticism.[1] Briefly, it is that his so-called explanation of space-conception really presupposes space. Hamilton had pointed this out in his Kantian moods.[2] The difficulty is obvious. In a scientific theory a statement in terms of space is an ultimate statement. We do not try, nor does it appear to be possible, to get behind it. When I have said that a body moves in an ellipse, I do not go on to express the ellipse in terms of 'muscular sensation.' That would be to substitute for a definite measure one essentially fluctuating and uncertain. I can define a given muscular sensation as that which corresponds to a certain distance; but to reverse the definition—to express the distance in terms of the pure sensation, excluding all reference to distance, is surely impossible. Now, it may seem that Mill is here attempting just this impossible feat. Therefore he is really still on the same side of the gulf, though he supposes himself to have crossed it. His 'pigtail'— according to the famous apologue—still 'hangs behind him.' In other words, he is mistaking a psychological for a metaphysical explanation; an account of how it is that we come to perceive space, assuming space to exist, with an explanation of what space is; and a resolution of the perception into a set of sensations associated in time. Here, again, he is under the great disadvantage of supposing the space-perception to have been made within the limits of a lifetime. If it were possible to look into the mind

---

[1] Made especially familiar in recent English speculations by T. H. Green's criticism of Hume. [2] *e.g.* Reid's *Works*, p. 869.

of an infant we could, he thinks, see how the idea was formed.[1] A modern psychologist can at least help himself by looking indefinitely further back and tracing the whole history of the organism to the earlier forms of life; and the space-perception ceases to imply a preternatural or *a priori* capacity. Something more is surely wanted, though I do not venture to say precisely what. Mill's doctrine that my belief in a external world is a belief in ' a permanent possibility of sensation ' may be accepted in some sense. When, for example, I believe in the existence of Calcutta, I mean that I believe that if I were transported to the banks of the Hoogly, I should have the sensations from which Calcutta is inferrible.[2] In other words, in making a statement about the external world, I construct a hypothetical and universal consciousness. When I exchange the geocentric for the heliocentric view, I am imagining what I should see if I were upon the sun instead of the earth. Instead of regarding my own series of sensations as the base from which to measure, I regard them as deducible from the series which would be presented to a different and, of course, incomparably more extended consciousness. I can thus fill up the gaps in my own experience and get a regular series instead of one full of breaches and interruptions. That I do this somehow or other is Mill's view, and I should admit with him that I do no more. But, then, the question remains whether Mill can account for my doing even this. It supposes, at least, a power of forming what Clifford called 'ejects,' as distinguished from ' objects.' I must be able to think not of things outside consciousness but of my own consciousness under

---

[1] *Examination*, pp. 146-47.   [2] *Ibid.* p. 235.

other conditions, and of other centres of consciousness than mine. But this ability is not explicable from sensations, as ultimate atoms, combined in various ways by 'association'; for that process, it would seem, might take place without in any way suggesting an external world or a different consciousness. Here Mill, like his father, is trying to explain thoughts by dealing with sensations as things and refusing to admit any action of the mind in order to keep to the unsophisticated facts. He will not allow the mind to have even an organising power, even though it be a power which cannot be separately revealed or give rise to independent truths, but appears simply as implied in its products. The mind *is* the cluster of atomic sensations. It must not tamper with the facts in any way, on penalty of causing illusion. I can only associate simple atoms, and the world remains a chaos of independent and incoherent fragments. They stick together somehow, but the division into the external and the internal world still remains an unsolved problem. The 'attribute' will not distinguish itself from the 'sensation.' We are still unable, that is, to explain the metaphysical puzzle left unsolved in the *Logic*.

Another question arises : If the world is still an incoherent heap of 'attributes' or 'sensations,' what are we to say of the mind? With his usual candour Mill applies his principles to the problem. We get, as he admits, to a real difficulty. The mind, in the phrase adopted from his father, is a 'thread of consciousness.' It is a series of feelings with the curious peculiarity that besides 'present sensations' it has 'memories and expectations.' What are these? he asks. They involve beliefs in something 'beyond themselves.' If we call the mind 'a series of feelings,' we have to add that it is a series which is 'aware of itself as past and future.' Is it, then, something different from the feelings, or must we accept the paradox that something 'which in hypothesis is a series of feelings can be aware of itself as a series?' Here is the final 'inexplicability' which must arrive, as he admits with Hamilton, when we get to an ultimate fact. The 'wisest thing we can do is to accept the inexplicable fact without any theory of how it takes place.'[1] That what we call personal identity is 'inexplicable' will hardly be denied. Yet Mill's position seems to make the paradox something nearly approaching to a contradiction. If the mental processes are to be described as feelings, separable but simply forming clusters more or less complicated and linked to each other, we seem to get rid not only of a something which organises experience, but of organisation itself. It becomes difficult to understand not merely what the mind or soul can be, but what are the mental processes to which the conception corresponds. This, however, leads to a different set of questions and one of far greater interest.

IV. THEORIES OF THE ABSOLUTE

Discussions such as I have touched often seem to be little more than a display of dialectical skill. Hamilton and Mill probably believed equally and in the same sense in the reality of Edinburgh or London. When a belief is admitted, the question why we believe is of interest chiefly in so far as the answer may give canons applicable to really disputable questions. Now the application of

[1] *Examination*, p. 248.

Hamilton's theories to theology certainly involved issues in regard to which men generally suppose themselves to be profoundly interested. We clearly believe in an 'external world,' whatever precisely we mean by it. But do we believe in God? or, if we believe, what precisely is meant by believing in God? That is a problem upon which turn all the most important controversies which have divided men in all ages—and the controversy which now raged over Hamilton's theory between Mill and Mansel corresponded to vital issues. Hamilton's essential position was given in the famous Cousin article in 1830. He frequently repeats, but he never much modifies or develops the argument. In the course of lectures repeated for twenty years, he divides his subject into three departments: 'empirical psychology' and 'rational psychology'; or the facts and laws of consciousness; and thirdly, 'ontology,' which was to deal with the ideas of God, the soul, and so forth.[1] This third department was never written; and though we may guess at its general nature, his doctrine is chiefly indicated by his criticism of Cousin.

One result is unfortunate. I doubt whether so many sayings capable of different interpretations were ever brought together in the same space. The art of writing about 'ontology' is, it would seem, to disguise a self-evident truism by pompous phrases till the words are vague enough to allow the introduction of paradoxical meaning. Schelling and Cousin between them had provided a sounding terminology; and Hamilton, though his main purpose is to show that these fine phrases were only phrases, takes them up, tosses them about as if they had a

[1] *Lectures* (Preface).

real meaning, and leaves us in some doubt how far he is merely using the words to show their emptiness, or suggesting that, when the bubbles are burst, there is still some residuum of solid matter. 'The unconditioned,' he says (giving his own view), 'is incognisable and inconceivable.'[1]   What, then, is 'the unconditioned'? 'The Unconditioned is the genus of which the Infinite and the Absolute are species.'[2]   These technical phrases are the balls with which the metaphysical juggler plays his tricks till we are reduced to hopeless confusion. Mill gives the straightforward and, I think, conclusive criticism.[3]   What is the sense of talking about 'The Absolute' or 'The Infinite' as hypostatised abstractions? Apply the epithets to concrete things or persons and we may understand what is really meant.   A predicate going about at large cannot be really grasped; and the discussion would only be relevant if we were speaking of something which is absolute and nothing but absolute.   The words themselves have meanings which become different when they are parts of different assertions. 'Inconceivable' is a word which varies from self-contradictory to mere difficulty of imagining. 'Absolute,' according to Hamilton, has two chief meanings, one of which is not opposed to the Infinite and the other contradictory of the Infinite.   Mansel takes Mill to task for not seeing that Hamilton uses the word in two 'distinct and even contradictory senses,' and for not perceiving which meaning is implied in which cases.[4]   It may be very wrong of Mill, but Hamilton's practice is certainly confusing.   There is Cousin's 'Absolute' and Hamilton's 'Absolute' and

[1] *Discussions*, p. 12.   [2] *Ibid.* p. 13.
[3] *Examination*, pp. 58, 73.   [4] *Philosophy of the Conditioned*, p. 95.

Mansel's own 'Absolute';[1] and the difference is to be inferred from the nature of the argument. There is a false Infinite and a true Infinite; and this suggests another difficulty. The obvious 'contradictory' of infinite is finite; but words cannot be really contradictory at all till they form part of a proposition. It is contradictory to call a thing finite and infinite in the same sense; but, if we admit of infinite divisibility, a thing must be at once infinite in comparison with an infinitesimal, finite in relation to other things, and infinitesimal in relation to those which in relation to it are infinite. Some words, again, refer to our knowledge of things, and are meaningless when predicated of objects. A fact may be 'certain' to me and only 'probable' to you, simply because the probability to each depends upon the evidence which he possesses. When this is supposed to correspond to some difference in the facts themselves, endless fallacies are produced. 'The certain' is contradictory of the 'uncertain'; but a given fact may be both 'certain' and 'uncertain.' A discussion naturally becomes perplexed, which is really treating a question of logic in terms appropriate to a question of fact.

I will not attempt to follow a controversy so perplexed in itself and in which the antagonists seem to be normally at cross purposes. I must try to bring out the main issue which is obscured by the singular confusions of the contest; and to this there seems to be a simple clue. Hamilton's theory is admittedly a 'modification of that of Kant,'[2] and intended to eliminate the inconsistency by which Kant had left an opening for the systems

[1] *Philosophy of the Conditioned*, pp. 108, 147.
[2] *Ibid.* p. 67.

of Schelling and Hegel.   Now Kant's famous argument, given in the *Critique of Pure Reason*, is a most crabbed piece of writing.   It makes an English reader long for David Hume.   Still, beneath its elaborate panoply of logical technicalities, it contains a very clear and cogent argument, which gives the real difficulty and which is strangely distorted by Hamilton.

According to Kant there are three Ideas of the pure Reason—the Soul, the World, and God.   Nobody really doubts the existence of the world; but doubts as to the existence of the soul or of God are possible and have been met by professedly demonstrative arguments.   The 'dogmatists' whom Kant criticised had, as they thought, proved the existence of a monad, an 'indiscerptible' unit called the soul; and of a Supreme Being, or 'Ens Realissimum,' who is taken to be in some sense absolute and simple.   Kant holds these arguments to be essentially a misapplication of logical method.   It is the function of the reason to unify our knowledge.   The ideal would be reached if all knowledge could be regarded as a system of deductions from a single principle.   This, in reasoning about the soul, produces a 'paralogism.'   All our thoughts and faculties are bound together into a unity which is consistent with multiplicity.   We interpret this unjustifiably as implying the existence of an absolutely simple unit.   We hypostatise the unity and regard it as a thing when, in truth, it represents a complex system of reciprocal relations.   The arguments upon the supposed proofs of the existence of a supreme Being, though they are expanded and considered in many different forms, reach a similar conclusion.   We are perfectly right in unifying as much as possible our whole knowledge of the

world, but though we may continue the process indefinitely, we can never logically arrive at the knowledge
of a single Being existing independently as the foundation of all other being. In this sense, Kant calls the
idea 'regulative.' It corresponds to the legitimate process of thought ; we must unify, but no reasoning can
reveal an entity lying beyond all experience. We are
thus led to 'irresistible illusions,' from which, however,
we can escape, though only ' by the severest and most
subtle criticism.' Kant compares this to the illusion
produced by a mirror, which makes objects really in
front appear to be behind it, or to the apparent
increase of the moon's size when near the horizon.
Still, it is impossible, as he emphatically says, that
reason should be itself undeserving of confidence. It
is only from its misuse in an inappropriate sphere, or,
in other words, from its attempt to transcend experience, that the fallacy arises.[1]

It is needless to ask how this argument can be reconciled with the theism which Kant accepts. Hamilton's
criticism of Cousin is essentially a statement of the con-
verse argument. Schelling and Cousin had taken up

---

[1] Hamilton strangely declares that Kant makes the speculative reason an
' organ of mere delusion ' (*Discussions*, p. 18, *Lectures*, i. 402), and Mansel says
that if we accept Kant's doctrine we must believe ' in a special faculty of lies,
created for the express purpose of deceiving those who believe in it.' For
Kant's statement that the reason cannot be itself untrustworthy, see Appendix
to *Transcendental Dialectic* (section on ' the ultimate end of the natural dialectic
of human reason,' and for the comparisons above quoted the same Appendix
(section on ' the regulative employment of the ideas of pure reason ') and the
Introduction to the *Transcendental Dialectic*. Bolton (*Inquisitio Philosophica*,
ch. iv.) quotes many passages from Kant to illustrate this point, which seems
to confirm Stirling's opinion of the superficiality of Hamilton's knowledge of
his author.

Kant's challenge, not by inferring the simple being from the complex of experiences, but by professing to show how multiplicity might be evolved out of absolute simplicity.   This feat, as Hamilton held, and as Mill of course held with him, could only be accomplished by a palpable juggle.   Clearly you cannot count, if you are restricted to the use of an absolute 'one.'   The germ from which an organic system is developed cannot be itself absolutely simple.   Knowledge can only be made out of rules; and a simple 'is' gives no rule.   Hamilton tries to express the principle implied in such instances in the proper pomp of metaphysical language.   Cousin starts by admitting that knowledge supposes 'plurality,' that is, an object and a subject.   Now, says Hamilton,[1] the 'absolute' must be identified with the subject or with the object, or with the 'indifferency of both' (whatever that may be).   On the first or second hypothesis, the absolute is not, as it ought to be, a unit, for it is one of a pair; on the other hypothesis, you suppose that consciousness does not imply plurality.   A man, let us say in humbler language, if he thinks, must think about something.   If so, we start from a man and a something. But suppose him to think about himself.   Then there must be something to say about himself; and he will have nothing to say if he is absolutely simple.   That seems to be true enough.   Every proposition asserts a relation of some kind, and a proposition cannot be got at all if no relation be given.   This, therefore, is one meaning of the 'relativity' of thought.   'To think is the condition'; that is, you cannot affirm or deny unless you deny or affirm something.   If you try then to get

[1] *Discussions*, p. 33.

to the absolute by stripping off all relations, you really get to zero. We think only by the attribution of certain qualities, and the negation of these qualities and of this attribution is so far a negation of thinking at all. Kant's arguments duly carried out prove 'the unconditioned,' says Hamilton, to be a mere 'fasciculus of negations.' [1] Clearly, we reply, if the unconditioned is reached by unsaying all that we have said. A plain person is, indeed, chiefly astonished that such arguments should be required. Schelling's system, says Hamilton himself, is only fit for 'Laputa on the Empire,' [2] but Schelling at least invented a supernatural faculty to perceive an 'incogitable' hypothesis. Cousin's hypothesis, which tried to omit this faculty, is worse, for it is self-contradictory. [3] The spectacle of three of the most distinguished men in Germany, France, and England joining in this game, and even of Hamilton winning a 'European reputation' by declaring that we cannot believe two contradictory propositions at once, or make something out of nothing, is not edifying to a believer in philosophy.

V. ANTINOMIES

Mill does not want all this apparatus to get rid of the transcendental world. It is for him too obviously superfluous to require to be exploded. How then does he come into conflict with Hamilton? We must turn for explanation to another of Kant's arguments. The universe must be regarded as in some sense one, though that does not prove the existence of a simple and absolute Being as its ground or principle. On the other

---

[1] *Discussions*, p. 17.   [2] *Ibid.* p. 20.   [3] *Ibid.* p. 32.

hand, the universe is an indefinitely complex multitude
of reciprocally dependent things. We can bring the
'laws' into unity and harmony ; but the things through
which the laws are manifested are themselves infinitely
numerous. We may then ask whether the universe is
not only one but a whole; whether its unity entitles us
to call it a single object. This leads to the famous
'antinomies.' They have been familiar enough in many
forms since speculation began. The universe is given
in space and time. Now, we cannot think of space and
time either as finite or infinite. We cannot think of
space as finite because, however far we go, there is still
space beyond. We cannot think of space as infinite,
because to imagine infinite space would require an infinite mind and infinite time. Space must be either
infinite or finite, because one of two contradictories must
be true, and yet each is 'inconceivable.' I must confess
with due humility that I could never see any antinomy
at all. In this I agree with Mill,[1] though I cannot agree
with his attempt to explain our beliefs in the infinity
of space by an 'inseparable association.' The apparent
antinomy is due, I fancy, to a shift in the meaning of
'infinite.' The mathematician calls space 'infinite'
because space is limited by space, and there cannot be
a 'whole' of space. If by 'infinite' I mean the completion of a process which *ex hypothesi* cannot be completed,
I become self-contradictory. There is no meaning in 'a
whole' of space, though every particular space is a whole.
Acuter reasoners, however, can see the difficulty, and we
will therefore admit the 'antinomy.' Then we must
observe that, according to Kant, the antinomies apply

[1] *Examination*, p. 103.

solely to the cosmological idea. There is nothing, he says,[1] antinomial in the psychological and theological ideas ; for they 'contain no contradiction.' He infers that their reality can be no more denied than affirmed. If from the organism I infer a soul I fall into a 'paralogism,' but not into an 'antinomy.' We do not prove that soul and no-soul are necessary alternatives and both 'inconceivable,' but simply that the soul, as a monad, is a superfluity which explains nothing—a thought interpreted as a thing. The antinomy occurs only when we deal with the perceived universe, and ask whether it has or has not limits. It has no application to the argument about God or the soul. Since they are not in space they have no concern with the antinomies involved in the conception of space.

Hamilton's misappropriation of this argument is the master fallacy of his system. In the Cousin essay he lays down a dogma without the slightest attempt to prove it. 'The conditioned is the mean between two extremes—two inconditionates—exclusive of each other, *neither of which can be conceived as possible*, but of which, on the principles of contradiction and the excluded middle, *one must be admitted as necessary*.'[2] He adds that our faculties are thus shown to be weak, but not deceitful. We learn, moreover, the 'salutary lesson' that the capacity of 'thought is not to be constituted into the measure of existence,' and we are warned from 'recognising the domain of our knowledge as necessarily coextensive with the horizon of our faith.' In a note we are invited to accept as true the declaration 'of a pious

---

[1] 'An ultimate end of the natural dialectic,' etc.
[2] *Discussions*, p. 14.

philosophy—a God understood would be no God at all';
and we are told that 'the last and highest consecration
of all true religion must be an altar to the unknown
God,'—which does not appear to have been St. Paul's
opinion. This doctrine was repeated again and again
in various lectures and notes. It was applied by Mansel
to defend Christianity, and was in a sense accepted by
Mr. Herbert Spencer as a support of Agnosticism.[1]
Yet it is sprung upon us in this abrupt fashion, not only
without proof, but without any clear statement of its
meaning; and, as I think, is really the expression
of a confusion of two lines of argument. An exposition
of this great axiom, he says,[2] would show that 'some
of the most illustrious principles' are only its 'subordinate modifications applied to certain primary notions.'
Among such notions are those of 'cause and effect'
and 'substance and phenomenon.' The discussion of
Cause and Effect[3] illustrates sufficiently the curious
shifting of the argument. Our inability to conceive a
beginning either of time or of the existence of things in
time gives the apparent necessity of causation. But as
we cannot suppose an infinite regress, the necessity
corresponds only to an 'impotence' of our minds.
Hence, he argues, in the case of the human will, we
must admit the possibility, though not the conceivability,
of an absolute beginning, and therefore of freewill. The
argument, if sound, is applicable to cause in general as

[1] I may say that although I am an 'Agnostic' I cannot accept Mr.
Spencer's version of Hamilton's doctrine. But I must not attempt here to
estimate the value of Mr. Spencer's theory.

[2] Reid's *Works*, p. 743 *n.*

[3] *Lectures*, ii, 376-413; *Discussions*, pp. 604-28.

well as to the will. Hamilton may mean that since an absolute beginning is possible at some time, it is possible at any time. We might then have an antinomy. One of the propositions, 'things are caused' and 'things are not caused,' must be true, and both are inconceivable. But this would be to destroy the axiom of causation. The appearance of an antinomy is obtained by changing the question. Instead of asking why we take things to be caused, we ask whether we can imagine an infinite series of causes. The antinomy in this case is simply the old formula over again. This central position of Hamilton's philosophy is thus an illegitimate application of Kant's argument. Kant admits an antinomy only where it is at least plausible, namely, as applied to the universe which we clearly have to extend indefinitely if not to absolute infinity. But no such difficulty is involved in the problem of unity. Hamilton seems to have been so delighted with the 'antinomy' that he 'enounces' it as a general law; applies it where it has no meaning whatever, and invariably 'illustrates' it by repeating the case in which it is plausible.

Hamilton thus contrives to blend two arguments into one. His view is the germ of inextricable confusions, and, one might have thought, too obvious a bit of logical legerdemain to impose even upon a metaphysician. It plays, however, a most important part in the attempt made by Mansel to bring Hamilton to bear against the unbeliever. Mansel's whole aim is to put his antagonists in a dilemma. They must not be allowed to say simply that an argument becomes meaningless; they must be taken to say that it leads to a balance between two alternatives. We therefore get a double result. On

the one hand, we are reduced to complete scepticism—
that is, reason is made impotent in regard to a question
which necessarily arises.   On the other hand, we are
left with an impression that we are compelled to take
some position in this region of inconceivables, and this
is translated into the pious assertion that 'belief' extends
beyond 'knowledge.' Thus Hamilton emphatically declares that it is the 'main scope' of his speculation to
show articulately that we 'must believe as actual much
that we are unable (positively) to conceive as actual.'[1]

To follow him through the maze of 'inconceivables,' 'absolutes,' 'infinites,' 'unconditioneds' and so
forth would be idle.[2] I shall be content with one
argument which in Mansel's hands led to an important
conflict with Mill. The Infinite, says Mansel, 'if it is
to be conceived at all, must be conceived as potentially' everything and actually nothing ; for if there
is anything in general which it cannot become, it is

[1] Letters to Calderwood in *Lectures*, ii. 530-35.

[2] One specimen of Hamilton's method may be given for those who care for
such things. In the essay on Cousin he opposes ' the Infinite ' as the ' unconditionally unlimited' to the ' Absolute' as the ' unconditionally limited.' In both
cases we have simple negations of thought, and therefore reach the inconceivable. If I say a thing and then unsay it, I get simple zero. That is obvious.
If, again, the absolute asserts the same limit which is denied by the ' infinite,'
they are of course contradictory. And, in this case, we get the old antinomy,
which he accordingly introduces in the next sentence about the impossibility
of conceiving space either as infinite or finite. But here the contradictory
of infinite ought to be—not ' absolute' but ' finite.' Having thus got an
' antinomy' by making ' the absolute' equivalent to ' the finite,' Hamilton
apparently assumes an antinomy between absolute and its contradictory everywhere. But I am not compelled to think of a thing either as being some
quality and so far ' conditioned,' or as being no quality at all. The alternative
is either to think of it or not think of it and that leads to no antinomy. So
again (pp. 29, 30) infinite time is identified with endless time, and absolute
with ended time.

thereby limited ; and if there is anything in particular which it actually is, it is thereby excluded from being any other thing.[1] It must also be conceived as 'actually everything and potentially nothing; for an unrealised potentiality is likewise a limitation.' Hamilton had put the same argument. 'The infinite is conceived only by thinking away every character by which the finite was conceived.'[2] That is, the 'infinite' is equivalent to the 'indeterminate,' or the result of unsaying all that you have said. This logically leads to pure nothing, not to an antinomy. We are told that we must believe something where we get not to a contradiction but to an absolute vacuum. Mill makes an obvious criticism.[3] When I talk of infinite space, I do not 'think away' the character of space, but I only think of an indefinite extension of space. To believe in infinite space would otherwise be to disbelieve in geometry. We cannot think at all about an utterly indeterminate object, but we can think of space without asking how much space there is in the universe. 'The Infinite' may be meaningless, but to predicate infinity of space does not destroy the space conception. If, then, the infinity of space does not hinder us from obtaining a perfectly accurate knowledge of its properties, does the infinite or absolute nature of the Deity prevent us from understanding his attributes ? Here is the real problem ; and it leads to the odd spectacle of the sceptic arguing on behalf of theology against the divine. There is no contradiction, as Mill argues, in speaking of an infinitely knowing or power- ful or good being. A being has infinite knowledge if

---

[1] *Bampton Lectures* (3rd edition, 1859), p. 71.
[2] *Lectures*, iii. 103. [3] *Examination*, p. 105.

nothing is unknown to him; and is infinitely powerful if nothing is impossible to him. That gives a plain meaning on the human side, though we are of course unable adequately to imagine the result on the divine side. Infinite goodness is, indeed, a less natural phrase than 'absolute,' because absolute does not suggest a numerical measure of 'goodness.' Goodness is a quality, not a quantity. But, understood as meaning the absence of even an infinitesimal degree of badness, it may be called infinite, and the 'limit' which is denied is not that implied by 'good,' but by the degree of goodness. Infinite, if it means anything, must mean an infinite amount or degree of something definite.

Mill thus appears to argue that theology is not as irrational as its defender supposes. The introduction of such predicates as infinite and absolute do not make knowledge of their subject impossible. It would have cleared the matter if Mill had gone on to explain his own view of the 'Absolute.' We may guess what he ought to have said in conformity with his principles. If all knowing is essentially a knowledge of relations, it is idle to seek for an 'absolute' in the sense of a thing which (on Mansel's definition) 'exists in and by itself, having no necessary relations to any other being.'[1] Since, in saying anything about it, we assert a relation, we cannot even speak of such an 'absolute' without contradiction. 'Absolute,' like certain, necessary, and so forth, is a name referring to our knowledge. An assertion about facts may be 'absolutely' true, however trifling the fact. It may be as absolutely true that a sparrow fell to the ground at 9 A.M. on the 1st of January last as that

[1] *Bampton Lectures*, p. 45.

the sun exists or that two and two make four. Knowledge implies not an 'absolute fact' but an 'absolute truth'—a truth which requires no qualification not explicitly given in the proposition asserted. To say that a thing exists absolutely is to add nothing but emphasis to the statement that it exists. Nor does the statement that it exists 'conditionally' alter the case. It is conditional in so far as it has a cause, or as from its existence we may infer some previous state of things. If, however, it exists, the conditions have *ex hypothesi* been fulfilled. It exists now 'absolutely,' however it came to exist. It is a part of the whole system of interdependent and continuous processes which make up the universe.[1] If we know that anything, then, is part of the actual world, we have all 'the absolute' required ; and this is an 'absolute' which is perfectly compatible with any complexity of relations. The clue is given by getting hold of any bit whatever of the actual web, not by getting into some transcendental world beyond. The error of supposing that we must find an 'Absolute' somewhere, and that we cannot find it in any part of our experience, is the same as would be the error of supposing that because we cannot fix a point in absolute space, we cannot get any valid space measures. The centre of the sun or Greenwich observatory will do equally well, though we cannot even speak intelligibly of their absolute position in the universe. To give a scientific account of astronomy we do not require an absolute centre of space.

---

[1] Cf. Tennyson's 'Flower in the Crannied Wall'—

'. . . If I could understand
What you are, root and all, and all in all,
I should know what God and man is.'

This is what I take to be implied in Kant's argument about the idea of God. We cannot get to an 'absolute' Being outside of the universe, but the whole must be regarded as a single and self-supporting system. This argument is distorted in the elaborate argumentations of Hamilton and Mansel against the attempts to get to an absolute Being outside of things in general. Such an absolute as they attack is doubtless an absurdity; but neither are we, as they urge, compelled to believe in it. If we still use theological language, we must say that God is not a Being apart from the universe, but implied in the universe; the ground of all things, the immanent principle whose 'living raiment is the world.' Mill of course holds that we must abandon 'transcendentalism' or the search for 'things in themselves' outside of the phenomenal world. Mansel often seems to agree. Philosophers who indulge in these freaks try, he says, to lift up the curtain of their own being to view the picture which it conceals. 'Like the painter of old, they knew not that the curtain *is* the picture.'[1] That sounds like good positivism or phenomenalism. It should give the deathblow to all 'ontology.' He assures us over and over again that the 'Infinite' is a 'mere negation of thought';[2] that contradictions arise whenever we attempt to transcend the limits of experience; that human reason is so far from being able to construct a 'Scientific Theology, independent of and superior to Revelation, that it cannot even read the alphabet out of which that Theology must be framed.'[3] We can know the laws of nature or the phenomena, but we can know nothing of the substance or noumenon which lies behind

[1] *Bampton Lectures,* p. 89.   [2] *Ibid.* p. 72.   [3] *Ibid.* p. 61.

them. Then, is the natural query, why not leave it out of account altogether? Why venture into this region, where, as Mansel admits, we find only 'antinomies' or 'contradictory inconceivables'? Why not, in short, be agnostics like Mr. Herbert Spencer, who based his *First Principles* on the Hamilton - Mansel doctrine? This gives the secret of the whole procedure.

'The cardinal point,' says Mansel, 'of Sir W. Hamilton's philosophy . . . is the absolute necessity, under any system of philosophy whatever, of acknowledging the existence of a sphere of belief, beyond the limits of the sphere of thought.'[1] Faith, then, remains when reason disappears, though faith cannot solve the doubts suggested by reason.[2] What 'faith' tells us, in fact, is that we must believe one of two propositions, though we cannot conceive the possibility of either. Can it possibly, we ask, much matter whether we believe that there is or is not an X of whom nothing more can be intelligibly said? A belief which extends beyond 'the sphere of thought' is a belief which we can afford to leave to itself. But Mansel has to declare that we are forced to believe where we cannot even properly think. 'We are compelled by the constitution of our minds to believe in the existence of an absolute and infinite Being,'[3] though, as we learn, to 'think of the infinite' is really a negation of thought. A decision to accept one of the contradictory beliefs is yet of the highest practical importance. The schemes of Freewill and Fatalism, says Hamilton,[4] are 'theoretically balanced,' though the fatalist inconceivability is the 'less obtrusive'; but

---

[1] *Philosophy of the Conditioned*, p. 51. [2] *Bampton Lectures*, p. 8.
[3] *Ibid.* pp. 67, 68. [4] Reid's *Works*, p. 974.

'practically' we must accept freewill on penalty of admitting the moral law to be 'a mendacious imperative.' That is, right and wrong become meaningless unless you accept one of two equally inconceivable doctrines. So Mansel declares freewill to be 'certain in fact' though 'inexplicable in theory.'[1] Why 'certain,' if, as he also declares, it is part of the 'fundamental mystery' of the coexistence of the Finite and the Infinite?[2] According to Mansel, again, the denial that an infinite Being exists, is simply the acceptance of one of two 'equally inconceivable alternatives.'[3] It is, he declares, 'our duty' to think of God as 'personal' and to believe that he is 'infinite.'[4] It is a duty, then, to accept as a certainty what reason declares to be only one of two equally probable alternatives.

The general attitude is familiar enough. Pascal has put it in his famous 'wager.' Believe a thing because it is impossible. You must back one side ; and reason is too imbecile to settle which. Then give up reasoning. The argument is persuasive if not logically convincing. Hamilton was too much of a philosopher and a rationalist to accept it in that form. His application remained ambiguous. Probably he would have approved a rather vague theism, which might be interpreted in terms of many religious creeds. Mansel, unluckily, had to get from his philosophy to the position of strict Anglican orthodoxy ; from the contradictory inconceivables to the Thirty-nine Articles. His method of performing this

---

[1] *Bampton Lectures,* p. 228. Yet he positively asserts (*e.g.* p. 220) that free-will is a 'fact of consciousness.'   [2] *Ibid.* p. 217.

[3] *Ibid.* p. 121. Though, as he adds, of that alternative which renders that very inconceivability 'itself inexplicable.'

[4] *Ibid.* p. 89.

feat has little interest now ; but I must notice it enough
to show the relation to Mill.

VI. REVEALED RELIGION

How is this Infinite and Absolute Being to be brought
into any relation whatever with facts ? How, by accepting
one of two equally inconceivable alternatives, can we
throw any light upon the truth of a historical statement ?
Mansel protests that he is not arguing as to the truth of
any particular revelation. Though he is not bound to
prove the truth of the Christian revelation, he is clearly
bound to show that a revelation is probable, and to
suggest the criterions by which its reality must be tested.
A religion, as Kant had said, could not be true which
conflicted with morality.[1] If morality binds me to be
merciful, and a god orders me to be cruel, he cannot be
the true God. The deist Tindal had argued long ago
that Joshua could not be justified by a divine command in
exterminating the Canaanites.[2] In answering this difficulty,
Mansel hit upon the unlucky phrase ' Moral Miracles.' [3]
A ' moral miracle,' a conversion of a bad act into a good
one, was, he admitted, not the kind of experiment to be
used too often. Every scoundrel can work ' miracles '
of that kind. He can break the divine law though he
cannot break the ' law of nature.' How are we to know
that in a given case the divine law has been sus-
pended by the supreme ruler and not really broken by
the wicked subject? By what logical feat can we show
the identity of Jehovah with the Absolute and Infinite ?
The deity of Joshua was frankly anthropomorphic ; the

[1] *Bampton Lectures*, p. 202.   [2] *Ibid.* p. 12.   [3] *Ibid.* p. 244.

(generally) invisible deity of a tribe. We can judge of his
character as we can judge of the character of Joshua
himself, or of the character of Baal, or Moloch, or Zeus.
If we argue that all the deities represent an imperfect
feeling after a supreme Being, our judgment would not
be affected. The deity would still be imperfect. The
commands obeyed were still cruel and immoral, as conceived at the time. To argue that they were good
because somehow or other Jehovah was the Inconceivable
seems to be too obvious a fallacy even for a Bampton
Lecturer. Mansel denounces the 'morbid horror of
what they (philosophers) are pleased to call Anthro-
pomorphism.' 'Fools, to dream that man can escape
from himself, that human reason can draw aught but a
human portrait of God.'[1] They really argue that the
portrait has at any rate very ugly features, and doubt
whether it is possible to draw any portrait whatever of
the Inconceivable.

Mansel makes play with this 'antinomy.' The God
of his philosophy is too inconceivable to be a moral law-
giver. But, says Mansel, he is also Jehovah. Jehovah,
it is replied, is immoral. But, says Mansel, he is
also the Inconceivable. This singular mode of eluding
difficulties can of course be expressed in edifying language. The 'caviller,' for example, had objected to
'vicarious punishment.' Mansel says[2] that this supposes
that nothing can be compatible 'with the boundless
goodness of God, which is incompatible with the little
goodness of which man may be conscious in himself.'
The ingenious argument, in spite of this way of putting
it, excited Mill's very justifiable wrath. 'I,' he said,

[1] *Bampton Lectures*, pp. 17, 18.   [2] *Ibid.* p. 212.

'will call no being good, who is not what I mean when I apply that epithet to my fellow-creatures; and if such a being can sentence me to hell for not so calling him, to hell I will go.'[1] Mansel is amazed at this 'extraordinary outburst of rhetoric'; he will not 'pause to comment on its temper and good taste'; but he suggests a parallel.[2] It is that of an 'inexperienced son' taking moral advice from an 'experienced father,' or believing that the elder man is acting rightly though his motives are not fully intelligible to the younger. This, as Mill replies,[3] assumes that the father is 'good' in the human sense, although with more wisdom or knowledge. To make the parallel close we should have to suppose a son who only knows that it is an equal chance whether his father exists or not, and is told by somebody who is equally ignorant that the father desires him to cut a man's throat and appropriate his wife. If the morality of God be absolutely inscrutable, we must fall back upon the conclusion that we are entitled to criticise not the moral contents but the external evidences of a religion.[4] Mansel tries to compromise. We may argue from the morality of religion within limits; the argument may prove that a religion cannot be divine; but not that it is divine. For that we must go to 'external facts.'[5] Our knowledge of God, he still asserts, is derivable from our 'moral and intellectual consciousness'; from the 'constitution and course of nature' and from revelation. These generally agree. When they appear to differ, we must not settle *a priori* which is to

---

[1] *Examination*, p. 129.
[2] *Philosophy of the Unconditioned*, p. 167 (also quoted in Mill's note to above).
[3] *Examination*, p. 123 n.   [4] *Bampton Lectures*, p. 234.
[5] *Ibid.* p. 239.

give way.[1]   Mr. Herbert Spencer, as Mansel thinks,
went wrong because he took only the 'negative position'
of Hamilton's philosophy, and did not see, for example,
that the belief 'in a personal God is imperatively
demanded by the facts of our moral and emotional consciousness.'[2]   Mansel was trying to escape from his own
logic under the shelter of 'vague generalities.'   Mr.
Herbert Spencer, I think, was perfectly right in holding
that when our Deity is the 'Unknowable,' he cannot
be made to take sides even in a moral controversy and
certainly not identified with the anthropomorphic deities
of popular mythology.

The Hamilton-Mansel controversy has become a weariness to the flesh.   The interest which it still possesses is
only in the illustration of the conflict between different
lines of development.   The position of Hamilton and his
disciple means a desperate attempt to escape from a
pressing dilemma.   Kant's theology represents the deistic
rationalism of the eighteenth century.   The metaphysical
argument necessarily tends to some form of pantheism,
such as that of which Spinoza is the most complete
representative.   Carry out the logic and God is identified
with Nature, and is not a being who can be conceived as
interfering with the laws of Nature.   The growth of
science had made it essential to widen the theological conceptions, and to invest the supreme ruler with attributes
commensurate with the new universe, which had been
growing both in vastness and regularity.   The result of
attempting to fulfil that condition was inconsistent with
the common-sense theology of the Scottish philosophy,
which tried, by help of 'intuitions,' to preserve a 'personal

---

[1] *Philosophy of the Conditioned*, p. 245.   [2] *Ibid.* p. 39 *n.*

deity,' a being still individual and therefore conceivable as
interfering; and which, finding the metaphysical argument
dangerous, was inclined to fall back upon the merely
empirical argument of Paley.   I have shown, at fully
sufficient length, how by substituting an antinomy for a
paralogism, Hamilton manages verbally to evade this
difficulty; and by extending the sphere of belief beyond
the sphere of reason, justifies belief in a God who is at
once unknowable and yet may be an object of worship.
Mansel's audacious extension of this to the historical and
mythological creeds, and the consequent identification of
Jehovah with the Absolute and Infinite, can only be
regarded as a logical curiosity.   The only results were,
on the one hand, Mr. Herbert Spencer's agnosticism,
and on the other, perhaps, some impulse to the speculation
of the rising generation.   Hamilton and Mansel did something, by their denunciations of German mysticism and
ontology, to call attention to the doctrines attacked.
The Germans might after all give the right clue; and it
might be possible, by substituting a new dialectic for the
old logic, to regard the universe as still woven out of
reason, and to preserve a theological or at least an idealist
mode of conception.   With that, however, I have no
concern.

VII. MILL ON THEOLOGY

Hamilton's theory at least recognised the inevitable
failure of the empirical or Paley theology which virtually
makes theology a department of science.   Mill, as a
thorough empiricist, might have been expected to
abandon theology along with all transcendentalism and
ontology.   In fact, however, his position was different.   I

have already pointed out that at one part of his argument he appears to be defending orthodox views of theology as against Mansel. This argument might appear to be merely *ad hominem*, as intended to show the absurdity of Mansel's doctrine of inconceivability ; not to deny the inconceivability itself. Mill, however, really goes further. He approves Hamilton's strange assertion that ' religious disbelief and philosophical scepticism are not merely not the same, but have no natural connection,'[1] and holds that all the real arguments for the existence of God and the immortality of the soul remain unaffected by the association theory. In his *Logic* Mill had accepted Comte's ' law of the three stages ' ; but in his later study of Comte he expressly declares that this doctrine is reconcilable with the belief in a ' creator and supreme governor of the world.' It implies a belief in a ' constant order,' but that order may be due to a primitive creation, and even consistent with the continual superintendence of an ' intelligent governor.'[2] In the posthumous essays this position was developed in such a way as to give some scandal to his disciples.[3] He not only leaves room for theistic beliefs, but he seems even to sanction their acceptance.

In the *Three Essays on Religion* Mill is clearly treading unfamiliar ground. He refers to the arguments of Leibniz, Kant, and Butler, but, as Professor Bain remarks,[4] was a comparative stranger to the whole

---

[1] *Examination*, pp. 170, 240 ; Hamilton's *Lectures*, i. 394. I do not try to reconcile Hamilton's ' Obiter dictum ' in this passage with his assertion in his second lecture that ' philosophy ' and ' psychology ' give the only possible proofs of theology ; or with his claim to have met Kant's scepticism.

[2] *Auguste Comte* (1865), pp. 14, 15.

[3] See Mr. John Morley's article in *Critical Miscellanies* (second series).

[4] Bain's *J. S. Mill*, p. 139.

sphere of speculation. He is not so much at home
with his subject as he was in the *Logic* or the *Political
Economy*; and therefore scarcely appreciates certain conditions of successful navigation of these regions made
sufficiently obvious by the history of previous adven-
turers. Yet his candour and his resolution to give fair
consideration to all difficulties are as conspicuous as his
wish to appreciate the highest motives of his antagonists.

Of the three essays, the first two, written before 1858
(on 'Nature' and the 'Utility of Religion'), show less
disposition than the last (upon 'Theism') to compromise
with orthodoxy; and yet their principles are essentially
the same. Mill, of course, is still a thorough empiricist.
One version of theology is therefore inconsistent with
his most essential tenets. The so-called *a priori* or ontological argument is for him worthless. It involves, he
thinks, the unjustifiable assumption that we can infer
'objective facts from ideas or convictions of our minds.'
The 'First Cause argument,' again, can only upon his
view of causation suggest an indefinite series of antecedents, and one in which the 'higher' as often follows
the 'lower' cause, as the lower the higher. Matter may
be the antecedent of mind, as well as mind of matter.
Moreover, no 'cause' is wanted for that which has no
beginning; and as our experience shows a beginning for
mind but no beginning for force or matter, the presumption is against mind.[1] If, indeed, the world be
simply a series of separate phenomena, connected solely
as preceding and succeeding, there is no possibility, it
would seem, of inferring any unity or underlying cause
or ground. The very attempt to reach unity is as hope-

[1] *Three Essays*, pp. 142-54.

less as is the proverbial problem of weaving ropes from
sand. The possibility of philosophical theism is thus
destroyed ; for the God of philosophy corresponds to the
endeavour to assert precisely the unity thus denied in
advance. By ' God ' Mill must really mean, not Spinoza's
necessary substance nor Kant's ' Idea of the pure Reason,'
but a being who is essentially one factor of the universe.
The confusion is of critical importance. It is constantly
assumed, as Mill assumes, that the ' *a priori* ' and the
empirical arguments are different modes of proving the
same conclusion. The word ' God ' is no doubt used in
both cases ; but the word covers entirely different senses.
The existence of Jehovah might be proved or disproved
like the existence of Moses. The God of Spinoza is
proved from the logical necessity of the unity and
regularity of the universe. One Being may interfere or
superintend because he is only part of a whole. The
other corresponds to the whole, and interferences or
miracles become absurd. Mill, therefore, by calmly
dismissing the *a priori* argument is really giving up
the God of philosophy, and trying what he can do with
the particular or finite being really implied in Paley.
Theology on this showing can be only a part of natural
science, and precisely that part in which we know
nothing.

To know anything of God, in whatever sense, we
must go to ' Nature.' In the first essay Mill discusses
the question whether anything can be made of the
various systems which prescribe ' imitation of Nature '
or obedience to the laws of Nature. If Nature be taken
in the widest sense, as including man, such systems are
nugatory. Disobedience to a ' law of Nature ' is not

wrong but impossible. We may, however, take Nature
in the narrower sense in which it is the antithesis of art ;
or, as he puts it, as meaning ' that which takes place
without human intervention.'[1] It is plain that, in this
sense, the whole aim of all human endeavour must be
to improve Nature. Mill emphasises this by expanding
the indictment against Nature, which has become more
familiar in discussions of the ' struggle for existence.'
The ' absolute recklessness of the great cosmic forces,'[2]
the variety of torments, such as the worst tyrants have
hardly used, inflicted upon all living beings without the
slightest regard to justice, are amply sufficient reasons
for not 'imitating Nature.' Hence Mill protests emphatically against the notion that ' goodness is natural.'[3]
All the virtues are in his sense ' artificial.' Sympathy
begins as a form of selfishness—selfishness for two—and
the sentiment of justice is developed by the necessity
of external law. It is the pressure from without, the
interest of each in the goodness of others, which has
really created the moral world. The ' germs' of all
these virtues must, it is true, have been present ; the
species could not have existed had it not been endowed
with desire for useful ends ; but then, we must also
admit the existence of bad instincts, producing ' rankly
luxuriant growths' of vice against which a long and
precarious struggle must be carried on.[4]

  Mill is thus saying emphatically much that has been
said by later evolutionists. One remark is obvious.
The distinction between ' Natural' and 'Artificial' in
this sense is clearly arbitrary for one who, like Mill,
rejects the doctrine of Freewill. If Nature makes men

---

[1] *Three Essays*, p. 19.   [2] *Ibid.* p. 28.   [3] *Ibid.* p. 46.   [4] *Ibid.* p. 53.

with certain capacities, Nature must also be taken to be the cause of all human ' intervention.' The sphere of the ' artificial' is merely one part of the sphere of the ' natural.' ' Sympathy' and ' justice' are not the less natural because they are in this sense artificial. Mill is, of course, fully aware of the fact that his ' nature' is here at most a department of Nature in the wider sense. Yet the illegitimate distinction seems more or less to affect his conclusions. He comes to speak as if the distinction corresponded to a line between different worlds. In the non-human world we appear to catch ' Nature' alone and unaided ; we can see what it can do by itself, and judge, if not of its justice, at least of its benevolence. He is thus led to use language about men amending Nature or ' co-operating with the beneficent powers,'[1] which would be more consistent in a thorough-going advocate of Freewill, but which in his mouth must be taken as a metaphorical or provisional mode of speech. To one who uses ' nature' in the widest sense as implying a conception of the universe as a whole, the narrower use would be meaningless. But, as we shall now see, the unity of nature is a conception which Mill virtually rejects.

Mill has shown conclusively that it is impossible to interpret Nature as the work of omnipotent Benevolence. So far, he agrees with many predecessors, including Hume and Mansel ;[2] but he does not with Hume become

---

[1] *Three Essays*, p. 65.

[2] ' Why,' asks Hume, ' is there any misery in the world ? Not by chance, surely. From some cause, then ? Is it by the intervention of the Deity ? But he is perfectly benevolent. Is it contrary to his intentions ? But he is Almighty. Epicurus's old questions,' he says, ' are yet unanswered.' ' If,' says Mansel, ' an infinitely powerful Being wills evil, he is not perfectly good. If he wills it not, his will is thwarted and his sphere of action limited.'—Hume's *Works* (1874), ii. 440, 442 ; *Bampton Lectures*, p. 51.

simply sceptical, nor follow Mansel in pronouncing that
we must believe a doctrine which we are unable to ' con-
strue to the mind' as conceivable. He suggests an
alternative view. It is possible to believe in a God who
is benevolent though not omnipotent. This, he declares,
is the only ' religious explanation of the order of Nature,'
which is neither self-contradictory nor inconsistent with
facts.[1] He ' ventures to assert,' moreover, that it has
been the real faith of all who have drawn a worthy support from trust in Providence ; ' they have always saved
[God's] goodness at the expense of His power.' This,
for example, is the true meaning of Leibniz's ' best of
all possible worlds.'[2] Mill declares that the doctrine
of the Manichæans, which he knows to have been
' devoutly held by at least one cultivated and conscien-
tious person of our own day,' is the only ' form of belief
in the supernatural which stands wholly clear both of intellectual contradiction and moral obliquity.'[3] He points
out, too, that even Christianity admits a devil, though it
places upon the Creator the responsibility of not annihi-
lating him.[4] Now Manichæism is a clear confession of
philosophical bankruptcy. The whole aim of reasoning
is to reduce the universe to unity, and this is to admit
that there is an ultimate and insoluble dualism. From
the point of view of the ontologist, indeed, the moral
difficulty which Manichæism is supposed to meet is
irrelevant. God is the ground or First Cause. Evil
is caused as much as good, and if a first cause or an
absolute substance be a necessary assumption, we must
ascribe to it the whole system of things, good or bad,

[1] *Three Essays*, p. 39. [2] *Ibid.* p. 40. [3] *Ibid.* p. 116.
[4] *Ibid.* p. 184. Friday asks Robinson Crusoe why God did not kill the devil.

painful or pleasurable, without trying to separate what is inextricably intertwined. An argument from causation leaves no *locus standi* for any moral objection. Mill, however, denies the necessity for, or indeed the possibility of, such reasoning. He is fully prepared to admit that in the last resort we come to independent and equally uncaused factors. The question, then, remains, what positive ground we can assign for a belief in any first cause or causes or 'supernatural entities.'

Having rejected the metaphysical arguments for a Deity, we reach at last, says Mill, an argument of a really scientific character—the argument, namely, from design.[1] That is to say, he tries to find room for an empirical deity, who must therefore correspond to a part of nature, not to the whole. He does not hold that the knowledge of nature anywhere involves antinomies or contrary inconceivables. It is a coherent and throughout intelligible system, but it would correspond to the ideal of completed science, not to any metaphysical belief. Within this system there is room for a being who, though he is limited by something external to himself, may yet be an object of worship. In fact, there can be no *a priori* objection to the theory of a powerful being, who may be discovered, like any other beings known to us, by his action in particular cases. Metaphysicians may decline to call such a being God; but a proof of superhuman wisdom and power may be enough for practical purposes.[2]

The proof, then, that such a being exists, must be made

[1] So in the *Examination of Hamilton* (p. 567) he says that this is 'by far the best' and 'by far the most persuasive argument.'

[2] *Examination*, p. 246.

by induction ; and, as Mill explains, by the first of the
famous 'four methods,' namely, by that of Agreement.[1]
This argument, though generally the weakest, is in this
case 'strong of its kind.' He illustrates it by the
familiar case. The eye is a complex structure which, as it
began in time, must have had a cause or causes. 'Chance'
is eliminated by the number of instances, and therefore
there must be some causal connection between the 'cause'
which brought the elements together and the 'fact of
sight.' Mill, that is, thinks it necessary to prove what
science takes for granted. No man of science disputes
that there is some cause of eyes and of every eye. But
here we have the curious transition into another order
of thought, which corresponds to the passage from the
empirical to the transcendental meaning. It is clear that
so long as we are in the sphere of science, the only 'cause'
of the existence of an eye is the sum of the preceding
organic processes. A given animal has eyes because the
processes of reproduction involve resemblance to its
parents. If we go back to eyeless ancestors, we have
the problem how eyes were developed ; but the purely
scientific answer would still consist in assigning the
previous conditions or the precedent stage in the whole
process of nature. How do we get out of this series ?
The argument, according to Mill, would proceed by saying
that, as sight follows the eye, the cause must be a 'final'
cause ; or, in other words, correspond to an 'intelligent
Will.' But what is the relation of this Will to the
admitted series of events ? Causation always sends me
back along an indefinitely producible series. Am I to
interpret this cause as an 'alternative' to what may be

[1] *Three Essays*, p. 170.

called the natural cause ; or as corresponding to a general power, which is manifested through the whole series ? In the latter case we may consider the God of nature as an 'immanent' power. His operation is manifest in the general wisdom of the whole system. It is not only consistent with, but implies, the persistence of the 'laws of nature,' and therefore the evolution of eyes, if there was a period before eyes existed. If that view be tenable, we may save 'teleology' by applying it to nature as a whole, but there is no intervention in the actual series of natural events. On the view which Mill accepts, we have an intervention, at some particular point. But how is this to be inferred, or what can it mean ? I have already noticed the familiar difficulties in speaking of ' Philip Beauchamp.' The philosophical objection is clear,[1] and in science ' creation ' can be only a word ; it introduces an arbitrary and unmeaning interruption, and, under the form of explaining, declares explanation to be impossible.

In fact, when such conceptions are brought into the argument, when ' creation ' is used as an alternative hypothesis to a permanent order, the answer of the evolutionist is conclusive. Here, accordingly, Mill finds himself confronted by Darwin. He admits that the doctrine of the 'survival of the fittest' would 'greatly attenuate,' though it would be in ' no way whatever inconsistent with creation.'[2] This means, apparently, that Darwinism does not prove that there was not a ' creation ' at some indefinite time ; though it does show that there is no need for supposing a creation since the existing order began.

[1] The 'ingenious simile,' says Mansel, 'by which God is compared to a mechanic fails only in this particular, that both its terms are utterly unlike the objects which they profess to represent.'—*Bampton Lectures*, p. 188.

[2] *Three Essays*, p. 174.

I have already noticed Mill's view of this 'remarkable speculation.' Here he virtually admits that his theology, such as it is, and, indeed, his whole conception of nature, is virtually opposed to evolution. Science, he says, most truly, leads us to regard nature as 'one connected system, not a web of separate threads in passive juxtaposition with one another, but rather, like the human or animal frame,' in perpetual 'action and reaction'; and the natural version of this, he adds, is theism. The unity of nature, that is, has enabled monotheism to supersede polytheism, because it corresponds to the scientific view.[1] Yet, while saying this in general terms, he cannot reconcile it to his own theories; he still talks of 'laws of nature' counteracting each other;[2] he can speak of some things as 'uncaused'; and of a 'permanent' and 'a changeable' element in nature, as though persistence was not a case of causation. He is willing, as we have seen, to assume that anything may be the cause of anything else. The universe is therefore ultimately a struggle between independent forces, and God becomes a being who has to struggle against antecedent or independent things. When science is regarded, not as a system of interdependent truths, where the value of every theory must be judged by the way in which it affects and is affected by all other ascertainable truth, but as an aggregate of purely empirical observations of the order of succession of otherwise unrelated facts, it is easy to introduce such conceptions as 'creation,' which virtually deny the continuity and reasonableness of the order

[1] *Three Essays*, p. 133.

[2] *Ibid*. pp. 16, 17. Observe the language about 'conforming to the laws of equilibrium among bodies,' instead of 'conforming only to the law of gravitation,' as though we did not necessarily 'conform' to all 'laws of nature' in all cases.

generally, and tend to confuse, as his antagonists would say, Nature with a particular element in Nature ; and to make noumena take a side in the struggle between phenomena.

Mill is thus able to hold that the adaptations 'in nature afford a large balance of probability in favour of creation by intelligence.'[1] It is, he grants, only a probability, and not strengthened by any independent arguments. It still remains to consider whether we can find reasons to believe that the creator is moral. He thinks that most ' contrivances ' are for the preservation of the creatures, and that there is no reason for attributing the destructive agencies to one Being, and the preserving agencies to another. We may therefore give up Manichæism, or a conflict between good and evil powers ; but we may still have an uncreated set of things with which the good being must struggle. We must be content to believe in a Being of great but limited power— how limited we cannot even conjecture ; whose intelligence may be unlimited though it may also be more limited than his power ; who desires the happiness of his creatures but has probably other motives. If he shows benevolence, there are no traces of justice.[2] Of immortality we can learn nothing, unless from revelation. He denies that a revelation, conflicting with morality, can be divine; but this forces him to limit the power of the Deity. His God desires morality. How can we discover that he desires it? Can these vague surmises be helped by any direct revelation or miraculous intervention? Mill

---

[1] *Three Essays*, p. 174.

[2] Mill has here come to speak of ' Nature ' in the narrower sense, as opposed to art or to nature working through man.

discusses the argument of Hume's essay and reaches, what
I take to be the true conclusion, that the real question
is whether we have independent reasons for believing in
a Deity whose intervention is conceivable.[1]   Considering
that we have some reason for believing in such a being,
he at last concludes that, in spite of most serious
difficulties, historical and philosophical, we are ' entitled
to say that there is nothing so inherently impossible or
absolutely incredible in the supposition that the " extremely precious" gift of Christianity came from a
divinely commissioned man as to preclude any one from
hoping that it may be true.'   He can go no further, for
he sees no ' evidentiary value' even in the testimony of
Christ himself.   The best men are the readiest to ascribe
their own merits to a higher source.   Mill, of course,
does not believe in the divinity of Christ; he holds
that Christ himself would have regarded such a pre-
tension as blasphemous ; but it remains possible that
' Christ actually was what he supposed himself to be
. . . a man charged with a special, express, and unique
commission from God to lead mankind to truth and
virtue.' [2]

Mill, we see, declared positivism to be reconcilable
with theism.   Comte himself, who declared atheism to be
the most illogical form of theology, would have agreed
that positivism does not disprove God's existence.   But
Comte would have said that an unverifiable hypothesis
about an inconceivable being was simply idle or ' otiose.'
Mill seems to treat the absence of negative proof as
equivalent—not indeed to the presence of positive, but—
to the existence of a probability worth entertaining.   His

[1] *Three Essays*, p. 232.   [2] *Ibid.* p. 255.

theism, if so vague and problematical a doctrine can be called theism, is defended as neither self-contradictory nor inconsistent with fact. Now a theory which is self-contradictory is really no theory at all. Nor is a theory scientifically valuable simply because 'consistent' with facts. A theory must have some definite support in facts. It must at lowest be not only consistent with the known facts, but inconsistent with some otherwise imaginable facts. If it fits every conceivable state of things, it can throw light upon none. But this is obviously the case with Mill's theory. He makes way for a good being by an arbitrary division of nature into two sets of forces. He saves the benevolence by limiting the power of the deity ; but then the limits are, by his own admission, utterly unknowable. A power, restrained by unknowable bounds, is a power from which nothing can be inferred. Whatever its attributes, we do not know whether they will affect any state of things. The goodness may be indefinitely frustrated. In fact, on Mill's showing, a power omnipotent but not bene- volent, or an indefinite multitude of powers of varying attributes, or a good and a bad power eternally struggling, or, in short, any religious doctrine that has ever been held among men, would suit the facts. Mill's 'plurality of causes' might have suggested this difficulty. I see a corpse. The death may have been due to any one of an indefinite number of causes. What right have I to select one ? I am in the same position when I regard the whole of nature as what Hume called a 'unique effect.' The four methods of induction become inapplicable, for there are no other universes and I have no compass to steer by in the region of the unverifiable.

What, then, can be the advantage of any belief where conflicting hypotheses must be all equally probable? The question is partly discussed in the second essay upon the utility of Religion. Here Mill takes up the old argument of 'Philip Beauchamp,' the 'only direct discussion' of the point with which he is acquainted,[1] and endeavours to state the case more fairly and in a less hostile spirit. His argument, however, is in general conformity with Bentham and Grote, and is very forcibly put. One point may be noticed. He virtually identifies 'religion' with a belief in 'the supernatural.'[2] He compares the efficacy of such beliefs with the efficacy of education (which, as he characteristically says, is 'almost boundless')[3] and of public opinion, and shows with 'Beauchamp' that when conflict occurs, these influences are stronger than those derived from supernatural sanctions. Now when we believe in a revelation it is intelligible to ask, What is the influence of a creed? It represents a new force influencing men's minds from without. But when the creed is supposed to be generated from antecedent beliefs, the argument must be altered by considering what are the true causes of the belief. How did it come to prevail? An admirer of Comte might have brought out more distinctly the fact that such beliefs mark an essential stage of progress, that what are now sporadic superstitions were once parts of a systematic religion and represented the germs of science. They were approximate hypotheses which had to be remodelled by extricating or dropping the 'supernatural' element. A full recognition of this would diminish the paradoxical appearance of the statement from which he starts, that 'a religion

---

[1] *Three Essays*, p. 76.   [2] *Ibid.* p. 100.   [3] *Ibid.* p. 82.

may be morally useful without being intellectually sustainable.' The truth surely is that we cannot separate the two elements of a creed. Doubtless there were no such beings as the Zeus or Apollo of popular belief; but polytheism may still have provided the only form in which certain truths could be presented; and was, as Comte would have said, a stage in the process from fetichism towards monotheism and positivism. A discussion of the utility of belief in the 'supernatural' without reference to the place of the supernatural in the whole system of belief must be necessarily inadequate. Mill admits this in substance, and argues that the moral truth may survive the superstitions in which it was bound up.[1] He goes on to argue, as Comte had argued, that the instincts which once found their sanction in the supernatural world might find their embodiment in the 'Religion of Humanity.'[2] This he holds to be not only entitled to the name of religion, but to be 'a better religion than any of those ordinarily called by that title.' It is disinterested and does not tend to cramp the intellect or degenerate into a worship of mere power. Mill says emphatically that the Bentham mode of considering religion as a supplement to police by providing 'sanctions' is inadequate; and that religion, like poetry, is valuable as suggesting higher ideals and gratifying the craving for knowledge of corresponding realities. To the selfish, supernatural religion offers heaven; and to the 'tender and grateful' it offers the love of God. He points out that it does not follow that we must 'travel beyond the boundaries of the world we inhabit' in order to obtain such consolation.[3] And the essay con-

---

[1] *Three Essays*, p. 97.   [2] *Ibid.* p. 111.   [3] *Ibid.* p. 104.

cludes by saying that, though the 'supernatural religions' have always the advantage of offering immortality, the value set upon immortality may diminish as life becomes higher and happier and annihilation may seem more desirable.[1]

Yet in the middle of this argument we have the defence of Manichæism as a possible creed,[2] and in the last essay we seem to reach the true account of his leanings to such a belief. He still, that is, requires a breathing-space for the imagination. 'Truth is the province of reason,' but 'in the regulation of the imagination literal truth of facts is not the only thing to be considered.'[3] Reason must keep the fortress, but the 'imagination may safely follow its own end and do its best to make life pleasant and lovely inside the castle.' Thus, though we are only entitled to hope as to the government of the world and a life after death, the bare hope may have a beneficial effect. 'It makes life and human nature a far greater thing to the feelings, and gives greater strength and solemnity to all the sentiments which are awakened in us by our fellow-creatures and mankind at large.' Aspirations are no longer checked by the disastrous feeling of 'not worth while.' Religion, too, has set before us a 'Divine Person, as a standard of excellence and a model for imitation.'[4] The ideal, it is true, would remain, even if the person were held to be imaginary ; and would not be encumbered by theological difficulties. Yet there is an advantage in the belief that a perfect being really exists and represents the ruler of the universe, which cannot be shared by the rationalist.[5] Hence as, after all, the truth of the

[1] *Three Essays*, p. 122.   [2] *Ibid.* p. 116.   [3] *Ibid.* pp. 248-49.
[4] *Ibid.* p. 253.   [5] *Ibid.* p. 252.

belief is possible, it may be combined with the Religion of Humanity. That religion, 'with or without super-natural sanctions,' will be the religion of the future ; but it will be strengthened by the feeling that we are 'help-ing God' and supplying 'co-operation' which 'he, not being omnipotent, really needs.'[1] Truly, Mill was nearly qualified for a place among the prophets.

Mill's arbitrary assumptions, like the metaphysical wiredrawings of Mansel, are rather unprofitable in them-selves : few people will care to follow them in detail ; and neither could boast of many converts. Believers soon became aware of the real scepticism of Mansel's position ; and positivists saw that Mill left an opening for superstition. Both Mansel and Mill were troubled about the Religion of Nature. It is abundantly clear, as Mill might have foreseen, that such a theology as he contemplates could be of no real value. It depends essentially upon compromises and arbitrary distinctions. It is still within the sphere of science, though doomed to disappear as science advances, and from the first is inconsistent with the very aims which are proposed by theology. God is admittedly not omnipotent, and his existence is no guarantee for morality or optimism. And hence there is an odd approximation between Mill and Mansel.

Mill observes[2] that the moral character of an alleged revelation cannot be of itself a proof of its divinity. The importance of the 'internal evidence' is therefore 'principally negative.' So says Mansel. 'The evidence derived from the internal character of a religion, what-ever may be its value within its proper limits, is, as

[1] *Three Essays*, pp. 256-57.   [2] *Ibid.* p. 216.

regards the divine origin of the religion, purely negative.' [1]
Where is the difference ? If the morality of a revelation
be bad, Mill argues that the revelation must be at once
rejected. Mansel thinks that although the morality be
not clearly good, it may in some way represent a divine
command. Immoral laws cannot be divine, says Mill,
though a good law may be human. A law apparently
bad, replies Mansel, may be divine, though, of course,
the badness can only be apparent. Here, as elsewhere,
the believer in the empirical character of morality appears
to attribute most certainty to the moral judgment. The
solutions differ accordingly. Mill supposes that God
must be good, but reconciles this to facts by assuming
that God is not all-powerful. Mansel will not give up
the power, and to preserve the goodness has to assume
a radical incapacity in the intellect—a necessity of believing where there is an impotence of conceiving.
Mill, that is, is content with the empirical deity, who
is necessarily limited ; and Mansel keeps the deity of
ontology but admits that he cannot be known. Mill's
conception is purely arbitrary, though he keeps within
the limits of conceivable experience ; while Mansel preserves the language appropriate to the conception of
absolute unity, and yet admits that it can mean nothing
for us. 'Agnosticism' seems to be an easier and more
rational alternative; if it means an open admission that
we know nothing, when we can only save our appearance
of knowledge by arbitrary assumptions or by the use of
meaningless words. Of Mill's position it must be frankly
admitted that his desire for a religious and even supernatural belief is a proof of dissatisfaction with his own

---

[1] *Bampton Lectures*, p. 238.

position. He felt here, as elsewhere, that something was wanting in his philosophy. What that really was may partly appear by considering other contemporary solutions. Mansel represents a particular phase of thought which is already extinct, and views differing both from theirs and from Mill's had in practice a far wider influence than either.

The Utilitarian view naturally identifies a religious creed with a belief in certain historical statements of fact. If the facts be provable the religion is true ; if disproved it is false. If there was such a being as Jehovah, it was desirable to worship him ; and the creed would then be useful. If there was no such being, worship was folly. The test of the utility of a religion was, therefore, simply the truth or falsehood of its historical statements. If its gods were made by the fancy, not by the reason, the result is a condemnation of religion in general. That is simple and logical, and recognises an indisputable truth. So far as a religion makes false statements, they must be abandoned ; and so far as its influence depends upon the falsity, it is pernicious.

A religion, however, represents more than can be estimated by this simple test. The poetical value of Homer is not destroyed by disproving the existence of the Pagan deisms, nor the value of the Hebrew Scriptures by disproving the existence of Jehovah. The facts alleged may be fabulous and absurd ; but they are also symbols for setting forth views of the world and of conduct, and so giving emphatic utterance to important truths. The old religions were attempts of men, in early stages of thought, to embody ideals of conduct which may really have been of the highest value to mankind. They were essential, again, to the social bonds which have, in fact, determined the formation of society and facilitated the growth of sympathy and philanthropy. Therefore, if a religious creed be false when interpreted as a simple statement of fact, we have not exhausted its significance or even touched the really most important significance of the religion itself. Believers felt more or less clearly that such attacks as 'Philip Beauchamp' affected only externals, and left the need for religion unsatisfied. Only as the actual creed was pledged to maintain the truth of certain statements, which were daily becoming more incredible, the necessity appeared of finding some stronger position than the old Paley scheme, which virtually regarded religion as a mere statement of historical fact, or as a department of natural science. To trace the consequences would be to write a history of modern theology. I shall try only to indicate the relation to the Utilitarians of a few thinkers. Two main lines of thought were conspicuous in Mill's generation, and correspond to what Newman called 'liberalism' and 'dogmatism.'

A very instructive example of one phase of liberal thought was Frederick Denison Maurice (1805-1872). Before Mill's attack upon Mansel, Maurice had been engaged in a sharp controversy invoked by the Bampton Lecturer. No two men could be more thoroughly at cross-purposes. In their arguments each word bears a different signification for the two disputants. Each, of course, vehemently disapproved the other; and Mansel

was provoked to call Maurice a liar[1] in direct terms.
The real difficulty is to reduce the argument to any
common measure; and Maurice's position, though not
easy to define, is significant. Maurice,[2] as I have said,
was one of Mill's friendly adversaries in the early
debating society. His references to Mill are always
respectful, little as could be their intellectual sympathy;
while Mill's judgment was that 'more intellectual power
was wasted in Maurice than in any one else of my
generation.' Deep respect for Maurice, admiration of
his subtlety and power of generalisation, only increased
Mill's wonder that he could find all truth in the Thirty-
nine Articles.[3] Maurice had been brought up as a
Unitarian, and was profoundly impressed by the barren
wrangling over the dogmatic partitions of various sects.
After long hesitation he at last found satisfaction in the
Church of England and, as he declared, by accepting the
Anglican formulæ in their obvious and most natural
sense. To men of other persuasions, his interpretation
appeared on the contrary to amount to a complete transformation of their natural meaning. Maurice was
therefore excluded from all the higher preferment, and
passed for an insidious heresiarch. He replied by a full
and frank, though hardly a lucid, assertion of his own
convictions; and gradually proved, even to his enemies,

[1] *Examination of the Reverend F. D. Maurice's 'Strictures'* (1859), p. 80.
This is a reply to Maurice's *What is Revelation?* (1859). Maurice in a *Sequel*
(1860) answers this and other accusations with dignity; though his remarks
upon Mansel were certainly sharp enough.

[2] Maurice's most complete book, the *Kingdom of Christ* (1838, enlarged
1842), is less rhetorical and more logical than its successors. The *Theological
Essays* (1853) gives his teaching in the shortest compass.

[3] Mill's *Autobiography*, p. 153.

his entire superiority to any worldly motives. He was expelled in 1853 from his professorship at King's College for denying the truth of the popular version of hell, a little before the denial had become a commonplace. Disciples had already gathered round him and regarded him with the reverence due to the purity and loftiness of his character. As the head of the Christian Socialists in the critical period of 1848, he had at least given a proof that divines could take a genuine interest in the great social problems of the day. Maurice himself was little qualified for business details, and the whole movement failed for the time, like most others which start from the sympathy of the outsiders instead of the actual experience of the actual sufferers. It was, however, significant of a most important change, more easily underestimated than exaggerated. Maurice deserves all respect, as Mill observes, for his action, of which, moreover, it is only just to say that it was really characteristic of his whole position.

What, then, was Maurice's position in theology? In the first place he recognised most fully a truth which, in various forms, gives the real strength to all great religious teachers. He held that the value of a religion depends upon its congeniality to the highest parts of human nature. He is thus at the opposite pole to the Philip Beauchamp doctrine, according to which the essence of religion is to create a spiritual police, and to add the sanction of hell to the sanction of the gallows. Maurice is equally opposed to the sacerdotalism which makes the essence of religion consist in a magical removal of penalties instead of a 'regeneration' of the nature. He takes what may be vaguely called the 'subjective' view

of religion, and sympathises with Schleiermacher's statement that piety is 'neither a knowing nor a doing, but
an inclination and determination of the feeling.'[1] It
is evident, again, that Maurice could as little base his
belief upon external evidence as his morality upon external
sanctions. So far he may be said to coincide with the
philosophical view. A religion must be an expression of
general truths accessible to all men, and independent of
time and place. Maurice had been a wide reader of philosophy ; he spent much time upon a history of 'Metaphysical and Moral philosophy'[2] which, if vague in the
statement of definite theories, shows wide sympathy and
desire to enter into the spirit of the various schools.
In the *Kingdom of Christ*[3] he declares that 'eclecticism is
a necessity of the age' ; meaning by eclecticism a doctrine
which shall discover what is the truth contained in all the
partial systems and creeds of all ages. Here, again,
Maurice was sharing the best liberal impulses of the day,
and sharing them because they were congenial to a
generous and tender-hearted nature. The same tendency
makes him averse to any definite system of metaphysical
dogmas. The dialectical wranglings over dogmas which
disgusted him in his youth appeared again in Mansel's
metaphysics. The Bampton Lectures showed, according
to him, that we cannot leave the ground of solid fact for
the 'logical ground without being involved in a series of
hopeless quibbles which no human being ought to trouble
himself with, unless he means to abandon the business of

---

[1] i.e. *eine Neigung und Bestimmtheit des Gefühls,* quoted in *What is Revelation?* p. 316. Maurice defends this against Mansel.

[2] Begun about 1835 for the *Encyclopædia Metropolitana.* The whole
collected in an edition of 1871-72.

[3] *Kingdom of Christ* (1842), p. 253.

existence and to give himself up to feats of jugglery.'[1]
In such regions no lasting foundation can be found.
Nor, on the other hand, can we be satisfied with the
mere historical critics who, like Strauss, pick holes in the
gospels or, like Strauss's opponents, manage to mend
them ; or with the philologists who argue whether 'the
line in the O can be detected with the aid of spectacles or
not.'[2]   A religion which is to move men's hearts must
have some wider and deeper basis.

So far Maurice's teaching would command the sympathy of all who called themselves liberal.   But what
becomes of Logic?   Can philosophy dispense with it
altogether?   Maurice professedly appeals to the heart.
The appeal is made over and over again in a great
variety of forms : to the 'great human heart,' to 'bed-
ridden sufferers,' to 'peasants, women, and children,'[3]
and we are told that it is the 'office of the theologian'
to appeal not to his own judgment or that of the ages,
but to the 'conscience, heart, reason of mankind.'[4]
Nothing can be more to the purpose if we are considering the efficacy of a religious belief ; but we must
ask how this appeal is related to the question of its
truth.   The emotions are not reason, though they are
bound to be reasonable.   The position is that of all
mysticism.   The mystic is one who virtually dethrones
reason in favour of the heart.   Therefore mysticism
leads to all the varying beliefs which are suggested by
our unguided feelings.   When Maurice was charged
with being himself a mystic or neoplatonist, his reply

[1] *What is Revelation?* (1819), p. 275.
[2] *Theological Essays*, pp. 65, 119.
[3] *Ibid.* pp. 113, 338, 465.   [4] *What is Revelation?* p. 232.

was that the error of the mystic is not in recognising
an 'inner light,' but in supposing that his intuition is
something personal and private, and not a universal
faculty of the human heart.[1] He admits, that is, that
all religion implies the direct recognition of divine
influences by the human heart, though it is terribly
apt to confound the true intuition with certain erroneous
doctrines. By what test, then, are we to separate the
true light from the misleading gleams of human passion
and prejudices? How can we know that it is the divine
Logos which is speaking to us, and not some sophist
substituting a mere human theory?

This gives Maurice's characteristic doctrine, repeated
in countless forms with most genuine fervour, and yet
leaving the painful impression that we can never get a
distinct meaning. He tells us again and again that we
require not a system but a revelation ; that we are
to believe in God, not in a theory about God ; not in
'notions' but in principles ; that a theology is ground-
less which 'accepts as a tenet what is revealed as a
truth,'[2] and that we shall be 'driven to creeds' by
'weariness of tenets.'[3] These, and countless variations
upon the same theme, involve a puzzling distinction.
How, precisely, does the belief in God differ from the
acceptance of a theory about God? Maurice, I may
perhaps say, takes the belief in God to be an operation,
not a mere bit of logic; an act of the man's whole nature,
not a purely intellectual process such as the deduction of

---

[1] *Kingdom of Christ*, i. (1842) 41. This book, first published as a series of
letters to a Quaker, is an exposition of the way in which the mystical doctrine
of Fox and Barclay degenerated from the confusion between a valid, because
universal, principle and a claim to a private or individual application.

[2] *What is Revelation?* p. 228.   [3] *Theological Essays*, p. 316.

the conclusion of a syllogism. It is the apprehension of the 'inner light,' always perceptible if the eye be opened, and which is in the same indissoluble moment not merely enlightening but life-giving. The vision is also 'dynamical': the submission of ourselves to a force as well as the recognition of the existence of certain outward facts. It implies not merely the admission of a new theory about the universe, but the bringing ourselves into harmony with the one central force of the universe—that is with the God who is Love as well as power and wisdom. This is the true mystical doctrine; and that doctrine, if not the most logical, is the most unanswerable form of religious belief. If a man believes that he has the 'inner light,' he is in his own court beyond appeal. But the difficulty of making his decisions valid for others cannot be evaded, and implies some use of logic. If the inner light implies knowledge as well as an emotion, it should be expressible in forms true for all men. The mere formula by itself may be barren, or merely subordinate; but if any definite creed is to emerge, it must include tenets capable of logical expression. This is, in fact, the problem round which Maurice is always turning.

The result is indicated in his little book upon the *Religions of the World*.[1] It embodies one of the most marked tendencies of modern thought. No divine can now speak of strange religions as simply devil-worship, or limit divine truth to his own set of dogmas. The simple or logical rationalist had inferred that the true creed must be that which is common to all religions. But to reject all special doctrines was to leave a blank

[1] Originally the Boyle Lectures for 1846. Fourth edition in 1861.

residuum of mere abstract deism, if even deism could survive. It was but another road to the 'religion of nature.' Yet that was the tendency of most liberal divines within the church. The 'broad church' party, as it was called, was getting rid of 'dogma' by depriving the creed of all meaning. Maurice's method is therefore different. The element of truth in all religions is not any separable doctrine common to all. It is to be found by regarding all creeds as partial or distorted expressions of the full truth revealed in Christ. On this showing therefore Buddhism testifies to the truth of Christianity, but Christianity does not testify to the truth of Buddhism. Or, to take a trifling but characteristic argument,[1] Wilberforce and the Unitarian, W. Smith, were colleagues in a great benevolent work. Does that show that the doctrine of the Trinity is unimportant? No; Smith should have seen that the zeal of Wilberforce 'manifestly flowed out of the faith' in the divinity of Christ. Wilberforce, on the other hand, should see that Christ might rule in the heart of the Unitarian though the Unitarian knew it not. The divine influence may operate upon the heart which does not recognise its true nature. Thus Wilberforce, instead of becoming 'latitudinarian,' could escape 'latitudinarianism.' This may be true, but it would clearly not convince Smith. If you appeal to your heart, why may I not appeal to mine? Is not your conviction, after all, 'subjective' —as representing your own personal prejudices—and would it not be just as easy, with equal skill, to invert the argument? Or is not the real source of action in both cases the benevolence which has nothing to do with

[1] *Theological Essays*, p. 211.

either set of dogmas? This unintentional shifting is implied in the process by which Maurice manages to accept the Thirty-nine Articles. Taken as truths, they utter the voice of the heart, or imply an apprehension of the divine light. Taken as merely logical, they are but tenets or ' notional' dogmas. The doctrine of the Atonement, for example, as made into a quasi-legal theory by Archbishop Magee, is simply horrible : it deserves all that Paine could have said of it, and actually ' confounds the evil spirit with God.' But take it in another sense—not as proclaiming the supremacy of a harsh and unjust ruler, but as declaring the process by which the love of God and of his son reconciles men to himself—and it becomes infinitely comforting, and expresses the feelings of ' tens of thousands of suffering human beings.'[1] So the doctrine of ' endless' punishment is horrible and revolting. But eternity has properly nothing to do with time. ' Eternal punishment is the punishment of being without the knowledge of God.'[2] That knowledge does not procure but constitutes the life. This is no metaphysical theory, but gives the natural meaning which commends itself to ' peasants, women, and children.'[3] To the ordinary mind, the natural inference would be that we should throw aside dogmas so capable of misinterpretation, and which admittedly have, as a historical fact, covered a confusion between God and the devil. The Athanasian Creed appears to be at least an awkward and ambiguous mode of expressing a universal benevolence and an aversion to metaphysical

[1] *Theological Essays*, p. 145.

[2] Maurice, as I remember Carlyle saying, thought that you might be eternally damned for five minutes.

[3] *Theological Essays*, pp. 430, 450, 480.

dogma. But to reject it would be, as Maurice thinks, to fall into mere rationalism. The formulæ which are so revolting in the mouth of the mere dogmatist are essential when read as utterances of the deepest feelings of the human heart. We can only hold to their true meaning and denounce their misapplication.

After all comes the real difficulty of fitting a 'subjective' religion to a historical religion. The Christian creed does assert facts, and facts to which historical evidence is applicable. A dogma can be made into an utterance of sentiment. A statement that there was a deluge in the year 4004 B.C. must be decided by evidence. Maurice was painfully shocked when the excellent and simple-minded Colenso brought up this plain issue.[1] Though Colenso had stood by him generously in the King's College time, Maurice, who had fully recognised the generosity, felt himself bound to protest. The dilemma was, in fact, most trying. To declare that historical evidence is irrelevant, that our faith is independent of the truth of the Old Testament narrative, is really to give up historical Christianity. On the other hand, to argue that the criticisms are trifling or captious is to stake the truth of the religion upon the issue of facts. Maurice complains of Colenso for beginning at the wrong end.[2] As, however, Colenso has made certain statements, whatever his method, the truth must be either denied or admitted. Are they true but irrelevant, or relevant but false? Maurice cannot unequivocally take either side. He appears to hold that we may accept the deluge

---

[1] Maurice's criticism is in a little book called *The Claims of the Bible and of Science* (1863).

[2] *Claims of Science*, etc., pp. 76, 125.

because it teaches us a good lesson (that bad people will be drowned, apparently), that is, to accept whatever is edifying; or to think perhaps the deluge was a little one, that is, to put himself on the ground of historical criticism. Here, in fact, was the growing difficulty. Mansel could still speak scornfully of the quibblings of Strauss. But historical criticism had now to be reckoned with, and subjective religion must consent to be merely subjective, or submit to have its results tested by the broad daylight of common sense.

From Maurice I turn to Carlyle, the beacon-light of the age, according to his disciples—the most delusive of wildfires, according to his adversaries; but in any case the most interesting literary figure of his time. Extraordinary force of mind and character are manifested in the struggles with inward difficulties and external circumstances, which made much of his life tragic and his teaching incoherent. With the imagination of a poet he yet cannot rise above the solid ground of prose: a sense of pervading mystery blends with his shrewd grasp of realities; he is religious yet sceptical; a radical and a worshipper of sheer force; and a denouncer of cant and yet the deviser of a jargon. Such contrasts are reflected in his work, and are not really hard of solution. A spiritual descendant of John Knox, he had the stern sense of duty, the hatred of priestcraft, and the contempt for the æsthetic side of things which had been bred in or burned into the breed. He came into the outer world, like his hero Teufelsdröckh,[1] as a 'Baptist living on locusts and wild honey,' and occasionally presented himself to others as a dyspeptic polar bear.[2] He had im-

---

[1] *Sartor Resartus*, ch. iv.; cf. Froude, i. 334.　　　[2] Froude, iii. 67.

bibed radicalism in a home of sturdy peasants, pinched by all the sufferings of the poorer classes in the war time. When the yeomanry was called out in 1819 he was more disposed to join the sufferers than the guardians of order.[1] So far, Carlyle was in sympathy with James Mill, whose career also illustrated one mode of passage from Puritanism to political radicalism. Nor would Carlyle differ from Mill widely on certain religious points. The conventional dogmatism of the kirk had lost its savour for both, and meant a blind tradition, not a living force. Carlyle only went with the general current of youthful intellect in abandoning the dogmatic creed. When Irving made a painful effort to put life into the dead bones, Carlyle recognised the hopelessness of the enterprise. But he was no nearer to Mill. Carlyle's 'conversion' took place in Leith Walk in June 1821.[2] It followed three years of spiritual misery ; and it is recorded in the famous chapter in *Sartor Resartus* on the 'Everlasting No.'[3] That passage is, indeed, the keynote to Carlyle's history. Briefly, he had found himself face to face with materialism and atheism. The weapons of defence afforded by such teachers as Brown were futile. Carlyle felt that he too was drifting towards the abysses whither they were being dragged by Hume. The word duty, so sceptics would persuade him, had no meaning, or was the name for a mere calculation of pleasure ; an exhortation to build not on morality but on cookery. The universe seemed to be 'void of Life, of Purpose, of Volition, even of Hostility : it was one dead, unmeasurable steam-engine, rolling on in its dead indifference, to grind me limb from limb. O

---

[1] Froude, i. 73. [2] *Ibid.* i. 101. [3] *Sartor Resartus*, ch. vii.

the vast solitary Golgotha and Mill of Death !' The nightmare was broken by an act of will. The 'Everlasting No' pealed 'authoritatively through all recesses of my Being, of my Me ; and then it was that my whole Me stood up in native God-created majesty and with emphasis recorded its protest.' The result is noteworthy : ' Even from that time the temper of my misery was changed : not Fear or whining sorrow at it, but Indignation and grim fire-eyed Defiance.'

Carlyle had won not peace but a 'change of misery.' He could look at the enemy with ' fire-eyed defiance ' but not with the calm of settled victory. His emancipation was not won by a reasoned answer to doubt. In the earlier essays Carlyle shows apparent sympathy with German philosophy.[1] He speaks with profound admiration, though in general and popular language, of the doctrines of Kant, Novalis, and Fichte, and seems to accept Coleridge's theory of a Reason superior to the Understanding.[2] Carlyle, however, was still less of a metaphysician proper than of a poet. He is a man of intuitions, scorning all logical apparatus in itself, and soon afterwards appears to regard metaphysics in general as a hopeless process of juggling which tries to educe conviction out of negation and necessarily ends in scepticism.[3] To him Goethe rather than any metaphysician presented the true solution. No two men of genius, indeed, could be more unlike. The rugged, stormy Puritan could hardly, one would have thought,

---

[1] Essays on 'State of German Literature' (1827); 'Novalis' (1829); 'Signs of the Times' (1829).

[2] Novalis, *Essays*, ii. 76.

[3] ' Characteristics' (1831); *Essays*, iii. 20.

breathe the serene atmosphere of the prophet of culture. But the very contrast fascinated him. Goethe had cast aside all the effete dogmas, and had yet reached the victorious position in which symmetrical development was possible. Carlyle remained to the end desperately struggling, full of 'fire-eyed defiance,' but never getting outside the chaotic elements. The metaphysical systems of Kant's successors attracted him as protests against materialism, but he preferred a shorter cut to the end, and his Scottish common sense was always whispering that philosophy was apt to be mere 'transcendental moonshine.'

Carlyle therefore was essentially protesting against the mechanical doctrines embodied in Utilitarianism. But he saw the hopelessness of meeting the attack in the old-fashioned armour of theology. The dogmas of the churches were dead, beyond all hopes of resuscitation. The verse in *Past and Present* gives his view :—

'The builder of the Universe was wise,
He planned all souls, all systems, planets, particles ;
The plan He shaped all worlds and æons by,
Was—Heavens !—was thy small nine-and-thirty Articles.' [1]

An earlier version of these lines speaks of the 'logic of Maurice,' who had characteristically proved that the articles were a charter of religious liberty.[2] Carlyle rejected formulas. The Maurician rehabilitation led to mere cant. Like Maurice, he was in principle a mystic, and holds that mysticism may be taken in a true sense,[3] in which it seems to be much the same with an Idealist as contrasted with a materialist doctrine. When he first

[1] *Past and Present*, ch. xv.   [2] Froude, iii. 40.
[3] 'Novalis,' in *Essays*, ii. 72, etc.

made Mill's acquaintance, it was under the erroneous impression that Mill too was a mystic.[1]

I have spoken of Carlyle's personal relations to Mill. His judgment of the Utilitarians generally is significant. Froude publishes some entries from Carlyle's journal of 1829-30, a time when the prophet was only preluding his fuller utterances.[2] The Utilitarians, he holds, exhibit tendencies spread over the whole intellect and morals of the time. Utilitarianism must collapse, because the reason will triumph over the senses, and the angel at last prevail over the brute. The moral nature of man is deeper than the intellectual ; the significance of Christ, he says, is altogether moral, and the significance of Bentham 'altogether intellectual, logical.' Where logic is the only method, the resulting system can be only mechanical. 'Alas! poor England! Stupid, purblind, pudding-eating England,' Bentham with his *Mills*[3] grinding 'thee out morality—and some Macaulay, also be-aproned and a grinder, testing and decrying it.' The mention of Macaulay reminds him that the Utilitarians have a relative merit. 'They *have* logical machinery,' and do grind ' fiercely and potently on their own foundation, whereas the Whigs have no foundation. . . . The Whigs are amateurs, the radicals are guild-brethren.'[4] The public utterances are versions of the same doctrines. In *Sartor Resartus* Teufelsdröckh would consent that the ' monster *Utilitaria*' should trample down palaces and temples 'with her broad hoof,' that new and better might be built.[5] So in the

---

[1] Mill's *Autobiography*, p. 175, etc.

[2] The journals have been separately printed in America for the Grolier Club (edited by Prof. Norton).   [3] Carlyle, I fear, is punning.

[4] Froude, ii. 79, 90.   [5] *Sartor Resartus*, bk. iii. ch. iv.

Hero-Worship[1] he calls 'this gross steam-engine Utilitarianism' an approach towards a new faith. It is at least a 'laying down of cant,' an honest acceptance of the belief in mechanism : 'Benthamism is an *eyeless* heroism ; the human species, like a hapless blinded Samson, grinding in the Philistine mill, clasps convulsively the pillars of its mill, brings huge ruin down, but ultimately deliverance withal. Of Bentham I meant to say no harm.' In later years Carlyle insists more emphatically upon the bad side of Utilitarianism. He had grown more bitter, and was more alienated personally. In the *Chartism* (1839) he attacks the 'Paralytic Radicalism'—paralytic being substituted for 'philosophical'— which has sounded statistically a 'sea of troubles' around us, and concluded that nothing is to be done but to look on. Paralytic Radicalism, accordingly, is 'one of the most afflictive phenomena the mind of man can be called upon to contemplate!'[2] The summary of his later view is given in the famous summary of the 'Pig Philosophy' in the *Latter-day Pamphlets*. The universe is regarded as an 'immeasurable swine's trough,' and the consequences deduced in a kind of Swiftian catechism.[3] Utilitarianism means mere sensualism. Carlyle's interpretation, true or false, reduces the issue to the simplest terms. Will you accept the mechanical or the mystical view? Carlyle's metaphysical leanings were to some forms of transcendental idealism. Time and space, as he says in the *Sartor Resartus*, are the canvas on which our life-visions are painted. They are mysterious 'world-embracing phantoms,' to be rent asunder

[1] Lecture v.
[2] *Chartism*, ch. x.
[3] *Latter-day Pamphlets*, 'Jesuitism.'

by the seer who would pierce to the Holy of Holies.
They are illusions, though while we are on earth we try
in vain to strip them off. Men are spirits ; the earth
but a vision. We issue from and fall back into mystery.
' We are such stuff,' in his favourite quotation,

> ' As dreams are made of, and our little Life
> Is rounded with a sleep.'[1]

This is poetry rather than philosophy; and though the
thought is always present to Carlyle and constitutes one
secret of his most powerful passages, it would be impossible to grasp it as a logical theory or imprison it in
any formula whatever. All systems and formulas are
suspicious to him. He is a ' seer' who not only does
not require any logical apparatus, but holds that to
require one is to give up the point. It is the sense of
the ephemeral nature of man, of his suspension in the
midst of infinities, which stimulates or overpowers him.
That sentiment lies deeper than all reasoning. The
' mechanical' view has the advantage derived from the
authority of the physical sciences ; but the sciences, he
holds, lie in a superficial region ; they belong to the
world of appearance, not to the world of reality.
When the mystic ventures into the ordinary daylight
and fights the man of science with his own weapons,
he will get the worst of it. Science must have its
rights on its own ground ; and to suppose the supernatural intruding here and there into natural phenomena is to court defeat. There are no ' miracles,' but
the universe is itself miraculous. His great message,
given in *Sartor Resartus*, is that the natural *is* the supernatural.[2] We are not to pick up ' intuitions' here and

---

[1] *Sartor Resartus*, bk. i. ch. viii. ; bk. iii. ch. viii.   [2] Froude, ii. 345.

there; but we have one intuition, that the world is not a mechanism but a revelation of God. No set of words can hold the great mystery. They are hopelessly inadequate, and the sooner they are swept into oblivion the better. But the one profound mystery remains.

Even such a vague indication of Carlyle's general meaning is an attempt to define an imaginative tendency which shrinks from definite formulation. The more practical application is perhaps more definable. The 'Everlasting No' means: I will not believe that the world is a mere dead mechanism, nor that the sole forces by which society is moulded are the sensual appetites. Rightly or wrongly, Carlyle attributed those views to the Utilitarians. They had a certain negative merit, in so far as they took their own line directly and consistently. The ordinary theology was a mass of 'shams' and 'cants'—a collection of subterfuges by which men could blind themselves for the time to the necessary drift of the current. The way to meet the Utilitarian was not to compromise or to argue, but to leave the world of outward fact and to plant yourself on a deeper base : the direct, imperative, and unassailable conviction or intuition of the divine order implied everywhere beneath the 'living raiment.' The issue then becomes simple and absolute. No set of creeds and 'formulas' can matter ; 'evidences' are an absurdity ; the one formula is the divinity of the universe ; the only evidence, the direct intuition of the eternal verities. The religions of the world are good so far as they recognise this truth ; bad so far as they try to imprison it in any sort of formula or make it dependent upon any particular fact. To Maurice, as to others, this attitude seemed to be hopeless. Does it not become mere pantheism—a sentiment too vague to be efficient?

Pantheism is a phrase scarcely appropriate for Carlyle's creed. If Carlyle believed in God, he also believed for practical purposes in the devil. He might have been expected to accept some such pessimistic scheme as Schopenhauer's. He was deterred by his innate Puritanism. The voice of God for him, however vaguely defined, is heard in morality. God is essentially the giver of the supreme laws of human conduct, however much the legislator may be wrapped in mystery. The 'simple creed,' according to his chief disciple, which was the 'central principle' of all Carlyle's thought, was the creed of the Jews and the Puritans, namely, that obedience to the divine law is the one condition of human welfare, and that nations who worship Baal even in the guise of art or of material prosperity are on the road to destruction.[1]

Carlyle, then, is so far like Coleridge and Maurice, that he feels that a religion must find some deeper and more universal base than can be discovered in the region of empirical fact. It must correspond to an imperative dictate of the whole heart or the intellect. He carries out the principle with incomparably more vigour by rejecting all historical supports and particular formulas. Neither the Thirty-nine Articles nor the decrees of councils or popes can be adequate to express the mystery ; nor can the religious sentiment be dependent upon particular events and 'miracles.' It is the difficulty of all such methods that the appeal to the heart comes to be the appeal to the prejudices

[1] Froude, iii. 12.

of the individual prophet.   In a man of such marked idiosyncrasies as Carlyle's this is of course conspicuous. His version of history and of philosophy reflects his inherited prepossessions.   It is enough here to mark one or two of the main points upon which he came into conflict with contemporaries.   A characteristic result is his theory of hero-worship.   The divine element in the world cannot be enshrined in one sacred book or a single supernatural order.   The revelation comes not only through Moses or Christ, but through every great man.   Odin, Mahomet, Dante, Shakespeare, Luther, John Knox, Johnson, Rousseau, Burns, Cromwell, and Napoleon are his chief instances in the ' lectures ' : each, more or less perfectly, was the vehicle of a more or less partial revelation.   But then, may we not see gleams of the same light in all the multitudinous strugglings of the poor human beings who have more or less consciously co-operated in the world's progress?   Here and there his shrewd commonsense leads him to recognise the value even of the stupid and the formula-ridden.[1]   But, as a rule, he thinks of the world as a collection of ' dull millions ' who ' as a dumb flock roll hither and thither,' led by little more than ' animal instincts.'   Among them at rare intervals are scattered men of intellect and will.[2]   The great men, as he says elsewhere, are ' children of the idea '—such a one as Ram Dass, who set up for a god because he had ' fire enough in his belly to burn up all the sins in the world.'[3]   Inspiration belongs to the inspired few, who have to struggle amid the vast

[1] e.g. *Past and Present,* bk. ii. ch. xvii., and bk. iii. ch. v., with the humorous description of John Bull, who manages to settle down with his centre of gravity lowest.

[2] *Essays,* iii. 69 (Boswell).   [3] *Essays,* iv. 146 (Scott).

chaotic masses incapable of originating thought or action. To Carlyle, the essence of history was biography ; the personal influence of a small minority of great men. The view condemns scientific modes of history. To disbelieve in the importance of great men is supposed to show materialistic principles. A 'law' of human development denies the importance of individual peculiarities. To hold that Cromwell or a Napoleon was a relatively insignificant accident, the mere fly on the wheel of great evolutionary processes, seems to be to lead to the exclusion of all action of the will or of thought. To Carlyle accordingly the historical method in some of its tendencies was profoundly antipathetic. To diminish the power of the individual was, in his view, to deny the spiritual forces upon which society is dependent. Inspiration, therefore, though no longer confined to a particular church, is still confined to the elect who stand out as burning and shining lights in the dim twilight of his Rembrandtesque pictures.

The great movements, then, of modern times correspond to the blind ' animal instincts' of the ' dumb flock.' They are good as the Utilitarians were good, or as the French revolutionists were good, so far as their blind action leads to the deposition of the false leaders and the destruction of their effete systems. The French Revolution is ' the crowning phenomenon of our modern time ; the inevitable stern end of much : the fearful but also wonderful, indispensable, and sternly beneficent beginning of much.' [1] This is a brief summary of the great prose epic, than which no book, as he truly declared, had for a hundred years come more direct and flamingly ' from the

[1] *Chartism*, ch. v.

heart of a living man.'[1]   The passage from which I
have quoted, however, indicates a further point.   The
French Revolution, he holds, was essentially part of the
revolt of the oppressed classes of Europe against their
oppressors.   But the positive doctrine of the 'rights of
man,' theories which denied the need of government or
demanded simply to throw the reins upon the neck of the
governed, could lead only to chaos.   The reconstruction
must be by a new government; by a government of
wisdom or, what to him seems the same thing, a
government by the wise.   The 'new Downing Street,'
as he puts it, is to be a Downing Street inhabited by the
'gifted of the intellects of England.'[2]   Nothing therefore could seem more contemptible than the doctrine
of *laissez faire*.   That is simply to leave the fools to
themselves.   Modern parliaments, with twenty-seven
millions mostly fools listening to them, fill him with
amazement.[3]   A definition of 'right,' then, which makes
it ultimately depend on the wishes of the fools, is simply
absurd.   Not the 'animal instinct' but the conformity
to the divine law is the test of morality; and therefore
not obedience to the majority but loyalty to the 'hero.'
But how is the hero to be known?   Could he tell us
that, he replies, he would be a Trismegistus.   No 'able
editor' can tell men how 'to know Heroism when
they see it that they might do reverence to it only, and
loyally make it ruler over them.'[4]   Here is, however,
the difficulty.   Obedience to the hero is our only
wisdom, and obedience to the quack is the road to

[1] Froude, iii. 84.
[2] *Latter-day Pamphlets*, 'The new Downing Street.'
[3] *Ibid.*, 'Stump Orators.'   [4] *Past and Present*, bk. i. ch. 19.

destruction. One is, it may be said, obedience to right, and the other obedience to might. How are we to tell right from might? The statement that Carlyle confused the two, that he admired might in reality, while professing to admire right simply, was the most popular and effective criticism of his opinions. He is constantly accused of approving mere brute-force. Nothing could less correspond to his intention; but he is puzzled in particular cases. He declares again and again that they coincide in a sense. 'Might and right do differ frightfully from hour to hour; but give them centuries to try it in, they are found to be identical.'[1] 'That which is just endures,' is an edifying statement, and one which he constantly emphasises; but may we not infer that that which endures is right, and be led to admire very questionable proceedings? Does the success of a Cromwell for his life-time, or the more permanent success of a Frederick, justify their proceedings? Carlyle may have often begun at the wrong end; but the curious point is that this part of Carlyle's teaching approximates so closely to a doctrine which he first detested. Froude tells us that he fought against Darwinism, but apparently 'dreaded that it might turn out true.'[2] Yet is not the doctrine of the 'survival of the fittest' just the scientific version of Carlyle's theory of the 'identity of Right and Might'? Was not evolution really in harmony with his conclusion? To him, according to Froude, it seemed that Science led to 'Lucretian Atheism.' He still believed in God, but when Froude once said that he could only believe in a God who did something, Carlyle replied 'with a cry

[1] *Chartism*, ch. viii.   [2] Froude, iv. 259.

of pain which I (Froude) shall never forget, He does nothing!'[1] The reconstruction which was to follow the destruction was indefinitely delayed. The hero did not come; and Carlyle was a prophet who had led his followers into the desert, but found that the land of promise always turned out to be a mirage. Carlyle held that hypocrisy was still worse than materialism; but, as he grew older and watched modern tendencies, he became less hopeful of the 'Exodus from Houndsditch,' and sometimes wished the old shelter to remain standing. He shrank even from the essayists and reviewers and from Colenso, though he had rejected historical creeds far more summarily than they had done.

Carlyle, then, and Maurice might both be called 'mystics' in the sufficiently vague sense used by Carlyle himself. They object to logic on principle. They appeal to certain primitive instincts which can be over-ridden by no logical manipulations or by any appeal to outward facts. Both, after all, are forced in the end to consider the plain, simple, 'objective' test. Maurice finds that he must answer the question of the historical critic : are the statements of fact true or false? Carlyle, not seeking for a base to support any particular creed, can throw the Thirty-nine Articles overboard, but finally comes into conflict with scientific conceptions in general. He finds himself opposed to the scientific view of historical evolution, and sees in the most conspicuous tendencies of modern thought the disappearance of all the most ennobling beliefs. The 'supernatural' and 'transcendental' have, after all, to conform to the prosaic matter of fact understanding. Accepting, as I do, what I suppose to be the scientific view, I fully believe that Carlyle's method is erroneous; that in denouncing scientific methods as simply materialistic, he is opposing the necessary logic of intellectual development, and that his hero-worship and theory of right really lead to arbitrary and chaotic results.

There is, however, another remark to be made. If Carlyle's view of a scientific doctrine be correct; if its legitimate result be the destruction of morality, of all our highest aspirations, even of any belief in the reality of the mind or the emotions; if the universe is to be made into a dead mechanism or a huge swine's trough, we are certainly reduced to a most terrible dilemma. It was really the dilemma from which Carlyle could never escape, and the consciousness of which tormented him to the last. He had to choose between allegiance to morality and allegiance to truth. Scientific tendencies, especially as embodied in Utilitarianism, seemed to many men, and, as Carlyle's case shows, to the men of the highest abilities, to have that tendency. The absolute sincerity of that conviction is unmistakable. I do not doubt that men, holding the conviction sincerely, were bound to seek some escape; nor could I condemn them if under so terrible a dilemma they allowed their love of truth to be partly obscured. In fact, too, I think that it cannot be denied that many of the men to whom we owe most, whose morality was the highest and most stimulating, and who, moreover, were most hostile to the lower forms of superstition, did in fact take this position. Though Maurice was far from clear-headed, I fully believe that his liberal and humane spirit was of the greatest value, and that he did more than most men to raise the social tone in regard to the greatest problems. Carlyle's doctrine is, I equally believe, radically incoherent; but I am also convinced that Carlyle's impetuous and vehement assertion of certain great social, ethical, and political principles was of the highest value. It must be allowed, I think, that such men as Carlyle and Emerson, for example, vague and even contradictory as was their teaching, did more to rouse lofty aspirations and to moralise political creeds, though less for the advancement of sound methods of inquiry, than the teaching of the Utilitarians. There was somewhere a gap in the Utilitarian system. Its attack upon the mythological statements of fact might be victorious; but it could not supply the place of religion either to the vulgar or to the loftiest minds. Then the problem arises whether the acceptance of scientific method, and of an empirical basis for all knowledge, involves the acceptance of a lower moral standard, and of a materialism which denies the existence or the value of all the unselfish and loftier elements of human nature? Can we adhere to facts without abandoning philosophy; or adopt a lofty code of ethics without losing ourselves in dream-land? Some thinkers sought a different line of escape.

IX. DOGMATISM

The 'Oxford Movement,' according to Newman, was really started on the 14th July 1833 by Keble's sermon on 'National Apostasy.' The 'movement' has become the subject-matter of vast masses of literature, as becomes a movement among a cultivated class. While Mill and his friends were under the impression that reason was triumphant and theology effete, the ghost of the old doctrinal disputes suddenly came abroad. Learned scholars once more plunged into dogmatic theology, renewed the old claims of the church, and seriously argued as to what precise charm would save an infant from the wrath of a righteous God. What explanation can be given of this singular phenomenon? There was clearly a 'reaction,' but why should there be a reaction? The Evangelical movement had been mainly ethical or philanthropical. It protested against evils when the national conscience was already in advance of the actual practice. That was its strength; its weakness was that it accepted, without examination, the current beliefs of the day, and simply did without philosophy. The Oxford movement, though many of its leaders were keenly awake to social evils, did not start primarily from a desire for social reform. Nor can its origin be traced directly to a philosophical development. Its leaders had, of course, been influenced by literary and speculative developments. They had, as Newman tells us, been stirred by Scott and Wordsworth and by Coleridge's philosophy. And yet it is plain enough that the impulse did not start from philosophical speculation. The movement corresponded to changes which would be part of the whole history of European thought. I have said enough of the Utilitarians to indicate the special English conditions. The Utilitarians saw in the established church the most palpable illustration of a 'sinister interest.' Bentham was attacking 'Church of Englandism'; James Mill was proposing to apply Bentham's principles by substituting an ethical department of the State for a church, and replacing the sacrament by tea-parties; the radicals of all varieties regarded disestablishment and disendowment as the natural corollary from the Reform Bill, and a Whig statesman significantly advised the prelates to put their house in order. It was taken as a hint to prepare for confiscation.

Yet the Church was enormously strong ; it was interwoven with the whole political and social organisation, and the genuine radical represented only a fraction of the population. Oxford in particular, the very focus of conservative and aristocratic interests, the favourite place for such culture as was popular with the landowners, the clergy, and all the associated classes, was startled and alarmed, and began to rouse its latent energy. Into Oxford no serious philosophical movement had penetrated. It had been slowly amending its system, but it still adhered in substance to the ancient traditions. Dimly it knew that infidels and rationalisers were preaching dangerous theories. Pusey visited Germany in 1825-27, and had come back with some knowledge of German thought. He was even accused, very superfluously, of rationalism. Of that there was no real danger[1] for a man thoroughly steeped in the Oxford spirit. A sufficient illustration of Oxford education may be found in the curious controversy between Copleston, who had done much to rouse his University, and the Edinburgh Reviewers. Copleston replied vigorously, and yet his boast is a tacit confession. He declares that Oxford possesses good classical scholars, and we need not inquire how far they were really abreast

[1] See Pusey's (afterwards suppressed) *Historical Inquiry* into German rationalism (1828). H. J. Rose had attributed the evil to want of bishops. Pusey thought it was due to 'dead orthodoxism.' He looked leniently for the moment upon the attempt to infuse a little philosophy into the creed, but soon perceived that the Thirty-nine Articles would be more to the purpose.

of the day. Oxford men had to get up logic in Aldrich and make some acquaintance with Aristotle; and he argues that the mathematical studies of the place were more than 'elementary.' They were even beginning to include 'fluxions.' If this were a matter for boasting, it could not be seriously held that Oxford was doing anything comparable to the German universities as an adequate organ of the national intellect.[1] In point of fact, the system allowed the great majority to remain in complete ignorance of any recent movements of living speculation, a century or two behind-hand in philology, and absolutely indifferent to science. Naturally, when the champions of the Church came out to fight, they were armed with antiquated weapons. Yet many of them were men of great ability, and one at least a man of most indisputable genius.

The alarm spread by radical assaults upon the Church was equally felt by the liberal divines. No one, for example, was more alarmed than Dr. Arnold. But Arnold, a man of lofty and generous instincts and strong political interests, took the essentially liberal view. The Church, as all active-minded men agreed, was in danger. It was threatened by 'the godless party,' the radicals and revolutionists who were the heirs of Jacobinism, and were as hateful to him as to the high-

---

[1] Oxford had been incidentally attacked in the *Edinburgh Review* in an article upon 'Laplace' by Playfair; in a review by R. Payne Knight of an Oxford edition of Strabo; and by Sydney Smith in a very amusing review of a book upon education by Edgeworth. Copleston replied, and was answered in an article by the three conjointly. The controversy wandered into various small points. Newman, in his *Idea of a University*, quotes Copleston with deserved respect for his general principle. But the application to the Oxford system is less cogent.

churchmen. But here his diagnosis becomes essentially different. Arnold thought that the Church had become a separate sect because it adhered to old prejudices and to sacerdotalism. His remedy was to make it truly national, by widening its borders, admitting dissenters, and encouraging philosophic thought. The Church should be, as Coleridge urged, an essential part of the State organism; not a close corporation belonging to a priestly order. It was properly identical with the State. It must be liberalised that the State might be made religious, and drop the antiquated claims to magical authority which opposed it to the common sense of the masses and the reason of the thinkers.[1] This was precisely the antithesis to the view taken by the leaders of the 'movement.' They held that the Church was weak, precisely because it had been unfaithful to its higher claims and made an alliance with the State, which had passed into a bondage. This, then, is one aspect of the division between the liberals and the dogmatists; and what I have now to do is to endeavour to indicate the dogmatical view.

I confine myself to two representatives of the movement: Newman, whose literary genius needs no emphasis; and W. G. Ward, conspicuous as one who never shrank from an inference, and who, to do him bare justice, was incapable of supporting logic by misrepresenting his opponents. He represents the forlorn Hope, and

---

[1] See especially Arnold's pamphlet on *Principles of Church Reform* (1833), reprinted in *Miscellaneous Works* (1845), pp. 257-359. Arnold's aversion to sacerdotalism was most vigorously expressed in an article in the *Edinburgh* for April 1836, entitled (by the *Edinburgh*) 'The Oxford Malignants and Dr. Hampden.' It was not reprinted in his works. See Stanley's *Life of Arnold*, ii. 9.

reveals the tendencies which frightened his less daring comrades.

The true starting-point of the 'movement' can hardly be given more distinctly than in Ward's *Ideal of a Christian Church*.[1] It represents the stage at which Ward was becoming fully aware of the consequences of his own logical position. The *Ideal* has ceased to be lively reading; it Is like an echo from old common-room disputations of young men intensely interested in the ecclesiastical movements of the day. Ward contrasts the actual Church of England with the ideal Church of Christ, and already finds in the Church of Rome a more promising embodiment of the true spirit. The true Church is of divine institution, the channel of super-natural graces, and independent of all human authority. The Church of England, if not the creature, has become in fact the slave, of the State. It claims a parliamentary title, and in return for privileges has abandoned its rightful authority. Above all, a true church is known by its discipline. It should be the incarnate conscience of the society, and should superintend, enforce by its sanctions and stimulate by its example, the spiritual nature of its members. A true church should exercise an omnipresent spiritual authority, reaching every detail of life and organising the perpetual warfare against the world, the flesh, and the devil. The utter decay of any such power is the most fatal symptom of the Anglican body. From a contemporary book,

---

[1] The *Ideal* (1844) was a defence of articles contributed by Ward to the *British Critic* against the 'Narrative' of William Palmer (1803-1885). It led to the final catastrophe, and was soon followed by the conversions to Catholicism of Ward and Newman.

Ward extracts a ghastly account of the misery, vice, and spiritual degradation of the mass of the population.[1] To remedy such evils, he declares, the ' science of dogmatic theology ' is more essential than the science of political economy.[2] Dogmatic theology is in fact the basis of ' ascetic theology,' or of the whole theory of religious discipline. If, indeed, the Christian theology be taken seriously, if spiritual degeneration has an importance altogether out of proportion to material progress, and the salvation of souls be the one thing necessary, the conclusion is inevitable. To enforce those truths upon the reason, to impress them upon the imagination, and to ensure a constant reference to them in all our conduct, must be the essential work of an authoritative church. Ward expatiates enthusiastically upon the ceaseless activity of the Church of Rome ; upon the elaborate training of the priesthood ; upon the catechising of children, the daily meditations, the constant practice of confession, and the various methods by which the church fixes the eyes of believers steadily upon spiritual realities. A church incapable of this can no longer be the salt of the earth, and, in fact, the Church of England, though it has boasted of being ' the poor man's church,' has been utterly blind to the ' accumulated mass of misery which has been gradually growing to a head for the last sixty years.' ' Through no agency of hers,' attention has been roused by such men as Lord Ashley; and yet the church has shown no symptoms of shame at such important neglect.[3] What else can you expect from the organ of the comfortable classes ?

[1] *Ideal*, p. 27. The *Perils of the Nation* (1843) is the book quoted.
[2] *Ibid.* p. 416.   [3] *Ibid.* p. 420.

The social evils were serious enough. Dogmatic theology may not seem at first sight to be the most appropriate remedy ; but, if it were, it certainly needed a better army of defenders. The ideal church must have a theological school, a body of trained teachers capable of meeting the assaults of unbelievers, of pointing out the true results of biblical criticism, of scientific and historical inquiries, and of defining the attitude of the church in regard to them.[1] Ward is awake to the growth of a new infidelity, more dangerous than that of the last century. Carlyle, Kant, Michelet, and Milman are mentioned as representing different manifestations of this evil spirit. Strauss, too, is selling more rapidly than any foreign work.[2] Moreover, 'Protestantism,' as he maintains, is utterly effete and unable to cope with the antagonist. The 'theory of private judgment' involves doubt, and will tend inevitably to 'Comte's philosophy.'[3] Comte was represented in England by Mill, who was accordingly the butt of Ward's sharpest attacks.

If Ward thus expresses the seminal principle of the movement, Newman was the most efficient leader. Newman, as he tells us in the *Apologia*, held three doctrines : first, the 'principle of dogma,' which was the 'fundamental principle' of the movement of 1833, and was the antithesis of 'liberalism'; secondly, the principle, implied by this, of a 'visible church'; and thirdly, the doctrine that the Pope was antichrist.[4] The last, of course, vanished ; but the two others remained and only took a sharper form in his mind. The history of his

[1] *Ideal*, pp. 34-44.   [2] *Ibid.* p. 266.
[3] *Ibid.* p. 504.   [4] *Apologia*, p. 121.

thought is simply the history of his growing conviction that the true authority was that of Rome, not of the Anglican Church.[1] The 'principle of dogma' is equivalent to the statement that 'religion as a mere sentiment' was to him 'a dream and a mockery.' The liberal principle applied to theology means the substitution of vague feeling for definite truth. But to speak absolutely of a 'principle of authority' is to raise a difficulty. To believe in authority is to ground my belief on the belief of some one else. Therefore the questions remain : why does the authority believe, and why should I accept its belief as authoritative? The Church must be competent to judge, and I must be able to judge of its competence.

The special answer given by Ward and Newman to these points gives their true position. First of all the dogmatists, agreeing so far with the liberals, were convinced that the ordinary opinions of the day led to infidelity or to complete scepticism. A perfectly consistent mind must, as Newman declared, accept Catholicism or Atheism. Anglicanism is 'the half-way house to Rome, and Liberalism is the half-way house' to Atheism.[2] Protestantism, again, as involving the right of private judgment, must lead, as Ward agreed, to Comte. Taken simply, such sayings amount to pure scepticism. To admit the consistency of Atheism is to admit that you have no grounds of confuting the Atheist. Upon the assumptions common to both, the sceptic would get the better of the Protestant. The rationalised theology of Paley had really given away the key of the position. It could not permanently hold out against

---

[1] *Apologia*, p. 205.   [2] *Ibid.* pp. 322, 329.

the legitimate development of the eighteenth century infidelity. 'As a sufficient basis for theism,' says Ward, the argument from final causes is 'absolutely and completely worthless';[1] and he declares that Paley's argument is quite unable to prove God's love, or goodness, or justice, or personality.[2] But Paley and his contemporaries had explicitly given up any other argument. A Protestant, then, was logically bound to Atheism. Newman agrees. 'I have ever viewed this argument with the greatest suspicion,' he says, and for good reasons. It may prove the power and, in lower degrees, the wisdom and the goodness of God; but it does not prove his attributes as judge and moral legislator.[3] So again, Newman declared[4] that it was 'a great question whether atheism is not as philosophically consistent with the phenomena of the physical world, taken by themselves, as the doctrine of a creative and governing power.' Paley's proof of Christianity is naturally as unsatisfactory as his proof of theology. In one of the *Tracts for the Times*,[5] Newman applied what he called a 'kill-or-cure' remedy. He argued, that is, that if his antagonists rejected his doctrines for want of Scripture proof, they would have to abandon their own for the same reason. After recalling and enforcing a number of the objections made by sceptics to the historical evidence, he concludes that the evidence is by itself insufficient. Shall we for

---

[1] *Ideal*, p. 277.

[2] *Ibid.* p. 499. Ward would apparently have modified these statements at a later period.

[3] *Idea of a University* (1875), p. 453.

[4] *University Sermons* (1843), p. 186. In the later edition this phrase is carefully qualified as referring only to an illegitimate use of reason.

[5] No. 85 (1838), reprinted in *Discussions and Arguments*, 1872.

that reason refuse to believe? No, we must begin by believing. If we refuse 'to go by evidence in which there are (so to say) three chances for revelation and only two against it, we cannot be Christians.'[1]

Hume, then, or Mill or Comte, can at least hold his own upon empirical ground. Unaided reason, as Newman says in the *Apologia*,[2] can indeed discover sound arguments for theology, but historically and in practice it will tend towards simple unbelief. The 'liberals' endeavoured to meet the enemy by appealing to some philosophical or quasi-mystical doctrine; but in so doing they either dropped dogmatic and historical creeds altogether, or saved them by non-natural interpretations. Religion sublimated into philosophy becomes a mere sentiment, or a system of subtle metaphysics. It cannot effectively discipline the ordinary mind or inspire a church to meet the world. Yet some philosophical principle is necessary. To the Oxford men philosophy meant chiefly some modification of Aristotle. They held, of course, that the necessity of a first cause was demonstrable, and that a theology could be constructed by the pure reason.

This, however, leads to the old difficulty, the perplexity which runs through Christian theology in general. It is forced to combine heterogeneous elements. Philosophy must be combined with mythology; and the first cause identified with the anthropomorphic deity. Your metaphysic proves the existence of God in one sense, and your concrete creed assumes the existence to

---

[1] In *Discussions and Arguments*, p. 249, the curious correction is made of substituting twelve for three. That marks without mending the blot.

[2] *Apologia* (1864), p. 380.

be proved in a sense quite inconsistent. By calling inconsistency mystery, you verbally force contradictions into a formula, and speak of a God-man ; but the difficulty of getting from the metaphysical to the historical theology is thus only masked. How is it to be overcome ?

Ward, laying the greatest stress upon the metaphysical argument, came into conflict with Mill. Ward and Mill always spoke of each other with marked respect. They communicated their writings to each other before publication. Ward reviewed Mill's *Logic* in the *British Critic* in the most complimentary terms. Mill wrote to Comte in hopeful terms of the services to be rendered to speculation by the new school of divines. Ward thought Mill by far the most eminent representative of the 'antitheistic school,' and spoke with generous warmth of his high moral qualities.[1] The point, however, upon which Mill specially valued himself was just the point upon which Ward took him to be utterly in the wrong. Mill denied the existence of 'necessary truths.' Ward believed in the existence of a great body of 'necessary truth.' Ward argues forcibly for the 'necessity' of mathematical truths, and denies the power of association. Ward, in short, is Mill's typical 'intuitionist.' Intuitions, he says, are truths which, 'though not parts of present consciousness, are immediately and "primarily" known with certitude.'[2] He adopts from Lewes the word 'metempirical,' as expressive of what lies beyond the sphere of phenomena ;[3] and holds that all 'intuitions' give us 'metempirical' knowledge.

[1] Ward's *Essays on the Philosophy of Theism* (1884), pp. 120-125.
[2] *Philosophy of Theism*, pp. 143 *n.*, 304.   [3] *Ibid.* ii. 87.

Lewes invented the phrase to express the difference between the legitimate 'intuitions' implied in experience and the illegitimate, which are 'metempirical' as professing to transcend experience. Ward holds that 'metempirical' truths are valid and essential to reason.

Morals, again, says Ward, are as certain as mathematical intuitions; the truth that 'malice and mendacity are evil habits' is as necessary as the truth that 'all trilateral figures are triangular.'[1] Further, I 'intue' that 'all morally evil acts are prohibited by some living Personal Being'; and from this axiom it follows 'as an obvious inference' 'that this Person is the supreme Legislator of the Universe.'[2] The obvious difficulty is that Ward proves too much. His argument is leading to an independent theism, not a theism reconcilable with an historical creed. Accordingly he has to limit or resist his own logic. He admits the uniformity of nature as 'generally true,' but makes two exceptions, in favour, first, of 'an indefinite frequency' of miracles, and secondly of the freedom of 'human volitions.'[3] The Freewill doctrine leads to an elaborate and dexterous display of dialectic, though he must be a very feeble determinist who could not translate Ward's arguments into his own language. Beyond this we have further difficulties. If the creed be as demonstrable as Euclid, how can anybody deny it? Ward has to account for the refusal of those who do not accept his intuitions by some moral defect; they are like blind men reasoning upon colours. Mill's 'antitheism' shows that he was guilty of 'grave sin'; for, on the Catholic doctrine, there can be no 'invincible ignorance of the one true

[1] *Philosophy of Theism*, i. 50.   [2] *Ibid.* i. 90, 94.   [3] *Ibid.* i. 315.

God.'[1] Many men, however, condemn the creed of revelation precisely upon the moral ground. The Utilitarians denounced the profound immorality of the doctrine of hell and of vicarious punishment. Ward's argument requires such a conscience as will recognise the morality of a system which to others seems radically immoral. The giver of the moral law is also the giver of the natural law. But it seems to be as hard to show that Nature is moral in this sense as to show that the moral legislator, if omnipotent, can also be benevolent. The one great religious difficulty, as Ward allows, is the existence of evil. He quotes Newman's statement that it is a ' vision to dizzy and appal ; and inflicts upon the mind a sense of a profound mystery, which is absolutely beyond human solution.'[2] Plainly, it comes to this : the ' intuitions ' are in conflict with experience. They assert that the creator is omnipotent and infinitely just and benevolent. The admitted facts are incompatible with the theory, and are therefore declared to imply an ' insoluble mystery.' Ward intimates that he can show the true place of this difficulty after setting forth the ' impregnable basis on which Theism reposes.' But he does not appear to have found time for this ambitious enterprise.

This introduces the more special problem. How from your purely metaphysical position do you get to the historical position ? What is the relation between the authority of the Church and the authority of the pure reason ? Though Ward was perfectly satisfied with his

---

[1] Philosophy of Theism, i. 121. Ward, we are told, subsequently ceased to hold this opinion 'with any confidence,' or abandoned it altogether. Ibid. ii. 132.   [2] Ibid. i. 359.

own metaphysics, it was of course evident to him that such reasoning was altogether beyond the reach of the mass of mankind. If you are to prove your creed by putting people right about Freewill and the uniformity of nature, you will adjourn the solution till the day of judgment. An essential point of his whole argument is the utter incapacity of mankind at large to form any judgment upon such matters. The Protestant 'right of private judgment' means scepticism. Everybody will have his own opinion if nobody trusts any one else. If the truth of Christianity is to be proved by the evidences after Paley's fashion, nobody has a right to believe who has not swallowed whole libraries and formed elaborate canons of criticism. The peasant who holds opinions about history, to say nothing of science and philosophy, must obviously take them on trust. Hence we must either give up the doctrine that 'certitude' is necessary, or we must find some proof accessible to the uneducated mind. But it is an essential point of Catholicism, if not of Christianity, that faith is necessary to salvation. If wrong belief be sinful, right belief must be attainable. But men by themselves are utterly impenetrable to right reason. We have, then, to combine scepticism as to the actual working of the human intellect with dogmatism as to the faith. How is that feat to be accomplished?

Ward replies, by the doctrine of 'implicit reasoning.' Acceptance of the intuitions implies acceptance of all legitimate deductions. But this position is more fully 'drawn out' (in his favourite phrase) by Newman. It runs through a whole series of the writings in which the delicacy and subtlety of his style are most fully displayed,[1] and the difficulty of the position most fully exhibited. Chillingworth had stated the Protestant argument. To admit the infallibility of the Church, he had said, takes the individual no further, unless he is infallibly certain of the infallibility. To this Newman replies[2] that I may be certain without claiming infallibility. Certainty that two and two make four is quite consistent with a power of mathematical blundering. Perhaps it should rather be said that, if there be necessary truths, every one must, within their sphere, be infallible. But no one asserts that the infallibility of the Church is a necessary truth. If real, it is a concrete fact to be proved by appropriate evidence. After exhausting your eloquence in proving the fallibility, and indeed the inevitably sceptical result of 'private judgment,' you are bound to show how, in this case, the individual can attain certitude. The judgment that 'the Church is infallible' has been disputed by reasonable people. How are we to show that, in this case, their doubts are unreasonable, if not wicked? Why do not the proofs of the weakness of private judgment apply to this as to every other judgment? Have you not really cut away the foundation on which sooner or later your argument must be based? Yet certitude is made out to be a moral duty even for the average believer.

The theory is most explicitly worked out in the *Grammar of Assent.* Newman exerts all his skill in expounding a very sound doctrine. As a matter of fact, we form innumerable judgments by what he calls the

[1] Especially the *University Sermons*, the *Essay upon Miracles*, the *Essay upon Development*, and the *Grammar of Assent.*

[2] *Grammar of Assent* (1870), p. 219.

'illative sense'; that is to say, not by formal argument, but by a complex system of 'implicit' reasonings. 'Logic,' as he says, 'does not really prove. It enables us to join issue with others . . . it verifies negatively'; and for 'genuine proof in concrete matter we require an organism more delicate, versatile, and elastic, than verbal argumentation.'[1] Logic is a chain which 'hangs loose at both ends,'[2] for the first principles must be assumed, and the abstract concept never fits the actual complexity of concrete fact. By the 'illative sense,' again, we reach innumerable truths. We hold that England is an island, or that the man whom we see is our brother, with a faith indistinguishable from absolute conviction. We go further; we believe that a friend is honest, or, say, that Cæsar crossed the Rubicon, without admitting the slightest scruple of doubt. All knowledge whatever of fact plainly implies something different from formal logic; and, so far, the only question seems to be why so palpable a truth needs so elaborate and graceful an exposition. The answer is indicated by the polemic against Locke. Locke had proposed, as a test of a love of truth, the refusal to hold any proposition 'with a greater assurance than the proofs it is built on will warrant.'[3] The statement seems to be not only unassailable but in conformity with Newman's doctrine. Should we believe England to be an island? When Julius Cæsar landed, it was not proved; and he would have been wrong to be certain. When did it become right to be certain? Surely at whatever moment it was adequately proved. It is never so proved that to deny it would be self-contradictory, but

[1] *Grammar of Assent* (1870), p. 264.   [2] *Ibid.* p. 277.
[3] *Ibid.* p. 155. See also *Essay on Development,* p. 328.

by this time it is as much proved as any fact can be proved. Locke would simply justify himself by saying that in this case our 'assurance' does not exceed the 'proofs on which it is built.' The approximation to demonstration is indefinitely close, though never absolute, and the difference becomes too small to be perceptible. A difficulty emerges only if we at once admit the rightness of belief and deny the sufficiency of the evidence.

Newman, having shown that we believe in concrete truths not proved by abstract logic, argues that we also assume many truths not proved even by sufficient empirical evidence. We have what Locke called a 'surplusage of assurance.' The fact, again, is undeniable. We believe implicitly in countless things upon insufficient evidence. This, as Locke would add, is one main explanation of the prevalence of error, and also a proof that error may be innocent. It is a duty to be candid; it cannot be a duty to be right. We must listen to reason; but the effect of reasoning must depend upon the constitution of our minds, and the various beliefs with which they are already stored. Now to Newman this doctrine always seems to be sceptical. It amounts to the 'liberalising' view that all creeds are equally good if only they be equally sincere. Hence he lays stress upon the doctrine that 'assent' is a volitional as well as an 'intellectual act.' It is our duty to obey the reason; and when the 'illative sense' declares the truth of a proposition, we are bound to an 'active recognition' of the truth.[1] Locke, on the contrary, holds that if we listen to reason, the assent follows automatically by a non-voluntary act.

[1] *Grammar of Assent*, p. 337.

On Newman's showing, an element of volition intrudes into logic. Belief belongs to action as well as to pure speculation. 'To act you must assume,' he says, 'and that assumption is faith.'[1] If acting upon an hypothesis is the same thing as believing the truth to be demonstrated, this leads to a singular result. A judge, says Newman, acts upon the assumption that a criminal's guilt is proved.[2] Yet, as it is never mathematically demonstrated, he has a 'surplusage of assurance.' The judge may be of opinion that the prisoner's guilt is highly probable and yet be bound to acquit. Is he to believe that the prisoner's innocence is demonstrated? The case really shows the opposite : simply that as we have to act upon probabilities, we are not the less, but the more, bound to guard against the illusion that they are certainties. At every moment and in every relation of our lives, we are forced to act upon imperfect knowledge. The obvious inference is that we are bound to keep in mind that it is imperfect; or otherwise we shall be morally bound to commit intellectually error. If, therefore, a creed be not demonstrably true, we may wisely act as if it were true, but have no right to deny that we are acting upon probability. Butler's famous doctrine that 'probability must be the guide of life,' is true if 'properly explained.' But the difficulty is that, in religious questions, 'certitude' is declared to be essential ; it must correspond to something more than a 'balance of arguments' ;[3] and yet the certitude rests upon faith, and faith is 'assumption.' The probability must be somehow converted into certainty. In the *Essay on Development*, Newman meets Locke by declaring that 'calculation never made a hero,'

[1] *Grammar of Assent*, p. 92.   [2] *Ibid.* p. 320.   [3] *Ibid.* p. 231.

and praising the Fathers for 'believing first and proving afterwards.'[1] Though calculation does not make a hero, it is essential to making heroism useful. The true hero is the man who is ready to act, though he fairly estimates the chances and knows perhaps that they mean a probability of death.

This gives the real dilemma. Allow conviction to be influenced by the will, and you must admit that a belief morally right may be intellectually wrong. You justify the judge for mistaking presumption for demonstration, and the child for believing that a drunken parent is strictly sober. If so, you sanction erroneous beliefs. And this admittedly applies in particular to religious beliefs. The world, it is granted, is full of false beliefs, attained precisely by your method. Not one man in ten of all that have lived has belonged to the true Church. Newman, in fact, admits that his ultimate proof is 'subjective.' There is no ultimate test of truth beside 'the testimony borne to truth by the mind itself.'[2] He does not, indeed, deny the possibility of demonstration : he often asserts it ; but he holds that the demonstration will not in fact convince. Men differ in their first principles, and he cannot change a man's principles more than he can make a crooked man straight or a blind man see.[3] Hence we have the final answer. We have really to desert a logical ground and to take our stand upon instinct. Our instincts are in one respect infallible. Belief in revealed religion depends upon belief in natural religion. Natural religion is founded on the conscience. The conscience means the sense of

---

[1] *Development*, pp. 328, 331.
[2] *Grammar of Assent*, p. 343.　　　　[3] *Ibid.* pp. 405, 408.

sin, and therefore the desire for intercession which is
satisfied by the priesthood.   The religion of philosophy
ignores the conscience, though it recognises the moral
sense.[1]   The order of the world, indeed, seems to contradict this.   What strikes the mind 'so forcibly and so
painfully' is God's absence from His own world.   He
has left men in ignorance, and is a 'hidden God.'   We
are forced to the conclusion that 'either there is no
Creator or He has disowned His creatures.'[2]   Such
doubts 'call for the exercise of good sense and for
strength of will to put them down with a high hand as
irrational or preposterous.'[3]   Why 'irrational,' if they
cannot be answered?   Newman, indeed, declares that
he is as certain of the existence of God as of his own,
although he has a difficulty in putting the grounds of
his certitude into 'mood and figure.'[4]   The position
is illustrated by a remarkable sermon[5] in which, after
his conversion, he again applies the old 'kill-or-cure'
remedy.   He puts the various difficulties of theistic
belief with his usual force.   He declares that there are
'irrefragable' demonstrations of the doctrine ; but he
admits the difficulties.[6]   They are so great, indeed, that
if you once believe in God you need not shrink from
accepting any of the mysteries of the Catholic creed.
The result seems to be that while Newman declares that
'demonstrations' exist, he also emphatically declares

---

[1] *Grammar of Assent*, p. 391.   [2] *Ibid.* p. 392.   [3] *Ibid.* p. 211.
[4] *Apologia*, p. 377.   [5] *Sermons to Mixed Congregations*, No. xiii.
[6] In one of his famous phrases, Newman says that ten thousand difficulties
do not make one objection (*Apologia*, p. 374).   This is clearly true in a sense.
I may find it impossible to solve a mathematical problem without doubting
that a solution exists.   But it suggests a very convenient logical device.   An
unanswerable objection can always be met by calling it a difficulty.

that they will not practically convince. The proof for
the ordinary mind must depend upon the 'illative sense';
and the illative sense implies the existence of the conscience, and, moreover, of the conscience as distinguished
from the 'moral sense.' The 'moral sense' leads only
to the hollow morality of 'so-called civilisation' and of
superficial philosophy. To convince men we must appeal
to their conscience. But for the conscience he would be
'an atheist, a pantheist, or a polytheist when he looked
into the world,' that is, if guided by experience alone.[1]

What, then, is, as he puts it, the 'burdened conscience'
which is my true informant?[2] The conscience is the
sense of sin. It tells us of a judge; of one who is
'angry with us and threatens evil.' It tells us of the
need of atonement, and yet of the absence of God from
the world. Natural religion, the foundation of revealed
religion, is therefore, as Lucretius said, a yoke; it
'burdens and saddens the religious mind.' It proves,
too, the doctrine of which Butler was the 'great master,'
the absolute necessity of 'vicarious punishment.'[3] Thus,
as he says, in another famous passage, natural religion
teaches gloom and horror of ourselves. To be 'superstitious . . . is nature's best offering, her most acceptable service, her most mature and enlarged wisdom, in
the presence of a holy and offended God. They who
are not superstitious without the gospel, will not be
religious with it.'[4]

This is, indeed, the real pith of the doctrine. Without
asking what may be the logical demonstration, the actual
persuasive force is the appeal to the conscience as a

[1] *Apologia*, p. 377.
[2] *Grammar of Assent*, p. 392.
[3] *Ibid.* p. 401.
[4] *University Sermons* (1872), p. 118.

'sense of sin.' Starting from the conception of the Church implied in Ward's *Ideal*, that is the foregone conclusion. We accept the Church theology, because we feel the terror which the Church soothes. Newman, as was inevitable from the confusion between rules of conduct and canons of logic, has given us the real cause of belief, but not a good reason for believing. And here the apologists are precisely at one with the ordinary deist of the eighteenth century. They agree that the doctrine was accepted because it fell in with 'natural religion' in 'superstition.' The power of the Church, or the power of priest-craft, depends essentially upon the belief in its power of pardoning sin and reconciling man to God. The difference is that the deist asserted the superstition to be false, and pardon a quack remedy; whereas Newman sees a fundamental truth in the superstition, and the full explanation in the revelation committed to the Church. How, then, is the issue to be decided? You are wrong, says Newman, as a blind man judging of colours is wrong. You have quenched the conscience, and therefore have no guide. Yet, if a blind man can never realise what sight is, no blind man ever doubts that sight exists. Nothing is easier than to prove to him that I have means of knowledge which he does not possess. Why, if conscience reveals truths, cannot the truths be impressed even upon those who have no conscience? Why should I believe that your theory is right, when the ultimate test is one which, by its nature, can appeal only to its own authority? If men have radically different instincts which can be brought to no common measure, scepticism is the inevitable result, unless a supernatural authority can be applied. That is precisely Newman's conclusion ; leave men to themselves, he says, and they will have no 'common measure,' unless controlled by a supreme power. The 'absolute need of a spiritual supremacy' is the 'strongest argument in its favour.'[1]

This gives Newman's relation to the philosophy of the time. The 'irrefragable demonstrations' of the schools are left in the background. Granting them to be irrefragable, do they prove or disprove his point? Does the 'first cause' argument properly lead to Nature or to the God of Catholicism? To overlook this is to assume that your reasoning is confirmed by the very logic to which it is radically opposed. Is Newman really sceptical when he denies the validity of the scientific view, or the man of science when he denies the validity of Newman's? What is the relation of 'science' to philosophy? Private judgment is said to lead, in religion, to scepticism. The obvious reply is that in the physical sciences it has led to indisputable truths. Whence the difference? Newman speaks as though the proofs of scientific truths rested exclusively upon the arguments for each proposition separately. Men of science accept Newton's theory, he says, without rigidly testing it each for himself, and assume that it conforms to the facts, even if the conformity be not obvious.[2] Believers in theology should make similar assumptions. But this omits the real ground of conviction. We believe in Newton's theory of gravitation, not simply because we have read the Principia ; not even simply because the

---

[1] Development, pp. 127, 128.

[2] Essays on Development, p. 129. Laplace and Lagrange had a different opinion.

argument is part of a whole system of consistent and independent truths; but also because it can be verified by proofs intelligible to all, and because it can predict facts open to the severest tests. The enormous authority of science is not due to the fact that it is believed by this or that expert or body of experts, but because it manifests its power by working wonders which are not miracles. It can appeal to a criterion which is not supernatural, and is as valid for the sinner as for the saint.

Here is one result of the Oxford indifference to science. When Newman was invited by innocent people to appear as the champion of faith against science, he refused, for the reason (among others) that he could not tell what was the position to be assailed. He would not deny that 'science grew, but it grew by fits and starts,' and threw out hypotheses which 'rose and fell.'[1] He supposes science to represent a fluctuating set of guesses. Even if it appeared to contradict revelation, the contradiction could be evaded by an easy device. Science and Scripture contradict each other as to the motion of the earth. We cannot decide till we know what motion is, and then it may turn out that science is false or reconcilable to Scripture.[2] This saying alienated Froude and Kingsley, and, I fancy, with good reason; but we can see how Newman came to it. Theology, he thought, rested on a deeper foundation than science. It represented a single body of deductive truth; while science represented a set of detached conclusions formed upon particular facts.

This appears to reverse the truth. 'The scientific

---

[1] *Apologia*, p. 404.   [2] *University Sermons* (1872), p. 348.

principle, in the first place, is at issue with the theology
not upon this or that point, not on the conflict between particular statements, but all along the line. Two
differing conceptions of the universe are at issue, and
one must be accepted. Newman substantially replies
that science has its own—a lower—sphere.[1] In the
Idea of a University he argues that theology must be
admitted into the course, because it deals with the
realities underlying phenomena, and is therefore the
rightful queen of sciences. The history of the actual
relations of science and theology would supply a curious
commentary upon this opinion. Newman meanwhile
holds that the conflict arises from a scientific misconception. The latest infidel device, he says, is to leave
theology alone. The man of science trusts to the interest
of his own pursuits to distract the mind from theology,
which then perishes by inanition.[2] His error consists
in leaving the higher study out of sight, or applying
methods legitimate in one sphere to those of the other
sphere. Science, then, does not give certainty, or gives
certainty which has no bearing upon the higher orders
of truth.

The reply is obvious. The physical sciences, in the
first place, give a body of consistent and verifiable truth,
and the only such body of truth. In the next place, it
is impossible to assign science and philosophy to two
different provinces. The scientific doctrines must lay
down the base to which all other truth, so far as it is
discoverable, must conform. The essential feature of
contemporary thought was just this : that science was
passing from purely physical questions to historical,

[1] *Idea of a University* (1875), pp. 428-455. [2] *Ibid.* pp. 401, 402.

ethical, and social problems. The dogmatist objects to private judgment or free thought on the ground 'that, as it gives no criterion, it cannot lead to certainty. His real danger was precisely that it leads irresistibly to certainty. The scientific method shows how such certainty as is possible must be obtained. The man of science advocates free inquiry precisely because it is the way to truth, and the only way, though a way which leads through many errors. His test is that which so impressed Newman himself, *Securus judicat orbis terrarum*; only *orbis terrarum* must not be translated one European Church during a few centuries. The man of science fully agrees with Newman that there is a true ' illative sense ' ; that men can reason implicitly before they can reason in logical form, and make approximately true formulæ though involved in innumerable superstitions and errors. The ultimate criterion is the power of verifying conclusions, of testing truth by its capacity to explain phenomena, and by its conformity to the scientific truth already established beyond dispute. But there is no royal road to truth in philosophy any more than in science; or, rather, it must be far longer and more difficult to reach it. Therefore we must not lay down rules as absolutely certain, but subject them to perpetual examination, to what Newman calls ' the all–corroding force' of the intellect, in the conviction that by that process we are slowly approximating to sounder belief. The errors have to be ' corroded.' This is admittedly true of all the natural sciences ; we have to puzzle out the truth in every development of thought, from astronomy to physiology, by a slow and painful process. Moreover, it is true of all the religions of the world

except, as Newman would say, the Catholic. Why is
that to be an exception? Newman candidly admits a
difficulty. The suggestion that a religion to be universally accepted should be universally revealed, as though
written 'on the sun,' is, he admits, plausible.[1] He
urges that there always was a revelation somewhere,
though a revelation in Jerusalem was not of much use in
Peking. Yet the admitted fact seems to be a fatal objection to the *a priori* probability which he assumes of a
revelation. To nine-tenths of the world there has been
only a 'virtual,' that is to say, no revelation. How, then,
does he try to make room for the one exceptional case?
The secret is to keep to the geocentric point of view.
Shut yourself up within the Church, interpret the world
by reference to it, instead of interpreting it by its place
in the world; pronounce the instincts by which it has
been supported to be ultimate and infallible, instead of
listening to the obvious explanation, and you can certainly
escape self-contradiction—as it is still always possible on
the same terms to hold to the Ptolemaic astronomy.
You have only to assume as a first principle that the
earth does not move, and the facts can always be forced
into conformity. To outsiders this is to confuse the
causes with the reasons of belief. So Newman in his
famous development theory provides a kind of parallel
to the scientific theory. He shows with the greatest
clearness how a certain body works out the properties
implied in the type, and so obeys an implicit logic. He
illustrates the case by analogies with other bodies, such as
the Anglican Church.[2] But why stop there? How did

[1] *Grammar of Assent*, pp. 372, 426.
[2] *Essay on Development*, pp. 102, 108, 170.

the first beliefs arise from which the full theological
doctrine expanded? Newman again suggests the answer.
They arise from the 'natural religions' or superstitions,
many of which were admittedly embodied in the Church.[1]
We have only to carry out his view logically, and the
'supernatural' element becomes needless. Christian and
Hebrew legends take their place in the general process
of human thought, and the assertion of the ultimate
authority of one particular body is simply the description
of the arbitrary claims which it developed under natural
conditions. If we keep the earth in the centre of our
system, we require a supernatural force to make the sun
revolve. Let things fall into their right order and all
becomes harmonious.

The positions thus occupied by the leading writers of
the time indicate the true issues. The 'dogmatists,' the
'liberals,' and the 'Utilitarians' are virtually agreed
upon one point. The Paley theology was in a hopeless
position. Protestantism could only lead to infidelity.
The arguments from design and from miracles are
radically incoherent. They confuse a scientific with a
philosophical argument, and cannot lead legitimately
to proving the existence of a supreme or moral ruler of
the universe. While accepting scientific methods they
are radically opposed to scientific results, because they
tend to prove intervention instead of order, and disappear as scientific knowledge extends. Mill's attempt to
suggest some kind of tentative and conjectural theology
was obviously hopeless, and interesting only as showing
his sense of the need of some kind of religion which
would embody high ethical ideals and stimulate the purest

[1] *Essay on Development*, pp. 358-365.

emotions. Empiricism was destructive of the historical
creeds, but could not of itself supply the place of the
old faiths.

Here then we come to the great problems by which
men are still perplexed. The Utilitarian, which is the
scientific view, lays down an unassailable truth. A
religious creed, so far as it is a statement of fact, must
state facts truly, and be in conformity with the results
of scientific teaching. Moreover, no theology can be
legitimately constructed upon this basis. The gods become figments; and theology is relegated to the region
of the unknowable. If that be the whole truth, religious
creeds are destined to disappear as knowledge is extended
and organised systematically. 'Philip Beauchamp' gives
the true Utilitarian position. Religion, however, as J.
S. Mill felt, is a name for something far wider. It
means a philosophy and a poetry; a statement of the
conceptions which men have formed of the universe, of
the emotions with which they regard it, and of the
ethical conceptions which emerge. It has played, as it
still continues to play, a vitally important function in
human life, which is independent of the particular statements of fact embodied in the historical creed. The
'mystical' doctrine, represented by Carlyle, corresponds
to this element of religion. Men will always require
some religion if religion corresponds not simply to
their knowledge, but to the whole impression made upon
feeling and thinking beings by the world in which they
live. The condition remains that the conceptions must
conform to the facts; our imagination and our desires
must not be allowed to override our experience; or our
philosophy to construct the universe out of *a priori*

guesses. What doctrine can be developed upon those terms, whether a 'religion of humanity' in some shape be possible, is still an open question. To the dogmatist this view seemed to be equivalent to the simple evaporation of all religion into mere vague emotional mist. To him a religion appeared essentially as a system of discipline or a great social organism, governing men's passions and providing them with a cult and a concrete vision of the universe. The difficulty is that such a creed cannot be really deduced from a general philosophy. The dogma has to be based upon 'authority,' instead of basing the authority upon proof. That is a radically incoherent position, and leads to the acceptance of the dogmas and traditions which have become essentially incredible, and to a hopeless conflict with science. To found a religion which shall be compatible with all known truth, which shall satisfy the imagination and the emotions, and which shall discharge the functions hitherto assigned to the churches, is a problem for the future. I must be content with this attempt to indicate what was the relation to it of the Utilitarian position.

INDEX

INDEX

2 K

INDEX